CHINA'S WEAPONIZATION OF TRADE

CONTEMPORARY ASIA IN THE WORLD

CONTEMPORARY ASIA IN THE WORLD

David C. Kang and Victor D. Cha, Editors

This series aims to address a gap in the public-policy and scholarly discussion of Asia. It seeks to promote books and studies that are on the cutting edge of their disciplines or promote multidisciplinary or interdisciplinary research but are also accessible to a wider readership. The editors seek to showcase the best scholarly and public-policy arguments on Asia from any field, including politics, history, economics, and cultural studies.

For a complete list of books in the series, please see the Columbia University Press website.

CHINA'S WEAPONIZATION OF TRADE

Resistance Through Collective Resilience

VICTOR D. CHA, ELLEN KIM, AND ANDY LIM

Columbia University Press

New York

Columbia University Press
Publishers Since 1893
New York   Chichester, West Sussex
cup.columbia.edu

Cataloging-in-Publication Data is available from the Library of Congress.

ISBN 9780231222396 (hardback)
ISBN 9780231222402 (trade paperback)
ISBN 9780231564205 (epub)
ISBN 9780231564939 (PDF)

LCCN 2025032115

∞

Cover image: Shutterstock

GPSR Authorized Representative: Easy Access System Europe,
Mustamäe tee 50, 10621 Tallinn, Estonia, gpsr.requests@easproject.com

For Andy's beloved family, Cindy, Tony, Melissa,
Jimmy, and Yumi

For Ellen's mother, Im-Chung, and in loving memory
of her father, Wye-Shick

For Victor's loving family, Andrew, Hyun Jung,
Patrick, and Kalea, and in joyful memory of his parents,
Soon Ock and Moon Young

CONTENTS

....

ILLUSTRATIONS AND TABLES

FIGURES

TABLES

PREFACE

This book emerged not from a theory but from data. One afternoon three years ago at the Center for Strategic and International Studies (CSIS), Victor and Andy were perusing some international trade data. We discovered an interesting pattern in China's trade. While the dominant narrative is that every company and government in the world is dependent on the massive Chinese market, thus giving China extraordinary leverage, we found something different in the data. There was a subset of goods that China imports from its trading partners on which it was highly, and in some cases wholly, dependent. Under normal circumstances, this would be the natural manifestation of healthy trading relations between China and its partners. But the current environment is far from normal. Indeed, China has weaponized its large and coveted market against many other countries, governments, companies, and individuals. This practice became known to the Western world in 2019 when China sanctioned the National Basketball Association (NBA) Houston Rockets over a single tweet by one of its staff supporting democracy protests in Hong Kong. For many smaller companies and countries in Asia and Europe, China's bullying forced economic actors to kowtow to the China market. Companies lived in fear of China's wrath and avoided anything that might offend China's authorities.

Maybe it is an American attribute to root for the underdog, but we thought that our data could provide a strategy for these small actors to stop China's weaponization of trade. We started to collate lists of trading items that were of value to China from the very countries it had coerced. We constructed a strategy to restore rules and trust in the international trading order, which we lay out in this book. Of course, China is not the only culprit when it comes to weaponizing trade. There are many other actors, including the United States. In that sense, the strategy and methodology we lay out in these pages could be applied to stop any actor from turning the liberal trading order into a weapon rather than an instrument for mutual benefit.

The earliest versions of our research appeared in the policy journals *Foreign Affairs* (Victor) and the *Washington Quarterly* (Victor and Andy).[1] We are grateful to the editors Daniel Kurtz-Phelan and Alexander Lennon, respectively, for their support of these publications. A more theoretical and data-heavy version by Victor appeared in *International Security* in 2023.[2] We are grateful to the editors Jacqueline Hazelton, Amanda Pearson, Monica Achen, and the anonymous reviewers at the journal for shepherding that manuscript to publication. As none of us are political economists, trade experts, or China experts, these publications gave us confidence that the research project had some value. Indeed, we knew we had something of value when one of these editors noted that their esteemed journal received maybe one hundred manuscripts on China annually, all saying pretty much the same thing, but identified our manuscript (and data) as saying something different.

This feedback gave us confidence to pursue the book manuscript. Both the data and the argument in this book have been revised, refined, and updated, making it somewhat unrecognizable from the earlier article iterations. Victor had the opportunity to present the project's data and arguments to numerous audiences. Comments provided by participants at the following institutions only made the manuscript better, for which we are immeasurably thankful: the Institute of International Studies and Institute of East Asian Studies at the University of California at Berkeley; the Center for International Studies at Princeton University; the East-West Center, Hawaii; the Kennedy School of Government at Harvard University; the German Marshall Fund in Washington, DC; the Freeman Spogli Institute for International Studies at Stanford University; and the Stiftung Wissenschaft und Politik in Berlin. Victor was also provided with the privilege of presenting the argument before Congress in May 2023.

For comments on draft chapters of the manuscript and the project overall, Victor thanks Nick Anderson, Kurt Campbell, Sungmin Cho, Tom Christensen, Zack Cooper, Dan Drezner, Bonnie Glaser, Brad Glosserman, Mike Green, Mary Alice Haddad, John Hamre, John Haslam, Joel Hellman, Dave Kang, Philip Luck, Abe Newman, Laura Rosenberger, Dick Samuels, and Al Song. The authors also thank Hyunsoo Cho, Grace Chung, Yeji Chung, Elisha Yeonsoo Ham, Minchi Hyun, Junah Jang, Seiyeon Ji, Shelley Kim, Romy Koo, Jifan Li, Anthony Hyunjin Park, Joshua Park, Seungmin Ryu, Yujin Son and Hyunseung Yu for their excellent research assistance. We thank CSIS and the Smith Richardson Foundation for their generous support of the project. At Columbia University

Press, we are indebted to Caelyn Cobb for her support and enthusiasm for the project from commission to publication.

Victor takes special pleasure in working with coauthors Ellen Kim and Andy Lim, who have been stalwart colleagues at CSIS. For Ellen, this is her second book and for Andy, his first. The grind of writing a book requires discipline, constant communication, rigorous and detailed attention, and collegiality—skills that are useful in life. For both, Victor hopes that this experience inspires them to pursue great things in the future.

Andy is forever grateful to Victor Cha, his coauthor, boss, and mentor for the invaluable opportunity to write his first book, hopefully the first of many so he can catch up, and for being the paragon of expertise and scholarship that many aspiring scholars and practitioners have looked up to. Everyone aspires to be the next Victor Cha, but there is only one. Andy is also thankful for the incredible work of his CSIS colleagues, including Minchi Hyun and coauthor Ellen Kim, for allowing him the bandwidth to focus on the book. He thanks his office mate Seiyeon Ji for her patience, collegiality, and friendship throughout the writing process. He thanks his family for giving him the lifelong opportunity to pursue a career he wants and hopes he can repay their sacrifices by being the first book author in the family. Most importantly, Andy is thankful to his wife Yumi Ko, whose constant encouragement and steadfast belief in his potential have made this possible. She is the epitome of patience, intelligence, and unwavering support—someone anyone would be lucky to have in their life.

Ellen is profoundly grateful to her two coauthors for making her second book possible. This marks her first publication with a university press since completing her PhD. None of this would have been achievable without Victor, to whom she feels deeply indebted. Ellen also thanks Andy Lim for his active leadership and tireless hard work, which helped ensure the smooth progress and completion of this book project. She cannot forget to thank Seiyeon Ji and Minchi Hyun for their strong support of her and others while working on this book.

ABBREVIATIONS

ACI	Anti-Coercion Instrument
ALD	atomic layer deposition
ASML	Advanced Semiconductor Materials Lithography
BDA	Banco Delta Asia
BIS	Bureau of Industry and Security
BRI	Belt and Road Initiative
CCP	Chinese Communist Party
CCTV	China Central Television
CFIUS	Committee on Foreign Investment in the United States
CFSP	Common Foreign and Security Policy (European Union)
CML	critical mineral list
CRMA	Critical Raw Materials Act (European Union)
DCTs	designated critical technologies
DEI	diversity, equity, and inclusion
DMZ	demilitarized zone
DSB	Dispute Settlement Body
DUV	deep ultraviolet
EC	European Commission
ESG	Environmental, social, and governance
ESPA	Economic Security Promotion Act (Japan)
EU	European Union
EUV	extreme ultraviolet
EVs	electric vehicles
FAO	Food and Agriculture Organization

FDI	foreign direct investment
FinCEN	Financial Crimes Enforcement Network
GATT	General Agreement on Tariffs and Trade
G7	Group of Seven
HTSUS	Harmonized Tariff Schedule of the United States
IAEA	International Atomic Energy Agency
ICT	information and communications technology
IEA	International Energy Agency
IEEPA	International Emergency Economic Powers Act
IPEF	Indo-Pacific Economic Framework
IP-2	Indo-Pacific 2 (Australia and South Korea)
IPR	intellectual property rights
ITA	International Trade Administration
JARE	Japan Australia Rare Earth
JOGMEC	Japan Organization for Metals and Energy Security
JU	Joint Undertaking (Chips)
MAD	mutually assured destruction
METI	Ministry of Economy, Trade and Industry (Japan)
MFN	most favored nation
MPIA	Multi-Party Interim Appeal Arbitration Arrangement
MSP	Minerals Security Partnership
MSS	Ministry of State Security (China)
NAIF	Northern Australia Infrastructure Facility
NATO	North Atlantic Treaty Organization
NBA	National Basketball Association
NGOs	nongovernmental organizations
NSC	National Security Council (United States)
OECD	Organisation for Economic Co-operation and Development
PNTR	permanent normal trade relations
PPE	personal protective equipment
PRC	People's Republic of China
REEs	rare earth elements
ROK	Republic of Korea
RR	replacement ratio
SBS	Seoul Broadcasting System
TECRO	Taipei Economic and Cultural Representative Office in the United States
THAAD	Terminal High Altitude Area Defense

TSMC	Taiwan Semiconductor Manufacturing Company
TWEA	Trading with the Enemy Act
UNGA	United Nations General Assembly
USGS	United States Geological Survey
USTR	United States Trade Representative
WHA	World Health Assembly
WHO	World Health Organization
WMD	weapon of mass destruction

CHAPTER 1

WHAT DO PELOSI'S TAIWAN TRIP, BANCO DELTA ASIA, AND TRUMP'S MEXICO TARIFFS HAVE IN COMMON?

In August 2022, United States House of Representatives Speaker Nancy Pelosi became the highest-level lawmaker to visit Taiwan in some twenty-five years. In a brief, unannounced, but widely leaked stop during an official trip to Asia, Pelosi met with President Tsai Ing-wen and with opposition party leaders; she also visited Taiwan's National Human Rights Museum for a roundtable discussion with human rights activists; delivered a speech at the Legislative Yuan, and had lunch with President Tsai, Taiwan Semiconductor Manufacturing Company (TSMC) founder Morris Chang, and other business leaders.[1] As she stood with President Tsai, the veteran House Speaker announced, "Today our delegation, of which I'm very proud, came to Taiwan to make unequivocally clear we will not abandon our commitment to Taiwan and we're proud of our enduring friendship."[2]

Beijing viewed the trip by America's second in line to the presidency as intimating de facto acceptance of the island nation as independent from China and a major affront to the "one China" policy. It responded with military exercises, ballistic missile launches, and naval maneuvers along Taiwan's territorial waters.[3] Of equal significance, however, was a battery of economic measures against the island. Beijing suddenly banned thousands of food imports from Taiwan, including fish, citrus fruits, pastries, instant noodles, tea, and honey.[4] The Ministry of Commerce blocked more than a hundred Taiwanese food brands, beer and distilled spirits from eleven Taiwanese suppliers, and more than a hundred beverage products. It also stopped exports of natural sand, which is a key component in the production of semiconductor chips, a vital Taiwanese export, and suspended the export licenses of more than two thousand (out of more than three thousand) Taiwanese producers.[5] Beijing initially made no announcement of the sanctions;

when called out on it, Chinese authorities later cited concerns ranging from pest safety issues to Covid prevention to incomplete paperwork. The purpose of these trade sanctions was clear: to remind Taipei of the considerable economic pain that China could inflict as its top trading partner, accounting for almost 23 percent of Taiwan's total trade.[6] Taiwan's political leaders declared defiantly in response: "We will not be intimidated by [China's] weaponization of trade."[7]

❧

In September 2005, representatives from the United States, China, Japan, Russia, South Korea, and North Korea gathered at the Diaoyutai state guesthouse in Beijing to sign the Six-Party Talks Joint Statement on denuclearization of North Korea. The agreement called for North Korea to freeze operations at the Yongbyon nuclear complex and disable core components of the program as requisite steps to an eventual declaration and dismantlement of all nuclear weapons–related programs. In return, the five other countries would provide the impoverished North Korea with economic and energy assistance, security assurances of nonhostile intent, and normalized political relations on a path to welcoming the self-isolated country into the community of nations.[8] Academics heralded the agreement as a major step toward stabilizing the security situation in Korea and welcomed the Six-Party Talks as the embryo of the first multilateral security institution in East Asia.[9]

At the same time, however, the U.S. Treasury Department issued a public notice of rulemaking by its Financial Crimes Enforcement Network (FinCEN) prohibiting U.S. financial institutions from relationships with a small bank licensed in the Macau Special Administrative Region of China named Banco Delta Asia (BDA).[10] The department announced that this bank was a conduit for North Korean money laundering for drug trafficking, counterfeiting of U.S. hundred-dollar bills, and other financial crimes.[11]

The announcement went virtually unnoticed by the media and governments (including North Korea), given the hoopla over the denuclearization agreement. But the impact of these financial sanctions soon became clear. BDA immediately froze some $25 million of North Korea–linked accounts for investigation. Fearful of being designated similarly by the Treasury authorities, other banks in Asia and Europe froze North Korean accounts.[12] Soon enough, North Korea was cut off from nearly all dollar transactions. The impact this was having on the North Korean elite's personal fortunes was made obvious by the way the release of the $25 million became the singular purpose of United States' counterparts in the denuclearization negotiations. The stress of unwinding a new form of U.S.

financial sanction they did not fully understand was palpable, Victor recalls from his time as a member of the U.S. negotiating team.[13]

❧

Fast-forward to November 2024. In a decisive electoral victory and historic political comeback, Donald J. Trump, the forty-fifth president of the United States, returned to the White House as the country's forty-seventh president. During the transition period, his advisers forecast that the second coming of Trump would augur unprecedented policy changes in the first hundred days. True to this prediction, less than two weeks after taking office, the president made a bombshell announcement that foretold the chaos to come over the following months. On February 1, 2025, the White House announced 25 percent tariffs on Mexico and Canada, America's two closest trading partners. The administration defiantly stated that access to the American market was "a privilege," not a right.[14] But the reason for the new tariffs (unlike the reciprocal tariffs against the world he announced two months later) had little to do with trade; instead, the tariffs were meant to punish the two U.S. neighbors for what Trump saw as undesirable Mexican and Canadian behavior. Specifically, Trump intended the tariffs as a form of punishment, holding the two countries accountable for not stemming the flow of illegal migrants and the drug fentanyl precursors into the United States. The White House accused the Mexican and Canadian governments of providing safe haven to narcotics production facilities and fentanyl and nitazene synthesis labs operated by drug cartels that led to the seizure of more than 21,000 pounds of fentanyl at U.S. borders. Trump also accused both countries of allowing more than ten million migrants to attempt to enter the country illegally during the previous U.S. administration. To accentuate the point, Trump declared, "[I will] sign all necessary documents to charge Mexico and Canada a 25% tariff on ALL products coming into the United States, and its ridiculous Open Borders. This tariff will remain in effect until such time as Drugs, in particular Fentanyl, and all Illegal Aliens stop this Invasion of our Country!"[15]

❧

We open with these three vignettes to highlight a particular phenomenon in international politics that has emerged as states and businesses have become more interconnected through globalization and economic interdependence—the exploitation of the law of comparative advantage. Think back to your college economics class. Nineteenth-century theorist David Ricardo developed the theory of comparative advantage to explain why states engage in international trade. Comparative advantage refers to one economic actor's ability to produce a good or service at a lower opportunity cost than another. So, the actor trades these goods or services for ones that others have an advantage in producing. The same applies to investment. Capital moves from places with excess savings to places experiencing net capital deficits. The resultant trade and investment patterns are mutually beneficial to all parties.

The United States' financial sanctions against North Korea and China's trade actions against Taiwan are effectively both forms of *economic coercion* that weaponize the liberal international economic order for political benefit. These actions exploit the dependencies and latent vulnerabilities created by participation in the global economy to affect the sovereign political choices of states or firms. It should be noted that economic coercion is different from protectionism, and that an economic sanction used in the former case is similar in form but different in purpose from the latter.[16] Economic coercion has very little to do with protection of domestic industry. It is a political act designed to achieve political goals. It is a form of economic statecraft short of war that is designed to punish a counterpart. It is a form of "gray-zone" coercion that is impactful enough to regulate the behavior of the target state but not so escalatory as to incite a military response.[17] What is different now is the use of such economically coercive tactics by two of the world's largest powers, suggesting that the world is on the threshold of a new era of "predatory liberalism" in which actors are capitalizing in potentially destructive and harmful ways on the integration, interdependence, and mutual prosperity created by eight decades of post–World War II neoliberal institutions.[18] This leads not only to a politicization of the global economic order but also to a weaponization of economically interdependent trade and investment ties such as we have never witnessed in recent history.

Are the actions of the United States and China really the same? Are Trump's tariff wars against Mexico and Canada the same as China's weaponization of trade against Taiwan? Are these forms of gray-zone coercion? Is Washington's use of sanctions against North Korea to counter foreign money laundering the same as Beijing's use of sanctions to punish others for allegedly violating the "one China" principle? What are the implications of the weaponization of economic interdependence by two of the leading powers in the international system? Is the postwar neoliberal global order being permanently eroded by new norms of predatory liberalism? If so, how can the world counter the phenomenon of economic coercion to preserve the liberal trading order?

These central questions inform this book on the weaponization of economic interdependence. The book describes, theoretically and empirically, the origins of this practice and its implications for the global order. We look at how and in what ways two leading powers in the international system, the United States and China, have used economic coercion. We argue that there have been fundamental differences in the employment of this tool of economic statecraft by Washington and Beijing. In particular, we focus on the latter's prevalent use of economic coercion over the past twenty-eight years and its impact on the rules-based liberal international order. This book assembles, for the first time, comprehensive data on all of China's acts of economic bullying against other states, as well as against private companies and individuals. We investigate, in both theory and practice, strategies for countering the weaponization of interdependence by the United States, China, or other actors. Synthesizing this trade data with traditional deterrence theory in the national security field, this book introduces the concept of *collective resilience* as a strategy for combating the weaponization of economic interdependence.

WHY THIS BOOK IS IMPORTANT

There are many reasons weaponization of economic interdependence is a critical topic of study for international relations and why it is important to devise a strategy for countering it. As noted above, the prevalent use of economic coercion by states constitutes a threat to the liberal international order by devaluing the premium placed on openness, integration, and trust among actors. If the shadow of economic coercion looms, states will become increasingly wary of developing mutually beneficial ties that can achieve higher productivity and profit for all.

Second, the absence of a strategy to counter economic coercion will allow the two most powerful actors in the international system to continue using it, setting an example for others to follow. The creation of such norms will lead states to seek autarkic solutions, devalue investments in relationships, and prefer coercion to negotiation. An illiberal international order is built on the judgment by states that interdependence is a liability rather than an asset.

Third, the means of countering trade weaponization thus far concocted by governments is deficient. These measures largely focus on maintaining cradle-to-grave control over everything in a key supply chain, from raw materials to finished products (e.g., medical equipment, memory chips), in order to protect against predatory acts by other potential suppliers. While this strategy protects one supply chain, it still leaves a universe of others as targets for coercion. The result is doubly negative: Targets do not feel safe from coercers; coercers feel emboldened to coerce again. New strategies are needed.

Fourth, most of the best scholarship in the field has focused on the United States' weaponization of the global economy.[19] While this is important, path-breaking work and might seem all the more timely given the tariff actions taken by the Trump administration against the world in 2025, there is another actor in the international system that has been weaponizing trade in major ways, for a protracted period of time, and against many targets. China has used economic coercion against a plethora of countries, companies, and individuals to suppress support for Hong Kong, Taiwan, Tibet, and Xinjiang. Despite tariff actions by the United States during the second Trump administration, China is by far the more active and ubiquitous coercer, yet there is no comprehensive understanding of all these cases. This book attempts to fill this void.

Fifth, from a U.S. national security perspective, dealing with China's weaponization of economic interdependence is critical to competing successfully against China. The willingness of countries to join U.S.-led supply chain coalitions, challenge China's militarization of the South China Sea, safeguard against Huawei's access to domestic 5G markets, support Taiwan's defense, and speak out for democracy in Hong Kong or against genocide in Xinjiang ultimately depends on how fearful countries and companies are of Chinese economic retaliation. Economic decoupling from China is not a silver bullet, despite Trump's attempts to do so, because no other country can completely cut its trade ties with one of the largest economies in the world. The solution, then, lies in trying to stop China's economic coercion without completely severing all links.

COLLECTIVE RESILIENCE

This book introduces a strategy of collective resilience to counter the weaponization of economic interdependence. The strategy borrows from conventional theories of deterrence in the international security field and applies them in the political economy field. Collective resilience promises a multilateral response in the trade space to the prospect of economic bullying. What informs this strategy is the understanding that interdependence, even asymmetric interdependence, is a two-way street. The target state, or ideally a collection of target states, can promise retaliation on things of value to the coercer to deter the coercer from acting.

We apply this simple concept to the case of China. From 1997 until 2025, we count a total of 605 cases of economic coercion by China. There have been twenty-three cases of coercion against eighteen governments and 582 cases of economic coercion against 470 private-sector companies and individuals (in forty-one countries plus Taiwan), with many companies being coerced on more than one occasion.[20] However, the fact that most targets of Chinese economic coercion are asymmetrically trade-dependent on China tends to obscure the reality that many of these countries also export items to China upon which the Chinese market is highly dependent, and in some cases almost 100 percent dependent. Original trade data presented in this book shows that the previous and current targets of Chinese economic coercion export more than $43.06 billion worth of goods upon which China is more than 70 percent dependent, as a proportion of its total imports of those goods, and more than $20.94 billion worth of goods upon which China is more than 90 percent dependent (based on 2024 data). These target states can band together and practice a collective economic deterrence strategy, modeled on NATO's Article 5, promising retaliation should China act against any one of the alliance members.[21] Forcing China to find a new supplier or pay a higher price for one item is, of course, not enough to change behavior; thus, operating alone against China would be foolhardy. However, sanctions on an aggregation of these high-dependence items would threaten enough inconvenience for Beijing that it might deter future predatory behavior. The barriers to collective action of this sort are undeniably high, but overcoming these barriers is necessary if countries want to stop forever living in the shadow of Chinese economic bullying. While the collective resilience strategy is intended to be applied to China, the same strategy to deter economic coercion could be employed against any potential violator, including the United States.

We begin with a conceptual look at the sources of predatory liberalism in the global order (chapter 2): what has enabled states to weaponize trade, and why have they chosen to do so? While economic coercion is a proactive policy choice, there are important facilitating conditions that deserve highlighting. In chapter 3, we take a deep dive into the case of China, which is the most blatant example of an economic coercer today. We provide the first-ever full accounting in the open source of 605 discrete acts of bullying, largely by the Xi Jinping regime, against targets on all continents except Antarctica. This is accompanied by a unique and original dataset of the universe of cases. Chapter 4 looks at how states have countered the weaponization of interdependence and why these strategies are deficient. In this chapter, we introduce the strategy of collective resilience. We again apply it to China, creating a unique dataset of China's trade vulnerabilities based on the UN Comtrade database. Chapters 5 and 6 are additional case studies of collective resilience. Chapter 5 looks at the prospect of building collective resilience among the Western economies, in particular the Group of Seven (G7) countries (United States, United Kingdom, France, Germany, Canada, Japan, and Italy) and other victims of economic coercion (particularly Australia and South Korea). Chapter 6 looks at the prospect of building collective resilience in the global critical minerals sector, where China holds a dominant position. Chapter 7 concludes with an assessment of the theoretical and policy challenges associated with stopping the weaponization of trade, general observations on how the United States and the European Union (EU) can contemplate a strategy of collective resilience, and the implications of Trump's tariff wars for the book's argument.

CHAPTER 2

THE SOURCES OF PREDATORY LIBERALISM IN THE GLOBAL ECONOMY

WHAT IS ECONOMIC COERCION?

We begin by defining our terms. The *weaponization of economic interdependence* refers to a conscious choice made by a state in the international system to exploit for strategic gain the vulnerabilities in trade patterns and financial interactions created by globalization. An act of *economic coercion* is the government's use of discriminatory actions in the trade of goods, services, and technology against a target. These actions can take a wide variety of forms, including tariffs, nontariff barriers, financial sanctions, export controls, trade embargoes, restrictions on market access, and social media campaigns against a target. The *target* is defined as a government, a private business, or an individual. In general, these actions are not taken for trade-related reasons (e.g., protection of domestic markets) but are designed to achieve specific strategic or political objectives by compelling the target to either take actions or withhold actions deemed contrary to the coercing government's interests. *Predatory liberalism* refers to the norm that is created when the weaponization of trade becomes common practice among governments in the global economic order to infringe on the sovereign political choices of another actor. This can happen when leading powers in the international system undertake these predatory practices, causing others to follow suit. For the targeted, predatory liberalism refers to the adoption of new norms of self-censorship, decoupling or disengaging from the economic order to minimize vulnerability to coercion.

Economic coercion is, of course, not a new practice in international affairs and generally falls under the category of economic statecraft and economic sanctions.[1] Classic works by the likes of David Baldwin, Robert Keohane, and Joseph Nye acknowledged the potential for weaponization of trade and finance, noting that economic interdependence between states in the international system, while mutually beneficial, also entails latent vulnerabilities in that this dependence could be exploited.[2] Henry Farrell, Abraham Newman, and Anne-Marie Slaughter, among others, have written more recently on how openness and borderless economic intercourse have created globalized networks of trade, finance, and information that can be exploited by actors occupying key nodes in that network to leverage power over others.[3]

Economic coercion is a sanction levied in the trade space, but it is not about trade per se. A trade tariff is usually about gaining more market share, countering dumping, or advantaging domestic goods in terms of price. When the United States pursues countervailing duties against a country for dumping a product below market prices, this is a trade-related act of compellence.

Economic coercion, by contrast, is politically motivated; it is a form of compellence aimed at infringing on sovereign political choice by punishing the target for some non-trade-related action or statement. The sanction can span the spectrum from formal and announced to informal and unannounced.[4] The latter end allows the coercer plausible deniability, which might make it easier to use or remove the sanction. As noted previously, economic coercion is classified as a gray-zone tactic in the uses-of-force taxonomy: it falls short of war and is purposefully modulated to compel a target without risking escalation to conflict.[5] In the BDA case in chapter 1, the United States pursued financial sanctions to denuclearize North Korea rather than, for example, positioning aircraft carriers off the Korean peninsula, which might be interpreted as an escalatory act of war.

Examples of economic coercion for political purposes abound in international politics. Virtually every trade or financial sanction by the United States against another country's political acts is a form of economic coercion. In 2019, the Trump administration sanctioned Turkish officials, government agencies, individuals, and businesses in specified sectors to reverse Turkey's military incursions into northeastern Syria. Russia's threat to block supplies of gas to Eastern European economies in wintertime is a perennial form of economic coercion. Russia's 2014 ban on the import of EU agricultural products is another type of coercion. The ban was presumably over "health inspections" but was implemented to alter the EU's position on the war in Crimea.[6] The difference between economic coercion and reciprocal tariffs is subtle. In April 2025, when the second Trump administration declared "Liberation Day" reciprocal tariffs against the world, the intended purpose was to get trading partners to lower their tariff and nontariff barriers to U.S. goods. As much as these actions were denigrated by some as unilaterally provoking a global trade war and as a mercantilist exercise of U.S. power, they were arguably not a form of economic coercion, because the White House justified the tariffs as retaliation for years of unfair practices by America's trading partners. When Trump cites the imbalance in the average tariff rates of the United States compared with countries like India and South Korea as the reason he loves tariffs, he is making an argument for trade protectionism, not economic coercion.[7] However, when the Trump administration declares 25 percent tariffs against Mexico until it curtails fentanyl flows into the United States and unless it receives illegal migrants being deported from the United States, as discussed in chapter 1, this is an act of economic coercion because it is weaponizing trade for a political objective, not an economic one.

Extraterritorial export controls are another form of economic coercion. Both China and the United States can specify that European economies require authorization to reexport products to third countries because some element of the supply chain for that product originated in the United States or China. This is a form of economic control that can be used for political purposes.[8] Economic coercion can be a preventative act regarding protection of key technologies, supply chains, information networks, data, or critical resources. In the run-up to World War II, for example, Germany instituted export controls against the United States on copper sulfate, reducing U.S. supplies needed for munitions manufacturing. When the United States controls the production of high-end memory chips, or when China withholds the export of urea (used for diesel fuel), these are both acts of economic coercion. Both China and the United States have coerced the private sector to transfer sensitive data. In the latter case, the justifications come from sealed indictments, anti-bribery, antitrust, or other forms of litigation. In the former case, there is virtually no transparency with regard to the practice.

Economic coercion is within the reach of not only the most powerful actors. Anyone can coerce by virtue of occupying a critical node or hub in any network. Henry Farrell and Abraham Newman refer to this as the "panopticon effect," in which the central hub has an informational advantage, able to see and interact with all of the other actors while each actor can only interact with the central hub.[9] The CEO of a major company can exercise power, but so can the green-eye-shaded accountant in the back office if they occupy a lower-level but critical chokepoint in the company. Moreover, not all hubs are the same. An actor may be powerful within one hub but less powerful and even vulnerable in another. With the U.S. dollar as the reserve currency, the United States holds inordinate influence over the global financial system, but during the Covid-19 pandemic, the world learned that China occupied a central hub as the supplier of medical personal protective equipment (PPE). During World War II, Canada exercised inordinate leverage through its controls on copper exports to the United States, specifying that supplies would be made available for the United States to fill munitions contracts only for allied countries.[10] The Netherlands could be another example, in that it occupies a key node in the semiconductor supply chain. The Dutch company Advanced Semiconductor Materials Lithography (ASML) is currently the only company in the world that has the capacity to produce the extreme ultraviolet (EUV) lithography machine, which is essential to produce the most advanced microchips.[11] Because of ASML's market monopoly, the Netherlands has enormous leverage in the advanced semiconductor supply chain, which prompted the Biden administration to enlist them to join its export controls of advanced semiconductor manufacturing equipment to China in 2023.[12] There are many different hubs—information, development assistance, military security, global health, natural resources, financial services—in which different actors can wield power.[13]

In addition to occupying the hub, the coercer seeks tools that are least costly to them; otherwise, the coercion would be self-harming. When China in 2012, for example, withheld banana purchases from the Philippines, it did so with the knowledge that there were many alternative suppliers domestically or abroad. In 2010, China targeted Norwegian salmon imports when it disliked the Norwegian Nobel Committee's decision to award the Nobel Peace Prize to Chinese dissident writer Liu Xiaobo. The six-year boycott led to a collapse in Norway's share of the Chinese market, dropping from 90 percent to 25 percent within a year. Meanwhile, China simply increased its purchases of Scottish or Faroese salmon to meet domestic consumer demand.

Finally, economic coercion is usually targeted. It is carefully designed to locate a vulnerability on which the coercer can exercise maximum impact rather than broad-based sanctions. In 2019, for example, Japan retaliated against South Korea's cancellation of a political agreement on comfort women by imposing export controls on three key precursors chemicals—hydrogen fluoride, fluorinated polyimides, and photoresist—that are critical to Korea's semiconductor chip production.[14] This means that economic coercion can be taking place between two countries at the micro level even though overall bilateral trade can look normal at the macro level.[15] In this sense, economic coercion is the equivalent of using a scalpel rather than a blunt instrument, inflicting maximum pain on the target at minimum cost to the coercer.

NOT ALL ECONOMIC COERCION IS THE SAME

The weaponization of economic interdependence is an outgrowth of globalization and the creation of information and finance networks that can be leveraged as a source of power by actors with dominant access and control over key hubs.[16] In 2009, scholars like Anne-Marie Slaughter saw these networks in a positive light as giving the United States a distinct advantage in shaping the global agenda, setting the rules, and unlocking innovation and growth. However, with the advent of financial sanctions and other "smart sanctions" by the United States to counter terrorism and weapons of mass destruction (WMD) proliferation, the literature offers a less benign view of the role that trade interdependence and globalization can play in promoting cooperation and leveling development differentials.[17] As some scholars argue, weaponization of economic interdependence has long been a trait of United States policy.[18] Exhibit A is the Trump administration's use of tariffs in early 2025 against Mexico and Canada, but it is also evident in the administration's domestic practices such as the withholding of federal grants to universities for their diversity, equity, and inclusion (DEI) practices. Although the latter is not a weaponization of trade per se, it is the use of economic leverage to pursue a noneconomic, political objective. Economic coercion has also been evident in the widespread Western sanctioning of Russia for the war in Ukraine, or the aforementioned U.S. use of financial sanctions against North Korea.[19] Successive U.S. administrations have levied sanctions against Iran since the 1979 revolution and against Cuba for decades. The United States also has a long history of economic coercion against China, including the withholding of most-favored-nation (MFN) trading status in the 1990s and financial sanctions against Chinese entities for the transfer of dual-use technologies to countries like Algeria, Iran, and Pakistan.

But there is a qualitative difference in the way the United States and China weaponize interdependence. In form, economic coercion by the United States or China can look quite similar. Both countries sanction governments, private companies, and even individuals. With the exception of certain tariff actions starting in 2025 by the Trump administration, we argue that over the past three decades there are fundamental differences in both the means and purpose of how the two countries employ economic coercion.

For one, acts of economic coercion by the United States are usually formal rather than informal. That is, in most cases, the United States government is generally forthright and transparent about its actions: it announces the sanction it is employing, against which target, and for what reason.[20] Even in the case of Canada and Mexico, the administration was very clear about the reasons for employing sanctions, even documenting them in a White House fact sheet.[21] In the case of China, tactics such as the application of tariffs, the withholding of tourist travel, or a consumer boycott are usually opaque. They are not formally announced in terms of target or purpose. There is no accompanying Zhongnanhai fact sheet. Sometimes the target does not know it is being targeted until it is too late; or it may not want to draw public attention to the sanction for fear of escalation and will quietly succumb to what the Chinese government wants it to do. As one study noted, "vague threats, cancellation of high-level visits, selective purchases and non-purchases, and other informal measures are the common methods that China uses to impose a sanction."[22] If called out by the targeted government or company, the Chinese government will occasionally deny any involvement and attribute the sanction to the "anger" of the Chinese people; or it might deny any role in the social media frenzy swirling around an innocuous action by a Western company (examples discussed below). If it admits to the sanction, it will usually justify it after the fact by some unsubstantiated health or safety concern.

Second, the use of economic coercion by the United States usually has a legal justification for action, based in some existing law, act of Congress, or executive order. BDA sanctions against North Korea, for example, originated from legal authority provided by the PATRIOT Act regarding money laundering and counterfeiting of U.S. currency.[23] In 2025, Trump levied 25 percent tariffs against Mexico and Canada and 10 percent additional tariffs on China using the International Emergency Economic Powers Act (IEEPA), which allows the president to regulate economic transactions pursuant to a declaration of a national emergency such as war (Trump's use of IEEPA is being contested in the courts at the time of this writing).[24] Other sanctions might derive their authority from the State Sponsors of Terrorism legislation or the Trading with the Enemy Act (TWEA).[25] Even the U.S. call for export controls on critical and emerging technologies to China, as anathema as they may appear to free traders, are based in legislation and clear about their purpose.[26]

Chinese economic coercion is rarely based in any legal and legitimate authority, which is also why it is applied informally and opaquely. Instead, Chinese sanctions are carried out in naked self-interest without any further need for justification. The informality and nonlegal basis of Chinese coercion serve a purpose. Informality allows the People's Republic of China (PRC) government to deny any responsibility, to avoid World Trade Organization (WTO) adjudication for unfair trade practices, and also to roll back coercion if it is unsuccessful (or successful) without losing face.

For example, despite an eighteen-month coercion campaign against South Korea over the deployment of a U.S. missile defense battery in the country that dealt Korean businesses billions of dollars in damage, the informal sanctions were never acknowledged by Beijing, nor imposed through existing legal conventions.[27] The PRC government instruction to travel agencies to stop selling group tourism packages to Korea was never delivered in a written, public communication, according to scholars, and instead was conveyed verbally along with the threat of fines if not followed.[28] According to one excellent study, when China stopped imports of Norwegian salmon in 2010 over the awarding of the Nobel Peace Prize to an imprisoned Chinese dissident, the order was quietly issued by the Beijing Capital Airport Entry-Exit Inspection and Quarantine Bureau, dated December 8, 2010, mandating blanket restrictive scrutiny of all agricultural products coming from Norway. The order applied to no other country.[29] When China sanctioned the export of rare earth elements (REEs) to Japan in 2010 over a territorial dispute, it not only never announced the action but also denied its existence when called out.[30] The coercion only came to be known through Japanese organizations like the relevant metals industry associations and the Ministry of Economy, Trade and Industry (METI), which confirmed publicly that Chinese exports had dried up. METI officials believed an order had been given verbally by the PRC government to its exporters to avoid any paper trails.[31] When called out for the coercion, Chinese leaders merely denied the allegation. In response to French president Nicolas Sarközy's meeting with the Dalai Lama in December 2008, China held up an order of 150 airplanes from Airbus and canceled a trade delegation trip to France, while spending $15 billion in trade deals in other European Union capitals during the same trip. These were all informal and unannounced measures, but when Chinese prime minister Wen Jiabao noted that his European itinerary skipped France, he reportedly scoffed, "We all know why."[32]

Third, the purpose of economic coercion by the United States and China is different. U.S. actions are usually to counter or punish some violation of U.S. law or international norm, whereas China's are pursued largely for narrow and parochial reasons. As one author noted, "in theory and largely in practice, [U.S. coercive practices] are intended to uphold the integrity of the international financial system and certain multilateral red lines, not the raw 'realpolitik' national interest of the United States."[33] U.S. sanctions are usually levied against deviant behavior in the international system and/or in compliance with UN Security Council resolutions. Financial sanctions against North Korea and Iran, for example, are meant to counter WMD proliferation and human rights abuses. Economic coercive measures against Russia are intended to punish for Vladimir Putin's unprovoked invasion of a neighboring country. The juridical nature of U.S. economic coercion is made all the more apparent by the outrage at home and abroad at Trump's unilateral tariffs at the beginning of 2025 against Canada, Mexico, and China. While formally announced, these tariffs were not justified as a response to some violation of existing international law, norms, or existing U.S. law. Instead, they were justified as emergency measures taken in the name of U.S. national security. While this rationale may make sound political sense, they exude an arbitrary and unilateral vibe that makes them unlike past U.S. practice and more akin to China's mercantilist mindset.

This makes Trump's actions more resonant with China's economic coercion, which is generally not in support of international norms or laws but narrowly focused on a handful of issues meaningful to China, largely related to sovereignty, territorial disputes, and the integrity of the Chinese Communist Party (CCP) leadership. This type of coercion is non–WTO conforming because it is discriminatory against a WTO member and not based on a trade-related matter, making it difficult for victims to take their grievance to the international organization for dispute resolution. China offers no apology for this behavior, as one author notes: "While the United States tries to justify its unilateral sanctions as upholding international issues like human rights or nonproliferation, China simply points to its own national interests."[34] Moreover, what distinguishes China's weaponization of economic interdependence is its incorporation by Beijing as a regular, routine tool of diplomacy to achieve foreign policy goals, not just as a sanction against deviant behavior in the international system like war, illicit activities, or WMD proliferation.

There are, of course, exceptions to these generalizations. The United States has used economic coercion out of naked self-interest—in addition to Trump's 2025 tariffs, the 2020 sanctioning by the first Trump administration of an International Criminal Court prosecutor for investigating the United States for war crimes in Afghanistan being one recent example.[35] And China has used coercion in support of international norms—such as sanctions against Iran after discovery of the Natanz nuclear program in 2003 or compliance with sanctions mandated by UN Security Council resolutions against North Korean nuclear proliferation. Not every Chinese sanction is informal and devoid of legal justification, just as not every U.S. sanction is levied on behalf of the good of the world. On balance, however, the differences in weaponization of economic interdependence are real and significant. Up until recently, the U.S. government would not orchestrate a social media campaign to boycott a foreign company because of satirical criticism of its president; China would. Or, as one author summarized the difference, the Treasury Department would not freeze the assets of a foreign or domestic entity "because of a tweet comparing the U.S. president to a cartoon character."[36] Not only has China done so, but it has also amassed an unprecedented record of weaponizing economic interdependence.

CHINA'S ECONOMIC PREDATION

China uses access to its large market to project influence and affect the political choices of others outside its borders. The purpose is to compel the target (whether foreign governments, private companies, or individuals) either to reverse actions or to withhold actions deemed contrary to China's core interests. These interests are largely defined as (1) recognizing Taiwan, Hong Kong, and Macau as part of China; (2) suppressing dissent in Hong Kong; (3) acquiescing to China's actions in Xinjiang and Tibet; (4) stifling the memory of the Tiananmen Square democracy protests; (5) suppressing homegrown democratic voices; (6) protecting China's territorial claims; (7) preserving the reputation of the CCP leadership and the Chinese people; and (8) defending Chinese national champions such as Huawei. Anyone who contravenes these policies is subject to Chinese coercion of the worst kind.[37] China's self-professed core interests also extend to broader military and strategic objectives, including undermining the legitimacy of U.S. alliances in Asia, expanding the surveillance state, and influencing international institutions.[38]

While China exercises power in many different forms, it employs economic coercion in two general ways.[39] In the largely nonwhite Global South, China uses financial capital through initiatives like the Belt and Road Initiative (BRI) to exercise influence. By funding the construction of seaports, railways, highways, stadiums, and other trophy projects of cash-needy developmental economies, China captures the loyalty of local political and business elites to ensure respect for Chinese interests.[40] China complements its BRI strategy with a massive disinformation campaign in Africa, Latin America, the South Pacific, and Southeast Asia, manipulating the public narrative on social media, in the press, and among politicians in ways favorable to China and critical of the West. Many observers, including the U.S. State Department, have written on these aspects, which are not the focus of this study.[41]

In the largely white Global North, China has used a different form of economic coercion. These countries are not as capital-poor as their developing counterparts, elite interests are not as easily captured, and media industries are not as easily penetrable. Instead, China weaponizes trade dependence to get what it wants. This could entail a sudden stoppage of imports from a particular country, a reduced flow of Chinese students and tourists to the target state, a consumer boycott of purchases, an embargo on exports, or any number of nontariff barriers based on arbitrary health and safety standards.[42] China does not discriminate among its targets, ranging from states to private-sector actors. In each case, its goals are rarely economic; instead, the aim is to achieve political and security goals.[43] While plaintiffs can take China to WTO arbitration for patent protection in Chinese courts, they have little recourse if tourists or students suddenly stop showing up in their country for holidays or for the new academic semester, or if Chinese consumers stop eating bananas for "health" reasons.

While unannounced and informal, Chinese sanctions are imposed swiftly and impactfully. This practice has been used against a host of Western and Asian countries, usually much smaller than China. After Taiwan opened a representative office in Vilnius in 2021, Lithuania saw a 91 percent drop in exports to China.[44] Andreas Fuchs and Nils-Hendrik Klann have found that countries whose leaders met with the Dalai Lama saw a subsequent decline in exports to China by 17 percent in the first year and an average of 12.5 percent over the next two years.[45] Another study by the Mercator Institute for China Studies identifies 123 cases of coercion since 2010, finding that China follows a two-pronged strategy: it uses popular boycotts targeting products and services against private companies (what one scholar has called "purchasing diplomacy"), and it uses a combination of restrictions on trade and tourism against governments.[46]

China's predatory actions are carefully designed to hit countries where it hurts most. In 1992, it cut France out of a major infrastructure project, while inviting other EU countries to participate, because of France's sale of Mirage fighter jets to Taiwan.[47] When it sanctioned the import of Philippine bananas in 2012, it did so with the knowledge that agriculture is one-fifth of the Philippine economy, that it employs one-third of the population, and that half of all Philippine bananas go to the Chinese market.[48] Similarly, when China stopped importing grouper fish from Taiwan in 2022 in response to the Pelosi visit, it knew that Taiwan was 91 percent dependent on the Chinese export market.[49] China has even leveraged its beloved pandas as a tool of coercion.[50]

China seeks deference by routinely warning countries about what it can do to them. For example, in response to Sweden's granting a human rights prize in 2019 to Chinese-born Swedish citizen Gui Minhai, who was detained in China, Beijing's ambassador to Sweden, Gui Congyou, announced publicly in an interview, "We treat our friends with fine wine, but for our enemies we have shotguns."[51] In an interview in the *Australian Financial Review* in April 2020, the Chinese ambassador Cheng Jingye levied unapologetically (and prophetically) the threat of sanctions after Canberra's call for an independent investigation into the origins of Covid-19 in China: "Maybe the ordinary [Chinese] people will say 'Why should we drink Australian wine? Eat Australian beef?'"[52] This threat was accompanied by social media posts on Weibo by the editor of *Global Times* with the full-throated warning: "[Australia] is a bit like chewing gum stuck to the bottom of China's shoe. Sometimes you have to find a stone to scrape it off."[53] In 2016, the Chinese ambassador to South Korea, Qiu Guohong, warned that if the Terminal High Altitude Area Defense (THAAD) battery were deployed in Korea, then Beijing would ensure that relations would be "destroyed in an instant."[54] When the Czech Senate Speaker Miloš Vystrčil visited Taiwan in August 2020, the Chinese Foreign Minister Wang Yi, who was in the middle of a trip to Europe, said the Czech Republic would "pay a heavy price."[55]

The threats and warnings proliferate in China's interactions not just with governments but with private companies and individuals as well. When China took clothing retailer H&M off all Chinese e-commerce sites and social media platforms in 2021, its kill-the-chicken-to-scare-the-monkey tactic was clear: "H&M was large enough in China to be noticed and made an example of [for other Western retailers]."[56] In 2020, like a scene out of a Triad movie, China sent a letter to the Czech president warning about the consequences of a visit by top legislators to Taiwan: "China is the largest foreign market for many Czech companies like Skoda Auto, Home Credit Group, Klaviry Petrof, and others . . . [these companies] will have to pay for the visit to Taiwan by Chairman Kubera."[57] Former Singaporean prime minister Lee Kuan Yew put it frankly when describing what sort of coercion can be levied by China: "As in the case of Hong Kong, if necessary the tap could be turned off."[58] When Norway gave the Nobel Peace Prize to jailed dissident Liu Xiaobo, China first warned the selection committee that there would be consequences of the choice; once the award was announced, China warned all foreign diplomats in Oslo not to attend the ceremony (the prize was to be awarded in absentia) or, said then vice foreign minister Cui Tiankai, they would "have to bear the consequences."[59] The reported remarks in New Zealand in May 2022 by the Chinese ambassador Wang Xiaolong are typical of a practice that seems to be reserved for China's top envoys in targeted countries: "An economic relationship in which China buys nearly a third of the country's exports shouldn't be taken for granted."[60]

SOURCES OF CHINA'S PREDATORY LIBERALISM

How did we get to this point of China's predatory use of economic coercion? While the practice has heightened dramatically under Xi Jinping, it goes back for decades. The sources of the behavior certainly have to do with conscious policy choices made by the PRC government, but several permissive conditions have facilitated the environment for such choices that can only partially be attributed to China and sit more squarely on the shoulders of the West.

One specific source of China's economic predation is the externalization of its domestic authoritarian practices. Foreign policy often reflects the political values of an actor in international politics, and China is no exception to this generalization. While trade policy may itself be neutral, it can be manipulated in ways that reflect illiberal practices and values at home.

Another source relates to China's unique strategic culture (defined as the historical and cultural framing of a country's security policy). Informed by its difficult past experiences as the "sick man" of Asia carved up by Western powers and Japan, China views economic coercion as a way to manage a hostile external environment. At the October 2022 Twentieth Party Congress, Xi Jinping replaced customary references to China's "favorable" external environment with statements about "worst-case scenarios" and "potential dangers." In the March 2023 National People's Congress, the PRC leader emphasized "severe challenges" to China's development path.[61] And in his 2025 New Year speech to the Chinese people and to the world, Xi talked about a "world of both transformation and turbulence" and emphasized the need for China to "rise above estrangement and conflict."[62] China may see economic coercion as a handy tool of statecraft in an uncertain threat environment.

A third source of China's economic predation stems from its integration into the global economy. The irony is that Beijing used to oppose economic sanctions as "illegal" tools of diplomacy. But since the late 2000s, the perspective has changed. James Reilly cites the Chinese legal scholar Jian Jisong as an important voice reflecting this change: "As China increases its economic influence, China should increase its use of unilateral economic sanctions in order to maintain its legal international interests and achieve its foreign policy objectives."[63] This change is a function of China's increased economic power, as well as lessons learned from the U.S. use of economic sanctions as a compellent tool of statecraft. As four decades of economic integration with the global economy made China critical to low-cost manufacturing product chains, a massive market for the world's exports, a destination for foreign capital, and a major supplier of critical minerals, China saw opportunities to leverage its centrality for political gain.[64]

The sources of China's predatory economic behavior, however, go beyond China's policy choices to theories, assumptions, and strategies held by the United States in its building of the postwar global order. Together, as Bethany Allen observes, these pathologies created "blind spots" for the West to China's economic coercion.[65] First, at the level of theory, a permissive condition of China's economic coercion is the West's overconfidence in neoclassical economics as the backbone of the liberal order. As Robert Atkinson notes, the premium placed on laissez-faire economics compelled policymakers to believe that all would aspire to minimize government intervention in the economy and economic policies. Any attempts to intervene in the economy or trade policy would, therefore, be temporary and nonthreatening because, in the end, market forces, if left alone, would offer the best outcomes in terms of productivity and profit for all. This created an environment, Atkinson observes, in which China's illiberal system and actions were viewed as nonthreatening to the postwar order. At worst, it was the exception that proved the rule.[66]

The same could be said about faith in the law of comparative advantage. The postwar global trading order was built on the notion that economies would specialize in the production of goods and services they could produce most efficiently and then trade with others. Few saw security implications to trade patterns that would allow one country (even an illiberal one) to develop a chokehold on supply chains. In short, it did not matter who made potato chips or memory chips. Economies would trade with each other to maximize efficiency and output. Related to this was the West's deregulation of the private sector and promotion of the free market, in which the firm reigned supreme. Milton Friedman and other economists wrote in the 1970s about how the singular purpose of firms should be to make profits, oppose regulation by the government, and allow for the free flow of capital, trade, and investments to wherever efficiency and margins are maximized.[67] Any restrictions on trade with and investment in China were considered anathema as one of the largest markets in the world started to open its doors to the West. As Allen observes, this undying faith in laissez-faire economics, private innovation, and private capital to expand the global economy created blind spots to the potential threats posed by government intervention or industrial policy: "The U.S.-led global embrace of a too-lightly regulated capitalism allowed the [Chinese Communist] party to develop and deploy its toolkit of economic coercion."[68] Dogmatic belief in liberalism cultivated blind spots and a "nonchalance" to China's interventionist trade practices and industrial policy.[69]

The second blind spot to China's economic coercion relates to the West's overconfidence in its grand strategy of transformative capitalism for China. To put it simply, the world expected that as China got rich, market liberalization would lead to political liberalization. When President Bill Clinton celebrated China's accession to the WTO in March 2000, he opined that this would eventually make China more like the United States: "The more China liberalizes its economy, the more fully it will liberalize the potential of its people. . . . And when individuals have the power not just to dream, but to realize their dreams, they will demand a greater say."[70]

The supreme confidence in the "more like us" thesis fostered magnanimity when it came to Chinese actions that ran contrary to free market or liberalism principles. These were things to be tolerated for now because in the end, China's path was assumed to be determined. Again, the Clinton administration's experiment with linking MFN trade status to human rights was illustrative. The rationale for eventually delinking the two, absent progress on the latter, was that promotion of trade and economic growth of China would eventually lead to political liberalization.[71]

Decades of American strategic thinking by the likes of Richard Nixon, Henry Kissinger, Zbigniew Brzezinski, and former World Bank president Robert Zoellick asserted that wealth and growth would eventually make China a "responsible stakeholder" in the international system.[72] Liberal international relations theorists wrote about how China would remain a rule-abider within the postwar order from which it had tremendously profited. The historic rise out of poverty by 800 million Chinese was the empirical proof of this thesis, so that even if China had revisionist intentions, the benefits of staying within the current order outweighed the tremendous costs of trying to overturn it.[73] The blind spots to China's coercion were reinforced by a theoretical and policy dogmatism in the West that China needed just a little more time to engage with the world to effect the transformation.

These passive attitudes toward China's predatory behavior have dissipated over the past half decade, for five reasons. First, policymakers realized the failure of the China experiment that dated back to Nixon's fateful opening in 1972.[74] China's economic development and wealth did not precipitate liberalization; instead, it empowered illiberal political forces at home that would become externalized in its bullying of other states. Second, the failure of globalization to close the wealth gaps in the global economy, encouraging privatization at the expense of labor and environment in the Global South, highlighted China as a culprit along with Wall Street and international financial institutions. Third, the 2008 financial crisis weakened the United States in the eyes of China, leading Xi Jinping and the CCP to be more forceful in realizing China's own destiny, rather than following the traditional diffident posture of "biding time" and "hiding strengths" of Deng Xiaoping. Fourth, with Donald Trump's rise (and 2025 return) to the presidency, his anti-trade and "America First" policies demonized as predatory China's merchandise trade deficit with the United States. And fifth, the Covid-19 pandemic awakened the world to the vulnerability of supply chains with China as a chokepoint in everything from medical masks to critical minerals.

These factors effectively ended more than fifty years of a U.S. policy toward China that privileged engagement and discouraged naked competition. In the end, both the far-right and far-left ends of the political spectrum in the West grew hypersensitive to China's weaponization of interdependence. The question now is whether this realization came too late—whether countries can organize to prevent a new era of predatory liberalism in the global economy led by China's practices.

CHAPTER 3

CHINA'S ECONOMIC COERCION

In the most comprehensive database assembled, we count a total of 605 cases in which China has weaponized trade (as of June 2025). The targets have been private-sector companies and individuals in 582 cases (in forty-one countries plus Taiwan) and governments (including Taiwan and the European Union) in twenty-three cases; the countries affected, forty-four in all, are listed in table 3.1. New and original data presented in this chapter offers the first look at this complete universe of cases. Table 3.2 presents the known acts of coercion directly against governments. Appendix 1 presents all of the known acts of coercion against private-sector firms (some more than once) since 1997. While these datasets record more cases than any other existing study, they most likely still underestimate the number and extent of coercive measures taken by Beijing. Because China's economic predation is often unannounced and informal, some targets may not realize they are in China's crosshairs, and those that do may be afraid to report it for fear of escalation. In a study of China's unannounced actions against Norwegian salmon, for example, three of five company heads operating in China backed out of doing interviews with the media about the discriminatory actions for fear of additional sanctions.[1]

THE GOALS AND TACTICS OF CHINA'S ECONOMIC COERCION

Beijing has incorporated economic coercion as a regular tool of diplomacy to achieve foreign policy goals, not just as a sanction against deviant behavior in the international system like war, illicit activities, or nuclear proliferation. As table 3.2

TABLE 3.1 Forty-Four Countries (Plus Taiwan) Coerced by China

Australia*†	Finland†	Japan*†	Netherlands†	Saudi Arabia†	Taiwan*†
Austria†	France*†	Jordan†	New Zealand*†	Singapore†	Thailand†
Belgium†	Germany*†	Latvia*	Norway*†	South Korea*†	Turkey†
Brazil†	India†	Lithuania*†	Palau*	Spain†	United Arab Emirates†
Canada*†	Indonesia†	Luxembourg†	Philippines*†	Sri Lanka†	United Kingdom*†
Czech Republic*†	Ireland†	Malaysia†	Poland†	Sweden*†	United States*†
Denmark†	Israel†	Mauritius†	Qatar†	Switzerland†	
Estonia*	Italy†	Mongolia*†	Russia†		

Sources: Victor D. Cha, "Collective Resilience: Deterring China's Weaponization of Economic Interdependence," *International Security* 48, no. 1 (2023): 91–124; Appendix 1.

Note: This list includes eighteen governments directly coerced by China (plus Taiwan and the European Union), and forty-one countries (plus Taiwan) whose firms have been targeted by China. Fifteen of the eighteen governments targeted directly overlap with the list of forty-one countries whose firms were targeted.
* Government directly coerced by China (including Taiwan)
† Company(ies) coerced by China

shows, the trigger for Chinese predation in most cases since 2008 is related not to trade or commercial disputes but to securing any one or a combination of political objectives:

- Opposition to Taiwan independence and acceptance that Taiwan is part of China
- Explicit recognition that Hong Kong and Macau are part of China
- Acceptance of China's exercise of sovereign actions over populations in Tibet and Xinjiang, even in the face of human rights abuses
- Respect for China's territorial claims on land, on water, and in the air (e.g., exclusive economic zone and air defense identification zone)
- Stifling domestic dissident voices, including the narrative and memorialization of the 1989 Tiananmen Square protests
- Preserving a positive image of the CCP leadership, including that of President Xi Jinping

TABLE 3.2 China's Economic Coercion Against Eighteen Governments
(Plus Taiwan and the European Union)

YEAR	TARGETED ACTOR	TYPE OF CHINESE ECONOMIC COERCION	ISSUE (NONECONOMIC)
2008	France	Street demonstrations and public boycott against French Carrefour in China	Tibet (pro-Tibet activists disrupted the Paris leg of the Beijing Olympics torch relay)
2010	Japan	Export embargo (rare earth minerals)	Sovereignty dispute (Senkaku/Diaoyutai)
2010	Norway	Import embargo (salmon)	Human rights (Nobel Prize awarded to Chinese dissident Liu Xiaobo)
2012	Philippines	Import embargo (bananas)	Sovereignty dispute (Scarborough Shoal)
2016	Mongolia	Nontariff actions (new border fees on commodity imports from Mongolia, cancellation of loan negotiations)	Human rights (Dalai Lama)
2016	South Korea	Discriminatory regulations; other nontariff actions (Lotte)	Political (emplacement of U.S. missile defense system in Korea)
2017	Palau	Nontariff actions (tourism ban)	Taiwan (Palau refuses to break its diplomatic ties)
2019	New Zealand	Nontariff actions (tourism ban and withdrawal of a tourism partnership agreement)	Political (exclusion of Huawei from 5G market)
2019	Sweden	Nontariff actions (canceled trade talks)	Human rights (prize to the Swedish-Chinese dissident Gui Minhai, jailed in China)
2019	Czech Republic	Nontariff actions (canceled Prague Philharmonic tour)	Taiwan (sister-city agreement)
2020	Canada	Nontariff actions (detention of two Canadian citizens); import embargo (soybeans, canola seed, meat)	Political (Canadian arrest of Huawei executive)

(continued)

TABLE 3.2 (*continued*)

YEAR	TARGETED ACTOR	TYPE OF CHINESE ECONOMIC COERCION	ISSUE (NONECONOMIC)
2020	Australia	Discriminatory tariffs against barley, beef, wine, and other exports	Covid-19 (Australian call for independent investigation; exclusion of Huawei from 5G market)
2020	Germany	Import embargo (pork)	Human rights (Xinjiang)
2020	Sweden	Discriminatory actions (Ericsson 5G contract awards reduced in China)	Political (exclusion of Huawei and ZTE from Swedish market)
2021	United Kingdom	Sanctions and assets freeze on organizations, individuals, and members of Parliament	Human rights (Xinjiang)
2022	Lithuania	Import embargo (including all EU imports that have parts made in Lithuania)	Taiwan (opening a representative office)
2022	Taiwan	Import embargo (fruits, fish); discriminatory regulations (suspension of export licenses); export embargo (natural sand)	Taiwan (Pelosi visit)
2022	Estonia and Latvia	Action undefined	Russia (leaving the China-CEEC framework)
2023	United States	Import restrictions on gallium, germanium, and two types of graphite (synthetic graphite material and natural flake graphite)	U.S. restrictions on AI chips and semiconductor manufacturing equipment
2024	European Union	Antidumping and anti-subsidy probes into brandy, dairy, plastic, and pork imports from the EU	EU restrictions on Chinese EVs
2024	Taiwan	Removed tariff exemptions on over 160 imports and other agricultural products	Election of new President William Lai

TABLE 3.2 *(continued)*

YEAR	TARGETED ACTOR	TYPE OF CHINESE ECONOMIC COERCION	ISSUE (NONECONOMIC)
2024	United States	Import embargo (antimony, gallium, and germanium)	U.S. restrictions on technology sales and transfers
2025	United States	Import embargo (other critical minerals such as tungsten, tellurium, bismuth, molybdenum, and indium)	U.S. restrictions on technology sales and transfers

Sources: All cases before 2022 are in Victor D. Cha, "Collective Resilience: Deterring China's Weaponization of Economic Interdependence," *International Security* 48, no. 1 (2023): 91–124.

For 2023 graphite, gallium, and germanium restrictions on the United States, see Emily Benson and Thibault Denamiel, "China's New Graphite Restrictions," *Center for Strategic and International Studies*, October 23, 2023, https://www.csis.org/analysis/chinas-new-graphite -restrictions. For 2024 anti-dumping and anti-subsidy probes into the EU, see Politico, "China Hits Back at Electric Vehicle Tariffs with Probe into EU Dairy," August 21, 2024, https://www .politico.eu/article/china-hits-back-at-electric-vehicle-tariffs-with-probe-into-eu-dairy/. For 2024 removal of tariff exemptions in Taiwan, see Foster Wong and Yian Lee, "China Ends Tariff Exemptions on Some Taiwan Agricultural Imports," *Bloomberg*, September 18, 2024, https://www.bloomberg.com/news/articles/2024-09-18/china-scraps-tariff-exemptions-on -some-taiwan-imports; Reuters, "China Suspends Tariff Concessions on 134 Items Under Taiwan Trade Deal," May 31, 2024, https://www.reuters.com/world/asia-pacific/china-suspends -tariff-concessions-134-items-under-taiwan-trade-deal-2024-05-31/. For 2024 import embargo on antimony, gallium, and germanium, see Reuters, "China Issues Rare Earth Regulations to Further Protect Domestic Supply," June 29, 2024, www.reuters.com/markets/commodities /china-issues-rare-earth-regulations-further-protect-domestic-supply-2024-06-29/; Gracelin Baskaran and Meredith Schwartz, "China Imposes Its Most Stringent Critical Minerals Export Restrictions Yet Amidst Escalating U.S.-China Tech War," *Center for Strategic and International Studies*, December 4, 2024, https://www.csis.org/analysis/china-imposes-its-most -stringent-critical-minerals-export-restrictions-yet-amidst. For 2025 import embargo on tungsten, tellurium, and more, see Juliana Liu, "China Proposes Fresh Export Curbs on EV Technology," *CNN*, January 3, 2025, https://www.cnn.com/2025/01/03/tech/china-ev-tech -export-controls-intl-hnk/index.html; Amy Lv, Lewis Jackson, and Ashitha Shivaprasad, "China Expands Key Mineral Export Controls After US Imposes Tariffs," Reuters, February 4, 2025, https://www.reuters.com/world/china/china-expands-critical-mineral-export-controls-after-us -imposes-tariffs-2025-02-04/.

There is a direct correlation between Chinese foreign and domestic policy goals and Beijing's weaponization of economic interdependence. It remains unapologetic about its use, does not acknowledge that these actions violate global trading norms, and remains undeterred in continuing the practice. The tactics employed by the PRC government against target governments, companies, and individuals in pursuit of these goals include:

- Ban on product of a target company
- Border entry ban for an individual
- Cancellation of contracts with a target company
- Consumer boycott on purchases from the target of select items already in China
- Embargo on exports to the target of select items from China
- Encouragement of domestic protests and vandalism in China against foreign targets
- Import embargo on select items from a target country or company
- Informal controls on tourism or student education flows from China to target country
- Investment ban against a target company in China
- Levying of tariffs on targeted goods entering China
- Online social media predation campaigns in China against the target
- Other nontariff barriers (e.g., related to "health" and "safety") that discriminate unfairly against target country or company
- Raids, arrests, and sanctions in China against a target company
- Refusal or cancellation of work permits for employees of a target company
- Revocation of press credentials in China of a target company
- Suspension of export licenses of a target company seeking to export to China
- Suspension of online sales platforms in China of a target company
- Suspension of streaming rights in China of a target company

CHINA'S THIRD FACE OF POWER

China's weaponization of economic interdependence is a source of power for four reasons. First, its market is extensive, and leveraging access to it is a tool of coercion. The Chinese market is arguably the largest in the world. For decades since the opening of the Chinese economy under Deng Xiaoping, companies have rushed to the country for a piece of the pie—over 900 million people made up the Chinese consumer class in 2024, more than one-fifth of the world's total.[2] Second, all of China's trade partners are asymmetrically dependent on it, providing another source of influence. In 2024, for example, China accounts for 27.98 percent of Australia's global trade, 20.75 percent of South Korea's, 20.12 percent of Japan's, and 11.18 percent of the United States', while these countries constitute a smaller fraction of China's overall exports.[3] Third, China executes its strategy in a dyadic format, ensuring that it maximizes its asymmetrical advantage over any one target government or company. It prefers to negotiate with countries individually and bilaterally, rather than as a group or collective, to cut deals that give it maximum leverage and intimidate the other side. Fourth, the illiberal nature of China's political system allows the government to implement directives with little pushback from consumers or civil society. If the PRC government mandates the suspension of travel by Chinese students to a particular country, it is unlikely to be criticized in the press or face pushback from civil society groups and political opposition parties. If it suddenly calls for the suspension of purchases of tropical fruits or beer from a particular overseas market, the political leadership does not expect to incur significant audience costs compared with a democratic leader considering such draconian acts.

The purpose of China's economic coercion is to achieve what scholars have called the third dimension of power by shaping how states view their own interests.[4] That is, China's use of economic punishment may not always be successful at changing the target state's behavior; however, over time, this bullying creates "an environment of self-censorship" among government and corporate leaders.[5] Beijing's actions set a precedent for others to anticipate, respect, and defer in advance to Chinese interests in all of their future actions. For these targets of coercion, there is very little they can do alone to resist, given the size and importance of the Chinese market. Countries simply accept China's threat of economic coercion as a new reality of the global trade order.

ECONOMIC COERCION WORKS

From Beijing's perspective, its predatory practices are working. The effect of economic coercion on state's choices is evident in actions and nonactions that defer to Chinese interests. Targets hardly ever stand up to China. They rarely protest China's characterization of an act as offensive to China's interests, however obscure or ambiguous the action might be. Instead, they accept China's claim, rescind the action, apologize profusely, and then self-censor subsequent behavior to avoid ending up in the crosshairs again. There are instances of resistance to China's coercion, such as Australia's efforts in 2020 or Lithuania's campaign in 2022, but these exceptions only prove the general rule.

For example, one journalist notes that between approximately 2010 and 2020, African governments with close economic ties to China routinely self-censored by avoiding political recognition of Taiwan, support of democracy in Hong Kong, condemnation of the treatment of Muslim minorities in Xinjiang, and opposition to militarization of the South China Sea.[6] Major democracies like South Korea and Germany remained silent and did not support U.S. sanctions against China when China passed the national security law in Hong Kong suppressing democracy in 2020.[7] Germany also apologized for Foreign Minister Heiko Maas's meeting with a Hong Kong democracy activist.[8] Brazil did not exclude Huawei from its 5G auction for fear of losing billions in business and promised cloud computing centers.[9] Italian prime minister Silvio Berlusconi reportedly once told the Dalai Lama in 1995 that he could not meet him anymore because of the need to maintain access to the Chinese market.[10] In 2009, French president Nicolas Sarközy issued an official statement confirming that from France's perspective, Tibet was unequivocally a part of China.[11] British prime minister David Cameron abstained from offering a statement of support for the 2010 Nobel Prize winner and Chinese dissident Liu Xiaobo because of an imminent visit by a PRC trade delegation that would make nearly three billion dollars' worth of trade deals with the UK.[12] In November 2024, German chancellor Olaf Scholz became the first Western leader to visit China after the three-year Covid-19 pandemic, bringing with him a delegation of the twelve largest German companies, even as Beijing was economically coercing Lithuania and had declared a "no limits" partnership with Russia, which had recently invaded Ukraine.[13] Germany—whose largest trading partner is China—was heading into a recession and needed Chinese business.

The willingness of both governments and private-sector firms to accommodate China with apologies and self-censoring is striking. Iconic French fashion house Givenchy issued a public mea culpa in 2019 for a T-shirt design that listed locations of its stores on the back of the shirt but did not list Taiwan and Hong Kong as part of China (i.e., "Hong Kong" as opposed to "Hong Kong, PRC"). Givenchy's corporate leadership stated it would immediately correct its "human negligence and mistakes" and that the company firmly adhered to the one-China policy.[14] In September 2019, French bank BNP Paribas went so far as to issue a public apology on behalf of the entire company for a pro–Hong Kong post by a single employee on their personal social media account.[15]

As Appendix 1 enumerates, there are many examples of corporate self-censorship being rewarded by China. Japanese clothing retailer Uniqlo remained silent about sourcing its supply chain from forced labor in Xinjiang despite mounting international pressure to stop the practice in 2020–2021. It was rewarded with an uptick in sales in the China market by 17 percent, while less silent companies like H&M, Nike, and others saw precipitous drops in sales.[16] In 2018, to preempt Chinese sanctions, the Gap clothing company issued a public apology and removed from sale a T-shirt design with a map of China that did not include

Taiwan and Tibet.[17] Marriott Hotels in 2018 also preemptively issued a public statement against separatism in China and took down its website that listed Hong Kong, Macau, and Taiwan as separate territories from China.[18]

Hollywood will not produce films that cast China in a negative light. A 2012 remake of the movie *Red Dawn*, about a group of teenage friends leading a guerilla resistance movement against a Chinese invasion of the continental United States, was delayed from release because the producers decided to recast the military invasion of California and Washington as from North Korea rather than from China.[19] After a harsh Chinese ban on films by Columbia Tristar Pictures for the release of a movie about Tibet in 1997, no motion pictures have since been made about Tibet or the Dalai Lama.[20] In fact, then Disney CEO Michael Eisner personally traveled to Beijing in October 1998 to apologize to PRC authorities for the making of *Kundun*, accepting blame for a "stupid mistake."[21]

The fruits of China's economic coercion strategy are also evident in various UN bodies. The vast majority of the fifty-three countries that read a statement in the UN Human Rights Council supporting China's national security law against democratic rights in Hong Kong in 2020 were recipients of BRI funding. A similar coalition came together in 2019 to support China's treatment of Uyghurs in Xinjiang before the UN High Commissioner for Human Rights.[22] China's financial support of the UN High Commissioner for Refugees office and its supporting NGOs effectively rendered the agency powerless in investigating Chinese practices of refoulement of North Korean escapees across the Sino–North Korea border.

In each of these cases, actors contextualize their choices to act in deference to China as "rational" self-interested economic decisions. But these choices are only deemed "rational" because (1) the immense size of the Chinese market is compelling and (2) they have accepted weaponized economic interdependence as the price of doing business with China. They act based on what they believe China wants. China exercises power without having to wield it.

CASES OF ECONOMIC COERCION AGAINST GOVERNMENTS

In this section, we profile selected cases of economic coercion against governments to illustrate the threshold for targeting, the tactics used by China, and the responses by targets (summaries of all cases are in table 3.2). The Lithuania case represents a form of Chinese economic coercion over Taiwan. The Norway case demonstrates coercion over domestic human rights issues. The embargo on Philippine bananas illustrates a case over territorial disputes. In the next section, the NBA case profiles China's reaction to a perceived infringement over Hong Kong.

Case Study 1: Lithuania and the Taiwan Question

The case of Lithuania illustrates what happens when countries cross China's redlines on Taiwan. In 2021, China promptly initiated an economic punishment campaign against the small Baltic country of 2.8 million people—unlike any other against a European economy—when Lithuania moved to establish official ties with Taiwan. Indeed, the PRC government's actions served as a wake-up call for the European Union, mobilizing Brussels to develop an action plan to counter China's economic coercion.

China has been on a campaign to coerce countries around the world to terminate their official ties with Taiwan. In March 2023, it succeeded with Honduras, thus reducing the total number of states that recognize Taiwan to twelve.[23] The list of countries that still recognize Taiwan is a hodgepodge of small island states in the Caribbean and the Pacific, three Latin American countries, Eswatini (the last absolute monarchy in Africa), and the Holy See, the seat of the Catholic Church.[24] This has been part of a broader effort by Beijing to further isolate Taipei internationally, either by pressure or with money. In countries that host a representative office of Taiwan (without formal diplomatic recognition), Beijing also undertook a campaign between 2017 and 2019 to expunge the word "Taiwan" from the names of these missions. This campaign succeeded in seven countries: Bahrain, Colombia, Ecuador, Jordan, Nigeria, Papua New Guinea, and the UAE.[25]

Against this backdrop, in March 2021, Lithuania announced that it planned to open a representative office in Taiwan.[26] Four months later, the Tsai Ing-wen government reciprocated with its own plan to open a corresponding office in Vilnius, calling it the Taiwanese Representative Office.[27] This was considered controversial because it would be the only office in the world to use the word "Taiwanese." For years, countries that have an office—a de facto embassy—for Taiwan have long avoided any iteration of Taiwan in its name. Often, these offices use the more acceptable capital city name "Taipei"—the most prominent example being the Taipei Economic and Cultural Representative Office for the United States (TECRO), the de facto embassy in Washington, DC. Lithuania's announcement immediately drew a stern rebuke from Beijing, which called on Vilnius to stay true to the "one-China principle" and not be taken advantage of by "Taiwan separatist forces."[28]

Lithuania's tilt toward Taiwan dates to 2019 when cracks opened in the Lithuania-China relationship. In February 2019, the Lithuanian government's annual national threat assessment spotlighted as a major concern China's increased intelligence activities in the country to discourage support for independence of Tibet and Taiwan.[29] This became evident in August 2019 during a violent counterprotest by the Chinese diaspora and embassy officials in Vilnius against a rally supporting Hong Kong democracy protests.[30] The Lithuanian police intervened, and the Lithuanian foreign ministry filed a protest with the Chinese embassy for its involvement.[31]

In April 2020, three months after the Covid-19 pandemic shut down the world, 204 Lithuanian politicians and public figures sent an open letter to President Gitanas Nausėda, asking him to support Taiwan's inclusion in international organizations such as the UN and the World Health Organization (WHO). The letter also called on Lithuania to support Taiwan's freedom and democracy, as Taiwan did in 1990 when Lithuania became independent from the Soviet Union. The request was eventually denied by President Nausėda, who responded with the technicality that only UN members can be WHO members (Taiwan is not). However, he indicated that Lithuania was open to cooperation with Taipei on Covid-19.[32]

China reacted very strongly to this issue. Shen Zhifei, the Chinese ambassador to Lithuania, told the press that the WHO letter is "an open provocation to the principle of one China."[33] On May 14, Lithuanian foreign minister Linas Linkevičius asked WHO director-general Tedros Adhanom Ghebreyesus to invite Taiwan to share its Covid-19 response measures at the upcoming Seventy-Third World Health Assembly (WHA) on May 18–19, while stressing that Lithuania respected the "One China policy."[34] China strongly protested again and blocked Taiwan's participation in the WHA.[35] Lithuanian support for Taiwan took a bigger leap after a new center-right government coalition won the November 2020 elections. The new government announced a "values-based foreign policy" and support for those "fighting for freedom around the world," including on behalf of Taiwan.[36]

All of these actions crossed obvious redlines for China, and Beijing lashed out with a major economic coercion campaign. In the summer and fall of 2021, China stopped purchases of Lithuanian timber and grain and stopped issuing export licenses to Lithuanian food companies.[37] In February 2022, it came to light that China had suspended all imports of beef, dairy, and beer. The Chinese customs agency initially offered no response when asked about the ban, denying any official embargo and attributing the actions to individual company and consumer choices. When pushed, it later cited an undefined "lack of documentation."[38] Lithuanian trade authorities believed the ban started in late 2021, speaking again to the informal and unannounced nature of China's coercion. The Lithuanian foreign minister criticized China for using trade as a weapon and received backing from the European Union, the United States, and the United Kingdom to file a case against China with the WTO on the grounds that the sanctions threatened the unity of the single EU market. EU members, the United States, Australia, Taiwan, and others purposefully increased their imports of Lithuanian goods to mitigate the effect of China's sanctions. Nevertheless, Lithuanian exports to China dropped 90 percent in December 2021 year-on-year as a result.[39]

China also implemented a secondary sanction campaign against the EU single market. It pressed multinationals to cut ties with the Baltic state by warning that any materials in the supply chain sourced from Lithuania could face Chinese sanctions. It made an example of German automotive parts companies Continental and Hella, whose parts were blocked from entry to China because of Lithuanian involvement in the supply chain.[40] This sanction was informal and unannounced, and German firms shied away from commenting on it publicly for fear of escalation by China.[41] The Chinese government also sanctioned Lithuania's deputy transportation and communications minister for a trip to Taiwan in August 2022.[42]

While China's explanation when called out about the trade embargo on Lithuania cited vague paperwork problems, the Chinese foreign ministry spokesman Zhao Lijian plainly stated the obvious motivation for the bullying, saying that Lithuania needed to "face up to facts, redress its own mistakes, and come back to the right track of adhering to the one China principle, instead of confusing right with wrong."[43] For these companies, the lesson is clear: the Chinese market is accessible only if they play by China's rules.

Case Study 2: Norway and Human Rights

The case of Norway demonstrates China's coercion against parties that are seen to intervene in domestic human rights issues. In 2010, the Nobel Committee awarded its annual Nobel Peace Prize to Chinese dissident writer Liu Xiaobo. Dr. Liu was an outspoken critic of China's political repression, often writing about how such actions violated China's own constitutional guarantee to its citizens of freedom of speech and freedom of assembly and association. The committee presented the award to Liu in absentia, symbolically placing the award on an empty chair as Liu was serving an eleven-year prison sentence for writing a manifesto in 2008 on the internet calling for political reforms that enshrined democracy, human rights, and the rule of law in China.

Beijing issued immediate threats about the award. It initially expressed disapproval at the nomination of Liu, accusing the Nobel Committee of meddling in Chinese internal affairs. The Chinese foreign ministry lodged a protest with Norway's ambassador in Beijing, and the Chinese embassy in Oslo warned that honoring a "criminal" would do significant damage to China-Norway bilateral relations. Beijing immediately canceled an impending visit by a trade delegation and refused to meet with the visiting Norwegian fisheries minister. In addition, after 2010, China canceled nearly all high-level official bilateral exchanges with the Norwegian government and would not approve travel visas, stating that Norwegians were "badly behaved."[44]

In 2010, Norway was by far China's largest source of salmon imports. Chinese consumers preferred it to all other salmon, and sales of Norwegian fresh chilled whole salmon accounted for more than 80 percent of China's market from 1997 to 2010.[45] In retaliation for the Nobel Committee's decision, however, China imposed unannounced restrictions on salmon imports that included enhanced licensing requirements, burdensome inspection and testing, and protracted quarantine periods. These measures led to a collapse in sales of Norwegian salmon by more than 60 percent year-on-year and decreased Norway's share of the Chinese imported salmon market from 90 percent to a meager 25 percent.[46] This action was clearly designed to punish the country for its award to Dr. Liu. The targeting of Norwegian salmon was selective, as China's overall imports of salmon grew from an average of 6,900 tons between 2007 and 2010 to more than 25,000 tons from 2011 to 2014.[47]

The manner in which China stealthily carried out the punitive action is also noteworthy. According to one excellent study, an order was quietly issued by the Beijing Capital Airport Entry-Exit Inspection and Quarantine Bureau dated December 8, 2010, mandating blanket restrictive scrutiny of all aquacultural products coming from Norway. The order applied to no other country. China followed this in January 2011 with a second order (Document 9) from the PRC Central Office of Quality Supervision, Inspection, and Quarantine calling for more stringent monitoring of salmon in general in order to circumvent charges of being non-compliant with WTO nondiscrimination rules, but the selective targeting of Norwegian salmon was clear.[48] Cases of Norwegian salmon suddenly piled up at Chinese ports as inspection times increased from three or four days to as much as twenty days. Approvals, moreover, came in small volumes of ten to thirty tons for Norway, while approval volumes were up to three hundred tons for salmon from other countries.[49] Because shipments are packed with enough ice to last only a few days, the customs delay basically left tons of Norwegian salmon rotting away in holding for reasons that the Chinese government felt no compunction to explain. This same treatment was not accorded to salmon imports from the United Kingdom, the Faroe Islands, and Chile, according to the case filed with the WTO by Oslo.[50]

China never acknowledged this act of economic coercion, which lasted for six years. Norway did everything it could to appease China. The Norwegian foreign minister apologized for the Nobel row and, reportedly, "deeply reflected upon the reasons bilateral mutual trust was harmed." Other government officials were quoted as saying "it's the fish that matters," downplaying the human rights agenda in bilateral relations.[51] Oslo responded to the Chinese government's demand that the Nobel prize never grace a Chinese dissident's hands by noting that the committee was independent from the government but that Oslo had initially opposed awarding the prize to Liu because of the negative impact on relations with China. In 2013, Norway supported China's membership in the Arctic Council to curry favor with Beijing. And when the Dalai Lama, a 1989 Nobel laureate, visited Norway in 2015 to celebrate the twenty-fifth anniversary of his prize, he might as well have been radioactive because no Norwegian government official would host a meeting for him.

Salmon exports to China did not reach 2010 level until 2016, at which point the government fully kowtowed to China, stating, "[Norway] attaches high importance to China's core interests and major concerns" and "will not support actions that undermine them."[52] Only then did Beijing acknowledge what it had done: "The sanctions on Norway that lasted for six years demonstrated China's firm determination against any external intervention into China's internal affairs."[53]

Case Study 3: The Philippines and Scarborough Shoal

The 2012 case of the Philippines showcases how China weaponizes economic coercion against claimants in territorial disputes and uses nonmilitary means to punish neighbors for infringing on Chinese sovereignty. China showed the world how quickly it can turn off the valve on a major agricultural product—in this case, Philippine bananas—at a moment's notice. Unlike in the case of Norway, it went beyond banning a single, but very important, agricultural product. Beijing also suspended Chinese tour groups to the Philippines, and Chinese hackers took down Filipino government, newspaper, and university websites.[54]

The genesis of this maritime dispute originated in the South China Sea, which has increasingly become a redline for Beijing and a hotbed of Chinese coercive actions, including diplomatic and economic sanctions and military actions in the past few decades.[55] The particular incident in question was a monthslong standoff between the Chinese and the Filipinos over the disputed Scarborough Shoal (Huangyan Island in Chinese and Panatag Shoal in Filipino)—over which, at the time, Manila held de facto control.

The standoff started on April 8, 2012, when Chinese fishermen were sighted anchored at the disputed territory by the Philippine Navy, which immediately dispatched a naval frigate to disrupt what it believed was illegal fishing.[56] A standoff ensued, with months of tense interactions between China and the Philippines at sea. Diplomatic negotiations were attempted, with the United States as an intermediary. Ultimately, the Philippines lost administrative control of the disputed shoal to Beijing and brought the case to international arbitration.

Throughout the standoff, the Chinese side was resolute and forceful in portraying the incident as an infringement on Chinese sovereignty and territorial integrity. Chinese vice foreign minister Fu Ying was unequivocal that the Philippines had made a grave mistake and misjudged the situation when it infringed on Chinese territory and that it should withdraw its ships immediately.[57] Right after the failed interception of the Chinese fishermen, the Chinese foreign ministry said the Philippines' attempt at "law enforcement" "infringed China's sovereignty."[58] The *People's Daily*, an official Chinese mouthpiece, feigned victimization, reiterating that China "would not give in to issues of sovereignty" and that the Philippines should not "view China's friendliness as weak and susceptible to bullying."[59] It prominently displayed these statements on the front page of its international edition for the world to read. Another official Chinese news organ, *China Daily*, published an op-ed in which it mused about the possibility of using force to resolve the situation, calling the Philippines' claim "groundless" and a "dangerous delusion."[60] Dai Bingguo, a high-ranking Chinese official, went even further, disparaging the Philippines by saying China should not be bullied by other countries, "especially small countries like the Philippines."[61] Beyond rhetoric, Beijing was not afraid to use a visible show of force, sending as many as seventeen ships to harass two Philippine vessels.

In addition to their physical presence and forceful rhetoric, the Chinese coupled their tactics with the full might of its economic prowess. As in the Norwegian salmon case two years earlier, China imposed sanctions where it hurt the target the most. In this case, it focused on the Philippines' large fruit industry, especially bananas, pineapples, and papayas.[62] Coincidentally in March, a month before the Scarborough Shoal incident, China had stopped a shipment of bananas after "finding" pests. As a result, Beijing implemented a more stringent quarantine inspection regime and targeted a larger batch of shipments, with any failing shipments to be either destroyed or sent back to the Philippines.[63] On May 10, the Chinese made public that 1,200 containers of Philippines bananas were being held in Chinese ports because of "quarantine concerns."[64] A few days later, the Chinese expanded the quarantine rules on other fruits after it claimed to have found mealybugs in Philippine papayas and pineapples.[65] Chinese authorities claimed to have found 104 types of harmful organisms in Philippine fruits.[66] These claims were disputed by Philippine agricultural officials, who argued that the alleged pest cited by the Chinese authorities—scale insect—actually "does not occur in bananas" (found only in coconuts). They also questioned why the shipments of the same bananas that were stopped by China had also gone to Japan and South Korea without any complaints.[67] In an effort to resolve the Chinese "health concern," Manila sent a delegation to China in late May to discuss the issue, but ultimately failed to convince the Chinese to lift the fruit quarantine.[68]

The damage to the fruit industry was swift. There were reports of tons of Philippine Cavendish bananas rotting at Chinese ports.[69] By mid-May, some experts estimated fruit exporters had already lost about 1.44 billion pesos ($33.6 million), with forty-three banana exporters told they could not export their bananas to the Chinese market.[70] Banana is an important agricultural product for the Philippine economy. It was their second-largest agricultural export, and the country was the second-largest exporter of bananas in the world after Ecuador.[71] In 2011, it exported about $2 billion worth of bananas to the world, about 19 percent ($367 million) of which went to China, its second-largest market after Japan. After the banana embargo, the Philippine share of the Chinese banana market dropped to 17 percent ($299 million) in 2012, and even further to 15 percent ($278 million) in 2013.

The sudden ban on banana imports had a devastating financial impact on Filipino banana farmers, many of whom are located hundreds of miles away from the Scarborough Shoal in Mindanao. They unwittingly became "collateral damage" in the maritime clash between the two neighbors. Stephen Antig, the executive director of the Pilipino Banana Growers and Exporters Association, estimated that two hundred thousand people would lose their livelihood if Beijing continued its ban.[72] The *Washington Post* interviewed a local Philippine banana grower who had staked his future on the Chinese market but now faced a "big disaster" after the Chinese stopped buying. Loads of China-bound banana shipments sat untended at Davao City port in Mindanao, leading to "free bananas" for the locals. Sara Duterte, then the mayor of Davao City (later vice president of the Philippines) admitted that her country was increasingly aware of the dangers posed by Chinese economic coercion—that China knows it has a "very big market" and "know their power and how to use it."[73]

Beijing did not stop at just banning fruits. It also targeted the tourism industry by abruptly issuing a travel warning and canceling all Chinese tour groups to the country, with travel agencies blaming "political uncertainty" and saying it was "too dangerous."[74] One Chinese travel agency admitted that government tourism authorities had asked them to suspend the tours. Chinese tourism to the Philippines is substantial: Chinese tourists make up the fourth-largest group to the country and account for as much as 60 percent of bookings at hotels and resorts.

The Chinese import embargo on the Philippines in 2012 had a lasting impact on the overall trajectory of the banana trade between the two countries. A 2023 Food and Agriculture Organization (FAO) report revealed that Chinese dependency on Philippines bananas dropped from an average of 50–75 percent in the 2010s to only 40 percent in 2022.[75] UN Comtrade data showed that in 2011, the year before the shoal incident, China was 91 percent dependent on the Philippines for bananas. That number dropped to 81 percent in 2012 and never fully recovered. Although China became the largest importer of Philippine bananas in 2019, its dependency on Manila that year was only 54 percent.[76] The FAO report attributed the change to a growing diversification of Chinese banana imports to new Chinese-owned banana plantations in Vietnam, Cambodia, and to a lesser extent, Laos. For China, these are more like-minded countries than the Philippines in Southeast Asia. Today, the Chinese banana market remains huge, the third-largest in the world after the European Union and the United States, but as China has shown the world in the past decade, its government, not the consumer, is the final arbiter of whom to buy bananas from. And sometimes the reason for not buying them is not economical, but political.

PRIVATE SECTOR: THE PROHIBITIVE PRICE OF DOING BUSINESS IN CHINA

China's predation is even more pronounced in the private sector. Table 3.3 summarizes, and appendix 1 presents in detail, an original collection of all known cases of economic coercion by the PRC government against private companies

TABLE 3.3 Private Sector: The Price of Doing Business with China

COUNTRIES (AND TAIWAN)	KNOWN CASES OF COERCION AGAINST FIRMS
United States	278
Japan	59
South Korea	33
Taiwan	33
France	30
United Kingdom*	25
Germany	22
Australia*	11
Switzerland	11
Netherlands	10
Italy	9
Spain	8
Sweden†	7
Canada	6
Czech Republic	3
Lithuania	3
Austria, Denmark†, India, Malaysia, New Zealand, Philippines, Russia, Saudi Arabia, Singapore, Thailand, United Arab Emirates	2
Belgium, Brazil, Finland, Indonesia, Ireland, Israel, Jordan, Luxembourg, Mauritius, Mongolia, Norway†, Poland, Qatar, Sri Lanka, Turkey	1

Source: Appendix 1.

Note: The total number of cases equals 585 in the table because cases against multinational companies Rio Tinto Group (British-Australian) and SAS Airlines (Denmark-Norway-Sweden) are counted for each country of joint ownership. We use 582 cases when we discuss in this book the total number of cases against companies.

* Includes coercion against Rio Tinto Group (British-Australian).

† Includes coercion against SAS Airlines (Denmark, Norway, Sweden).

and associated individuals. We count 582 cases, involving 470 companies (some companies coerced more than once). These companies are located in forty-one different countries (plus Taiwan) on all continents except Antarctica.[77]

Works by others have cited specific cases, but none have provided the data in its entirety.[78] In its 2022 report, the Mercator Institute for China Studies cited 123 cases between 2010 and 2022, but that data remains proprietary. Our dataset, though substantially larger than in previous studies, probably still underestimates the number of cases. This is because the coercion often goes unannounced by the PRC government, so it is difficult to track unless the targeted actor speaks out. Sometimes targeted actors are unwilling to publicize their concerns for fear of escalation, or a target may itself be unaware of the coercion taking place until it is too late.

The list of coerced companies runs the gamut from airlines, banks, conglomerates, gaming companies, and professional sports leagues to bakeries, bookstores, and bubble-tea chains. China is not intimidated by the size of its targets: the list includes five of the top ten companies on the 2024 Fortune 500 list (Walmart, Amazon, Apple, Exxon Mobil, Alphabet [Google]), and four of the top ten companies in the 2024 Fortune Global 500 list (Alphabet drops off the list).[79] American companies are the most targeted, with 278 cases, more than the next ten targets combined: Japan (59), South Korea (33), Taiwan (33), France (30), United Kingdom (25), Germany (22), Switzerland (11), Australia (11), Netherlands (10), and Italy (9). The G7 countries, Australia, and South Korea grouping account for 81 percent of all cases (473). Of the 470 companies on the list, eighty-five have been targeted at least twice, for different or similar infractions. Apple has suffered the most, with four cases, followed by twenty-eight companies with three cases each, including Amazon, FedEx, Intel, McDonald's, Mitsubishi, Nike, Nissan, Toyota, Walmart, and Zara. If you combine subsidiaries together, major U.S. defense companies would top the list in number of cases: Lockheed Martin (18), General Dynamics (13), Raytheon (9), and Boeing (5).

The actions that trigger China's coercion are not dissimilar to those of targeted governments in that the perceived offensive behavior has very little to do with trade competition or protectionism; instead, they are considered political offenses deserving of retaliation. These alleged offenses include actions or statements on Taiwan, Tibet, Xinjiang, Hong Kong, Macau, Tiananmen, territorial claims, or the CCP. We start with a case study of coercion against the NBA in the United States because it illustrates many of Beijing's bullying tactics, its political will, and the submissive responses by the targeted firms. The case study will be followed with supplementary observations about private-sector coercion.

Case Study 4: The NBA Houston Rockets and the Hong Kong Protests

During a trip by the Houston Rockets to Asia before the start of the regular season in October 2019, the team's general manager, Daryl Morey, shared a Twitter image with the words "Fight for Freedom, Stand with Hong Kong." That single tweet set off a firestorm for NBA-China relations that few could have imagined. Although the tweet was quickly deleted, the damage had been done. Morey's single tweet would eventually incur significant economic costs to the professional basketball league, estimated to be upwards of $400 million.[80]

China is unquestionably the largest foreign market for the NBA. More than three hundred million play the sport in China, about five to eight hundred million have watched an NBA game, and the league currently enjoys a larger social media following in China than any other sport.[81] The potential for growth, moreover, is large. More Chinese fans (twenty-one million) than Americans (eighteen million) watched the final game of the 2019 NBA Finals between the Toronto Raptors and the Golden State Warriors. A 2024 survey found that while only 10 percent of Europeans and 23 percent of Americans watched the NBA online, 52 percent of their Chinese counterparts did so.[82] The popularity of the professional teams and players among the Chinese is reportedly worth 10 percent of the NBA's revenue, $5 billion in business revenues, and an estimated $150 million in value for each of the thirty NBA franchises.[83] The NBA enjoys a multibillion-dollar streaming deal with Tencent in China, and NBA owners have invested more than $10 billion in the country.[84]

The Chinese market is also lucrative for NBA players. Since 2005, more than sixty players have signed deals with Chinese brands, including Anta, Li-Ning, Peak, and 361 Degrees, worth hundreds of millions of dollars.[85] Some of these players are All-Stars, household names, and Hall of Famers. One player reportedly said he made more money in one year from his Chinese deal than in eight years with Nike.[86] Dwyane Wade, a NBA Hall of Famer, signed a lifetime deal with Li-Ning in 2018 that includes his own sub-brand "Way of Wade," eleven signature shoes (so far), and more than ten physical stores in China.[87]

The NBA's popularity in China would normally be considered positively emblematic of globalization, a huge positive-sum economic opportunity for all parties, and a vehicle for promoting cultural diplomacy and people-to-people ties. But in the case of the Houston Rockets in 2019, China weaponized these economic ties against the NBA (and China's NBA fans) in unprecedented ways. The immediacy and fury with which the PRC government responded to the seemingly innocuous pro–Hong Kong tweet was disproportionate, to say the least. While Hong Kong is certainly a sensitive issue, Morey was not a global celebrity, a political figure, or a human rights activist. He did not give a major speech or stage a dramatic protest. He shared a single tweet, yet the PRC government unleashed massive coercion. The Chinese government immediately banned sales of all Rockets merchandise and stopped streaming all Rockets games. To put added pressure on the NBA commissioner Adam Silver, China stopped streaming *all* NBA games on the state-run CCTV. Chinese companies systematically dropped their sponsorships of the Houston Rockets team en masse, costing an estimated loss of about $25 million for the Rockets for the 2019–20 season.[88] The Chinese Basketball Association—headed by NBA Hall of Famer and former Houston Rockets center Yao Ming—suspended all cooperation with the Rockets.[89] Four days after the tweet, the bullying continued. China's state-run newspaper *Global Times* threat-tweeted at the NBA, insinuating more future punishment: "Freedom of speech is never free. The #NBA incident with China might help the Western world to at least pay attention to what and how Chinese ordinary people, including basketball fans, feel about #HK riots and why they are offended."[90]

Chinese representatives canceled all media appearances, NBA Cares events, and celebrity appearances at NBA fan events in Shanghai that week.[91] CCTV and Tencent suspended broadcasts of the preseason games with the Los Angeles Lakers and Brooklyn Nets in Shanghai and Shenzhen. Within a week of Morey's tweet, all eleven official Chinese sponsors of NBA China—Anta, Changhong, CTrip, Dicos, Luckin Coffee, Master Kong, Meiling, Mengniu Dairy, Wzun, Vivo, and X Financial—announced a suspension of ties with the league, with statements condemning the NBA for actions that "harm the interests of the motherland" or proclaiming that "national interest is above all else."[92] Some NBA players reportedly had their Chinese endorsement deals nixed at the last moment as retaliation.[93]

The NBA's response was hardly virtuous and reflected cold business decision-making to salvage the bottom line and cater to Chinese demands. The NBA's initial reaction was reportedly to do whatever was necessary to placate Chinese complaints and minimize the economic damage. NBA commissioner Silver eventually supported Morey's freedom of expression, but Morey's tweet was immediately taken down, as noted above.[94] More significantly, however, the sanctions against the Rockets created a pervasive culture of self-censorship among NBA teams and players about anything related to China. Player personnel and staff were under an implicit gag order on any political statements that might offend the Chinese government.[95] Sports agents advised their star clients to stay silent. Lebron James (who has visited China during the offseason for fifteen consecutive years) initially characterized Morey's tweet as "misinformed," before backtracking and clarifying that he did not want to talk about it.[96] James Harden, then a Rockets player who visits China once or twice a year, said, "I'm staying out of it [Hong Kong]."[97] Stephen Curry, who is one of the most popular current NBA players in China, and who had frequented China for the past six seasons prior to the incident for his Under Armour promotional tour, emphasized that he "just [doesn't] know enough about Chinese history and how that's influenced modern society enough to speak on it [Hong Kong]."[98] Houston Rockets owner Tilman Fertitta declared that Morey's views did not represent those of the team and immediately recanted Morey's controversial tweet on Twitter the same day, "Our presence in Tokyo is all about the promotion of the @NBA internationally and we are NOT a political organization."[99] In early 2022, when the U.S. Congress called out current NBA players with lucrative deals with Chinese companies for being complicit in human rights violations in China, none of these players or their representatives responded to requests for comments.[100]

China ultimately reinstated online broadcasts of the NBA on Tencent but continued the ban against the Rockets. This hardly represented a change in tactics. PRC authorities extended the ban to the Philadelphia 76ers in persecution of Morey, who moved to the team in 2020; in 2021, China continued to coerce the NBA, this time targeting the iconic Boston Celtics, because of a tweet by Celtics player Enes Kanter accusing the PRC of cultural genocide in Tibet.[101] On state TV, moreover, the Chinese blackout of NBA games lasted well over two years—it finally ended twenty-eight months later in March 2022—more than two years without an NBA game on Chinese state TV because of one tweet.

Thin-Skinned: China's Attack on Firms

The coercion against the NBA provides a window into a universe of Chinese bullying of private-sector firms around the world (see appendix 1 for a full list of cases). While it is understandable that any traversing of China's core interests in Taiwan or Hong Kong is well-known neuralgia for China, what is striking about the actions against private-sector actors is that the threshold for offense is very low: no perceived slight is too trivial. For example, in 2008, government-backed Chinese netizens organized a boycott of Coca-Cola's "shitty product" in response to a company advertisement showing Buddhist monks frolicking on a roller coaster—that was somehow interpreted as a subliminal message supporting Tibetan independence (Coke immediately pulled the ad to preserve its annual sales of 1.5 billion cases to the China market).[102] In 2017, the Chinese government forced Emirates Airlines to stop the companywide practice of its flight attendants' wearing pins of their home country because a handful of these employees were Taiwanese; in 2018, it blocked HBO and the John Oliver show because of an on-air joke about Xi Jinping; China even banned the universally lovable children's character Winnie-the-Pooh from China because of an image portraying Xi as Pooh (and Obama as Tigger).[103] In almost all cases of private-sector coercion, the companies "contort themselves to satisfy Chinese pressure," as one observer described it, issuing profuse apologies almost immediately and caving to all of the government's demands to rectify the offense.[104]

The tactics of Chinese economic predation against private companies range widely. One form of coercion is to block (or threaten to block) market access for foreign companies if they do not comply with China's demands. In 2018, for instance, forty-four air carriers, including American Airlines, United Airlines, and Delta Airlines, complied with China's demands to remove online references to Taiwan as a separate country by redesignating the destination on their websites as "Taiwan, China."[105] If they did not, then their airplanes might suffer the same fate as Shanghai-bound Air New Zealand flight 289, which was denied landing privileges and forced to redirect in midair back to Auckland because its documentation referenced Taiwan as if it were independent from China.[106] That same year, the PRC government put seventy-four global companies from sixteen countries on notice to change their websites to formally designate that Taiwan, Hong Kong, and Macau are part of China. The following year, it issued the same threat to ninety-two more global companies (see appendix 1).

The denial of market access is quite pronounced and long-standing in the media and entertainment industry, where Chinese viewership is coveted by motion picture and television companies and streaming platforms. The data shows at least a dozen cases of major coercive actions. As mentioned previously, China instituted a five-year ban on Columbia Tristar Pictures in 1997 after it released *Seven Years in Tibet,* starring Brad Pitt, because the movie's portrayal of government suppression "hurt the feelings of the Chinese people."[107] The PRC government banned Disney's release of *Kundun* because it positively portrayed the life of the Dalai Lama and banned Disney CEO Michael Eisner and director Martin Scorsese from entering China (the film and its trailer are no longer available online or in any format).[108] China also blocked the release of the 2019 superhero blockbuster *Shang-Chi and the Legend of the Ten Rings,* starring the Marvel Studio's first Asian American lead, Simu Liu, because the villain in the film franchise is portrayed as Chinese while the hero is Chinese American.[109] Another Marvel film, *Eternals,* as well as the Oscar-winning *Nomadland* have both been banned from China because their award-winning director Chloé Zhao, a

Chinese American, made critical comments about China's political system and suppression of speech. No Marvel movies (a total of seven) were released in China between July 2019 and January 2023—without any official explanation from Chinese authorities—likely costing Disney "hundreds of millions of dollars."[110]

Sometimes what is considered by China as offensive content and grounds for censorship is exquisitely trivial. A popular Korean variety show on SBS was censored in China in December 2020 because of a scene showing the characters playing a real estate board game (Blue Marble) on which a Taiwan flag piece appeared.[111] China harshly criticized Urban Works Media, the South Korean production company, as well as the distributor SBS, for "insulting China" and removed the episode from the Chinese streaming platform Bilibili. An August 2022 promotional video by Snickers for an online event with South Korean boyband BTS was targeted because it referred to Taiwan as a country—even though the video was meant for a non-Chinese audience. Mars Wrigley, the maker of the Snickers bar, offered not one but two apologies, emphasizing that "There is #OnlyOneChina in the world, and Taiwan is an inseparable part of Chinese territory."[112] Sony Pictures Entertainment's 2021 blockbuster *Spider-Man: No Way Home* contained a climactic twenty-minute fight sequence amid scaffolding at the Statue of Liberty in New York. Chinese authorities demanded that the image of the American landmark be digitally removed, presumably because it might be interpreted as a nod to the memory of pro-democracy demonstrations at Tiananmen Square (where pro-democracy supporters built a likeness of the statue). Sony refused to comply, and the film was not released in China.[113] *Doctor Strange in the Multiverse of Madness*, a 2022 Marvel film, received similar treatment because the titular character was spotted in a few-seconds-long scene with the *Epoch Times* (in the background), a newspaper run by the Falun Gong, which the PRC considers and persecutes as a religious cult. The *Global Times* promptly lambasted the depiction as a "shame" to Hollywood and the United States.[114] The June 2022 release of Paramount Pictures' *Top Gun: Maverick*, starring Tom Cruise, was not shown in China, presumably because of a scene in which Cruise's character, Pete Mitchell, dons a flight bomber jacket with patches on the back depicting the Taiwanese and Japanese flags alongside the American stars and stripes. But this was only after Tencent's 12.5 percent investment in the film's production was pulled for political reasons—prior to that, the scene was scrubbed to remove the offensive flags for a Chinese audience.[115]

In addition to blocking access to its market, China's coercive practices against private companies include nontariff barriers such as random health or safety inspections, new document requirements, or in some cases, draconian unexplained bans on sales of a foreign company's goods in China. This tactic was on full display with the sanctions placed on South Korea in 2016 because of the joint U.S.-South Korea deployment of a THAAD system in Seongju. The purpose of the system was to shore up deterrence and defense capabilities against the burgeoning North Korean ballistic missile threat; however, China claimed that the system's radar could look deep into China.

In response, China undertook an eighteen-month targeted economic coercion campaign against Lotte, the Korean company that originally owned the land on which the THAAD system was stationed (Lotte was asked to transfer title to the land to the government). Sanctions forced the closure of all of Lotte's 112 stores in China, ostensibly because of "fire safety" concerns, causing more than $7.5 billion in economic damage. Beijing also took informal coercive actions against many other Korean commercial enterprises. The government did not approve import licenses for nineteen cosmetic products from top-line Korean companies (Amore Pacific, Aekyung, CJ Lion, and Iaso, among others). China's State Administration of Radio, Film and Television verbally told distributors and agents to halt all invitations to K-pop music concerts in China, block all streaming platforms for the music, and cancel endorsement contracts for Chinese pop stars with Korean companies in China. The government took discriminatory action against South Korean electric vehicle (EV) batteries by denying subsidies for cars utilizing them. The government instructed all travel agencies to stop group tourism to South Korea. This was especially painful as it was intended to undercut Chinese tourist attendance and hotel revenues for South Korea's 2018 Winter Olympics in PyeongChang, causing an almost 50 percent drop in arrivals from China between 2016 and 2017 and an estimated $15.6 billion loss to the tourism industry.[116] The tourism ban also crashed sales revenue for Korea's major duty-free companies, Galleria, Lotte, and Shilla. China even banned the sale of toilet-seat bidets from Korea on the spurious grounds that the instruction manuals lacked mandated information for Chinese users.[117]

China carried out widespread import bans on thousands of food products and beverages produced by Taiwanese companies from August 2022 to January 2023 in response to Nancy Pelosi's visit to Taipei in 2022. The reasons given for the draconian import suspensions ranged widely from "excessive pesticide residue" for foods (including pastries and honey), "insufficient safety standards" (including bottled beer), and "improper paperwork" (which had been filed sufficiently prior to 2022).

An apology from the targeted company does not necessarily stop the coercion. Chinese authorities will hold the entire firm responsible for the actions of one individual and force management to take termination actions against the employee even after an apology has been elicited and the offending action has been stopped. Our database shows too many cases to enumerate, but a few examples illustrate the degree of Chinese scrutiny. In 2018, an employee of Dior used a map of China that did not include Taiwan as a part of China in a presentation before Chinese clients. A video of the presentation somehow got posted to Weibo and elicited mass criticism. Dior reprimanded the employee and posted an apology that looked as though it was drafted by the Chinese government: "Dior has always respected and upheld the principle of one China, strictly upholding China's rights and complete sovereignty, treasuring the feelings of Chinese citizens."[118] In 2019, even after coercing an apology from Cathay Pacific Airways for pro–Hong Kong statements by some of its workers, China threatened to close its airspace unless the company fired the two dozen employees.[119] When an employee of the Japanese fast-food chain Yoshinoya posted a pro–Hong Kong message on the Yoshinoya Facebook page, the viral outrage on Weibo and consumer boycotts continued until the company CEO terminated the employee.[120] In 2020, the art director of the activewear brand Lululemon posted a T-shirt design on their personal Instagram page showing a box of fried rice with batwings and chopsticks saying "No Thank You." This was interpreted by Chinese authorities as blaming China for the Covid-19 pandemic. "#LululemonInsultsChina" received hundreds of millions of views on Weibo along with viral calls for a consumer boycott. Lululemon removed the Instagram post and apologized on several online platforms, including Weixin (Instagram is banned in China): "The image and the post were inappropriate and inexcusable. We acted immediately and the person is no longer an employee of Lululemon."[121] During the 2024 Paris Olympics, a Chinese influencer worked with a CCP-backed local propaganda organization to target and boycott a hotel chain owned by a Taiwanese company in Paris.[122] The offense was the lack of a Chinese flag in the hotel lobby and the unproven claims that a Taiwanese hotel manager had removed the Chinese flag from the original display. The hotel apologized, but Chinese booking platforms had already removed it from their search results.[123]

In addition to going after similar offenses by a single staff member of the NBA Houston Rockets, described earlier, China not only blocked the social media account of Arsenal Football Club's star Mesut Özil for his online posts supporting Muslim Uyghurs, but it also removed his likeness from the video game Pro Evolution Soccer.[124] In both cases, the NBA and the English Premier League did nothing in response for fear of losing the lucrative Chinese market. Foreign journalists who write stories critical of Xi and his family see their press credentials revoked. U.S. consultancy firms doing due diligence work for client deals in China see their offices raided and employees imprisoned.[125] The list goes on (see appendix 1). The degree to which China exercises its coercion against private individuals is truly breathtaking.

It should be evident from the examples thus far cited that one of the main instruments of private-sector economic coercion is the manipulation of social media. Once an action is identified, the company is targeted, ridiculed, and sometimes vandalized through millions of social media posts. Prominent Chinese influencers join in the coercion, often ending any associations with the targeted company as a form of punishment. In 2019, T-shirt designs by French fashion icon Givenchy, Italian designer Versace, and American designers Coach and Calvin Klein appeared not to label Taiwan, Hong Kong, and Macau as part of China. Pictures of the T-shirts suddenly appeared on Weibo with viral calls for boycotts. Chinese brand ambassadors Jackson Yee (Givenchy), Yang Mi (Versace), and Jelly Lin (Calvin Klein) all severed their endorsement deals. In the Versace case, the T-shirt design labeled Hong Kong and Macau as locations for Versace without adding China (as opposed to, say, New York, USA and Milan, Italy). The story was picked up by *Global Times*, and the hashtag "Versace Suspected of [Supporting] Hong Kong and Macau Independence" received more than one billion views on Weibo. Actress Yang Mi slammed the Italian brand, stating, "The motherland's territorial integrity and sovereignty are sacred and inviolable at all times." The company, fearful of lost sales, issued a profuse apology, declaring that "we love China deeply and resolutely respect China's territory and national sovereignty."[126] Donatella Versace, co-owner of Versace, issued an additional apology on her personal Instagram page for "any distress that [the T-shirt] may have caused."[127] Bulgari, another LVMH brand like Givenchy, was targeted in 2023 because some of its websites listed China and Taiwan separately, with one social media hashtag on Weibo reaching more than eight hundred million views. The company quickly apologized, blaming "management negligence" for mislabeling the websites, and reiterated that it respects China's sovereignty "as always and unswervingly."[128]

When the clothing retailers H&M and Hugo Boss stated their intention in 2021 not to use Xinjiang-sourced cotton because of forced labor concerns, criticism on Chinese social media went viral, and media stars like actor-singer Li Yifeng terminated their endorsement deals. In China, H&M saw a precipitous drop in sales of more than 40 percent year-on-year, and sixty of its stores were forced to close.[129] China used this same tactic against seventeen companies in 2021 and 2022 over Xinjiang-sourced materials, including Adidas, Burberry, Calvin Klein, Intel, Lacoste, New Balance, Nike, Puma, Tommy Hilfiger, and Walmart (see appendix 1). During this nationalistic backlash, at least forty Chinese stars canceled their endorsement deals with these companies, which the *People's Daily* likened to "malicious backstabbers."[130]

In September 2024, Beijing ratcheted up its response, announcing it would formally investigate PVH, which owns Calvin Klein and Tommy Hilfiger, for "discriminatory measures" against Xinjiang-sourced products.[131] This marked the first time China had announced a formal investigation under its new Unreliable Entity List (UEL) regime.[132] Preliminary findings released in January 2025 accused PVH of "improper" conduct related to the Xinjiang region. A month later, China formally placed the company on a sanctions list. Beijing fined PVH, revoked work permits, denied employees (including the CEO) entry into the country, and prohibited import and export activities. For PVH, that meant the threat of shutting down its dozens of stores in China, hence losing access to the lucrative Chinese market.[133]

To many observers, China's actions in September 2024 and February 2025 against PVH were arguably timed to Washington's actions in the growing U.S.-China trade war—first the Biden administration's announcement of tariffs on Chinese EVs and then the Trump administration's declaration of additional tariffs on Chinese products. This marks a growing trend of tit-for-tat action by the Chinese government that is likely to continue over the next few years under a second Trump administration. Take, for example, the case of the American tech company Nvidia. In December 2024, the company, the most valuable publicly traded company in the world and a key player in the artificial intelligence race, was targeted by Beijing for antitrust violations it allegedly made in 2020. The case was conveniently opened just after the Biden administration expanded its restrictions on the sale to China of advanced chips, including Nvidia's, that are critical for AI and other advanced technologies.[134]

With this looming trade threat and a greater willingness by Beijing to use its growing economic coercion tool kit, companies globally are likely to tread more carefully to avoid being indirect casualties of geopolitics. The Japanese CEO Tadashi Yanai's November 2024 interview with the BBC provides a cautionary tale. In the interview, he admitted that his company, Fast Retailing (which owns Uniqlo), did not use cotton from Xinjiang, before realizing his mistake midway and stopping himself, saying, "Actually, it gets too political if I say anymore so let's stop here."[135] The second half of his response is a prime example of the type of self-censorship that we now commonly see and expect from company executives when it comes to sensitive Chinese issues: avoid it, don't talk about it. The Greater China market accounted for 22 percent of Yanai's company sales in the first eight months of 2024 and is home to more than a thousand of his stores. A few days after his BBC interview was published, Uniqlo put out a statement saying it was "monitoring the situation carefully" for a potential Chinese boycott as its shares fell on the Nikkei 225.[136]

There are countless other cases of such coercion, such as social media–inspired consumer boycotts of any product seen being used or consumed by Hong Kong protestors in 2019, Chinese brand ambassadors and athletes severing contract commitments in South Korea during the 2016 THAAD controversy, or the shunning of Japanese cosmetics during the public outrage over Japan's Fukushima nuclear wastewater plan in 2023 for "safety issues."[137] The incidents would play out the same way: viral outrage, followed by Chinese brand ambassadors terminating relationships, followed by profuse apologies by the targeted company.

In some cases, the coercion campaign would lead to violence. For example, when the Olympic torch relay for the Beijing Olympics was making its way through Paris in April 2008, the ceremonial procession was disrupted by pro-Tibet demonstrations. The incident sparked an uproar on Chinese social media demonizing France and calling for boycotts of all French products, including protesting and the burning of French flags at Carrefour supermarkets in China.[138] Peugeot and Citroën cars, though in partnership with a local Chinese carmaker, saw a precipitous drop in sales.[139] During the THAAD controversy in South Korea, viral boycotts led not only to a drop in sales by 30 percent year-on-year but also to random acts of vandalism destroying Hyundai and Kia cars, with pictures posted on the internet to encourage others to follow suit.[140]

The fates of Facebook and Zoom in the Chinese market provide a cautionary tale of economic coercion against not just any company, but against some of the biggest and most successful Western companies. In September 2019, the PRC government blocked Zoom's access to China on the grounds that "illegal" activities were taking place on its platform among users regarding demonstrations in Hong Kong, memorials for Tiananmen Square, and human rights in Xinjiang. Zoom promised to monitor content as a condition for reentering the Chinese market and agreed to migrate the data of one million Chinese users from American to Chinese servers inside China. After the Chinese government allowed Zoom to be used in China in November 2019, it pressed the company to shut down any meetings with content deemed hostile to China and to provide information about the users to the Ministry of State Security (MSS). The MSS also demanded user information about anyone from or related to Xinjiang. By contrast, Facebook did not agree to China's demands for monitoring, reporting user data, and censoring its platform. Facebook's website has consequently been blocked in China since 2009.[141]

BARK WORSE THAN BITE?

Some scholars have surmised that China's bark is worse than its bite—that Chinese acts of economic predation do not inflict much damage and are not very effective. For example, the rare earth minerals export ban against Japan in 2010 did not do much harm to the economy and was short-lived. The same was true for China's import ban against the Philippines in 2012, and even the suspension of imports of Taiwanese food products over Nancy Pelosi's visit to Taiwan in 2022. China's actions amount more to a signaling of the pain it can potentially inflict in order to shape future behavior of the target. In the latter two cases, it signaled largely through the agricultural market, where China's position as arguably the world's largest consumer gives it formidable power. In this sense, China ends up shooting itself in the foot because its predation alienates others and causes states to reduce dependence on the sanctioned goods, some experts argue.[142]

It is true that China is not aiming to weaponize all trade, instead weaponizing carefully selected trade patterns that can send a clear signal to the target. But to say that this is an unsuccessful tool is not true. For one, economic predation creates self-censoring, in which countries or companies are cowed into a mode of silencing their own statements or actions to a degree that is almost Orwellian. For example, in 2021, the photographic film company Kodak shared Instagram images of northwestern China by photographer Patrick Wack. Wack took the photos in 2016–2019, using Kodak film, as part of a book in which he described Xinjiang as a dystopian nightmare. Wack's ten images prompted viral outrage on Chinese social media directed at Kodak. The company not only immediately removed the Instagram post but also issued a self-flagellating public apology: "Kodak has maintained a good relationship with the Chinese government and has been in close cooperation with various government departments. We will continue to respect the Chinese government and the Chinese law. . . . We will keep ourselves in check and correct ourselves, taking this as an example of the need for caution."[143]

Second, for every case of a weak sanction, China has used strong ones (e.g., THAAD); moreover, the supposedly "weak" sanction is usually an effective signal to intimidate the target. It amounts to a shot across the bow: "Such acts . . . serve as a warning of stronger retaliation if a country does not reverse a certain action or if a country does not make an official gesture to improve relations."[144]

Third, China's economic coercion may be disproportionately effective against smaller countries that are allies or partners of the United States. If the U.S. government or firms are unwilling to help these targets of Chinese coercion through mitigation or trade diversification efforts (discussed in the next chapter), then losing access to the Chinese market for exports or imports may be unsustainable for them in periods of economic uncertainty. China's tactics may instill fear in these allies and partners against standing up for the defense of Taiwan or for human rights and democracy advocates in China. The result is that the United States may become more isolated and unable to build coalitions of like-minded partners in dealing with China. This outcome is the aggregate desired effect of China's coercion: Beijing takes actions against allies and partners that are low in intensity, so as not to elicit a strong U.S. response, but that incentivize compliance and self-censoring among the targets, slowly but surely shaping the global environment to China's advantage.[145] In this regard, those who belittle concern over China's economic coercion as unnecessary handwringing fall right into Beijing's gray-zone trap.

THE BUILDING OF AN ILLIBERAL INTERNATIONAL ORDER

China's economic predation is not to be taken lightly because it constitutes a key pillar of the emerging illiberal global order. The components of such an order, as described by scholars Elizabeth Economy, Bethany Allen, and others, are (1) the reinforcing of political and economic control by the state; (2) the limiting of individual freedoms; and (3) the constraint of open markets and free market forces.[146] Economic coercion is one of the primary tools used in China's building of this order. Along with the deployment of disinformation and BRI-type collateralized capital investments, China can secure compliant behavior, self-censorship, and acquiescence to a world order that replaces the Western postwar liberal system. The stakes in stopping China's economic coercion could not be higher.

CHAPTER 4

COLLECTIVE RESILIENCE

There are two basic ways to contend with the weaponization of economic interdependence. One is to decouple from the threat to make oneself invulnerable. This autarkic solution comes at an inordinately high cost (look at the example of North Korea's economic destitution), and if the threat is coming from China, it is virtually impossible to decouple oneself from one of the largest economies in the world. The other is to devise ways to protect or defend oneself against China's trade weaponization, either individually or with a group of other countries. Most countries have taken this latter path. For the most part, these measures are ad hoc and relatively recent in origin in response to China's weaponization of interdependence.

Thus far we have seen states take five measures to contend with economic coercion: (1) identifying economic security vulnerabilities; (2) practicing trade diversification; (3) devising impact mitigation measures, (4) securing supply chains through reshoring and friend-shoring, and (5) using export controls and investment screening. These strategies are pursued through individual national efforts or by using newly created institutions like the Quad, the Indo-Pacific Economic Framework (IPEF), the Minerals Security Partnership (MSP), and the "Chip 4" alliance. These strategies are designed to reduce dependence on Chinese import and export markets and thereby to minimize vulnerability.

While well-intended, these strategies do not fully address the problem; they are largely piecemeal and defensive in nature. Instead, we introduce *collective resilience* as a peer competition strategy designed to deter China's economic coercion. Collective resilience promises multilateral responses in the trade space to the prospect of China's economic coercion. Original and new trade data presented in this chapter shows that while most targets of Chinese economic coercion are asymmetrically trade-dependent on China, many of them also export items to China upon which China is highly dependent, and in some cases almost 100 percent dependent. Indeed, the eighteen governments (plus Taiwan and the European Union) targeted by China export tens of billions of dollars' worth of goods that Beijing is highly dependent on as a portion of its total trade in those goods. This gives states leverage in practicing an Article 5–type collective economic deterrence strategy that signals the threat of retaliation should China act against any one of the alliance members. Sanctions on an aggregation of these high-dependence items would threaten enough inconvenience for Beijing to deter future predatory behavior. We begin with a review of counter-coercion measures being practiced by states. We argue that these are necessary to contend with the problem, but not sufficient in themselves, and propose that they be complemented by a strategy of collective resilience. We then introduce the theory and data behind the strategy.

THE NEW IMPERATIVE OF ECONOMIC SECURITY

Countries have responded to economic coercion in five basic ways that have been categorized under the general rubric of *de-risking*. This term, coined by the Biden administration, distinguishes actions in the economic security domain from decoupling; it suggests a continued adherence to the norms of the liberal trading order, while at the same time reducing vulnerability.

Building Economic Security Bureaucracy

First, all countries have become much more attuned to the new imperative of economic security as a priority and have been developing capabilities to detect disruptions in advance. In November 2021, for example, South Korea was caught by surprise by Chinese-induced shortages of urea—a mineral used for emissions control in diesel fuel—that paralyzed retail, shipping, transport, and construction industries.[1] Everyone was caught by surprise when the pandemic-induced lockdown in China led to worldwide shortages of critical PPE such as surgical masks, hospital gowns, gloves, respirators, and face shields.[2] In the early days of the pandemic, toilet paper flew off the shelves, with manufacturers unable to respond to an overnight 40 percent increase in demand as people were mandated to stay home.[3] A global shortage of semiconductors, or chips, which power everything from cars, smartphones, and vacuums to computers brought to prominence the ubiquitous importance of this tiny silicon wafer, disrupting 169 industries.[4] The chip shortage hit the auto industry hard, with estimates ranging from $60 billion to $210 billion loss in revenue for the industry as automakers faced lengthy wait times for the hundreds of chips needed to power the infotainment systems, power steering and brakes, and other components of new vehicles.[5] This drove up prices for both new and old vehicles, with an average new vehicle hitting a record high of $48,681 in November 2022 and used cars increasing by 40 percent.[6] Limited inventory meant that even if you had the money, the waiting list for some new models stretched to months.

Thus, governments have created new bureaucracies and appointed new personnel to manage supply chain disruptions. "Tsars," or point persons, and early warning systems have emerged across capitals to plan for and to detect in advance economic disruptions. For example, Japan set up a new cabinet position for economic security in October 2021 and passed new legislation to guard critical supply chains and technologies.[7] This was a key priority for the Kishida administration (2021–2024), which appointed Takayuki Kobayashi, a former parliamentary vice minister of defense, as the first minister for economic security. In February 2022, the new legislation, the Economic Security Promotion Act (ESPA), was approved by the Kishida cabinet; it was passed by the Diet in May 2022 and went into force in August 2022. The law created a two-year implementation timeline and established four key pillars of economic security for Japan: (1) securing a stable supply chain of critical products; (2) safeguarding critical infrastructure; (3) supporting designated critical technologies (DCTs); and (4) creating a nondisclosure system for selected patents. Pillars one and three were put into force in August 2022, and an Economic Security Promotion Office was established within the cabinet to implement the law. Eleven products were designated as "critical"—antibacterial preparations, fertilizers, permanent magnets, machine tools/industrial robots, aircraft parts, semiconductors, storage batteries, cloud programs, natural gas, critical minerals, and ship parts—along with twenty-seven technologies in four domains (oceans, outer space/airspace, inter-domain and cyberspace, and bio).

In South Korea, the Yoon Suk Yeol administration (2022–2025) activated an early warning system for nearly four thousand key industry materials and created a new economic security position in the presidential office. Of the four thousand materials, about one to two hundred (including magnesium, tungsten, neodymium, and lithium hydroxide) were deemed critical to major South Korean industries such as semiconductors, autos, and battery cells; these materials were put under additional monitoring because of their heavy dependence (more than 50 percent) on imports from specific nations.[8] Seoul expanded the early warning system from twenty-three embassies to thirty-seven embassies by January 2022, three months after initial activation.[9] In May 2022, the Yoon administration appointed Wang Yunjong, a Chinese economy expert, to the new position.[10] He shepherded the Yoon administration's efforts to coordinate economic security–related agendas and develop strategies within the Korean bureaucracy, and spearheaded new bilateral and trilateral economic security dialogues with the United States and Japan.[11]

Wang's role was further elevated in early 2024 when he was promoted to the new position of third deputy director of the National Security Office (in charge of economic security), demonstrating the importance of this issue for South Korean national security.[12] Furthermore, Seoul amended and introduced three pieces of legislation to strengthen its capacity for addressing supply chain risks and resilience: (1) an amendment to establish a legal basis for supporting supply chain stabilization; (2) the Framework Act on Supply Chain, in December 2023, which established a pan-government Supply Chain Committee and a Supply Chain Stabilization Fund within the Ministry of Economy and Finance; and (3) the Special Act on National Resource Security, in February 2024, which designated petroleum, natural gas, coal, uranium, hydrogen, and "key minerals" as "core resources."[13] The supply chain stabilization fund provides financial support for Korean companies to diversify export destinations, domestic and overseas facility investments, and technology development. The committee is chaired by the deputy prime minister (dual-hatted as minister of economy and finance) and held its first meeting in June 2024.[14] During that meeting, the deputy prime minister introduced the four policy directions for the supply chain stabilization strategy: (1) increasing the total number of economic security items from two hundred to three hundred and providing a five trillion won (about $3.6 billion) budget for the stabilization fund; (2) expanding domestic manufacturing (reshoring); (3) supporting core supply chain technologies; and 4) promoting international cooperation through the IPEF Supply Chain Agreement and MSP. The deputy prime minister likened the committee to the "helmsman of an aircraft carrier" navigating the "turbulent waters of global supply chain risk."[15]

The European Commission (EC) has taken a leading role in many of the economic security initiatives of the European Union (EU) because of its executive powers in trade, competition, and foreign direct investment (FDI) policy, as well as its "power of proposal" to initiate parliamentary lawmaking.[16] The EU has prioritized enhancing supply chain resilience as a critical aspect of its economic security strategy. In May 2021, one year after Covid-19 disrupted the global supply

chains, the EC updated the 2020 industrial strategy, emphasizing the need to bolster the resilience of the EU's single market and safeguard its strategic autonomy
while giving additional support to accelerate the green and digital transition of
EU industry.[17] As part of this effort, the EC conducted a study that revealed its
strategic dependency on 137 critical items from foreign countries, more than half
of them from China.[18] The global semiconductor chips shortage as a result of
the supply disruptions during the pandemic also led to the EU's reckoning of the
importance of a robust semiconductor ecosystem for Europe's technological leadership and autonomy. In response, in February 2022, the EC proposed the European Chips Act, which came into effect in September 2023.[19] This legislation
established the European Semiconductor Board and the Chips Joint Undertaking
(JU)—a "tri-partite partnership" involving the EU, thirty-one member states and
partners, and industrial associations.[20] In April 2023, the EU also established a
semiconductor alert system to monitor potential disruptions.[21]

A month earlier, in March 2023, the EU announced a new action plan to
secure critical raw materials against unforeseen disruptions and shortages.[22] This
followed President Ursula von der Leyen's 2022 State of Union speech, in which
she introduced the Critical Raw Materials Act (CRMA) to enhance the EU's
resilience across the entire supply chain, especially in light of China's influence
in the global processing industry, and to reduce the EU's strategic dependencies.[23] To that end, the CRMA, which took effect in May 2024, set specific targets to increase the EU's domestic extraction, processing, and recycling of critical raw materials by 2030.[24] The law also imposed a cap, limiting the EU's
reliance on a single third country for processing any critical raw material to no
more than 65 percent of its annual consumption.[25] In addition, the CRMA
established the European Critical Raw Materials Board as a key body for purchasing critical raw materials for the EU.[26] This board, consisting of representatives from the member states and the EC, is responsible for monitoring supply
risks and coordinating strategic stockpiling to ensure the EU's access to these
vital resources.[27]

Promoting Trade Diversification

Second, states have practiced trade diversification, meaning that when China dis-
rupts trade with the target state, the target state finds alternative export markets
for those same goods in order to blunt the economic damage wrought by loss of
the Chinese market.[28] When China embargoes imports of goods from country

X, for example, China must meet domestic demand by sopping up the international supply of that good in other markets, thus allowing country X to backfill the global supply sucked up by China's demand.

This strategy has seen some success. One of the best-known cases is Australia. In 2020, at the onset of the Covid-19 pandemic, China delayed releasing the genome map for the virus and did not immediately provide the WHO with information about cases and patients. In response, Australia, which sat on the WHO executive board, called in April 2020 for an independent investigation into the origins of Covid-19 in China. Prime Minister Scott Morrison (2018-2022) also demanded that the WHO be given "special inspections" authority, akin to that of the International Atomic Energy Agency (IAEA)'s nuclear weapons inspections, to visit the Wuhan lab facilities and to interview the lab's scientists.[29]

China retaliated by slapping tariffs on Australian barley (80.5 percent) and wine (218 percent) and a partial import ban on beef (China suspended imports from eleven Australian abattoirs).[30] In 2019, China was Australia's largest beef export market at 27 percent.[31]

Australia responded to this act of economic coercion by redirecting these goods to the rest of the world.[32] In the case of wines, Australia increased sales to the UK, Canada, South Korea, Sweden, and the United States, making up about 80 percent of the lost revenue from Chinese sanctions, according to one of the major wineries.[33] For barley, Australia shifted sales to its customers in the Middle East and Southeast and East Asia, and also found new markets like Mexico.[34] An exceptional harvest for the 2020–2021 barley crop (exceeding thirteen million tons for the second time in history) also helped mitigate losses as barley exports increased by 105 percent between May 2020 (when tariffs were first imposed) and May 2021.[35] China never completely banned Australian beef. It banned beef from eleven abattoirs, and as a result, its share of the Australian beef export market only decreased from 19 percent in 2020 to 18 percent in 2022. Furthermore, the traditional markets of Japan, South Korea (which overtook China), and the United States accounted for about 60 percent of Australia's beef exports between 2020 and 2022, minimizing any potential fallout from China's beef bans and tariffs. Trade diversification in alternative export markets allowed Australia to lose just $1 billion against expected losses of more than $19 billion from Chinese sanctions.[36] Beijing slowly and quietly lifted these sanctions in 2023, a year after a change of government in Canberra.[37]

In another example, when China restricted rare earth mineral exports to Japan over a territorial dispute in 2010, Japan diversified its sources of critical minerals away from China to other suppliers. Japan Organization for Metals and Energy Security (JOGMEC) and Sojitsu invested $250 million in the Australian mining company Lynas to secure long-term supply contracts providing for 30 percent of Japan's consumption.[38] Japan also initiated crash programs to both reduce the demand for rare earths (e.g., decreased the use of dysprosium in batteries and magnets) and increase the use of substitute materials.[39] The government also directed more investment into domestic seabed exploration for rare earth excavation. According to one account, Japan reduced its demand for cerium (used for glass polishing) by 75 percent; neodymium and dysprosium by 70 percent; yttrium (fluorescent bulbs) by 60 percent; and lanthanum by 40 percent within three years of the rare earth minerals ban by China. In total, these practices reduced Japan's overall dependence on Chinese rare earth minerals from 90 percent to 58 percent in a decade.[40]

Using Impact Mitigation Measures

A third method states have adopted in response to Chinese economic bullying is impact mitigation. This is an ad hoc portfolio of preferential economic measures taken by friendly countries to blunt the impact of China's economic coercion against smaller countries. These measures include trade support, monetary assistance, and investment funding.

Lithuania is the best-known case thus far of impact mitigation. When Lithuania was targeted in 2021 with undeclared Chinese sanctions for its support of Taiwan, its central bank estimated that it suffered a 1.3 percent hit to its GDP in 2022–2023. In response, the EU provided a $140 million support package for those Lithuanian firms targeted by China, and the United States provided a $600 million export credit agreement with the Export-Import bank. Taiwan also created a $200 million investment fund for Lithuanian industry and a $1 billion fund for bilateral joint ventures.[41] According to Melanie Hart, a senior State Department official working on countering China's economic coercion, the United States organized B2B meetings between Lithuanian and American companies and activated embassy posts in the Indo-Pacific region to assist Lithuania in discovering new supply chains. As a result, according to Hart's speech at CSIS in February 2023, "Lithuania's GDP grew 2.2 percent [in 2022], and currently less than 0.5 percent of Lithuania's exports go to China. They have replaced the China gap by expanding their trade relationships and their exports to other partners."[42]

In some cases, impact mitigation can come from private-sector initiatives. A notable example is the Czech Republic. In September 2020, a Chinese piano trader canceled a bulk order from the Czech piano company Petrof amid heightened tension between the Czech Republic and China over Czech Senate president Miloš Vystrčil's visit to Taiwan.[43] Bilateral relations had already been strained following Prague's decision to sign a sister-city agreement with Taipei in January 2020, which prompted the Shanghai city government to suspend official contacts with Prague, including their sister-city agreement, citing a violation of the "one-China" principle.[44] Against this backdrop, in August Vystrčil led a ninety-member delegation—the largest ever—to Taiwan and delivered a speech at the Taiwanese parliament.[45] During his speech, Vystrčil expressed strong support for Taiwan, declaring "I am Taiwanese," echoing John F. Kennedy's famous speech in West Berlin in 1963.[46] Chinese state councilor Wang Yi strongly condemned Vystrčil's trip, warning that he would "pay a heavy price."[47] The piano maker faced a loss of nearly $23.8 million as a result of the canceled order.[48] In response, Karel Komárek, a Czech entrepreneur and billionaire, quickly stepped in, purchasing eleven pianos originally destined for China and donating them to schools in his country.[49] Komárek stated, "My wife and I agreed that our foundation would immediately donate them to Czech schools. We want the eleven instruments to become a symbol of Czech pride and cohesion."[50]

Reshoring and Friend-Shoring

Another measure adopted by countries in response to economic coercion is to protect production supply chains from disruption by effectively reversing the offshoring effects of globalization. This entails controlling the entire production chain by moving offshore elements back home or to partner economies where the chances of disruption are low. This "reshoring" or "friend-shoring" is more costly than offshoring where factors of production may be more efficient, but this is the price to be paid for moving key elements of a supply chain out of places where China may exercise inordinate influence, or for making critical supply chains less vulnerable to Chinese disruption. The supply chain is brought home or brought to trusted partner economies.

One example of friend-shoring is the Quadrilateral Security Dialogue, or Quad, involving the United States, Japan, India, and Australia, with its growing concentration on building resilient supply chains for Covid-19 vaccines, semiconductors, emerging and critical technologies, and clean energy.[51] The Quad launched the Quad Vaccine partnership at their first (virtual) summit meeting in March 2021.[52] To ensure that more people have access to necessary vaccines, the new Quad initiative aimed to produce at least a billion doses of vaccines within a year.[53] In doing so, they built the vaccine supply chain by expanding the vaccine manufacturing capacity in India, with the United States, Japan, and Australia all providing critical support in the form of vaccine technology, financial resources, and logistics support for vaccine delivery.[54] This division of labor was necessary to tackle the global health crisis but also reflected a lesson drawn from the pandemic experience that overreliance on a single country for critical sectors like public health could pose a national security risk. When the pandemic led to a shutdown of all factories in China, causing significant supply disruptions for almost every possible good, building a more diversified and resilient supply chain became an ever more urgent task.

In May 2022, the Biden administration also launched IPEF to build a resilient economy among fourteen member countries by "establishing an early warning system, mapping critical mineral supply chains, improving traceability in key sectors, and coordinating on diversification efforts."[55] After a year of negotiations, countries concluded the Supply Chain Agreement in May 2023, with a common goal "to work together collaboratively to make supply chains more resilient, efficient, transparent, diversified, secure, and inclusive, including through information exchange, sharing of best practices, business matchmaking, collective response to disruptions, and supporting labor rights."[56] To implement the vision laid out in the agreement, the three supply chain bodies—the Supply Chain Council, the Crisis Response Network, and the Labor Rights Advisory Board— were established.[57] Under the Supply Chain Council, which is responsible for policy coordination concerning supply chain activities, the United States in August 2024 drew up a list of critical sectors and key goods, such as advanced batteries, medical devices, and semiconductors.[58] The Labor Rights Advisory Board was launched to address labor rights as an important aspect of building resilient supply chains. The Crisis Response Network was created to establish an "emergency communication channel" that will give early warnings and facilitate coordinated response among IPEF partners to better manage and mitigate supply disruptions.[59]

In June 2022, twelve countries came together to launch the MSP to build sustainable and diverse critical mineral supply chains across the globe.[60] The MSP aims to develop and support joint projects that adhere to high environmental, social, and governance (ESG) standards, enhance collaboration with resource-rich countries for mutual benefits, and facilitate public and private partnerships and responsible investment in critical energy sectors. Most of the MSP's projects are related to clean energy industries focusing on critical minerals, such as nickel, lithium, and cobalt.[61]

During the Biden administration, the United States, Japan, South Korea, and Taiwan formulated a "Chip 4" alliance, or "Fab 4," to consolidate the semiconductor supply chain.[62] This strategic technological partnership has four primary objectives: (1) diversify the semiconductor supply chain (particularly away from China); (2) safeguard the intellectual property of the members; (3) coordinate export control policies (with regard to China); and (4) promote equitable supply chain distribution among the members.[63] The Chip 4 alliance is in the nascent stage compared to other initiatives. After the United States initiated discussions in 2021, the group held its first preliminary meeting in September 2022, followed by a second (virtual) meeting in February 2023.[64] During this meeting, senior officials met for the first time and discussed establishing an early warning system among the members to enhance semiconductor supply chain resilience.[65] Progress has been gradual and meetings infrequent, in part because of members' concerns about possible Chinese retaliation.[66]

Nonetheless, Chip 4 is an ambitious initiative that has the potential to reshape the global semiconductor industry because of the critical roles each of these four members plays in the global semiconductor value chain. The U.S. companies lead in semiconductor design and equipment manufacturing. Japan excels in semiconductor materials and equipment, commanding 56 percent of the global market share in materials and 32 percent in equipment, including 88 percent of the market for coater/developers, 53 percent for silicon wafers, and 50 percent for photoresists as of 2023.[67] South Korean companies, Samsung Electronics and SK Hynix, dominate the memory chip market, while TSMC is the world's leading semiconductor foundry. In sum, the United States, Japan, South Korea, and Taiwan collectively account for 82 percent of the global semiconductor market share and 74 percent of the global supply value chain.[68] In addition, they dominate other critical segments of the industry, holding 84 percent of the market in chip design, 77 percent in manufacturing equipment, and almost 99 percent in memory chips.[69]

Export Controls and Investment Screening

In relation to consolidating supply chains, the United States has also used export controls and investment screening as tools to protect against Chinese coercion. On October 7, 2022, the Biden administration introduced new sweeping export restrictions on certain advanced computing integrated circuits and semiconductor manufacturing items.[70] These expanded export controls, implemented by the Department of Commerce's Bureau of Industry and Security (BIS), were intended to "restrict the People's Republic of China's (PRC's) ability to both purchase and manufacture certain high-end chips used in military applications."[71]

To enhance the effectiveness of these export controls, the Biden administration sought policy coordination with key allies and partners. Specifically, the administration approached Japan and the Netherlands—two key producers of advanced chip manufacturing equipment, including the lithography machines—to align their policies with U.S. efforts in restricting their sales of advanced semiconductor equipment to China. At the same time, the Biden administration also sought compliance from South Korea, particularly from South Korean companies Samsung Electronics and SK Hynix, whose chip manufacturing facilities in China would be directly affected by the U.S. new export control rules. Although these Korean companies were granted a one-year license to import semiconductor equipment to maintain their business operation in China, their future operation after the expiration of the license remained uncertain.[72] Japan, the Netherlands, and South Korea were all reluctant to follow. However, from the U.S. government standpoint, securing their cooperation was critical to effectively curb China's access to advanced technologies while not putting U.S. companies at a disadvantage.[73]

The situation took a turn on January 27, 2023, when Japan and the Netherlands quietly agreed to restrict their sales of advanced semiconductor manufacturing equipment to China.[74] In late March, Japan announced new export restrictions on twenty-three types of chip manufacturing equipment, noting "[Japan's] responsibility as a technological nation to contribute to international peace and stability."[75] The new rules will apply to six categories of equipment, such as cleaning, deposition, lithography, and etching.[76] Japanese minister of economy, trade and industry Yasutoshi Nishimura noted, "If our exports are not being reappropriated for military use, we will continue exporting. We believe the impact on companies will be limited."[77] On June 30, the Netherlands also unveiled the government's new supplemental export controls "on national security grounds," requiring Dutch companies to apply for a permit when they export to non-EU countries.[78] The new measures will affect the Dutch company ASML's deep ultraviolet (DUV) lithography and atomic layer deposition (ALD), in addition to existing restrictions on the EUV machine, which had already been on the export control list since 2019.[79] In early October, the United States and South Korea also resolved their dispute with the U.S. decision to grant Samsung Electronics and SK Hynix an indefinite waiver from the export control requirements, allowing them to continue supplying semiconductor equipment to their Chinese facilities without disruption.[80]

Outbound investment screening is another tool to protect critical domestic industries from potential economic coercion. Outbound investment screening monitors and blocks U.S. outgoing investments to foreign entities, especially in "countries of concern," if such investments are assessed to undermine U.S. national security by supporting adversaries to develop "military, intelligence, surveillance, and cyber-enabled capabilities."[81] Although the United States has historically maintained a policy of open investment, there has been a growing call within the U.S. Congress since 2016 to enhance the power of the Committee on Foreign Investment in the United States (CFIUS) to restrict outbound investments, particularly in sensitive technologies.[82] This led Biden to issue Executive Order 14105 in August 2023, proposing (1) a prohibition on U.S. persons making outbound investments in sensitive technologies and products—namely, semiconductors and microelectronics, quantum information technologies, and artificial intelligence—in countries of concern; and (2) the mandatory requirement to notify the Treasury about such investments.[83] The executive order specifically designated China, Hong Kong, and Macau as a "country of concern."[84] In February 2025, the second Trump administration issued a national security presidential memorandum, titled "America First Investment Policy," calling for strengthening CFIUS authorities, including over "greenfield" investments, and restricting PRC investments in strategic U.S. sectors such as technology, critical infrastructure, health care, agriculture, energy, and raw materials.[85]

The U.S. initiative to establish a new outbound investment program has influenced other countries. For instance, in January 2024 the EC started discussion among the member states about outbound investment screening at the EU level, as part of five initiatives under the European Economic Security Strategy announced in June 2023.[86] In January 2025, the EC published a recommendation based on those discussion, calling on all EU members to review outbound investment (from January 2021 onward) in the three strategic technology areas of semiconductors, artificial intelligence, and quantum.[87] Although some member states, such as Germany, Austria, and Spain, already have some mechanism in place to monitor outbound investment at the national level, the EU is actively considering a unified regulatory framework after a period of monitoring outbound investments at the national level.[88]

THE SOURCES OF DE-RISKING

At their core, these multi-method de-risking strategies manifest a loss of trust in the norms and rules of the liberal trading order that privilege openness and free trade. Actors no longer believe that market forces alone can bring them maximum profit and efficiency. In fairness, this posture is not solely a product of China's economic coercion. While China's bullying may be the specific cause, several permissive conditions have led the world to this state of mind.

For one, the global pandemic made clear how critical health, technology, and minerals supply chains could suddenly become choked off without any scalable alternative sources. As Allen observed, advanced industrialized economies experienced material shortages for the first time in generations, and they had no solutions for their angry constituencies. "Policymakers concluded that they could no longer trust that the free market would speed needed supplies to them in times of need. As a result, there has been growing support for stockpiling . . . reshoring production domestically, and diversifying supply chains."[89] The pandemic lockdown prompted the EU to organize PPE on a scale not seen since World War II in Denmark, Sweden, Germany, Greece, Hungary, and Romania. The U.S. Department of Defense started a program of "homeshoring" PPE, providing billions of dollars in subsidies to domestic manufacturers as a matter of "national security."[90]

Another factor leading to skepticism and mistrust in free-market forces was the first Donald Trump presidency. With no foreign policy experience, the U.S. president looked at international relations largely through business profit-and-loss lenses. His former aides noted that he had a mercantilist view of foreign policy that distinguished countries only in terms of their trade balance with the United States rather than according to traditional categories like security allies and adversaries. According to former National Security Council (NSC) officials, the first bit of factual information required by Trump in all briefings to him before a leader-level meeting (after the name of the country and the leader) was the trade surplus or deficit with the United States.[91] This had ripple effects domestically in the United States as constituencies for free trade lost all voice. Trump alienated the traditional free-trade platform of Republicans and turned the party in the direction of protection of domestic industry and jobs, not terribly different from the Democratic Party. Indeed, the overarching strategic purpose of Trump's 2017 Indo-Pacific policy was not about America's alliances and promotion of freedom and democracy in Asia but expressly to build the financial and economic power of the United States.[92]

Trump viewed China's $500 billion trade surplus as the United States "losing" to China and was unwilling to count on market forces to rectify the imbalance. He effectively started a trade war by levying tens of billions in tariffs on China in 2018 that continued until the 2020 Phase One agreement, which lowered some barriers. The Biden administration through its last year in office did nothing to remove the Trump-era tariffs and instead increased them. The May 2024 Section 301 tariffs on $18 billion of imports from China included

100 percent tariffs on EVs, 50 percent on semiconductors, solar cells, and syringes, and 25 percent on batteries, PPE, graphite, and critical minerals, among other products.[93] In January 2025, the second Trump administration came into office and levied additional 10 percent tariffs against China a few weeks later.[94] At the time of this writing, Trump raised tariffs to 20 percent in March 2025 and 54 percent in April 2025. In response to Chinese retaliation, Trump further raised tariffs to 145 percent later the same month. A full-blown tariff war between the two largest economies in the world hardly provides an environment that engenders trust in free-market forces.

When the leading power in the international system enacts policies that move away from free-market principles, it creates an environment that invites others to do the same. And when the next leading power in the system, China, is politically illiberal and promotes a state-led industrial policy that directs market economic forces and capital in the direction of state goals, then the environment is not only inviting but ripe for non-market-based policies. China's economic growth has been fueled by companies that have become global in stature but are also heavily subsidized and supported by the state, far beyond any comparable support provided in the West. In order to remain competitive, companies and governments look to devise their own industrial policies. The result is that the traditional focus on free markets, private enterprise, innovation, and increasing production and efficiency are eclipsed by industrial policy reminiscent of wartime.

As noted earlier, the United States refers to the strategies of trade diversification, impact mitigation, supply chain reshoring, and export/investment controls as "de-risking" rather than decoupling. In reality, however, the last two are different from the others. Trade diversification and impact mitigation both seek to reduce the harm caused by China's coercion through market-based solutions, while still trading with China. Reshoring and export/outbound investment controls are also meant to reduce vulnerability to Chinese disruption, but this is accomplished through decoupling completely from China. Reshoring and export/investment controls arguably operate against free-market principles by artificially rejecting production efficiencies or potentially lucrative capital projects in the name of national security.

The Classic De-Risking Dilemma

The classic dilemma with these multi-method derisking strategies is that they are designed to defend against China's economic coercion, but none of them actually stops it. The distinction is not dissimilar to that between defense and deterrence in international security. States must defend themselves once the enemy has attacked, but they use deterrence to stop the enemy attack from occurring in the first place. Defense operates in the realm of action (thwarting the enemy's attack); deterrence operates in the realm of nonaction (preventing the attack from occurring). If states practice deterrence but then they have to use defense, then deterrence has failed. If a state's threat to retaliate against an adversary's attack causes the adversary to stand down, then deterrence has succeeded. What deters the adversary is the assessment that the costs of attacking (i.e., threat of unacceptable punishment) outweigh the benefits if it carries out the attack.[95] The evidence of failure is that you must fend off an attack. Evidence of success is a nonaction, but although that nonaction could be the result of your deterrent threat, it could also be the result of some other factor influencing the adversary's decision.

The success of conventional deterrence strategies on the part of the West was evident during the Cold War. The United States has maintained security commitments to its NATO allies in Europe and to South Korea and Japan in East Asia, promising to retaliate against any offensive attack by the adversary against allies in each theater. The costs associated with such a wider war with the United States have deterred adversaries from considering such action. The credibility of the conventional deterrent threat was based in the "tripwires" placed in each theater. Whether it was thirty to sixty thousand U.S. ground troops at the demilitarized zone (DMZ) on the Korean peninsula or more than 250,000 U.S. troops in West Germany, the automatic involvement of the United States in any conflict made the deterrent threat credible.[96] If the Soviets attacked Western Europe or the North Koreans again crossed the DMZ, then the deterrent threat would have failed and the United States and allies would have had to resort to defense to repel these attacks and retaliate by carrying out the deterrent threat.[97]

De-risking measures are largely defensive in nature. They are implemented in response to Chinese predatory actions. The measures aim to blunt the impact of sanctions, embargos, tariffs, nontariff barriers, and other tools used by China to hurt a country's economy. But these measures, while important, do not deter the *next* act of Chinese economic coercion. For example, providing ad hoc investment capital to an economy hurt by Chinese bullying may help in one particular instance, but this measure does not prevent the next act of coercion against this economy or against another one. De-risking measures try to help the victim, but they do not change or shape Chinese predatory economic behavior.

Similarly, supply chain resilience and ad hoc mitigation measures insulate certain lines of production from China's economic coercion without stopping the practice. Securing the supply of one product, such as medical PPE, does nothing to prevent China from finding another economic sector through which to coerce. Those same countries with secure PPE production chains may still be timid to speak out on behalf of Taiwan or Hong Kong to avoid further targeting by China. Backfilling precipitous drops in a country's exports to China with trade diversification to other markets helps the targeted country, but it imposes no costs on China's use of the predatory practice against the next target. Indeed, many countries' enthusiasm for participating in such mitigation measures is circumscribed by fears that China will retaliate by finding new areas with more economic coercion. For example, South Korea's initial hesitation at joining the Chip 4 alliance was in part due to concerns about Chinese economic retaliation along the lines of the frontal assault on consumer goods, tourism, and education in 2017 over THAAD. Surely enough, China later identified urea as another vulnerability where South Korea was highly dependent on Chinese supply that it could leverage for coercion over other issues.[98]

As noted earlier, the reshoring measures undertaken by countries on semiconductor chips are a form of decoupling because they seek to protect the entire supply chain from China. This is one effective way to stop economic coercion. But economic actors are at best willing to participate in such draconian measures only on a handful of key items, which the U.S. government has defined as artificial intelligence, synthetic biology, and quantum computing. But in all other areas of trade and commerce, the world has no desire to decouple from China.

Thus, while de-risking is necessary and important, it suffers from a fatal flaw: it can defend against coercion, but it cannot deter such coercion. The willingness of many countries to participate in building such supply chain networks outside of China or restricting critical technology exports to China is still limited by fears of Chinese economic retaliation on a multitude of other goods or services, since no country can truly decouple from one of the world's largest economies. What is needed is a strategy that can stop and not just insulate from this behavior, while still trading with China (i.e., not decoupling). Supply chain resilience, trade diversification, impact mitigation, and reshoring can be made more effective only if they are complemented by a competitive strategy to shape and deter Chinese predatory economic behavior. In short, the world needs to make Beijing recognize the high cost of doing business this way so that it refrains from practicing such extraordinarily predatory behavior and instead respects the norms of the global trading order.

The rest of this chapter lays out the theory of collective resilience. Collective resilience is designed to deter acts of economic coercion. It promises a multilateral response to the prospect of economic bullying. What informs this strategy is the understanding that interdependence, even asymmetric interdependence, is a two-way street: a target of economic coercion that is asymmetrically trade-dependent on the coercer may also export items to the coercer upon which the coercer is highly dependent. In the application of this theory to China's economic coercion, we present original trade data showing that the previous and current targets of Chinese economic coercion export more than $43.06 billion worth of goods upon which China is more than 70 percent dependent, as a proportion of its total imports of those goods, and more than $20.94 billion worth of goods upon which China is more than 90 percent dependent (2024 data). These target states can band together and practice an Article 5–type collective economic deterrence strategy by promising retaliation should China act against any one of the alliance members. Forcing China to find a new supplier or pay a higher price for one item is, of course, not enough to change behavior; thus, operating alone against China would be ineffective. However, sanctions on an aggregation of these high-dependence items might threaten enough inconvenience for Beijing to deter future predatory behavior. The barriers to collective action of this sort are undeniably high, but overcoming these barriers is necessary if countries want to stop forever living in the shadow of Chinese economic bullying.

Dealing with China's weaponization of economic interdependence is critical to competing successfully against China. The willingness of countries to join supply chain coalitions, challenge China's militarization of the South China Sea, safeguard against Huawei's access to domestic 5G markets, support Taiwan's defense, and speak out for democracy in Hong Kong or against genocide in Xinjiang ultimately depends on how fearful countries and companies are of Chinese economic retaliation. Economic decoupling is not a silver bullet because no country can completely sever its ties to one of the world's largest economies. A strategy of collective resilience, however, could neutralize China's coercive behavior while not decoupling from relations with China.

COLLECTIVE RESILIENCE

Collective resilience rests on the threat of an organized coalition response with trade tools to deter economic coercion.[99] It can be practiced by any group of countries that wants to protect the liberal international trading order from subversive economic bullying. Collective resilience rests on two bodies of theory in international security and international political economy. It borrows from traditional deterrence theory and builds on the literature on globalization and the weaponization of interdependence. The literature on globalization initially argued that the creation of fiber optic–capable superhighways of borderless information, finance, and production chains at the end of the Cold War would raise productivity for all, reduce costs, privilege open and free societies, and eliminate the prospect of war.[100] As true as this may have been, the enthusiasm was tempered by a subsequent wave of work that critically analyzed how networks of finance, information, and trade may not be a universally beneficial attribute of the global order. Instead, globalized networks can be weaponized; they can accentuate power differentials, especially for those who dominate key nodes in the network.[101] Whether the United States in global finance or China in global trade, actors who occupy key chokepoints exercise inordinate power over all others in the same network.

The theory of collective resilience responds to this literature by demonstrating that actors without a dominant hold on key nodes of an embedded network are not powerless. Even if they do not control a key node, they can still exercise leverage over the dominant actor if they (1) hold something of value to the hegemon for which exit options are costly (i.e., it is costly for the dominant actor to replace) and (2) are able to band together to send a credible deterrent signal. In short, there is power in numbers to create alternate networks or subnetworks within a network that at first glance may seem to be dominated by one actor.

Applied to China, collective resilience uses the threat of multilateral trade action as a deterrent to the dominant actor's predatory impulses. It features the credible threat of collective punishment in the form of trade retaliation—in an Article 5 deterrent framework—imposing significant and unacceptable costs if China attempts to coerce others economically. Collective resilience focuses not on the use of economic punishment—that is, it is not advocating a trade war. Rather, it is the credible threat by a collective of states to carry out the punishment in unison if and when China acts against any one of the states in the collective. Like deterrence theory, collective resilience operates in the realm of nonaction. It tries to elicit a nonaction from China (no economic predation) with nonaction (the threat of certain retaliation). If and only if the deterrent threat fails will the collective resilience partners actually impose sanctions on China.

To be successful, collective resilience requires both *capabilities* and *political will*. Regarding capabilities, no country on its own can deal with the Chinese economic behemoth, and no country can decouple fully from it. Every country is asymmetrically dependent on China in their trade balance. For example, as table 4.1 shows, China accounts for about 27.98 percent, 20.75 percent, 20.12 percent, and 11.18 percent of global trade in 2024 for Australia, South Korea, Japan, and the United States, respectively, while the share of China's global trade accounted for by each of those countries in the same year is approximately 3.43 percent, 5.32 percent, 5.00 percent, and 11.20 percent (2024 data).[102]

TABLE 4.1 China's Asymmetric Trade with Global Economies (2024)

OTHER COUNTRY AS A PERCENT OF CHINA'S TRADE			CHINA AS A PERCENT OF OTHER COUNTRY'S TRADE		
COUNTRY	TOTAL TRADE WITH CHINA (USD)	PERCENT OF TRADE	COUNTRY	TOTAL TRADE WITH CHINA (USD)	PERCENT OF TRADE
United States	$690,239,622,709	11.20	United States	$606,166,055,785	11.18
South Korea	$327,730,266,003	5.32	South Korea	$272,777,942,098	20.75
Japan	$308,250,470,198	5.00	Japan	$291,745,971,363	20.12
Australia	$211,534,397,164	3.43	Australia	$178,327,940,571	27.98
Germany	$201,857,852,292	3.28	Germany	$272,307,506,049	8.71
United Kingdom	$98,470,996,435	1.60	United Kingdom	$144,934,616,700	11.00
Canada	$93,009,304,957	1.51	Canada	$86,474,923,892	7.67
France	$80,175,190,086	1.30	France	$104,189,054,661	7.40
Italy	$72,549,245,908	1.18	Italy	$70,270,630,831	5.45

Source: Authors' original table with data derived from UN Comtrade database at https://comtradeplus.un.org/.

However, there is power in numbers. The United States, Japan, South Korea, and Australia together account for about a quarter of China's trade. Moreover, economic interdependence—even asymmetric interdependence—is still a two-way street. Even though countries like South Korea and Australia may export less to China than they import, China values and relies inordinately on some subset of this trade. In the words of Keohane and Nye, China experiences "vulnerability interdependence" on these imports in the sense that it would be sensitive to price changes or would need to seek alternative suppliers if it could not acquire those goods from the exporting country.[103] China sanctions Australian beef and barley, for example, but will not sanction Australian spodumene (used for lithium EV batteries) or iron ore imports because, as of 2024, China is more than 62 percent and 61 percent dependent, respectively, on these Australian sources as a proportion of its total supply. This potentially gives Australia leverage, as part of a collective of other like-minded partners with similar goods that China is dependent upon, to shape and deter China's economic predation.

Original data presented in this book shows that China is highly dependent on hundreds of items exported to it by countries that Beijing targets with economic coercion. Part of China's hubris in bullying its trade partners is the confidence that the targets would not dare to countersanction. But as Bonnie Glaser has argued, economic coercion has become so pronounced a Chinese practice that countries cannot just play defense by reshoring or fortifying supply chains; they need to play offense too.[104] Contrary to conventional wisdom, these trade partners of China have the tools to do so.

Collective resilience might not suit the tastes of liberals and globalists because of its anti–free trade premise. Our argument is admittedly controversial. But the strategy is designed to protect trading nations from China's predatory pathologies. It is a necessary competitive strategy for protectors of the liberal international order. As one author has noted, these supporters are out of practice with the sometimes illiberal nature of peer competition.[105] Collective resilience is not advocating a trade war or decoupling; instead, the strategy seeks to shape Chinese conformity with the liberal trading order.

CAPABILITIES OF CHINA'S TRADING PARTNERS

China is far more dependent on its trade partners than most people realize. Australia, Japan, and South Korea, for example, are like-minded U.S. democratic allies in Asia whose primary trade partner is China. Alongside the United States, in

2024 they constituted almost 25 percent of China's total global trade ($1.53 trillion in total trade).[106] Each has been subject to harsh economic coercion by China, costing billions of dollars. However, each country exports a wide variety of goods upon which China is highly dependent. Table 4.2 summarizes China's high-dependence trade (2024 data) with victims of its economic coercion. A high-dependence item is defined as a good that China imports from another country that constitutes more than 70 percent of its total trade in that good. Table 4.2 lists the total number and total value of high-dependence items imported from eighteen countries whose governments have been direct targets of China's coercion: Australia, Canada, Czech Republic, Estonia, France, Germany, Japan, Latvia, Lithuania, Mongolia, New Zealand, Norway, Palau, Philippines, South Korea, Sweden, United Kingdom, and the United States.[107]

This data is derived from UN Comtrade, an UN-based repository of official international trade statistics. Percentage dependence by China on a particular import from a given country is taken as a percentage of China's total imports of that good (e.g., the value of the imports from Australia of good X as a fraction of the total value of all imports of good X by China). The import data used is based on nomenclature (HS 2022) and all six-digit HS codes. Chinese high-dependence

TABLE 4.2 China's High-Dependence Imports from Eighteen Targets of Economic Coercion (2024)

CHINA'S LEVEL OF DEPENDENCE*	TOTAL NUMBER OF IMPORT ITEMS	TOTAL VALUE OF IMPORTS (USD)
At least 70 percent dependent	589	$43,065,872,182
At least 80 percent dependent	404	$27,038,015,882
At least 90 percent dependent	259	$20,946,686,774

Source: Authors' original table with data derived from UN Comtrade database at https://comtradeplus.un.org/.

Note: The eighteen countries included are Australia, Canada, Czech Republic, Estonia, France, Germany, Japan, Latvia, Lithuania, Mongolia, New Zealand, Norway, Palau, Philippines, South Korea, Sweden, United Kingdom, and United States. These countries have all experienced broad-based coercion directed against the government. Including all countries in which specific firms have been targeted would raise the number to forty-one, but private-firm cases are dealt with separately below.

* China's dependence on a particular import from a given country is defined as a percentage of total imports (e.g., the value of China's imports from Australia of good X as a fraction of the total value of all imports of good X by China). The import data used was based on nomenclature (HS 2022) and all six-digit HS codes.

trade is defined as 70 percent or greater. While this number is arbitrary, it is a fair indicator of Chinese trade dependence. By way of comparison, China is widely known to be dependent on Australian iron ore (61.45 percent) and Philippines nickel ore (about 60 percent). This makes the 70 percent threshold a reasonable metric.

In total, targets of Chinese economic coercion export 589 items upon which China is more than 70 percent dependent. The total value of this trade is not insubstantial at more than $43.06 billion. These countries export 404 items with a trade value of over $27.03 billion upon which China is 80 percent dependent, and 259 items valued at over $20.94 billion with 90 percent Chinese dependence. This gives these countries substantial leverage in dealing with Chinese bullying. Japan, for example, in 2024 exported to China 147 items, valued at over $9.44 billion, upon which China is more than 70 percent dependent as a percentage of China's total imports of those goods. These included forty-eight items, worth $4.61 billion, upon which China is more than 90 percent dependent. The United States in 2024 exported 132 items, totaling $5.71 billion, with greater than 70 percent Chinese dependency, including seventy-three items, totaling $3.36 billion, with greater than 90 percent Chinese dependency (see appendix 2). Table 4.3 summarizes the number and value of China's high-dependency imports in 2024 from the eighteen countries that have been victims of Chinese economic coercion. Breakdowns for each country are contained in appendix 2. Itemized lists of all of China's high-dependence goods for each of the countries are contained in appendix 3.

As the tables show, the numbers are not trivial. Of the eighteen countries targeted by Chinese economic coercion, eight of them export more than $1 billion worth of goods with Chinese dependency rates higher than 70 percent. Five of the targeted countries export more than $5 billion worth of high-dependency goods to China.

Strategic Value and Substitutability

Not every high-dependence item is costly to China. For example, China is 86 percent dependent on imports of ballpoint pens from Japan and 83.5 percent dependent on high-quality suitcases from Germany, but no one believes that cutting these off would alter Chinese behavior. For China to experience vulnerability interdependence, the items targeted in a collective deterrence strategy must meet two criteria. First, the good must have some *strategic value*, which is defined as a

TABLE 4.3 China's High-Dependence Imports by Country (2024)

COUNTRY	NUMBER OF ITEMS (GREATER THAN 70 PERCENT DEPENDENT)	TOTAL VALUE OF IMPORTS (USD)
Japan	147	$9,447,462,727
United States	132	$5,713,431,562
Germany	95	$1,430,635,581
South Korea	48	$8,577,531,035
France	38	$2,618,002,507
Canada	26	$5,457,672,022
New Zealand	23	$5,347,529,586
Australia	22	$2,357,003,034
Norway	16	$596,650,834
United Kingdom	13	$412,544,078
Mongolia	9	$474,174,554
Philippines	9	$294,055,795
Sweden	7	$321,842,049
Czech Republic	4	$17,336,818
Estonia	0	$0
Latvia	0	$0
Lithuania	0	$0
Palau	0	$0
Total number of items:	**589**	**$43,065,872,182**

Source: Authors' original table with data derived from UN Comtrade database at https://comtradeplus.un.org/.

Note: China's high-dependence trade is defined as 70 percent or greater. While this percentage is arbitrary, it is a fair indicator of Chinese trade dependence.

critical intermediary or end-product good, or a luxury good. We include luxury goods because, even though they do not meet the definition of a strategic good, they carry high audience costs. Because luxury goods are enjoyed by the political and business elite in any society, the inability to access these goods could create inordinate political pressures on the leadership, even in nondemocratic societies.[108] The deterrent effect associated with luxury goods could therefore be more significant than the trade value of the sanction itself. Second, the good must have low *substitutability*, defined as a lack of alternative suppliers.[109] We measure substitutability by looking at the next two or three largest alternative suppliers of the good to China and determine whether they are like-minded partners of the collective resilience coalition.

Using these criteria, the trade data shows many items that meet the threshold of high dependence and low substitutability. Table 4.4 provides a selection of items for which China is highly dependent on the eighteen countries whose governments it has directly coerced in the past—items that could be incorporated into a collective economic deterrence strategy. If China were unable to import these items from its top three or four suppliers, this could create significant transaction costs to find alternative sources. An expanded list of China's high-dependence items from these eighteen countries is provided in appendix 4.

As noted previously, the entire list of high-dependence goods from the eighteen countries whose governments China has economically coerced encompasses 589 items with a total annual trade value of over $43 billion (the full itemized list is available in appendix 3). This list includes ten items with trade values over $1 billion. Table 4.4, a selected list of China's high-dependence merchandise trade commodities, includes fifteen items with annual trade values each over $1 billion (including some noteworthy items under 70 percent dependency). These range from intermediary goods such as iron and nickel ores, spodumene (lithium), inorganic salts, ethylene, propylene, and acyclic hydrocarbons to advanced manufactured products like hybrid electric vehicles, OLED displays, turbojets, and turbojet turbines to agricultural products and luxury goods such as grain sorghum, brandy, milk powder, and rape seeds. While some of these items may seem trivial, China relies on quite a few of them for key parts of its economy.

For example, China is over 84 percent dependent on the supply of silver powder [HS 710610] from Japan as a percentage of its total imports of the commodity, and over 74 percent dependent on the supply of industrial robots [HS 847950] from Japan. Silver powder is a critical intermediary good used to produce photovoltaic and electronic conductive paste for solar panels, and industrial robots are critical for manufacturing and advanced industries. The EV battery market is very important to China, yet it is highly dependent on the Philippines—a country on which China has routinely applied economic coercion—for nearly 60 percent of its global supply of nickel ores and concentrates [HS 260400], with a trade value of almost $1.6 billion. Nickel ores and concentrates are used to produce battery cathodes. China is more than 62 percent dependent on Australia—another favorite target of China's coercion—for spodumene [HS 253090], which is processed to extract lithium chemicals that are a necessary component of lithium-ion

TABLE 4.4 China's Vulnerability Interdependence (Selected List, 2024)

COUNTRY AND ITEM (HS CODE)	PERCENT DEPENDENCE* (TRADE VALUE, USD)	REPLACEMENT RATIO[†]	SUBSTITUTE SUPPLIERS[‡] (PERCENT CHINA DEPENDENCE)	DESCRIPTION
AUSTRALIA Iron ores and concentrates (260111)	61.45[§] ($79,510,063,078)	0.020	Brazil (22.12) South Africa (3.36)	Critical component for steel (pig iron)
AUSTRALIA Other mineral substances (253090)	62.1[§] ($3,229,183,817)	0.024	Zimbabwe (15.22) Brazil (5.32)	Natural minerals including spodumene, a critical component of lithium (used for lithium batteries)
CANADA Rape or colza seeds (120510)	100.00 ($3,294,156,686)	0.000	N/A	Used for cooking oil (canola)
CANADA Cereals: wheat/meslin; durum wheat, non-seed (100119)	58.43[§] ($855,522,112)	0.000	Australia (30.89) United States (10.00)	Used for food products and agriculture
CANADA Lobsters, nonfrozen (030632)	78.96 ($609,077,551)	0.000	United States (20.69)	Luxury good
CANADA Semichemical wood pulp (470500)	76.81 ($470,210,161)	0.008	New Zealand (8.18) Sweden (5.49)	Used for the paper and packing industries

CANADA Coniferous wood: S-P-F, sawn or chipped (440713)	99.96 ($92,167,241)	0.038	N/A	Used for wood framing in construction
CANADA Coniferous wood: hem-fir species (440714)	98.35 ($61,866,957)	0.057	N/A	Used for wood framing in construction
FRANCE Spirits (220820)	99.21 ($1,223,858,496)	0.203	N/A	Strong distilled liquor (brandy). Brandy is the largest imported spirit in China.
FRANCE Broken or scutched flax (530121)	86.91 ($756,652,158)	0.000	Egypt (6.11) Belgium (5.48)	Used for production of linen fabric and paper
FRANCE Perfumes (330300)	63.80§ ($636,303,705)	0.511	Italy (13.26) Spain (11.26)	Fragrance products like perfume and cologne
FRANCE Champagne and sparkling wine (220410)	69.16§ ($46,495,694)	0.051	Italy (22.61) Spain (4.62)	Luxury good
GERMANY Gear machinery (846140)	64.48§ ($351,044,084)	0.169	Switzerland (18.15) Japan (13.92)	Used to cut, grind, and finish common gears: spur, helical, and bevel
GERMANY Fused quartz or silica tubes (700231)	77.82 ($61,302,573)	0.345	United States (11.16) Japan (5.95)	Used for semiconductor manufacturing, optical fibers, and laboratory equipment

(continued)

TABLE 4.4 (*continued*)

COUNTRY AND ITEM (HS CODE)	PERCENT DEPENDENCE* (TRADE VALUE, USD)	REPLACEMENT RATIO[†]	SUBSTITUTE SUPPLIERS[‡] (PERCENT CHINA DEPENDENCE)	DESCRIPTION
GERMANY Ingots, alloy steel (722410)	70.48 ($30,446,661)	0.266	Malaysia (10.23) India (5.29)	Primary forms of alloy steel used in construction and shipbuilding
GERMANY Tetrachloroethylene (290323)	98.54 ($17,487,779)	0.929	Japan (1.46)	A chemical commonly used to dry clean fabrics
JAPAN Hybrid electric vehicles (870340)	98.86 ($3,951,111,137)	1.154	United States (1.11)	Energy-efficient vehicles that use both an internal combustion engine and an electric motor for propulsion, such as the Toyota Prius
JAPAN Silver powder (710610)	84.69 ($892,448,804)	0.005	United States (9.99) Taiwan (2.58)	Used in photovoltaic and electronic conductive paste needed for solar panels
JAPAN Industrial robots (847950)	74.75 ($481,954,200)	0.888	Germany (5.66) France (4.44)	Important to manufacturing and advanced industries
JAPAN Plates, sheets, and film of cellulose acetate (392073)	77.93 ($466,056,030)	0.140	South Korea (10.27) Taiwan (6.19)	Used for packaging of food, beverages, and medical supplies and for textile treatment

Country / Product (HS code)			Partners	Description
JAPAN Textile lubricants (340391)	70.64 ($305,917,476)	0.160	Germany (16.55) Italy (3.72)	Used for the treatment of textiles and leathers
JAPAN Copper foil (741012)	77.07 ($202,555,244)	0.295	Germany (8.37) United States (6.84)	Used in construction to produce locks, wiring, doors, and electrical sockets
MONGOLIA Fine animal hair (510219)	94.26 ($135,861,149)	0.031	Peru (3.53) Bolivia (0.73)	Used for clothing, textiles, and makeup brushes
NEW ZEALAND Solid milk and cream (040221)	79.19 ($1,287,144,337)	0.038	Australia (12.69) Netherlands (4.73)	Milk powder or cream
NEW ZEALAND Butter (040510)	80.23 ($591,644,848)	0.016	France (8.64) Netherlands (3.38)	Food staple
NEW ZEALAND Fresh kiwifruit (081050)	98.64 ($590,226,297)	0.072	Italy (1.22) Greece (0.14)	Food staple
PHILIPPINES Nickel ores and concentrates (260400)	59.91§ ($1,597,758,356)	0.000	Russia (12.03) Australia (6.05)	Essential element in the battery cathodes used in the electric vehicle industry
PHILIPPINES Pineapples (080430)	97.70 ($198,918,517)	0.116	Indonesia (1.44) Thailand (0.64)	Fresh or dried fruit
SOUTH KOREA OLED panel displays, without drivers or control circuits (852412)	94.01 ($2,118,159,315)	0.185	Japan (3.64) Taiwan (2.05)	Used for smartphones, televisions, monitors, laptops, and other electronic devices

(continued)

TABLE 4.4 (*continued*)

COUNTRY AND ITEM (HS CODE)	PERCENT DEPENDENCE* (TRADE VALUE, USD)	REPLACEMENT RATIO[†]	SUBSTITUTE SUPPLIERS[‡] (PERCENT CHINA DEPENDENCE)	DESCRIPTION
SOUTH KOREA Other inorganic salts (284290)	93.67 ($2,060,419,042)	0.932	Japan (4.73) United States (0.57)	Used for various agricultural, industrial, and scientific applications, including fertilizers and glass
SOUTH KOREA Acyclic hydrocarbons: unsaturated, ethylene (290121)	69.87[§] ($1,383,967,103)	0.033	Japan (17.41) Oman (4.68)	Critical base product for petrochemicals
SOUTH KOREA Propylene, unsaturated (290122)	74.29 ($1,295,108,795)	0.044	Japan (18.3) Philippines (2.59)	Crucial building block for producing plastics and other chemicals
UNITED KINGDOM Whiskies (220830)	86.65 ($391,179,828)	0.153	Japan (6.71) United States (3.21)	Luxury good
UNITED STATES Turbojet turbine (841191)	62.81[§] ($4,057,954,464)	0.341	France (8.36) Germany (6.44)	Gas turbine engine used in aircraft
UNITED STATES Acyclic hydrocarbons (290110)	98.15 ($2,604,826,737)	0.034	Spain (0.77)	Chemical compound used in lubricants and polyethylene (plastic bags)

UNITED STATES Turbojets (841112)	48.86§ ($2,179,113,096)	0.129	France (43.09) United Kingdom (7.65)	Gas turbine with a propelling nozzle used in aircraft
UNITED STATES Grain sorghum (100790)	66.85§ ($1,733,210,890)	0.000	Australia (22.30) Argentina (10.81)	Used to produce traditional Chinese drink (*baijiu*)
UNITED STATES Amine compounds (292122)	85.07 ($95,557,095)	0.246	Germany (7.72) France (6.61)	Includes acyclic polyamines and HMDA that can be used for production of nylon 66 and as curing agent for epoxy resins
UNITED STATES Scintigraphic medical instruments (901814)	76.28 ($91,876,205)	0.681	Israel (9.19) Germany (8.38)	Used in nuclear medicine for diagnostic imaging, including cancer detection
UNITED STATES Bovine semen (051110)	91.93 ($53,535,288)	0.000	Germany (5.51) France (1.86)	Used for insemination of cattle
UNITED STATES Kentucky bluegrass seed (120924)	93.08 ($20,308,770)	0.000	Denmark (6.92)	Cool-season grass seed planted as turf in athletic fields

Source: Authors' original table with data derived from UN Comtrade database at https://comtradeplus.un.org/.

* China's dependence on the source country for the good as a percentage of China's total imports of that good.

† Domestic production of the good is measured using reported Chinese exports of the good as the proxy variable. The replacement metric is the exports/imports ratio. A number greater than 1 suggests a strong capacity to replace a loss of imports with domestic sources by diverting exports to fill demand.

‡ China's dependence on the next largest source country(ies) for the good as a percentage of China's total imports of that good.

§ Falls below 70 percent dependency, but included because (1) trade value is significant and/or (2) alternate supplier(s) is a coerced, like-minded country.

batteries.[110] China buys more than $3.2 billion worth of this commodity from Australia. Moreover, it exports almost none of these minerals, suggesting high vulnerability and replacement costs to find alternative sources.[111] South Korea supplies over 93 percent of China's inorganic salts [HS 284290], which are used for various agricultural, industrial, and scientific applications, including ceramics, glass, and refractories. Together with Japan, China's high dependence increases to 98 percent. South Korea also provides China with almost 70 percent of ethylene [HS 290121] and 74 percent of propylene [HS 290122], two critical building block chemicals for China's vast petrochemicals industry. Combined with Japan, its dependencies rise to 87 percent and 92.5 percent, respectively.

China is the world's largest steel producer, producing more than 50 percent of the global total.[112] But to keep its steel mills running, it needs iron ore, a vital component of steel. This is an inconvenient truth for China because it is almost two-thirds dependent on Australia for its iron ore. China imports about $79.5 billion worth of iron ore and concentrates [HS 260111] from Australia, or about 61 percent of its total global imports. Without Australia, the world's largest iron ore producer, China cannot produce enough steel to fuel its massive infrastructure boom. China also knows there are no easy alternate markets because their next biggest source is Brazil, which supplied 22 percent of its demand in 2024. Even if China completely shifted to the Brazilian market, there would still be a massive supply gap. In 2024, China imported about 272 million tons (valued at $28.6 billion) of iron ore from Brazil. That was 74 percent of Brazil's total exports of iron ore that year—nowhere close to the numbers needed to cover the additional 700 to 800 million tons that China imports from Australia.[113] When Beijing placed sanctions on Australian wine, beef, and barley in 2020, it never touched iron ore.[114] This gives all of China's trading partners a significant amount of leverage, probably more than each ever thought they had, if they can come together as a group.

China's high dependence on trade extends far beyond commodities needed for China's production of solar panels, robots, batteries, chemicals, and steel. While these other items are not "big ticket" in terms of trade value, they have symbolic meaning and would register political costs if all of a sudden China suffered displaced supplies. One of these is wood. China is over 98 percent dependent on Canada for its global supply of two types of coniferous woods (99.9 percent dependency on coniferous wood, S-P-F, sawn or chipped [HS 440713], and 98.3 dependency on coniferous wood, hem-fir species [HS 440714]). Both of these woods are used for framing in construction. With annual combined trade values of $154 million, the significance of these imports may seem minor, but

China shows no domestic capacity to produce these woods based on replacement ratios near zero (elaborated on in chapter 5).

Another one of these smaller but significant items is foodstuffs. China is 100 percent dependent (about $3.29 billion worth) on Canada for rape or colza seeds [HS 120510], a key ingredient for canola oil. It is more than 91 percent dependent for its supply of solid milk and cream [HS 040221] on New Zealand (79 percent) and Australia (12.6 percent), and more than 88 percent dependent on imports of butter [HS 040510] from New Zealand (80 percent) and France (8.6 percent). The Philippines and New Zealand provide China with 97 percent and 98 percent of its imported supply of pineapples [HS 080430] and fresh kiwifruit [HS 081050], respectively. China relies on the United States for almost 92 percent of its annual imported supply of bovine semen [HS 051110], used for maintaining a high-quality beef supply.[115] It relies on the United States for 93 percent of its Kentucky bluegrass seed [HS 120924] used for cool-season seeding of its soccer pitches.

Could the Chinese live without butter from New Zealand, rape seeds for cooking oil from Canada, or U.S. seeds for lush green soccer fields? Certainly. But a concatenation of pressures from different directions and different countries on such items would create transaction costs that China would have to calculate in considering its use of economic coercion against any of these economies.

Substitutability and Alternative Suppliers

A high-dependence item is defined not just by the percentage of trade but also by China's ability to find alternative suppliers. If Beijing can easily find substitute suppliers of the item, then China is not truly dependent on any one country's supply. This requires us not just to enumerate the percentage high-dependence trade items for China but also to measure China's substitutability of these items. That is, we must identify the next largest suppliers of China's high-dependence goods and whether these are like-minded partners of the West. This measurement of substitutability is a key prerequisite for collective resilience to be credible.

Figures 4.1 and 4.2 show examples of high-dependence items with low substitutability. As noted previously, China is over 84 percent dependent on Japan for its supply of silver powder. In addition, the next three largest suppliers of silver powder are the United States (about 10 percent), Taiwan (2.5 percent), and South Korea (2.1 percent). This means that the four partners in total account for over 98 percent of China's global supply (the issue of Chinese domestic production is

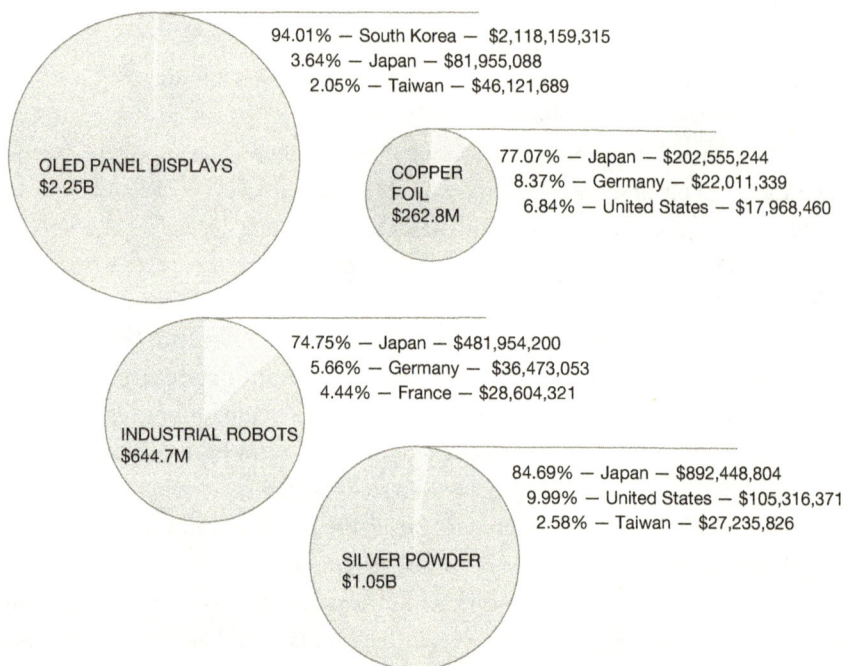

OLED PANEL DISPLAYS
$2.25B

94.01% — South Korea — $2,118,159,315
3.64% — Japan — $81,955,088
2.05% — Taiwan — $46,121,689

COPPER
FOIL
$262.8M

77.07% — Japan — $202,555,244
8.37% — Germany — $22,011,339
6.84% — United States — $17,968,460

INDUSTRIAL ROBOTS
$644.7M

74.75% — Japan — $481,954,200
5.66% — Germany — $36,473,053
4.44% — France — $28,604,321

SILVER POWDER
$1.05B

84.69% — Japan — $892,448,804
9.99% — United States — $105,316,371
2.58% — Taiwan — $27,235,826

FIGURE 4.1 Substitutability of selected high-dependence goods. Dark shading represents the combined share of China's total supply imported from the top three suppliers (2024).

Source: Authors' original figure with data derived from UN Comtrade database at https://comtradeplus.un.org/.

addressed below). Similarly, China exhibits 74 percent dependence on Japan for its supply of industrial robots [HS 847950]. China's next two suppliers are Germany (5.6 percent) and France (4.4 percent). The three like-minded partners provide 84 percent, which Beijing would find difficult to replace. As figure 4.1 shows, China relies on Japan for 77 percent of its imports of copper foil [HS 741012], used for construction wiring, locks, and electrical outlets. Together with supplies from Germany (8.3 percent) and the United States (6.8 percent), China's dependence reaches 92 percent. And in terms of high-tech products that are increasingly ubiquitous in Chinese daily lives, China is more than 94 percent ($2.11 billion) dependent on South Korea for OLED panel displays [HS 852412], a critical component of smartphones, smart watches, tablets, televisions, and increasingly of vehicle dashboards and infotainment systems. If you add Japan and Taiwan to the mix, China is more than 99 percent dependent on its three neighbors.

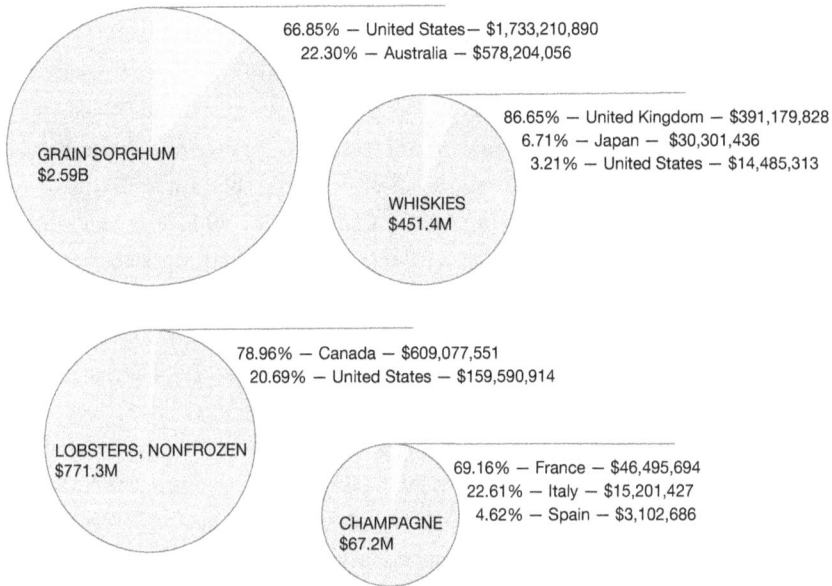

FIGURE 4.2 Substitutability of selected high-dependence luxury goods. Dark shading represents the combined share of China's total supply imported from the top two or three suppliers (2024).

Source: Authors' original figure with data derived from UN Comtrade database at https://comtradeplus.un.org/.

We noted earlier that luxury goods carry high audience costs and therefore could be an effective deterrent in a collective resilience strategy. The data shows that there are in fact many luxury goods that meet the vulnerability interdependence criteria (see figure 4.2). Take lobsters, for instance. China is 99.6 percent dependent on Canada and the United States for nonfrozen lobsters [HS 030632] and completely reliant (99.8 percent) on Canada for frozen ones [HS 030612]. For whiskies [HS 220830]—another luxury good—China is more than 86 percent dependent on the UK, with Japan (6.7 percent) and the United States (3.2 percent) the next largest suppliers. Together, the United States and Australia supply 89 percent of China's grain sorghum [HS 100790], used to produce the traditional Chinese alcohol *bai-jiu*. France, Italy, and Spain together account for more than 96 percent of China's champagne imports [HS 220410], and for fine spirits (e.g., brandy and cognac) [HS 220820], China is essentially wholly reliant on France (99.2 percent).

Again, an inability to acquire these items, or replacing them with lower-quality substitutes, could give rise to criticisms of the leadership and complaints about competence in that their policies have resulted in international retaliation. While China could certainly survive the absence of European fine spirits, the political cost would have to be calculated in the leadership's thinking every time it considered another act of economic bullying. Collective resilience's deterrent threat is to create such a cost calculation where one did not previously exist. Before collective resilience, our strategies focused on reducing the pain of China's bullying, but this imposed hardly any costs on China, so it could freely move on to coerce the next victim. Collective resilience aims at imposing a cost on this policy.

Two relevant points emerge regarding a collective resilience strategy. First, China could practice trade diversification in response, locating alternative foreign suppliers for one, two, or any handful of these items. But if a large coalition of countries threatened to act on an array of these goods (table 4.4 is a selective list only) in response to Chinese coercion against any one country, the costs of trade diversification might grow enough to alter Chinese behavior. Second, leveraging Chinese goods that are high-dependence, have strategic importance, and exhibit low substitutability lessens the burden on countries that participate in the collective resilience coalition. Each country would not need to threaten to cut off all high-dependence items it exports to China but only threaten action on one or two items that meet the vulnerability criteria (elaborated below). For example, Japan would not be required to sanction all 147 of the high-dependence items it ships to China; instead, it might be called upon to threaten to act on only three critical exports—copper foils, silver powder, and industrial robots—to signal credible deterrence against China's economic coercion of others.[116] Similarly, Australia, Canada, France, and South Korea would not be asked to threaten to retaliate on all of their high-dependence items, but only on one or two—such as spodumene (Australia), lobsters (Canada), brandy (France), and OLED displays (South Korea)—to minimize the pain to their own economies while presenting a credible deterrence signal to China. The upshot is that the targets of Chinese economic coercion have significant capabilities at their disposal to make credible deterrent threats of retaliation against Chinese bullying.

Having the capability to carry out a collective resilience strategy is only half the equation. A necessary condition is that states have the *political will* to commit to a collective stance in which they are willing to act not only for their own benefit but also on behalf of any other member of the collective, even if it means they will incur costs for doing so. Without such a commitment, the deterrent signals carry no weight, and the credibility of collective resilience is undermined. It is to this question we turn in the next chapter.

CHAPTER 5

RESILIENCE AND THE GROUP OF SEVEN (G7)

The previous chapter introduced collective resilience as a theory and as a strategy. Collective resilience is designed to resolve the dilemma of de-risking strategies by going beyond defending against China's bullying to adopting deterrence strategies commonly used in the security arena to stop such future acts. As in the military use of the strategy, collective economic deterrence requires the material capabilities to be effective. Our original data has shown that all of the countries that have been targeted by economic coercion, even as they are asymmetrically dependent on trade with China, simultaneously trade in high-dependence goods of strategic value to China. While this provides each country with a small amount of leverage, a coalition of countries similarly positioned vis-à-vis China would amplify the leverage to a point where it could impose enough costs for Beijing to reconsider its predatory actions.

But having the material capabilities to deter China's economic coercion is decidedly only half of the strategy. The other half relates to political will and commitment. Like deterrence in the security realm, collective resilience is only as effective as it is credible. This requires targets of economic coercion to make an Article 5–type commitment to the cause—that is, the economic security of one is related to the economic security of all. If China uses discriminatory trade practices to infringe on the sovereignty of any one country in the group, this will elicit a collective response from the others on China's high-dependence items.

Every country does not need to act on every high-dependence item that it trades with China. This could spark an all-out trade war—in security terms, the equivalent of mutually assured destruction (MAD). The strategy should be more subtle than that. As a group, each country could commit to acting on one or a handful of items, which in the aggregate could register significant deterrent costs for China to consider.

Achieving this level of political commitment is difficult but not impossible. The immediate reaction by some potential coalition participants, when asked to act against China on behalf of another country, may be to think only about their own immediate self-interest. Why should they incur China's wrath when it is directed at someone else? However, there are many incentives for forward-thinking leaders to see such participation in a coalition as being in their enlightened self-interest. Being present to help one coalition member under attack is the only way to ensure that members will come to your assistance when the situation is reversed.

We first look at the political commitments necessary for collective resilience. We then consider how China would respond to collective resilience actions. We conclude the chapter by looking at alternate groupings of countries that might be more prone to a political commitment to stand against economic coercion. Countries that share similar values and objectives might show greater interest in the effort than a random group of countries that have nothing else in common other than being victims of economic coercion. The G7 could be such a grouping.

POLITICAL WILL

The political requirements to pull together a collective resilience group are like those you would expect for compliance in any norm-based regime to circumvent the collective action problem. As noted above, the collective resilience group will be more cohesive if players operate on the presumption of enlightened self-interest, not just short-term myopic self-interest. Arguably, democracies have a higher tendency than nondemocracies to cooperate based on such long-term conceptions of self-interest rather than being narrow egoistic actors.[1]

There must be a strong reciprocity norm in the group too. The incentive for one player to cooperate in support of another is stronger if the player knows that its help will be reciprocated in the future. There are numerous determinants of what creates reciprocity within a group, but in the case of collective resilience, one could argue that three stand out: (1) a previous pattern of positive interaction among members of the group; (2) common interests in supporting a liberal, open, and nondiscriminatory trading order; and (3) belief in the integrity of the WTO as a regulatory body to ensure fair trade.[2] Support for the WTO forms a basis for reciprocity because the types of economic coercion discussed in this book cannot be easily adjudicated through the WTO mechanism, thereby undermining not just the organization but also confidence in the trading order.

An additional requirement for formation of the collective resilience group is that players need to be socialized to some sense of reputational or prestige costs for membership and compliance within the group. Players must care whether they would be identified as not carrying their fair share within the group. In addition, they must feel a sense of shame for being called out as "cheaters" in the group. Again, this is more likely to be the case among a group of like-minded players than not.

Should there be a group that operates on enlightened self-interest, strong norms of reciprocity, and a sense of reputational commitment, then this forms a good basis for trust among the collective resilience group's members. Trust would be the premise of the initial commitment to the project, and that trust would grow with each successful deterrent threat that stops a coercive economic act emanating from within or outside of the group. Any failed deterrent threat or act of free-riding in the group will reduce the level of trust and, ultimately, the viability of the group to stay together.

Trust would not be the only premise of the initial commitment to join a collective resilience group. As the liberal internationalist John Ikenberry writes, there would be significant "club benefits" from joining the group on the condition that members followed the rules.[3] First, members of the group would not have to feel they were dealing with the Chinese economic behemoth on their own and could find some confidence in the fact that while the threat of economic coercion is still present, it casts a shorter shadow than it did without the group. Those outside the club's protective walls would face a harsher environment in which they would have to kowtow to China's influence efforts or otherwise face economic pain. Second, the club members would no longer have to self-censor their political beliefs for fear of offending China. While the club does not give them license to attack or provoke China, it frees them from the discomforting self-censorship that many have thus far reluctantly accepted as the price of doing business with China. Third, the club allows members not to have to pay the ultimate price of decoupling from China as the only way to be free of economic coercion. While some decoupling choices have already been made in certain sectors like high-end memory chips, countries can still trade with China in everything else with less fear that the trade interdependencies incurred will be weaponized by Beijing for political purposes.

Fourth, being a member of the collective resilience club still allows countries to practice de-risking in terms of trade diversification and impact mitigation. A collective deterrence strategy does not preclude these de-risking strategies but supplements them. Indeed, club membership may improve de-risking strategies by providing a ready coalition of countries that can provide market access or additional investment. An impact mitigation strategy by the United States, for example, may promise U.S. support if one gets hit by economic coercion, but it does not guarantee that other countries will provide support outside of a collective resilience context. The club's assurance is clear: If you get hit, others will support you and retaliate on your behalf. This support also relates to cooperation on "backfilling." That is, club members commit not to backfill supplies to China from their own companies if China imposes sanctions on imports of the good from the targeted state.

Fifth, and perhaps most important, club membership offers a collective identity that allows each member to act like a "shaper" rather than a "taker" in the global trading order. Ikenberry writes, "In today's chess game to rewrite the rules of trade . . . , the side with the largest coalition will have the upper hand."[4] The club's benefits are that members will be part of the effort to sustain and shape trust in an open and rules-based trading order. While this trust is ultimately a public good that benefits all, it is appealing to leaders to be part of the rule-making and rule-shaping club.

There are no illusions that the political obstacles to a collective resilience club would be easily surmountable. There are many challenges to consider. All members would have to identify and agree upon the definition of economic coercion—which, as described in chapter 2, can take many forms—as well as agree upon what would be the trigger for collective action. Disputes over trade that could be decided by the WTO would not meet the threshold. Instead, deterrence would focus on those trade actions by China taken for political purposes.

Members would need to reassure each other, particularly the smaller powers in the group, that they would not be abandoned when Beijing tries to peel them off individually from the coalition with sanctions. Beijing would almost certainly look for the weakest link in the chain and target that entity first to try to break up the assembled coalition. This requires key members to commit to trigger actions if China bullies any other member, even if it is economically costly to them; otherwise, collective resilience will have little credibility.

It will be especially important for large powers like the United States and Japan to lead because of the nature of China's coercion strategy, which rarely targets the big economies, instead going after smaller partners of the United States. As one expert observes, "the PRC has repeatedly demonstrated its willingness to coerce American treaty allies. Meanwhile, it has stepped back from sanctioning the U.S."[5] Because these targets are smaller, weaker links (in China's eyes), Beijing calculates that the coercion will not elicit a U.S. response. And this calculation would not be wrong. When Beijing targeted Philippine bananas over a territorial dispute or the South Korean conglomerate Lotte over a missile defense battery, the United States did not step up to support its partners. Therefore, we learn from these experiences that large powers in the collective resilience club will need to demonstrate early commitment to the strategy to give confidence to others.

The incentives to free ride would be high. That is, some countries may want the direct benefits of the club but none of the obligations. Some entities may want to backfill, taking advantage of new export opportunities to China opened up by Beijing's closing its doors to goods from a targeted country. Some governments may oppose or want to de-escalate any collective resilience action in order to minimize collateral damage. For example, fearful of secondary sanctioning against its own companies by China, Germany pressured Lithuania to concede to Chinese demands on de-recognizing Taiwan and not to carry out the threat of Lithuanian companies leaving China.[6]

Larger powers would need to provide early and tangible signs of commitment to underwrite the coalition and create confidence. While some of this reassurance would certainly be political, it would also likely have to be material, as a tangible sign of commitment. For example, partners might invest in a collective fund to compensate smaller members for losses or offer alternative export or import markets to divert trade in response to Chinese sanctions. Otherwise, the temptation to defect when another is being coerced by China is high.

There is no denying that a collective resilience strategy would be domestically controversial. All members would need to build support at home for the strategy, which will not be easy because it may translate to some economic pain. A company in the United States, for example, may not be willing to sacrifice its quarterly earnings from its business in China to cooperate with the strategy, especially on behalf of a country or a competitor on the other side of the world being coerced by China. Political opponents will see significant opportunities to launch "my country first" attacks at the party in power for sacrificing domestic interests to some globalist ideal and for incurring China's wrath for no apparent reason. Leaders will have to make the case to their publics about how the broader threat to the rules-based order posed by China's weaponizing trade translates into threats to national interests in both the short and long term. They will have to work within their individual political constraints to legislate a mix of industrial policy, tax law, and corporate incentives to promote public-private sector partnerships in support of the strategy. Bethany Allen's recommendations in terms of legislation to enhance corporate transparency make sense. Because of China's stealthy methods to weaponize trade, requirements need to be put in place that both protect companies and hold them accountable. These could include, for example, that companies divulge any efforts by China to pressure them with sanctions or to recruit them to backfill for sanctions applied to another member of the club. Companies might also be required to report any contact with Chinese government authorities (e.g., law enforcement or national security entities, not trade agencies) and divulge the identity of any employees cooperating with such outside agents.[7] Legislation could also require the reporting of all investments made in China or Chinese companies operating outside of the country. There will likely be pushback from the private sector and from the political opposition, not to mention the general public, which will cause more than one leader to hesitate about burning the large amount of political capital necessary to accomplish the task.

It is undeniably harder for democracies to organize in this manner than China. In this regard, as a nondemocracy, China will be much more adept at a competing strategy of economic coercion because it faces fewer political obstacles to acting. It can decree that society and its companies bear the costs of any blowback from its coercive strategies. Yet as formidable as the obstacles are, surmounting them would send a very credible signal of the collective resilience group's political commitment and intent. Thus, the process of organizing—the seriousness and combative tone of the domestic debates, the purposeful conversations among members—could itself act as a deterrent to China's coercion.

Despite these challenges, what would hopefully motivate each party to stay the course is the desire to trade with China and, at the same time, to stop China's economic coercion and the deleterious effects such coercion has on the rules-based order. Every self-interested actor wants to remove the shadow of Chinese economic bullying. Knowing that this strategy works better as a group, given the combined capabilities of the economies, should create incentives to band together. Each member's political commitment to the collective is critical for the deterrent strategy to be effective. Any one country practicing this policy alone would do nothing to change Chinese behavior. But a group of countries working together would create problems for Beijing. As Ikenberry notes, the larger the coalition of countries, the more credible the deterrent threat will become.

WOULD CHINA CARE?

Altering the Payoff Structure of Coercion

Our analysis begs the question of whether threats to leverage China's high-dependency goods would register with Beijing. After all, acting on a handful of trade items constitutes such a small percentage of China's overall trade.

Collective resilience does not aim to cut off all or a substantial chunk of trade with China but seeks to alter the calculation that drives the deviant behavior. China's economic coercion follows a "minimax" strategy: it is designed to minimize costs for China while maximizing those for the target. Collective resilience alters this payoff structure by raising the costs to China of its policy choice.

When China targets countries, it usually focuses on restricting goods or services that have no major repercussions at home. China followed such a minimax strategy in its sanctions on Norway over the Nobel Prize awarded to dissident Liu Xiaobo. China could have blocked all seafood imports from Norway, but that would have incurred a cost for China, since some of these products are processed in China for reexport. Instead, it sanctioned only salmon, which had a huge cost for Norway but little cost for China.[8]

In a similar vein, those sectors that China targets are usually ones that matter more to the exporting country than to China. For example, China's ban on Canadian soybeans in 2019 over the detention of a Huawei executive was worth more than $1 billion to Canada but constituted only 3 percent of China's total trade in that product. China was only 36–40 percent dependent on Australian wines and only 19 percent dependent on Australian barley when it tariffed them in 2020, but the sanctions did substantial damage to those targeted, forcing many Australian producers to close shop. The PRC's sanctions against Czech pianos were of little cost to China, given alternative suppliers, but they threatened almost 40 percent of the revenues for the company Petrof.

The sectors most targeted by China are those in which there is low dependence or easy substitutability.[9] China rarely employs sanctions on its high-dependence goods. For example, in all its sanctioning of Australia, China has not leveraged its much-needed imports of Australian iron ore. China will not sanction Taiwan's TSMC or South Korea's Samsung because of its dependence on these memory chip suppliers. Indeed, while China's economic coercion campaign forced the closure of South Korea's Lotte stores over the THAAD deployment in 2017, South Korean chipmakers SK Hynix and Samsung reported no disruptions or irregularities to their operations in China because Beijing had no easy substitutes if it sanctioned these items.[10] By contrast, for many of the items that China did sanction (food marts, cosmetics, music, travel), easy substitutes were available. The point is that if Beijing is unwilling to locate alternative sources at this level of dependency, then one would expect greater sensitivity to dependency levels of 70 percent or higher. What distinguishes collective resilience from other impact mitigation and trade diversification strategies is that it focuses on raising costs to shape behavior. In short, "the most important feature of Beijing's coercion to date is economic costs to the PRC have been tiny. . . . One implication is that the

US can deter China in at least some instances by threatening to raise its costs to a noticeable level."[11]

Collective resilience thus alters the payoffs for Beijing's coercion strategy not by threatening all trade but by leveraging specific dependencies and vulnerabilities inherent in China's trading patterns. Sufficient evidence to indicate the efficacy of this approach is found in Chinese government and expert literature that shows China's acute awareness of its trade vulnerabilities. A study by Georgetown University's Center for Security and Emerging Technology identified scores of articles published in the government-run *Science and Technology Daily* [科技日报] newspaper detailing "chokepoints" in China's supply chains and core technologies. The government's response is to call for import substitution strategies, the use of lower-grade, domestically produced applications, or the acquisition of foreign companies. Chinese private firms are resistant to lower-quality domestic sourcing, complaining about inconsistent batch quality and the lack of adequate domestic research and development comparable to that of foreign firms with their decades of experimentation, data, and precision.[12] The point is that China cares about its trade vulnerabilities, and the literature indicates that domestic economic, business, and political factions would balk at losing access to key items, thus raising the costs to the Chinese government of an economic coercion act.[13]

Replacement Ratio

China presumably tolerates its reliance on the high-dependence goods because it is optimal in terms of price and efficiency. Beijing also assumes that no single trade partner would dare retaliate in what would amount to self-inflicted pain. But if these goods were leveraged by collective resilience partners, would China be able to replace a cutoff of imports with domestic production? Critics of our strategy would contend that Beijing could practice its own form of supply chain "homeshoring" and replace any imports of high-dependence goods with homegrown substitutes.

In order to measure the capacity for China to substitute domestic production for imports, we create a quotient called the replacement ratio. The replacement ratio (RR) measures the amount of domestic production of a good by using Chinese self-reported exports of the same good as a proxy variable.[14] The replacement metric is the quotient of exports (X) over imports (I).

An RR value less than 1 (China exports less of the good than it imports) suggests that China would have little or no capacity to replace its external

$$RR = \frac{X\,(\text{exports})}{I\,(\text{imports})}$$

FIGURE 5.1 Replacement ratio

dependence with domestic production; even if they diverted all of their exports of the good to domestic needs, they would still fall short. In this case, replacement would be *highly costly*. A value between 1 and 1.5 (China exports about the same amount or a little more of the good than it imports) suggests *costly* replacement; it would require a significant diversion of its exports to meet domestic need. A value higher than 1.5 (China exports much more than they import of the good) suggests *not costly* replacement capacity; China could meet domestic demand and still have some export capacity. An RR value of 0 means *no* replacement capacity; China depends entirely on its trading partner for that good.

Figures 5.2a and 5.2b categorize China's capacity to replace a cutoff of high-dependence goods with domestic production. The values are for a representative list of high-dependence goods from the eighteen countries targeted by China's economic coercion, as well as others (derived from table 4.4 and appendix 4).

Figures 5.2a and 5.2b show that out of the forty-five items on the high-dependency list, forty-two are *highly costly* or *costly* for China to replace. Forty-one of them have an RR metric lower than 1, meaning it would be very difficult for China to replace those items because shifting exports would not be enough to meet domestic demand. One item, with an RR metric between 1 to 1.5, could not easily be replaced by domestic production. Furthermore, there are eight items for which China has no replacement capacity (RR of 0). Lastly, there are three items with an RR metric over 1.5, meaning these are *not costly* items because China could easily mitigate the impact of a collective action. An example is ballpoint pens from Japan (RR of 11.76). China imports about $81 million worth from Japan, but it exports more than $1.1 billion worth to the world, meaning that Japanese ballpoint pens could easily be replaced by Chinese ballpoint pens, regardless of the pen quality.

The replacement ratio measurements indicate that China would feel the pinch of a collective resilience strategy. The purpose of such a strategy is not to create prohibitive costs for China but to create sufficiently troublesome transaction costs. The strategy also assumes such costs would be incurred by the leadership outside of the trade vacuum. From the Chinese leadership's perspective, they would have to consider taking on this additional problem amid tensions with Taiwan, the economic slowdown, corruption in the military, U.S.-China strategic

Replacement ratio
(total value of exports of good/total value of imports of good)

1.000

0.900

0.800

0.700

0.600

0.500

0.400   HIGHLY COSTLY

0.300

0.200

0.100

0.000

a	b	c	d	e	f	g	h	i	j	k	l	m	n	o	p	q	r	s	t	u	v	w
0.000	0.000	0.000	0.000	0.000	0.000	0.000	0.000	0.001	0.005	0.009	0.017	0.021	0.024	0.032	0.034	0.034	0.038	0.039	0.044	0.052	0.058	0.073

(a) Cereals: durum wheat, non-seed	Canada	(m) Iron ores and concentrates	Australia
(b) Broken or scutched flax	France	(n) Other mineral substances (e.g. spodumene)	Australia
(c) Oilseeds	Australia	(o) Fine animal hair	Mongolia
(d) Bovine semen	United States	(p) Ethylene, unsaturated	South Korea
(e) Kentucky bluegrass seed	United States	(q) Acyclic hydrocarbons	United States
(f) Nickel ores and concentrates	Philippines	(r) Solid milk and cream	New Zealand
(g) Lobsters, nonfrozen	Canada	(s) Coniferous wood: S-P-F, sawn or chipped	Canada
(h) Rape or colza seeds	Canada	(t) Propylene, unsaturated	South Korea
(i) Grain sorghum	United States	(u) Champagne and sparkling wine	France
(j) Silver powder	Japan	(v) Coniferous wood: hem-fir species	Canada
(k) Semichemical wood pulp	Canada	(w) Fresh kiwifruit	New Zealand
(l) Butter	New Zealand		

FIGURE 5.2A   China's capacity to replace high-dependence goods with domestic production (2024)

Source: Authors' original figure with data derived from UN Comtrade database at https://comtradeplus.un.org/.

Replacement ratio
(total value of exports of good/total value of imports of good)

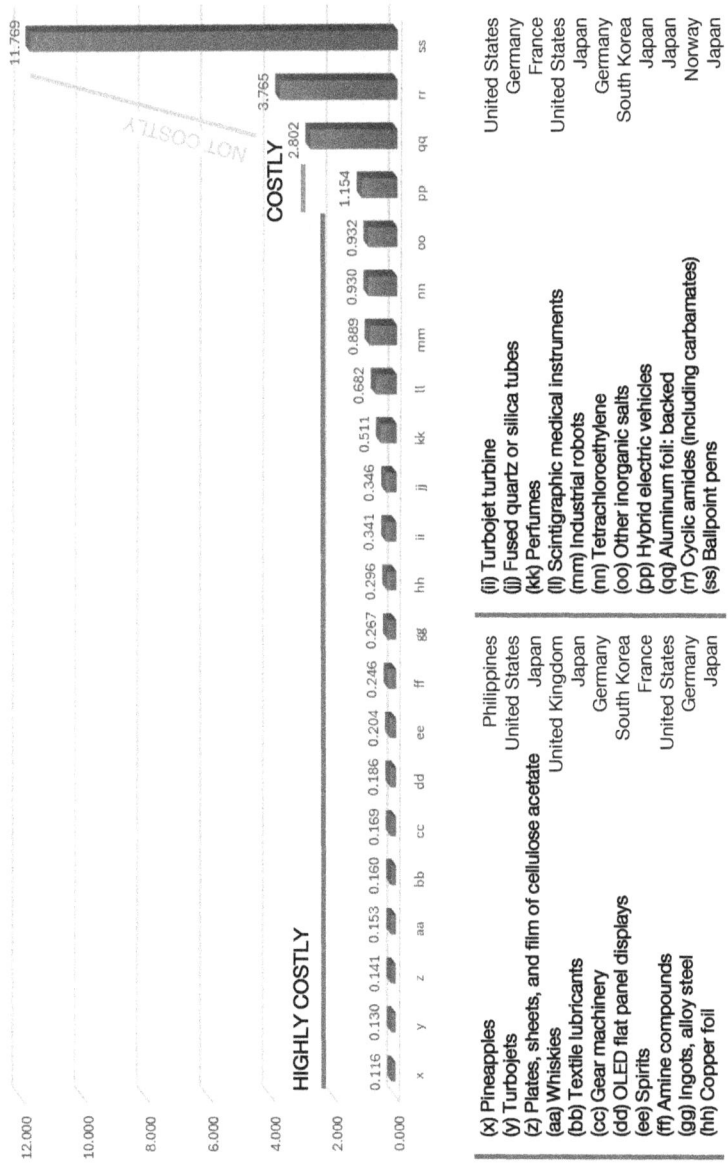

Label	Value	Good	Country
x	0.116	Pineapples	Philippines
y	0.130	Turbojets	United States
z	0.141	Plates, sheets, and film of cellulose acetate	Japan
aa	0.153	Whiskies	United Kingdom
bb	0.160	Textile lubricants	Japan
cc	0.169	Gear machinery	Germany
dd	0.186	OLED flat panel displays	South Korea
ee	0.204	Spirits	France
ff	0.246	Amine compounds	United States
gg	0.267	Ingots, alloy steel	Germany
hh	0.296	Copper foil	Japan
ii	0.341	Turbojet turbine	United States
jj	0.346	Fused quartz or silica tubes	Germany
kk	0.511	Perfumes	France
ll	0.682	Scintigraphic medical instruments	United States
mm	0.889	Industrial robots	Japan
nn	0.930	Tetrachloroethylene	Germany
oo	0.932	Other inorganic salts	South Korea
pp	1.154	Hybrid electric vehicles	Japan
qq	2.802	Aluminum foil: backed	Japan
rr	3.765	Cyclic amides (including carbamates)	Norway
ss	11.769	Ballpoint pens	Japan

HIGHLY COSTLY — COSTLY — NOT COSTLY

FIGURE 5.2B China's capacity to replace high-dependence goods with domestic production (2024)

Source: Authors' original figure with data derived from UN Comtrade database at https://comtradeplus.un.org/.

competition, territorial disputes with other Asian countries, and a host of other ongoing problems. Leaders prefer to avoid headaches if they can, and Beijing may choose not to act out on its bullying inclination.

❧

China could use trade diversification as a strategy to counteract collective resilience. Beijing could do this preemptively if it was aware of its vulnerability to collective economic deterrence by its trading partners. A longitudinal analysis of UN Comtrade data from 2022 to 2024 (table 5.1) shows that China's trade dependencies on so-called high-dependence items have changed over time. Indeed, in some cases, China has reduced its dependency on imports from countries that it has previously targeted with economic coercion.

Take the example of Australia. In 2022 and 2023, China imported 69 percent and 73 percent of non-durum wheat and meslin [HS 100199]—used for making buns and noodles in China—from Australia, totaling $1.86 billion and $2.13 billion, respectively. Australia was by far China's largest source, outpacing number two supplier France, which provided 22 percent ($608 million) in 2022 and 10 percent ($308 million) in 2023. But in 2024, China reduced its dependence on this staple food ingredient from Australia to 31 percent ($627 million) of total non-durum wheat/meslin imports, while increasing that from France to 35 percent ($707 million). There was a similar pattern in chemical contraceptives [HS 300660], which China imported primarily from Germany in 2022 and 2023 at a dependency rate of 74 percent ($255 million) and 64 percent ($162 million), respectively. But in 2024, China reduced its dependency on Germany to 31 percent ($64 million) and increased its imports from Hungary, making it the top provider at 32 percent ($65 million) of China's total imports of the item. Another example is harvesting machinery [HS 843359] for its farmland. China's reliance on the United States, which provided 72 percent ($211 million) and 76 percent ($325 million) in 2022 and 2023, dropped to only 18 percent ($18 million) in 2024. The United States was replaced by Germany, which exported 42 percent ($41 million) of harvesting machinery to China that year. In all three examples, China's dependency on these items has dropped below the 70 percent threshold and has instead become more evenly spread among multiple suppliers.

We have no idea if this is a conscious or unconscious strategy by China. Given the widespread criticism of China's coercive economic practices, Beijing may indeed be trying to use trade diversification to reduce vulnerability to others using the same playbook against China. But many other variables could be affecting trade dependency, including completely unrelated factors like the war in Europe.

TABLE 5.1 China's High-Dependence Imports from Eighteen Targets of Economic Coercion (2022–2024)

COUNTRY	# OF ITEMS 2024	TOTAL VALUE OF IMPORTS 2024 (USD)	# OF ITEMS 2023	TOTAL VALUE OF IMPORTS 2023 (USD)	# OF ITEMS 2022	TOTAL VALUE OF IMPORTS 2022 (USD)
Japan	147	$9,447,462,727	145	$10,164,641,805	124	$4,960,038,430
United States	132	$5,713,431,562	117	$6,459,718,028	87	$11,548,305,886
Germany	95	$1,430,635,581	85	$1,411,739,209	64	$827,620,276
South Korea	48	$8,577,531,035	47	$7,055,193,685	28	$5,354,364,494
France	38	$2,618,002,507	40	$2,860,590,490	27	$2,490,927,512
Canada	26	$5,457,672,022	25	$6,659,175,212	18	$5,090,898,875
New Zealand	23	$5,347,529,586	33	$5,198,558,890	20	$3,918,283,198
Australia	22	$2,357,003,034	19	$17,613,885,616	14	$10,562,817,896
Norway	16	$596,650,834	13	$486,067,836	7	$544,501,211
United Kingdom	13	$412,544,078	21	$503,556,314	6	$480,259,062
Mongolia	9	$474,174,554	10	$598,323,716	4	$409,607,128
Philippines	9	$294,055,795	8	$234,965,156	5	$185,491,811
Sweden	7	$321,842,049	5	$341,050,464	5	$270,750,988
Czech Republic	4	$17,336,818	7	$23,771,288	3	$7,118,606
Estonia	0	$0	0	$0	0	$0
Latvia	0	$0	0	$0	0	$0
Lithuania	0	$0	0	$0	0	$0
Palau	0	$0	0	$0	0	$0
Totals	**589**	**$43,065,872,182**	**575**	**$59,611,237,709**	**412**	**$46,650,985,373**

Source: Authors' original table with data derived from UN Comtrade database at https://comtradeplus.un.org/.

A potential case in point is Chinese imports of maize [HS 100590], which in 2022 showed heavy dependence on the U.S. market, with 74 percent of its total maize imports ($5.28 billion) coming from the United States. Since then, China's dependence on the U.S. market has dropped to 29 percent ($2.61 billion) in 2023 and 15 percent ($562 million) in 2024. In 2024, Brazil and Ukraine were China's top two sources of maize, providing more than 50 percent ($1.89 billion) and almost 30 percent ($1.11 billion), respectively, thereby weakening a potential collective resilience act on maize.

But it is important to note that these trade dependencies work in directions that do not just negate but may actually reinforce the collective resilience strategy. Over the past three years, China has become more reliant on some items from countries it has coerced. This includes marine propulsion engines [HS 840810] from South Korea. These fuel-efficient diesel or semi-diesel engines are critical components for China's growing shipbuilding industry, and it has become increasingly reliant on its neighbor, a major shipbuilding rival. China's dependence on South Korea grew from 52 percent ($298 million) in 2022 to 70 percent ($781 million) in 2024. Another example is China's import of liquefied petroleum gas (LPG) [HS 271112] from the United States, which has grown from 41 percent ($6.68 billion) in 2022 to almost 60 percent ($11.2 billion) in 2024.

OVERCOMING THE COMMITMENT TRAP: G7 PLUS AUSTRALIA AND SOUTH KOREA

Critics might argue that the collective resilience strategy, despite all of its supposed benefits, still faces a commitment trap. There are two aspects to this trap. First, China's counterstrategy will be to pick off the weakest countries in the coalition. While many countries are unhappy with Chinese bullying, few may be up to challenging China in this way. Some countries, particularly in Asia, have large Chinese expatriate communities, many are deeply penetrated by Chinese disinformation narratives, and many are distrustful of one another and of the continued commitment of larger powers, especially the United States, to the cause.

Second, it will be harder to build a coalition around countries that are not like-minded and that do not share the same threat perceptions of China. If we look at the eighteen governments cited in chapter 3 that have been targeted by China's economic coercion, they do not necessarily exhibit the traits of a group around which to build a collective resilience framework. The variations in economic size, political values, trade dependence on China, and relative differences in vulnerability to Chinese disinformation narratives greatly complicate the political obstacles and material leverage necessary to build a successful collective resilience coalition. Not that it could not be done, but it would not be easy *ceteris paribus*.

One way of circumventing the commitment trap would be to build coalitions around like-minded groupings of countries that have sizable economies and a history of working together. We propose the G7 countries plus two Indo-Pacific countries, Australia and South Korea, as one such grouping. The G7—the United States, the United Kingdom, Japan, Canada, France, Germany, Italy, along with the European Union/European Commission—comprise the world's leading advanced industrialized democracies. They have already developed strong bonds of trust and boast a long history of working together on global problems.

The G7 initially was an ad hoc gathering of the finance ministers of the leading economies in 1973, and then heads of state in 1975, to address the oil shock and to coordinate monetary policies.[15] Membership in the group has changed over time, most notably with the addition in 1998 and then removal in 2014 of Russia. The G7's signature trait has been its informality and yet its policy effectiveness, as leaders can discuss issues and coordinate economic policies in an intimate setting. In the past few years, however, G7 leaders' statements have taken on a more urgent, expansive, and unified tone as the world has grappled with a range of existential issues from the COVID-19 pandemic, financial crises, and climate change, to supply chain resilience, the Ukraine war, and the Gaza war.[16] Indeed, the G7's prominence as an institution of global governance has arguably grown as a result of the war in Europe, the Middle East, and the formation of a bloc of autocracies centered around China, Russia, Iran, and North Korea.[17] While the G7 has always seen its agenda as global, the leaders' summit in Hiroshima, Japan, in 2023 was a watershed. A recent Center for Strategic and International Studies study showed how the G7 at this meeting greatly expanded its mandate as a relevant global governance institution by enumerating nine issues considered critical to sustainment and future navigation of the rules-based order.[18]

This higher profile for the G7 as a global governance institution stands in contrast to the underperformance of other such groupings. The United Nations Security Council, once key to addressing global security challenges, is now obstructed by Russia and China, which have adopted a recalcitrant approach to diplomacy as strategic competition with the United States intensifies. This dynamic also applies to other institutions such as the G20, which played a pivotal role in response to the 2008 global financial crisis but is now hamstrung by geopolitical rivalry and demands for expansion to include more voices from the Global South. The BRICS construct, including Brazil, Russia, India, China, and South Africa, is also expanding to reflect the prerogatives of the Global South in an apparent attempt to supplant the advanced industrialized democracies as stewards of the global order.[19] And the WTO, established to uphold rules and norms for the global trading system, is ill-suited to govern the digital economy, norms for which are emerging haphazardly in a complex web of multilateral trade agreements.[20] In short, the institutional architecture of the international system is fraying, and competition for influence among international institutions has seemingly fostered an environment in which the G7 has emerged as the standard bearer for the traditional rules-based international order.

In this regard, building a collective resilience group around the G7 makes eminent sense. The members share common values and have identified their own self-interest with preserving the rules-based order. As noted, unlike a random collection of countries that have been targeted in the past by economic coercion, this group has a common collective identity based on a preexisting foundation of consultation, coordination, and trust that lends itself well to overcoming some of the significant commitment obstacles to building a collective resilience group. G7 members place positive value on membership, which also connotes certain reputational and prestige equities in complying with agreements made by the group. This also bodes well for organizing a collective resilience strategy. Finally, they are all medium-to-large economic players who cannot be easily picked off by China as a weak link in the coalition.

Most important, all G7 governments or their companies have been victims of China's economic coercion, which creates a tangible motivation for them to avoid repeating histories, as well as a degree of empathy for ensuring that others do not suffer a similar fate. Indeed, evidence of this intent is clear in recent statements by G7 members. At the 2023 G7 Hiroshima meeting, the leaders expressed "serious concern over economic coercion . . . which not only undermines the functioning of and trust in the multilateral trading system, but also infringes upon the international order centered on respect for sovereignty and the rule of law, and ultimately undermines global security and stability."[21] At Hiroshima, G7 leaders also agreed to launch the Coordination Platform on Economic Coercion for information sharing and response coordination, thus putting actions to the strong statements of intent.

Australia and South Korea

A collective resilience coalition comprised of G7 members could be made even stronger with the addition of two Indo-Pacific countries, Australia and South Korea (we refer to these as the Indo-Pacific 2 or IP-2). To start, both have been major targets of China's economic bullying. As discussed in chapter 4, Australia came under massive discriminatory and WTO-noncompliant tariffs over the Morrison government's call for an independent investigation into the origins of Covid-19 in 2020. South Korea similarly faced a two-year campaign of economic bullying as a result of the U.S. THAAD battery emplacement on the peninsula in 2016. Thus, both have strong motivations to stop future acts of coercion. Indeed, the G7 countries plus South Korea and Australia account for an astounding 80 percent of all our recorded cases of China's economic coercion (483 out of 605 cases). South Korea and Australia are respectively the twelfth and thirteenth largest economies in the world, giving them leverage that could contribute to a collective resilience strategy. Their economic size also makes them big enough not to be easily picked off or targeted as weak links in a collective resilience grouping. Both are already practiced in economic security and supply chain resilience policies, including membership in groupings like the Minerals Security Partnership.[22] Australia, in particular, has stood up to China's bullying with a successful trade diversification policy with regard to beef, barley, and wine that has reduced the harmful economic impact of Beijing's sanctions.[23] In addition, the two countries have much to offer in terms of building and protecting critical supply chains in emerging technologies, including high-end memory chips, artificial intelligence, critical minerals, quantum computing, and biotechnology.[24]

Finally, Australia and South Korea exhibit shared values with G7 members. They demonstrate a commitment to the rules-based international order and have followed through on this with concrete actions. The two countries have fought on the side of freedom and democracy in every war since the Korean War (Australia going back to World War I). Moreover, they have undertaken numerous actions that demonstrate their commitment as providers of public goods to the international system. Table 5.2 shows the level of commitment in recent years by both countries that overlaps with and substantially strengthens the agenda outlined in recent G7 summits. This engenders a level of trust shared among the G7 countries.

Capabilities of the G7 + IP-2

Should the G7 + IP-2 be brought together in a collective resilience coalition, they would possess significant capabilities to deter China's economic bullying. As a coalition, the G7 nations plus Australia and South Korea account for a significant

TABLE 5.2 Public Goods: Australia and South Korea

AUSTRALIA

NAME OF SUMMIT	MONTH AND YEAR
World Health Summit Regional Meetings	April 2024
ASEAN-Australia Special Summit	March 2024
Seventh Indian Ocean Conference	February 2024
2023 FIFA Women's World Cup	July 2023
Second ASEAN Regional Forum on Nuclear Risk Reduction	March 2023
First Indo-Pacific Economic Framework (IPEF) Negotiating Round	December 2022
Indo-Pacific Chiefs of Defense Conference	July 2022
Virtual WTO Ministerial Meeting	October 2020
G20 Brisbane Summit	November 2014

SOUTH KOREA

NAME OF SUMMIT	MONTH AND YEAR
2025 Asia-Pacific Economic Cooperation (APEC) Summit	October 2025
Responsible AI in the Military Domain (REAIM) Summit	September 2024
2024 Korea-Africa Summit	June 2024
AI Seoul Summit	May 2024
Third Summit for Democracy	March 2024
Sixteenth Seoul ODA International Conference	September 2023
Fourth Indo-Pacific Economic Framework (IPEF) Negotiating Round	June 2023
2023 Korea–Pacific Islands Summit	May 2023
19th International Anti-Corruption Conference	December 2020

Source: Authors' original table excerpted from Hamre et al., " 'Bending' the Architecture: Reimagining the G7," Center for Strategic and International Studies, June 12, 2024, https://www.csis.org/analysis/bending-architecture-reimagining-g7.

TABLE 5.3 China's High-Dependence Imports from
G7 + IP-2 Countries (Totals, 2024)

	NUMBER OF IMPORT ITEMS	TOTAL VALUE OF IMPORTS (USD)
At least 70 percent dependence	595	$37,056,545,782
At least 80 percent dependence	408	$23,436,883,835
At least 90 percent dependence	248	$17,492,865,578

Source: Authors' original table with data derived from UN Comtrade database at
https://comtradeplus.un.org/.

35 percent of China's global trade. As table 5.3 shows, the G7 + IP-2 countries have 595 items on which China exhibits 70 percent or more dependence, with a trade value of more than $37.05 billion (2024 data). This includes 408 items, valued at $23.43 billion, upon which China is 80 percent or more dependent and 248 items, valued at $17.49 billion, upon which China is 90 percent or more dependent. These numbers are comparable to those of the victims of Chinese economic coercion listed in table 4.2.[25] The difference is that these countries share more in common and are better socialized to work together to form a collective economic deterrence pact than a randomly assembled group that shares common victimization at the hands of China's bullying but perhaps little else.

Members of the G7 + IP-2 group could credibly signal a commitment to retaliate against any economic bullying. The purpose of the group would not be to coerce China. On the contrary, the threat of retaliation would only be carried out as a response to China's action, not as an offensive weapon. It would not be used against every Chinese tariff or embargo, but only against those that have political intent, no legal basis, and no trade-related basis. The purpose would be to signal to China that it will incur costs for using predatory bullying tactics against members of the coalition where heretofore no costs have existed. This will create hesitation on the part of Beijing's leaders.

The conjoining of this group's collective resilience capabilities offers a rich array of deterrent signals. For example, as table 5.4 shows, Australia exports twenty-two items, with a trade value of $2.35 billion, upon which China is 70 percent or more dependent, as a percentage of total trade in those goods. Canada exports twenty-six items to China, with a trade value of $5.45 billion, upon which China is 70 percent or more dependent. South Korea exports forty-eight items to China, valued at $8.57 billion, on which China is similarly dependent.

TABLE 5.4 China's High-Dependence Imports from
G7 + IP-2 Countries (Country Breakdown, 2024)

COUNTRY	NUMBER OF IMPORT ITEMS GREATER THAN 70 PERCENT DEPENDENCE	TOTAL VALUE OF IMPORTS (USD)
Japan	147	$9,447,462,727
United States	132	$5,713,431,562
Germany	95	$1,430,635,581
Italy	74	$1,042,263,236
France	38	$2,618,002,507
Canada	26	$5,457,672,022
United Kingdom	13	$412,544,078
Australia	22	$2,357,003,034
South Korea	48	$8,577,531,035
Total	595	$37,056,545,782

Source: Authors' original table with data derived from UN Comtrade database at
https://comtradeplus.un.org/.

But each government might balk at the notion that they would have to leverage all of these goods as part of a collective resilience strategy. What democrati-
cally elected leader would want to effectively sanction every high-dependence
item it exports to China in order to retaliate against China's bullying of another
country? Doing so would constitute political suicide, incur the wrath of business constituents at home, and potentially instigate an all-out trade war with
China. However, to deter China's coercion, G7 + IP-2 countries could employ a
scalpel rather than a blunt instrument. That is, they could join forces and act
with precision on a handful of key high-dependence items that are strategically
important to China. Table 5.5 offers some examples. The United States and
France, for example, could act on their exports of turbojet turbines [HS 841191]
and turbojets [HS 841112] to China (respectively, gas turbine engines and gas
turbine engines with a propelling nozzle). The two countries' exports comprise
71 percent of China's global supply of turbojet engines and almost 92 percent of
turbojets. Indeed, two other like-minded partners, Germany and the UK, are
the next alternate suppliers of these goods to China, and China's replacement

costs for alternatives through domestic production would be highly costly (replacement ratios of 0.341 and 0.129 respectively).

Japan has 147 high-dependence (70 percent or greater) exports to China, with a trade value of $9.44 billion. Germany's number is ninety-five items, valued at $1.43 billion. But each country would not have to leverage all of these items to deter China's bullying. While this could create some economic costs for China, it would also create pain at home across a multitude of industries and would be domestically unpopular. A more credible collective economic deterrent posture would be for Japan and Germany to combine their leverage in one or two key sectors. As noted in table 5.5, Japan and Germany could together act on gear machinery [HS 846140] exports to China. Gear machinery is used to cut, grind, and finish common gears (spur, helical, and bevel). The two countries' exports of gear machinery comprise 78.4 percent of China's total imported supply (or 96.5 percent if Switzerland also cooperates), which makes this a credible deterrent threat on a key strategic item for China (replacement ratio of 0.169).

Germany and Japan could also promise to respond to Chinese economic coercion by acting on their exports of textile lubricant [HS 340391] and offset printing machinery [HS 844313]. China uses the former as textile lubricant for leather and fur and the latter as tools for its printing industry (see table 5.5). In 2024, these two countries made up more than 87 percent of China's imported supplies of textile lubricant, with a trade value of over $377 million, and more than 99 percent of imports of offset printing machinery, with a trade value of over $590 million. Furthermore, China does not have readily available alternative domestic supplies to make up for the imports as Beijing has a replacement ratio of 0.160 for the textile lubricant and 0.391 for offset printing machinery.

As of 2024, the United States has 132 high-dependence exports to China, with a trade value of $5.7 billion. But it would be neither plausible nor desirable for Washington to leverage its entire list of high-dependence items to deter Chinese coercion. This would not be a credible deterrent threat in China's eyes because Beijing can forecast that domestic opposition in the United States would be strong. However, the United States could team up with others and leverage a handful of key items that would make any Chinese act of economic coercion costly for Beijing. For example, the United States and France could leverage their collective supply of aeronautical/space instruments [HS 901420] to China. Aeronautical/space instruments are used in China's inertial navigation systems, and China relies on American and French supplies for 91 percent of its total imports, with a trade value of $112 million. China's ability to replace this large volume of imports with domestic production is extremely costly, with a replacement ratio of 0.182. The United States could also team up with Germany on their supply of

TABLE 5.5 China's Vulnerability Interdependence to G7 + IP-2 (Selected List, 2024)

COUNTRY AND ITEM (HS CODE)	PERCENT DEPENDENCE (TRADE VALUE, USD)*	REPLACEMENT RATIO†	SUBSTITUTE SUPPLIERS‡ (PERCENT CHINA DEPENDENCE)	DESCRIPTION
AUSTRALIA Iron ores and concentrates (260111)	61.45§ ($79,510,063,078)	0.020	Brazil (22.12) South Africa (3.36)	Critical component for steel (pig iron)
AUSTRALIA Other mineral substances (253090)	62.1§ ($3,229,183,817)	0.024	Zimbabwe (15.22) Brazil (5.32)	Natural minerals including spodumene, a critical component of lithium (used for lithium batteries)
AUSTRALIA Greasy wool (510111)	79.22 ($1,543,854,694)	0.000	South Africa (8.56) New Zealand (4.67)	Source of lanolin, a natural wax used in personal care products like lip balm, lotions, and creams
AUSTRALIA Oilseeds (120729)	88.10 ($190,302,622)	0.000	United States (11.90)	Used for extraction of vegetable oils for cooking, industrial processes, and biofuel production
CANADA Rape or colza seeds (120510)	100.00 ($3,294,156,686)	0.000	N/A	Used for cooking oil (canola)
CANADA Cereals: wheat/meslin, durum wheat, non-seed (100119)	58.43§ ($855,522,112)	0.000	Australia (30.89) United States (9.99)	Used for food products and agriculture
CANADA Oil cake: from rape/colza seed (230641)	75.25 ($783,343,131)	0.002	UAE (17.33) Russia (4.77)	Used as animal feed

Product (code)	Value		Top importers	Use
CANADA Lobsters, nonfrozen (030632)	78.96 ($609,077,551)	0.000	United States (20.69)	Luxury good
CANADA Semichemical wood pulp (470500)	76.81 ($470,210,161)	0.008	New Zealand (8.18) Sweden (5.49)	Used in the paper and packing industries
CANADA Coniferous wood: S-P-F, sawn or chipped (440713)	99.96 ($92,167,241)	0.038	N/A	Used for wood framing in construction
CANADA Coniferous wood: hem-fir species (440714)	98.35 ($61,866,957)	0.057	United States (1.64)	Used for wood framing in construction
CANADA Frozen lobsters (030612)	100 ($31,401,447)	0.033	N/A	Luxury good
CANADA Lucerne (alfalfa) seed (120921)	86.79 ($8,439,692)	0.009	Australia (7.86) France (4.79)	Crop grown for feeding livestock and soil improvement
FRANCE Spirits (220820)	99.21 ($1,223,858,496)	0.203	N/A	Strong distilled liquor (brandy). Brandy is the largest imported spirit in China.
FRANCE Broken or scutched flax (530121)	86.91 ($756,652,158)	0.000	Egypt (6.11) Belgium (5.48)	Used for production of linen fabric and paper
FRANCE Perfumes (330300)	63.80$ ($636,303,705)	0.511	Italy (13.26) Spain (11.26)	Fragrance products like perfume and cologne

(*continued*)

TABLE 5.5 (*continued*)

COUNTRY AND ITEM (HS CODE)	PERCENT DEPENDENCE (TRADE VALUE, USD)*	REPLACEMENT RATIO[†]	SUBSTITUTE SUPPLIERS[‡] (PERCENT CHINA DEPENDENCE)	DESCRIPTION
FRANCE Champagne and sparkling wine (220410)	69.16[§] ($46,495,694)	0.051	Italy (22.61) Spain (4.62)	Luxury good
FRANCE Homogenized/reconstituted tobacco (240391)	100.00 ($8,814,292)	0.000	N/A	Brown shredded innards used as filler in cigarettes
FRANCE Vinylidene chloride polymers (390450)	76.82 ($26,030,212)	0.702	Japan (22.84)	Used to make plastics such as flexible films or wraps; also used in flame retardant coatings
GERMANY Offset printing machinery (844313)	74.70 ($444,424,041)	0.391	Japan (24.52)	Prints large quantity of items such as newspaper and magazines
GERMANY Gear machinery (846140)	64.48[§] ($351,044,084)	0.169	Switzerland (18.15) Japan (13.92)	Cuts, grinds, and finishes common gears: spur, helical, and bevel
GERMANY Fused quartz or silica tubes (700231)	77.82 ($61,302,573)	0.345	United States (11.16) Japan (5.95)	Used for semiconductor manufacturing, optical fibers, and laboratory equipment

Country / Product (code)	Value 1	Value 2	Top partners	Description
GERMANY Ingots, alloy steel (722410)	70.48	($30,446,661)	Malaysia (10.23) India (5.29)	Primary forms of alloy steel used in construction and shipbuilding
GERMANY Tetrachloroethylene (290323)	98.54	($17,487,779)	Japan (1.46)	A chemical commonly used to dry-clean fabrics
ITALY Leather footwear (640359)	89.55	($217,135,137)	Spain (4.53) Vietnam (1.79)	Luxury good: dress shoes, loafers, moccasins
ITALY Woven fabric from wool (511211)	84.23	($116,852,856)	Japan (7.00) United Kingdom (5.28)	Used to make luxury and high-end clothing
JAPAN Hybrid electric vehicles (870340)	98.86	($3,951,111,137)	United States (1.11)	Energy-efficient vehicles that use both an internal combustion engine and an electric motor for propulsion, such as the Toyota Prius
JAPAN Industrial robots (847950)	74.75	($481,954,200)	Germany (5.66) France (4.44)	Important to manufacturing and advanced industries
JAPAN Silver powder (710610)	84.69	($892,448,804)	United States (9.99) Taiwan (2.58)	Used in photovoltaic and electronic conductive paste needed for solar panels
JAPAN Plates, sheets, and film of cellulose acetate (392073)	77.93	($466,056,030)	South Korea (10.27) Taiwan (6.19)	Used for packaging of food, beverages, and medical supplies and for textile treatment
JAPAN Textile lubricants (340391)	70.64	($305,917,476)	Germany (16.55) Italy (3.72)	Used for the treatment of textiles and leathers

(continued)

TABLE 5.5 (*continued*)

COUNTRY AND ITEM (HS CODE)	PERCENT DEPENDENCE (TRADE VALUE, USD)*	REPLACEMENT RATIO[†]	SUBSTITUTE SUPPLIERS[‡] (PERCENT CHINA DEPENDENCE)	DESCRIPTION
JAPAN Copper foil (741012)	77.07 ($202,555,244)	0.295	Germany (8.37) United States (6.84)	Used in construction to produce locks, wiring, doors, and electrical sockets
JAPAN Staple fibers (550330)	62.68[§] ($71,891,880)	0.149	Thailand (11.86) Türkiye (8.98)	Acrylic, modacrylic, and nylon used in clothing
JAPAN Opium alkaloids (293919)	88.44 ($21,770,221)	0.001	India (8.02) Italy (1.36)	Used in pharmaceuticals
SOUTH KOREA OLED panel displays (852412)	94.01 ($2,118,159,315)	0.185	Japan (3.64) Taiwan (2.05)	Used for smartphones, televisions, monitors, laptops, and other electronic devices
SOUTH KOREA Other inorganic salts (284290)	93.67 ($2,060,419,042)	0.932	Japan (4.73) United States (0.57)	Used for various agricultural, industrial, and scientific applications, including fertilizers and glass
SOUTH KOREA Ethylene, unsaturated (290121)	69.87[§] ($1,383,967,103)	0.033	Japan (17.41) Oman (4.68)	Critical base product for petrochemicals
SOUTH KOREA Propylene, unsaturated (290122)	74.29 ($1,295,108,795)	0.044	Japan (18.3) Philippines (2.59)	Crucial building block for producing plastics and other chemicals

SOUTH KOREA Drawn/blown glass sheets, non-tinted (700490)	71.64 ($928,091,114)	Taiwan (19.49) Japan (6.96)	0.269	Used for buildings, mirrors, and windows
SOUTH KOREA Acrylonitrile-butadiene rubber (NBR), primary forms (400251)	78.23 ($106,583,920)	Malaysia (7.45) Japan (6.94)	0.220	Nitrile rubber, known for its resistance to oils and fuels, used to make disposable gloves, fuel hoses, and sealants
SOUTH KOREA Unsaturated acyclic hydrocarbons (290123)	82.52 ($19,297,048)	Japan (6.90) Singapore (6.90)	0.262	Butene, used to make polyethylene, common in plastic bags, film wraps, and containers
UNITED KINGDOM Whiskies (220830)	86.65 ($391,179,828)	Japan (6.71) United States (3.21)	0.153	Luxury good
UNITED STATES Turbojet turbine (841191)	62.81§ ($4,057,954,464)	France (8.36) Germany (6.44)	0.341	Gas turbine engine used in aircraft
UNITED STATES Acyclic hydrocarbons (290110)	98.15 ($2,604,826,737)	Spain (0.77)	0.034	Chemical compound used in lubricants and polyethylene (plastic bags)
UNITED STATES Turbojets (841112)	48.86§ ($2,179,113,096)	France (43.09) United Kingdom (7.65)	0.129	Gas turbine with a propelling nozzle used in aircraft
UNITED STATES Cereals: grain sorghum (100790)	66.85§ ($1,733,210,890)	Australia (22.30) Argentina (10.81)	0.000	Used to produce traditional Chinese drink (*baijiu*)

(*continued*)

TABLE 5.5 (*continued*)

COUNTRY AND ITEM (HS CODE)	PERCENT DEPENDENCE (TRADE VALUE, USD)*	REPLACEMENT RATIO[†]	SUBSTITUTE SUPPLIERS[‡] (PERCENT CHINA DEPENDENCE)	DESCRIPTION
UNITED STATES Pistachios (080251)	67.50[§] ($578,239,257)	0.024	Iran (30.63) Australia (1.79)	Fresh or dried, shelled
UNITED STATES Forage products (121490)	73.77 ($354,489,657)	0.002	Australia (15.99) Spain (5.23)	Root vegetables, legumes, and plants used for animal feed
UNITED STATES Oak wood (440791)	75.47 ($312,519,528)	0.008	Russia (16.20) Canada (3.84)	Sawn/chipped, used for furniture, flooring, construction, and wine/whiskey barrels
UNITED STATES Flours, meats, and pellets from meat/offal (230110)	78.17 ($237,897,016)	0.000	Uruguay (7.42) Australia (7.02)	Used as animal feed or fertilizers
UNITED STATES Non-plasticized cellulose acetates (391211)	85.67 ($207,245,157)	0.258	Japan (14.27)	Processed for common synthetic plastics
UNITED STATES Cherry wood (440794)	98.56 ($103,449,895)	0.000	Canada (1.36)	Sawn/chipped, used for furniture, flooring, and construction
UNITED STATES Aeronautical/space instruments (901420)	82.48 ($101,269,501)	0.182	France (8.82) Taiwan (1.71)	Inertial navigation systems

Source country (HS code)	Dependence (%)[*]	(Trade value)	Replacement metric[†]	Alternate suppliers[‡]	Description
UNITED STATES Amine compounds (292122)	85.07	($95,557,095)	0.246	Germany (7.72) France (6.61)	Includes acyclic polyamines and HMDA that can be used for production of nylon 66 and as curing agent for epoxy resins
UNITED STATES Scintigraphic medical instruments (901814)	76.28	($91,876,205)	0.681	Israel (9.19) Germany (8.38)	Used in nuclear medicine for diagnostic imaging, including cancer detection
UNITED STATES Raw ground nuts (120241)	98.46	($70,725,774)	0.521	Vietnam (1.54)	Peanuts used for snack foods, cooking, and oil production
UNITED STATES Gas turbines, power not exceeding 5MW (841181)	64.42[§]	($64,005,290)	0.380	France (21.67) Canada (4.53)	Engines used for power generation, mechanical drives, and cogeneration systems (heat and electricity)
UNITED STATES Bovine semen (051110)	91.93	($53,535,288)	0.000	Germany (5.51) France (1.86)	Used for insemination of Chinese cattle
UNITED STATES Kentucky bluegrass seed (120924)	93.08	($20,308,770)	0.000	Denmark (6.92)	Cool-season grass seed planted as turf in athletic fields

Source: Authors' original table with data derived from UN Comtrade database at https://comtradeplus.un.org/.

[*] China's dependence on the source country for the good as a percentage of total imports of that good.

[†] Domestic production of the good is measured using reported Chinese exports of the good as the proxy variable. The replacement metric is the exports/imports ratio. A number greater than 1 suggests a strong capacity to replace a loss of imports with domestic sources by diverting exports to fill demand.

[‡] China's dependence on the next largest source country(ies) for the good (after the primary source) as a percentage of China's total imports of that good.

[§] Falls below 70 percent dependency, but included because (1) trade value is significant and/or (2) alternate supplier(s) is a coerced, like-minded country.

scintigraphic medical instruments [HS 901814], upon which China is more than 84 percent dependent. These specialty medical instruments are used in nuclear medicine for diagnostic imaging. It would be highly costly for China to make up a loss of overseas supply through domestic production with a replacement ratio that is low at 0.681 (total trade value of $101.9 million). Together, the United States, Japan, and Germany provide almost 95 percent of China's total supply of fused quartz or silica tubes [HS 700231], with a trade value of $74.7 million, used for semiconductor manufacturing, optical fibers, and laboratory equipment. This would be a costly and credible deterrent to Beijing because China has minimal domestic production capacity (replacement ratio of 0.345). The United States, Germany, and France together provide a substantial 99 percent of China's demand for amine compounds [HS 292122], used for production of nylon 66 and as a curing agent for epoxy resins, which the three could wield effectively as a deterrent to economic coercion. Losing these supplies would be highly costly to China as it has little domestic capacity to supply them (replacement ratio of 0.246).

As noted earlier, luxury goods are a useful collective resilience tool. Though not strategically important to China's supply chains, they create elite audience costs for the leadership if supplies are curtailed. The Chinese government may be forced to think twice about using economic coercion against a member of the collective resilience coalition if it knows that it will face domestic criticism. Italy and France can leverage their exports of luxury goods like perfumes and colognes [HS 330300] and champagne [HS 220410]. As of 2024, these two G7 countries make up 77 percent and more than 91 percent of China's imports, and China's replacement costs would be very high (replacement ratio of 0.511 for perfumes and 0.051 for champagne). As noted in chapter 4, Chinese elite get 86.6 percent of their fine whiskies [HS 220830] from the United Kingdom (replacement ratio of 0.153). The next largest supplier is Japan at 6.7 percent, followed by the United States at 3.2 percent. Together, the three could leverage this supply to deter any act of economic bullying by China. Alternative supplies are certainly substitutable, but if tapped this could precipitate Chinese elite annoyance at having to drink Indian or other whiskey. This imposes a cost on China's economic coercion that did not exist previously, when Beijing would isolate a target country and apply pressure on it. Now that pressure will be met with counterpressure not just from the target but also from other countries.

Table 5.5 enumerates a list of high-dependence, low-substitutability, and strategic/luxury items for the G7 + IP-2 group. This G7 + IP-2 grouping arguably already has a high degree of cohesion among its members for collective action and could exhibit stronger political will than an ad hoc coalition of victims of Chinese economic coercion. At the 2023 Hiroshima G7 summit, G7 leaders adopted the first ever G7 Leaders' Statement on economic security and economic resilience.[26] In the statement, they agreed to launch a new Coordination Platform on Economic Coercion, and to increase their "collective assessment, preparedness, deterrence and response" to the "serious concern" of economic coercion." They warned that continued "attempts to weaponize economic dependencies . . . will fail and face consequences." The leaders also expressed that they will not only respond to economic coercion but also counter it where appropriate, supporting targeted states. This view was further supported by South Korea and Australia, which attended the G7 summit as guests. Based on the economic security issue alone, G7 members would be well-advised to advocate for South Korea's and Australia's membership in the group.

⟿

Collective resilience is not a trade war strategy; it is a strategy designed to stop China's economic bullying without decoupling from China. It rests on the threat to weaponize trade, not the actual use of sanctions. If China does not act, then there is no need to make good on the threat. The purpose of this strategy is not to target all Chinese economic behavior. As one of the world's largest economies, China will naturally have trade disputes with G7 + IP-2 partners. These should be resolved and negotiated bilaterally and through WTO adjudication. What collective resilience aims to deter are acts of economic coercion that are non-WTO-conforming and aimed at achieving goals not related to trade. Retaliation against Norway for awarding the Nobel Prize to a Chinese dissident, sanctioning Korean companies for emplacement of a THAAD battery for national defense, and embargoing imports from countries for speaking out on suppression of democracy in Hong Kong are the types of coercive actions that need to be deterred. Finally, collective resilience is not in lieu of trade diversification, impact mitigation, and supply chain strategies, but supplemental to them and hopefully will facilitate even more participation in these strategies among like-minded countries once the threat of Chinese economic bullying is deterred.

CHAPTER 6

COLLECTIVE RESILIENCE IN CRITICAL MINERALS

C ritical minerals have significant strategic value, serving as essential inputs for various high-technology and clean energy industries. In the United States, a "critical mineral" is defined as "(1) a non-fuel mineral or mineral material essential to the economic and national security of the United States, (2) the supply chain of which is vulnerable to disruption and (3) that serves an essential function in the manufacturing of a product, the absence of which would have significant consequences for our economy or our national security."[1] The United States Geological Survey (USGS) published the first U.S. critical minerals list in February 2018, containing a total of thirty-five minerals.[2] The second list, published in February 2022, expanded to include fifty critical minerals.[3] Other countries have begun to create their own critical minerals lists as well. Japan has maintained a critical minerals list since 1984; its current list includes thirty-four critical minerals and two mineral groups, platinum group metals (PGMs) and rare earth elements (REEs).[4] In 2023, South Korea announced thirty-three critical minerals and ten "strategic" critical minerals.[5] Australia has thirty-one critical minerals, including PGMs and REEs.[6] Since 2011, the European Commission has been regularly updating its critical raw materials (CRMs) list. As of 2023, it has thirty-four CRMs.[7]

Table 6.1 compiles the most recent lists of critical minerals for the United States, Japan, Australia, South Korea, and the European Union, including REEs and PGMs.

China has inordinate influence over many of these critical minerals. As a result, China's weaponization of critical minerals as a political and foreign policy tool has far-reaching consequences, potentially disrupting global supply chains of many industries and undermining the economic security of the United States and collective resilience partners. Since the summer of 2023, China has introduced a

TABLE 6.1 Critical Mineral Lists of Selected G7+IP-2 Countries

NO.	CRITICAL MINERALS	UNITED STATES	SOUTH KOREA	JAPAN	AUSTRALIA	EU
1	Aluminum	✓	✓			✓
2	High-purity alumina				✓	
3	Antimony	✓	✓	✓	✓	✓
4	Arsenic	✓			✓	✓
5	Barite	✓				✓
6	Barium			✓		
7	Beryllium	✓		✓	✓	✓
8	Bismuth	✓	✓	✓	✓	✓
9	Boron			✓		✓
10	Cerium	✓	✓REE	✓REE	✓REE	✓LREE
11	Cesium	✓		✓		
12	Chromium	✓	✓	✓	✓	
13	Cobalt	✓	✓	✓	✓	✓
14	Coking Coal					✓
15	Copper		✓			✓
16	Dysprosium	✓	✓REE	✓REE	✓REE	✓HREE
17	Erbium	✓		✓REE	✓REE	✓HREE
18	Europium	✓		✓REE	✓REE	✓HREE
19	Feldspar					✓
20	Fluorine			✓	✓	
21	Fluorspar	✓				✓
22	Gadolinium	✓		✓REE	✓REE	✓HREE
23	Gallium	✓	✓	✓	✓	✓
24	Germanium	✓		✓	✓	✓
25	Graphite	✓	✓	✓	✓	(natural) ✓
26	Hafnium	✓		✓	✓	✓
27	Helium					✓

(*continued*)

NO.	CRITICAL MINERALS	UNITED STATES	SOUTH KOREA	JAPAN	AUSTRALIA	EU
28	Holmium	✓		✓REE	✓REE	✓HREE
29	Indium	✓	✓	✓	✓	
30	Iridium	✓		✓PGM	✓PGM	✓PGM
31	Lanthanum	✓	✓REE	✓REE	✓REE	✓LREE
32	Lead		✓			
33	Lithium	✓	✓	✓	✓	✓
34	Lutetium	✓		✓REE	✓REE	✓HREE
35	Magnesium	✓	✓	✓	✓	✓
36	Manganese	✓	✓	✓	✓	✓
37	Molybdenum		✓	✓	✓	
38	Neodymium	✓	✓REE	✓REE	✓REE	✓LREE
39	Nickel	✓	✓	✓	✓	✓
40	Niobium	✓	✓	✓	✓	✓
41	Osmium			✓PGM	✓PGM	
42	Palladium	✓	✓PGM	✓PGM	✓PGM	✓PGM
43	Phosphate rock					✓
44	Phosphorus			✓		✓
45	Platinum	✓	✓PGM	✓PGM	✓PGM	✓PGM
46	Praseodymium	✓		✓REE	✓REE	✓LREE
47	Promethium			✓REE	✓REE	
48	Rhenium			✓	✓	
49	Rhodium	✓		✓PGM	✓PGM	✓PGM
50	Rubidium	✓		✓		
51	Ruthenium	✓		✓PGM	✓PGM	✓PGM
52	Samarium	✓		✓REE	✓REE	✓LREE
53	Scandium	✓			✓	✓
54	Selenium		✓	✓	✓	
55	Silicon		✓	✓	✓	✓

NO.	CRITICAL MINERALS	UNITED STATES	SOUTH KOREA	JAPAN	AUSTRALIA	EU
56	Strontium		✓	✓		✓
57	Tantalum	✓	✓	✓	✓	✓
58	Tellurium	✓		✓	✓	
59	Terbium	✓	✓REE	✓REE	✓REE	✓HREE
60	Thallium			✓		
61	Thulium	✓		✓REE	✓REE	✓HREE
62	Tin	✓	✓			
63	Titanium	✓	✓	✓	✓	✓
64	Tungsten	✓	✓	✓	✓	✓
65	Uranium			✓		
66	Vanadium	✓	✓	✓	✓	✓
67	Ytterbium	✓			✓REE	✓HREE
68	Yttrium	✓		✓REE	✓REE	✓HREE
69	Zinc	✓	✓			
70	Zirconium	✓	✓	✓	✓	

Sources: Each country's critical minerals list is derived from its own sources.

For the United States: United States Geological Survey, "U.S. Geological Survey Releases 2022 List of Critical Minerals," February 22, 2022, www.usgs.gov/news/national-news-release/us -geological-survey-releases-2022-list-critical-minerals.

For South Korea: ROK Ministry of Trade and Industry and Energy, Strategy for Securing Critical Minerals to Become a Global Leader in Advanced Industries, February 2023, https://www.motie.go.kr/kor/article/ATCL3f49a5a8c/166862/view.

For Japan: Japanese Ministry of Economy, Trade and Industry, Measures to Secure a Stable Supply of Critical Minerals, March 29, 2024, https://www.meti.go.jp/policy/economy/economic _security/metal/torikumihoshin.pdf; also see Masato Nagahara, Introduction of the Lists of Critical Minerals and Materials Around the World, January 14, 2025, https://mric.jogmec.go.jp /reports/mr/20250114/185205/.

For Australia: Department of Industry, Science and Resources, "Australia's Critical Minerals List and Strategic Materials List," February 20, 2024, https://www.industry.gov.au/publications /australias-critical-minerals-list-and-strategic-materials-list.

For the European Union: European Commission, "RMIS—Raw Materials Information System," 2023, https://rmis.jrc.ec.europa.eu/eu-critical-raw-materials.

Note: The most recent critical minerals lists were published in different years: United States (2022), South Korea (2023), Japan (2024), Australia (2024), European Union (2023). The U.S. 2022 critical minerals list published all REEs and PGMs as individual elements. The EU specifically lists titanium metal, silicon metal, and natural graphite in its critical minerals list, whereas other countries refer to these materials more generally as titanium, silicon, and graphite. For brevity, we have used the general terms across all entries.

series of export restrictions on critical minerals, beginning in July with gallium and germanium. These restrictions required local Chinese suppliers to apply for government-issued licenses to export these nonfuel minerals and related commodities.[8] Gallium and germanium are vital to U.S. high-tech industries, including semiconductor, defense, telecommunication, and clean energy sectors. Gallium is used to produce advanced semiconductor chips, next-generation missile defense and radar systems, mobile phones, and LED lighting.[9] Germanium is used in the production of a range of items including solar panels, semiconductors, fiber optics, and infrared sensors.[10] China has a chokehold on the global supply of gallium, accounting for 98 percent of the world's supply, and it dominates 68 percent of the global market on refined germanium.[11] In October 2023, China expanded its export restrictions to include natural and synthetic graphite used in lithium EV batteries, fuel cells, and lubricants.[12] In December 2023, China's new export ban included several technologies, specifically targeting those related to the production of rare earth magnets, as well as rare earth ore mining, selection, and refining—broadening the existing ban on extraction and separation technologies.[13] The REEs, which consist of seventeen metallic elements, are key components vital to many high-tech industries. In June 2024, China intensified its control over rare earths by declaring them state property and introducing a traceability information system for rare earth products.[14] In August 2024, China imposed another export ban on antimony, a silver metal widely used in the production of ammunition, infrared missiles, and night vision goggles.[15] In January 2025, China unveiled a plan to impose new restrictions on technology related to EV cathode batteries, lithium, and gallium, followed by announcing new export license requirements for twenty products related to tungsten, tellurium, bismuth, molybdenum, and indium.[16] These measures are expected to affect defense industries, clean energy, and other manufacturing industries (artillery shells, solar panels, medical treatments, missile components, and phone screens).[17] The Chinese Ministry of Commerce stated that all of these export controls are "in accordance with law" and intended to "safeguard national security," maintaining that these measures are "not targeted at any specific country or region, nor at any specific incident."[18] In April 2025, China announced export restrictions on seven additional medium and heavy rare earth minerals— samarium, gadolinium, terbium, dysprosium, lutetium, scandium, and yttrium— and related magnets targeted at the United States in retaliation for Trump's "Liberation Day" tariffs against China.[19] China is the leading producer of rare earth magnets, accounting for about 90 percent of the global annual production. Rare earth magnets, made with certain heavy earth minerals such as dysprosium and terbium, are crucial for electric motors, which are widely used in a range of important goods, such as EVs, drones, missiles, and jet fighters.[20]

China exhibits a history of weaponizing critical minerals. Recall China's rare earth export ban against Japan in September 2010 following a collision incident near the disputed Senkaku/Diaoyu Islands. Japan was caught off guard by China's economic coercion and was forced to release a Chinese fishing boat captain after China halted shipments of rare earth oxides, rare earth salts, and pure rare earth metals to Japan for nearly two months, affecting Japan's production of hybrid cars, wind turbines, smartphones, cameras, and other electronic goods.[21] Concerns about China's weaponization of rare earths resurfaced in May 2019 when Chinese president Xi and his trade minister visited a rare earth magnet factory in Jiangxi Province at the height of trade war tensions with the Trump administration. This was widely interpreted as a veiled threat, signaling that China could leverage its dominance in rare earths against the United States.[22] The Chinese foreign ministry suggested otherwise, but the *Global Times* editor Hu Xijin tweeted that the Chinese government was "seriously evaluating the need to do so."[23]

To be clear, China is not the only country that practices export restrictions on critical minerals and raw materials. According to an OECD report, the number of export restrictions on critical raw materials has increased more than fivefold in the past decade, with countries like India, Russia, Argentina, Vietnam, and Kazakhstan increasingly implementing such measures.[24]

In many other cases, restrictions on critical minerals are related to resource nationalism. For instance, in January 2020, Indonesia, the world's largest supplier of nickel, banned the export of unprocessed nickel ores, a key material for EVs. This move was intended to increase domestic processing and refining capabilities and stimulate economic growth.[25] Similarly, in October 2023, Malaysia announced export restrictions on raw rare earth materials while allowing the export of processed rare earth materials.[26] Malaysian prime minister Anwar Ibrahim stated that this decision was intended to "prevent any exploitation, loss of resources and in turn guarantee a maximum return to the country."[27]

But these actions pale in comparison to those of China. First, China accounts for 20 percent of the new export restrictions between 2009 and 2022.[28] Second, and more important, these restrictions are designed to target the economy of others to achieve China's political and foreign policy objectives, particularly in its strategic competition with the United States.[29] China's choice of gallium, germanium, graphite, REEs, antimony, tungsten, and bismuth targets significant U.S. dependencies. As table 6.2 shows, the United States is completely dependent on imports for gallium and (natural) graphite, and China was one of the top suppliers over the years between 2020 and 2023. In July 2023, the U.S. Department of Defense confirmed that the United States has no government stockpile of gallium.[30] Nearly 80 percent of REEs, 89 percent of (refined) bismuth, and

TABLE 6.2 U.S. Net Import Reliance on Critical Minerals Restricted
by China (2024)

CRITICAL MINERAL	U.S. NET IMPORT RELIANCE (NIR) AS A PERCENTAGE OF CONSUMPTION	PRIMARY SUPPLIERS TO U.S. IN 2020–2023 (IN DESCENDING ORDER)
Gallium	100	Japan, China, Germany, Canada
Germanium*	Above 50	Belgium, Canada, China, Germany
Graphite (natural)	100	China, Canada, Mexico, Mozambique
Rare earth elements (compounds and metals)	80	China, Malaysia, Japan, Estonia
Antimony (metal and oxide)	85	China, Belgium, India, Bolivia
Tungsten	Above 50	China, Germany, Bolivia, Vietnam
Tellurium*	Below 25	Canada, Philippines, Japan, Germany
Bismuth* (metal, alloys, and scrap)	89	China, South Korea
Indium*	100	South Korea, Japan, Canada, Belgium
Scandium	100	Japan, China, Philippines

Source: U.S. Geological Survey, *Mineral Commodity Summaries 2025*, 2025, https://pubs.usgs.gov /periodicals/mcs2025/mcs2025.pdf, 7, 23.

Note: China imposed export restrictions at various times, starting with gallium, germanium, graphite, and technologies tied to REEs in 2023. This was followed by new export controls on antimony in August 2024 and specific items and technologies related to tungsten, tellurium, bismuth, molybdenum, and indium in February 2025. Rare earth elements in the table include lanthanides cerium, dysprosium, erbium, europium, gadolinium, holmium, lanthanum, lutetium, neodymium, praseodymium, samarium, terbium, thulium, and ytterbium. China added seven of these rare earth minerals—samarium, gadolinium, terbium, dysprosium, lutetium, scandium, and yttrium—and related magnets to the export control list in April 2025.
* Refinery production.

85 percent of antimony consumed in the United States is sourced from foreign suppliers, with China as the primary source.

The economic costs of supply disruptions for these minerals are extremely high. According to a study by USGS analysts, a 30 percent disruption in the gallium market supply could have a ripple effect across the industry, resulting in a 2.1 percent decline in GDP ($602 billion). Similarly, a 30 percent supply disruption of graphite, antimony, and bismuth could lead to GDP declines of 2.8 percent ($816 billion), 1.9 percent ($544 billion), and 0.9 percent ($271 billion), respectively, in the United States.[31]

Indeed, China weaponized rare earth magnets during the escalating trade tensions over Trump's "Liberation Day" tariffs. China instituted retaliatory export restrictions on heavy REEs and magnets, leading to a 59 percent drop in the export volume of rare earth magnets to the United States in April 2025 compared to the same month a year earlier; the following month saw a 93 percent decline year-on-year.[32] This set off alarms across the United States and other countries, as a potential shortage of rare earth magnets, essential for everything from electric motors in EVs to smartphones, wind turbines, aerospace, and other key defense technologies, could bring industry-wide manufacturing to a halt. Understanding the detrimental impact of China's latest export curbs on U.S. key industries, the Trump administration reached a deal with China on May 12, 2025 to lower reciprocal tariffs for ninety days, including China's suspension of rare earth magnet export controls.[33] This trade truce did not last long, however, because China was not easing its export curbs on rare earth magnets.[34] On May 30, 3025, Trump wrote on Truth Social accusing China of having "totally violated its agreement" with the United States, and his administration swiftly responded with punitive measures, prohibiting U.S. sales of chip-designing software to China and announcing its plan to revoke visas for Chinese students in the United States.[35] This escalatory move eventually restored the truce following a phone call between Trump and Xi and another round of intense negotiations, during which China agreed to expedite export licenses for rare earth magnets in exchange for U.S. suspension of its punitive measures against China. As of this writing, the truce remains in place. However, this episode shows the United States's acute vulnerability to China's ability to choke off the supply of essential minerals and magnets, underscoring the inherent risk that China may use rare earth magnets as leverage in the future as the two largest economies continue to negotiate a solution to their trade dispute and strategic competition.

CHINA'S DOMINANCE IN THE GLOBAL CRITICAL MINERALS SUPPLY CHAIN

China's weaponization of critical minerals raises acute concerns because of its dominance of global supply chains. This position stems from three key factors. First, the country is a major producer, supplying nearly 60 percent of global

TABLE 6.3 China's Share of Global Mine Production (2024)

CRITICAL MINERALS	CHINA'S SHARE OF GLOBAL PRODUCTION (PERCENT)	APPLICATION
Gallium	99	Integrated circuits and optical devices
Tungsten	83	Metallurgy
Graphite (natural)	79	Batteries, fuel cells, and lubricants
Rare earths	69	Electronics, catalysts, permanent magnets, and defense system
Vanadium	70	Batteries, catalysts, and metallurgy
Fluorspar	62	Cement, industrial chemical, and metallurgy
Antimony	60	Flame retardants and lead-acid batteries
Tin	23	Metallurgy

Source: U.S. Geological Survey, Mineral Commodity Summaries 2025, 2025, https://pubs.usgs.gov/periodicals/mcs2025/mcs2025.pdf, 17, 23.

production.[36] China's significant production share is attributable to mining. As table 6.3 shows, China is the world's leading producer of gallium, tungsten, graphite, vanadium, fluorspar, antimony, and tin, all included in the U.S. 2022 critical minerals list, and its share of global mine production exceeds 50 percent for nearly all these minerals, except for tin. China also holds inordinate influence over REEs, which are indispensable components widely used in producing smartphones, computers, LCD screens, and defense systems. In 2024, China's documented rare earth mine production was 270,000 metric tons, accounting for 69.2 percent of global output.[37] China holds less than 48 percent of global reserves, estimated at forty-four million metric tons, which gives the country enormous leverage over these key strategic minerals.[38]

Second, China dominates the global processing and refining industry. The country controls nearly 85 percent of the global processing capacity.[39] This implies limited options for other countries that need to ship their raw ore to processing

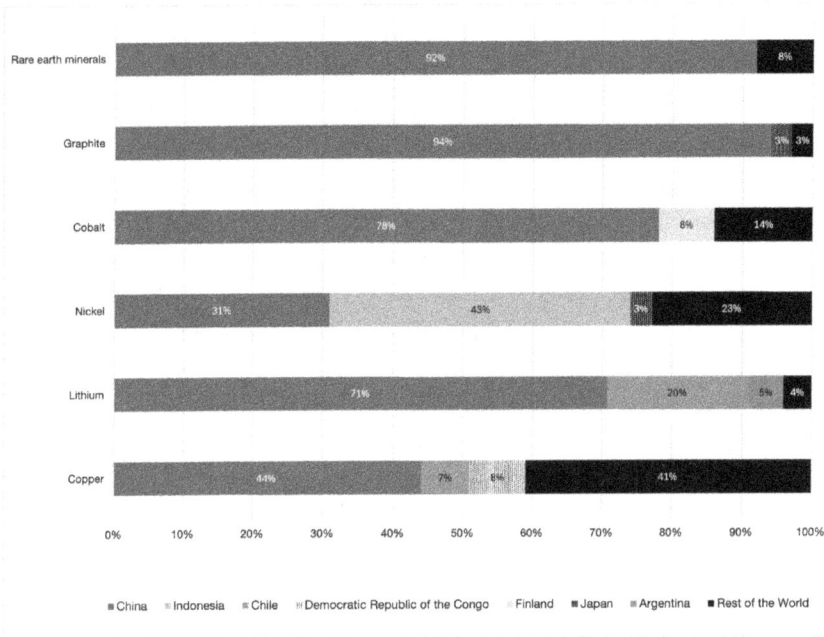

FIGURE 6.1 Share of refined key energy transition materials production by country (2024)

Note: Rare earth minerals refer to those used in magnet only. Graphite refers to battery-grade spherical and synthetic graphite.

Source: Original figure derived from International Energy Agency (2025) at "Geographical Distribution of Refined Material Production for Key Minerals in the Base Case," https://www.iea.org/data-and-statistics /charts/geographical-distribution-of-refined-material-production-for-key-minerals-in-the-base-case.

plants in China or those owned by Chinese companies abroad. China's dominance in this processing capacity is telling particularly because many critical minerals essential for the clean energy industry are dependent on China. Figure 6.1 shows that China accounts for more than 60 percent of refining cobalt, natural graphite, and lithium, as well as REEs.[40] The global refinery production of other minerals is also highly concentrated in China, including magnesium (95 percent), bismuth (81 percent), indium (70 percent), titanium (69 percent), and tellurium (77 percent).[41] China is the largest producer, in both mining and refining, of graphite and magnet rare earths, giving the country significant influence over these strategic minerals.[42]

China's dominance in global metal refining and processing poses a challenge to countries seeking to reduce their reliance on the country because China sits at a key node in the global critical minerals supply chain. That is, even though the United States has begun to increase domestic production of rare earths, most are still sent to China for separation and processing before being reexported to the United States.[43] As a result, China's export restrictions on these refined goods could create a choke point, leading to significant disruptions.

Third, Chinese companies have secured access to critical minerals in resource-rich countries through direct investment and interest acquisition in mining projects and metal sectors. Since the 1980s, private and state-owned Chinese companies have been active in outbound investments. In 2017, annual Chinese mining project investments surpassed $1 billion for the first time.[44] Between 2011 and 2020, nearly $16 billion was invested for mergers and acquisitions, predominantly focused on copper projects in Africa and Europe.[45] As of early 2021, Chinese entities owned forty-five copper projects.[46]

More recently, under the Belt and Road Initiative, Chinese investment in mining and metal projects has accelerated, reaching over $10 billion in the first half of 2023.[47] There has been a notable shift toward acquiring cobalt, lithium, and other metals critical to clean energy technology sectors, including EVs, solar photovoltaics (PV), and wind energy. A good example is the Democratic Republic of the Congo, the world's largest cobalt producer, where Chinese investments control nearly 70 percent of the country's mining sector.[48] In the global race for lithium, Chinese investors are also seeking to acquire lithium projects in Australia, Zimbabwe, Namibia, and Mali and are interested in Argentina, Chile, and Bolivia for significant lithium deposits.[49] These trends suggest that Chinese investments in critical mineral mining and processing will likely continue amid global competition for these essential resources.

In short, China holds a dominant position in the global critical minerals supply chain, ranging from mine production to refining and processing. Through overseas investments and mergers in resource-rich countries, the country also seeks to expand its global market share and meet surging domestic demand that it cannot meet based on domestic capacity. These factors, coupled with other countries' heavy reliance on China for critical minerals, have given China enormous influence in the global critical mineral supply chain, which Beijing has leveraged numerous times to create disruptions against other countries.

G7+IP-2 COUNTRIES' DE-RISKING STRATEGIES

Before China introduced export controls on critical minerals, countries had already begun addressing supply chain risks and vulnerabilities. These decisions were driven by increasing uncertainties from the intensifying U.S.-China competition, concerns about overreliance on a single country (China) for critical mineral supplies, and the economic imperative to ensure a stable supply chain for critical minerals amid the global race to support green energy and digital transitions. While some countries perceived greater threats from China than others, the shared need to reduce reliance on China prompted a range of precautionary measures. These de-risking strategies generally include (1) identifying strategic vulnerabilities in critical minerals, (2) diversifying trade partners, (3) engaging in friend-shoring and reshoring, and (4) stockpiling and investing in research and development. Four collective resilience partners—the United States, Japan, South Korea, and Australia—are featured here as examples of how they pursued de-risking in critical minerals supply chains.

United States

The United States undertook a massive reshoring effort with regard to critical minerals, beginning with a major step in December 2017, when President Donald Trump signed Executive Order 13817. The order highlighted the country's heavy dependence on foreign sources as a "strategic vulnerability for both its economy and military" and mandated that government agencies develop a policy to help reduce this dependency and improve supply chain resilience.[50] It also defined U.S. critical minerals and directed the Secretary of the Interior to publish a list.[51] In September 2020, Trump issued Executive Order 13953, calling the country's disproportionate reliance on China for many critical minerals, such as rare earths, barite, gallium, and graphite, "particularly concerning."[52] He then declared a national emergency and called for increased domestic production of critical minerals and the development of secure and resilient supply chains by establishing and enhancing U.S. domestic mining and mineral processing capabilities, among other measures.[53]

Efforts to address vulnerabilities in U.S. critical mineral supply chains continued and became more concrete under the Biden administration. Following a hundred-day policy review mandated by Executive Order 14017, the Biden administration announced a "Made in America Supply Chain for Critical Minerals" in February 2022.[54] This initiative sought to use public and private investments to build and strengthen domestic production capacity across the United States.[55] Existing legislation, such as the Infrastructure Investment and Jobs Act of November 2021, provided the necessary financing for mining, processing, and recycling projects.[56] In late March 2022, President Biden authorized use of the Defense

Production Act Title III to expand mining and processing capacity for lithium, cobalt, and other minerals used in large-capacity batteries.[57] Under the Inflation Reduction Act, enacted in August 2022, the Biden administration introduced sourcing requirements for EV batteries to build a strong and secure critical minerals supply chain with U.S. free trade agreement partners while reducing U.S. reliance on foreign entities of concern.[58]

The Biden administration also proactively pursued friend-shoring initiatives through bilateral, minilateral, and multilateral partnerships. Notable examples include signing a bilateral Critical Minerals Agreement with Japan in March 2023; establishing a Climate, Critical Minerals and Clean Energy Transformation Compact with Australia in May 2023; and launching an inaugural "C5+1" Critical Minerals Dialogue with Central Asian Countries in February 2024.[59] At the Camp David Summit in August 2023, Biden agreed with Japanese and Korean leaders to establish a pilot supply chain early warning system, which will allow for prompt information sharing to mitigate risks associated with supply disruptions in critical minerals.[60]

The United States also spearheaded MSP and IPEF to enhance cooperation with like-minded countries. The MSP aims to build sustainable critical mineral supply chains through joint projects in mining, extraction, processing and refining, and recycling, with a commitment to high environmental, social, and governance (ESG) standards.[61] After its establishment with twelve countries and the European Union in June 2022, the MSP gained further momentum when India and Estonia joined in June 2023 and March 2024, respectively. The United States and other MSP members invited mineral-rich countries to the principals' meetings to enhance cooperation with them. The MSP has also engaged private-sector entities and relevant stakeholders to promote public-private partnerships and "responsible" investment in critical mineral sectors. As of March 2024, the MSP was running twenty-three projects—sixteen in upstream mining and mineral extraction and seven in midstream processing, including seven projects involving recycling and recovery.[62] These projects focus on clean energy industries such as cobalt, copper, gallium, germanium, graphite, lithium, manganese, nickel, and rare earths.[63]

Japan

In Japan, the government and the private sector have employed a combination of diversification, friend-shoring, stockpiling, and mitigation measures to build secure and sustainable critical mineral supply chains. Given the country's lack of natural resources, including of critical minerals, energy security is closely linked to national security. As a result, securing access to oil and natural resources has been a priority for the Japanese government, which has led to the stockpiling of key minerals since 1983 and maintaining a critical minerals list since 1984.[64] Over time, Japan has focused on building a stable supply chain of critical minerals through "trade, investment in mining projects overseas, stockpiling, and R&D in substitutes and recycling technologies."[65] Notably, Japan's investment in overseas mining projects "using foreign aid, public finance, and trade insurance" began in 2008, even before China's rare earth embargo.[66]

The 2010 Chinese rare earth embargo had a significant impact on Japan. The rare earth prices jumped nearly tenfold, which then affected many Japanese industries reliant on these minerals.[67] The Japanese government quickly implemented a supplemental budget of 100 billion yen (about $1.2 billion at that time) and introduced five key measures: (1) reducing the use of rare earths through technology development and equipment investment, (2) developing technology to find substitutes for rare earths, (3) promoting the recycling of rare earths, (4) investing in and developing mining projects outside China, and (5) stockpiling rare earths.[68]

Trade diversification was spearheaded by the Japan Organization for Metals and Energy Security (JOGMEC) and Japanese companies. During the embargo, Japanese companies collaborated with the government to find alternative suppliers in places such as Vietnam, India, Brazil, and Central Asia.[69] In November 2010, the Japanese company Sojitz identified Lynas in Australia as a potential supplier and entered into a tentative agreement.[70] Four months later, Japan Australia Rare Earth (JARE), a joint venture between JOGMEC and Sojitz, reached a deal with Lynas. This agreement involved JOGMEC providing $250 million in exchange for a minimum of 8,500 tons per annum of rare earth products to Japan over the next ten years, covering nearly 30 percent of the Japanese market.[71] Since then, JARE's partnership with Lynas has ensured a stable supply of rare earths to Japan for more than a decade.[72] As a result of this and other government initiatives, Japan has reduced its dependency on Chinese rare earth imports from 85 percent in 2009 to 58 percent in 2018, with plans to bring it down below 50 percent by 2025.[73] Japan also diversified its rare earth suppliers to Vietnam (14 percent), France (11 percent), Malaysia (10 percent), and others (8 percent) by 2018.[74] By 2021, Japan had established several rare earth project partnerships overseas, including the Mount Weld project in Australia, the Dong Pao project in Vietnam, and the Indian Rare Earth project in India.[75]

Japan has also formed bilateral and multilateral partnerships with resource-rich and like-minded countries to diversify its trade partners. For instance, in October 2022, the Japanese and Australian governments concluded a critical mineral partnership. This partnership aims to promote the growth of Australia's critical mineral sectors and ensure Japan's access to a stable and sustainable supply of these minerals from Australia.[76] Under this partnership, the two countries established an official bilateral working-group-level dialogue on critical minerals and agreed to cooperate on joint projects, including project cofinancing and private-sector investment, research and development, information sharing, and streamlining the permit process.[77] In March 2023, Sojitz and JOGMEC enhanced their partnership with Lynas by reaching a new deal. Under this agreement, Lynas will supply Japan with heavy rare earths (dysprosium and terbium) to cover nearly 30 percent of the country's domestic needs.[78]

While Japan actively participated in the MSP, IPEF, and Quad to enhance the critical mineral supply chain, the G7 Hiroshima Summit showcased Japan's friend-shoring initiative. Japan launched the Coordination Platform on Economic Coercion to enhance "collective assessment, preparedness, deterrence and response to economic coercion" among the G7 members.[79] It also adopted the "Five-Point Plan for Critical Minerals Security" announced by the G7 climate, energy and environment ministers. This five-point plan aims to develop a plausible forecast on medium- and long-term supply and demand for critical minerals, develop resources and supply chains responsibly, recycle more and share capabilities, save resources through innovations, and prepare for supply disruptions.[80] Like other multilateral partnerships, these initiatives allow G7 members to better coordinate their response to coercion and take joint actions, making the G7 a possible platform for collective resilience in the future.

South Korea

Efforts to bolster and protect domestic critical minerals supply chains from China's coercion are also evident in South Korea. The country's poor resource endowment has precipitated dependence on external sources for key minerals and raw materials. South Korea acquires nearly 95 percent of its critical minerals and raw materials from abroad.[81] In particular, South Korea's dependence on China poses significant economic risks, as evidenced by the urea shortages in 2021 (discussed in chapter 4). In 2022, South Korea was reliant on China for more than 94 percent of its graphite supply.[82] For lithium hydroxide and cobalt hydroxide, critical chemicals used in lithium-ion battery production, China accounted for 84 percent and 69 percent of South Korea's imports, respectively.[83] Reducing this reliance, particularly in key advanced industries, such as semiconductor and EV batteries, has been very challenging.

The Yoon Suk Yeol government (2022–2025) took a number of steps to reduce the country's vulnerability to external pressure while enhancing the resilience of domestic supply chains. In February 2023, the Ministry of Trade, Industry and Energy unveiled a Supply Chain Stabilization Strategy to reduce South Korea's dependence on specific countries for key minerals, from 80 percent to 50 percent, and increase the resource recycling rate to 20 percent by 2030.[84] The strategy seeks to achieve three goals: (1) enhancing emergency response capability through the establishment of a comprehensive early warning system; (2) diversifying critical mineral acquisition by expanding bilateral and multilateral cooperation and through active participation in the MSP, IPEF, and International Energy Agency (IEA); and (3) establishing a systematic critical mineral infrastructure through the designation, management, and stockpiling of critical minerals, as well as the creation of a recycling cluster.[85] The Yoon government also planned to increase the strategic stockpiling target of rare metals to 100 days of use (180 days for some rare earth elements and cobalt) from the current level of 54 days.[86]

Following the passage of three key pieces of legislation, including the Framework Act on Supply Chain Stabilization Support for Economic Security in December 2023 and the Special Act on National Resource Security in February 2024, the Ministry of Economy and Finance held the first supply chain committee meeting in June 2024. During this meeting, the South Korean government announced a more detailed supply chain stabilization effort, including the expansion of key strategic items from two hundred to three hundred; development of self-sufficiency and diversification plans for key industries such as semiconductors and secondary batteries; the decision to use the $3.6 billion Supply Chain Stabilization Fund to support companies that help stabilize the supply chains of key strategic resources; and the provision of tax and other financial incentives to domestic companies to encourage domestic production.[87]

The Yoon government also focused on building bilateral, minilateral, and multilateral partnerships with resource-rich countries, resulting in several successes. For instance, South Korea and Mongolia signed a memorandum of understanding in February 2023 to cooperate on the rare metals supply chain, which was further solidified in November 2023 with the initiation of a joint center for rare metals.[88] In June 2023, South Korea held the first U.S.–Mongolia–Republic of Korea Critical Minerals Dialogue to discuss enhanced information exchange and joint projects.[89] South Korea also expanded its partnership with Vietnam, which has the world's second-largest rare earth reserves. After launching a research project in Vietnam on rare earth extraction technology, South Korea concluded a bilateral agreement with Vietnam in December 2023 to create a joint research center for critical mineral supply chains.[90] In June 2024, South Korea and forty-eight African countries agreed to launch a critical minerals dialogue to enhance cooperation on stable supply and development of critical mineral resources.[91] This initiative was followed by the signing of critical mineral supply chain partnerships with Kazakhstan, Uzbekistan, and Turkmenistan in the same month.[92]

South Korean companies have proactively moved to diversify their supply chains. For example, South Korean firm POSCO acquired interests in a lithium mining project in Australia.[93] In March 2022, the company announced a $4 billion investment in a lithium mining project at Salar del Hombre Muerto in Argentina, aimed at producing materials for EV batteries.[94] Concurrently, POSCO built a factory in South Korea to produce lithium hydroxide using lithium supplied from Australia. [95]

In March 2024, South Korea reported some progress in reducing its dependence on Chinese imports for critical minerals. Its reliance on Chinese imports of lithium hydroxide, used in EV batteries, decreased from 87.9 percent in 2022 to 79.6 percent in 2023.[96] This reduction was achieved through increased imports from Chile, which rose to 17.5 percent from 10.7 percent the previous year.[97] South Korea reduced its dependence on Chinese imports of neodymium permanent magnets, essential for making EV motors, from 87.5 percent in 2022 to 84.7 percent in 2023 through diversification of trade to the Philippines.[98]

In July 2024, the Yoon government announced the creation of a "crisis response network" within IPEF. Led by South Korea and Japan, this emergency response network is designed to assist the fourteen IPEF members in managing supply chain disruptions through coordinated responses. In the event of a supply disruption or shortage, this network will facilitate information sharing about inventories, coordinate stockpile sharing, and help members identify alternative supply chain routes.[99]

Australia

Australia is a key partner in other countries' de-risking plans and has been on the front lines of contending with China's economic coercion. Australia's mineral wealth puts it in a unique position to leverage its abundant resources to strengthen its critical minerals supply chains while helping other countries to diversify their own. As the world's largest producer of lithium, accounting for nearly 37 percent of the global supply in 2024, and home to abundant mineral deposits of cobalt, manganese ore, rare earths, and titanium, Australia has the wherewithal to become a leading country in the critical mineral industry. The global drive to enhance supply chain resilience presents Australia with an opportunity to expand its domestic critical minerals sector and potentially reshape the global industry.

This economic incentive has spurred Australia to develop ambitious government strategies, backed by the A\$4 billion Critical Minerals Facility and the A\$5 billion Northern Australia Infrastructure Facility (NAIF) to finance critical mineral projects in the country.[100] In June 2023, Australia released the Critical Minerals Strategy 2023–2030 to become a leading producer in raw minerals and processing.

Australia has actively pursued reshoring through both bilateral and multilateral engagement. In May 2023, Australia and the United States signed a Climate, Critical Minerals and Clean Energy Transformation Compact. This agreement established a ministerial-level Australia–United States Taskforce on Critical Minerals to coordinate their efforts and investment to "support the expansion and diversification of responsible clean energy and critical minerals supply chains."[101] To attract U.S. investment in domestic mining projects in Australia, Prime Minister Anthony Albanese announced in October 2023 the creation of a \$1.25 billion fund that will offer low-interest loans to mining and processing firms.[102]

In addition to the United States and Japan, India and South Korea have found Australia to be a crucial partner for their critical minerals supply chains. For instance, Australia and India signed a Critical Minerals Investment Partnership in 2022 to identify possible investment projects, which led them to find five target projects in 2023.[103]

Australia has actively pursued friend-shoring initiatives through various forms of engagement. In 2022, Australian rare earth company Lynas received \$120 million from the U.S. Department of Defense to build a rare earth processing facility in the United States. Another notable example is the Quad, which includes the United States, Japan, Australia, and India. Alongside the MSP and IPEF, the Quad has served as an active platform for discussing cooperation on critical minerals. This includes mapping the collective capacity and vulnerabilities of the Quad members in their semiconductor supply chains.[104] In March 2022, Australia, Japan, and India launched the Supply Chain Resilience Initiative and proposed trade and investment diversification to address supply chain disruptions in the Indo-Pacific.[105] In May 2023, the Quad members discussed creating a public-private Quad investor network for joint investment in semiconductor and critical minerals.[106] In July 2025, the four countries launched the Quad Critical

Minerals Initiative to diversify their supply chains and reduce their vulnerability to "economic coercion, price manipulation and supply chain disruptions" arising from heavy reliance on a single country.[107]

Meanwhile, inbound investment screening could become Australia's new de-risking strategy to limit China's influence over its critical infrastructure and reduce the risk of China's economic coercion. The case in point is when Australian treasurer Jim Chalmers, in June 2024, issued a divestment order mandating that Yuxiao Fund—specifically, Chinese national Wu Tao and four other foreign investors—sell off eighty million shares of Northern Minerals within sixty days.[108] Northern Minerals is one of Australia's key heavy rare earth producers. Amid growing concerns about China's dominance in the refining industry, the company holds strategic importance for Australia because the company's Browns Range project in Western Australia is set to become the country's first comprehensive rare earth refinery.[109] Against this backdrop, in February 2023, Chalmers disapproved, under the foreign investment law, Yuxiao Fund's proposed acquisition plan to increase its stake in Northern Minerals, although the fund acquired eighty million shares later in September to increase its stake from 9.81 percent to 19.9 percent. In explaining the divestment order, the Australian government emphasized that "the decision, based on advice from the Foreign Investment Review Board, is designed to protect our national interest and ensure compliance with our foreign investment framework."[110]

COLLECTIVE RESILIENCE IN CRITICAL MINERALS

In this section, we examine whether a collective resilience strategy by the G7+IP-2 countries could stop or deter Chinese weaponization of critical minerals. Admittedly, this is a bit of a "David versus Goliath" problem as these countries must be capable of standing up to China in a market dominated by China. As mentioned in the previous chapters, the collective resilience strategy rests on the premise that interdependence is a two-way street and that there are certain imports for which China is heavily dependent on other countries. If there are comparable items in the critical minerals sector on which China is dependent, this could be leveraged as part of a collective resilience strategy to deter China's own coercive practices with critical minerals. To identify high-dependence critical minerals for China, we have developed a set of four criteria (slightly different from those applied to merchandise trade in previous chapters): (1) high dependence, (2) capacity to find alternative suppliers (substitutability), (3) capacity to rely on domestic production (replacement ratio) and (4) total import trade value. Specifically, we define a critical mineral export as a *high-dependence* item for China if more than 50 percent of China's global imports of that mineral is provided by at least one major supplier.[111] We define a high-dependence critical mineral for China as having *low substitutability* when at least one of the alternative suppliers of the item to China is a G7+IP-2 country that would not cooperate with China's trade diversification, making it difficult for China to find alternate suppliers. We define a *low replacement ratio* as China's inability to replace external dependence with domestic production (using China's reported exports of the critical mineral as a proxy variable); for the collective resilience strategy to be effective, the replacement ratio should be less than 1.[112] Lastly, we set the *trade value* of a high-dependence critical mineral for China at a minimum of $10 million in annual trade. That is, China's imports of the high-dependence item from its primary suppliers should have a value greater than $10 million. We choose this threshold because while some items in our research fit the first three criteria, their total trade value is too insignificant to have any deterrent effect on China. Setting a minimum trade value of $10 million imposes a high enough replacement cost to be a significant consideration for China. We use trade data from the 2024 UN Comtrade database. To identify the critical minerals list, we use the Draft List of Critical Supply Chains prepared by the U.S. Department of Commerce's International Trade Administration (ITA), which encompasses four supply chains: public health and biological preparedness, information and communications technology (ICT), energy, and critical minerals.[113]

The critical minerals supply chain category includes a total of 271 products. This draft list is based on eight- and ten-digit tariff lines of the Harmonized Tariff Schedule of the United States (HTSUS). Since the UN Comtrade database uses six-digit HS codes, this study adjusted the HTS codes to conform to the HS codes. As a result of this adjustment, the final list of HS codes searchable within the UN Comtrade database consists of 170 products.

Out of these 170 products, this study identifies fourteen high-dependence critical mineral items that the G7+IP-2 countries could potentially leverage in a collective resilience strategy. The total value of these fourteen items imported from the G7+IP-2 countries is $9.55 billion, accounting for 60.39 percent of China's total global imports of these items.

Three items in table 6.4 do not meet the full collective resilience criteria but are included nonetheless. Spodumene mineral substance [HS 253090] is included because Australia alone supplies more than 62 percent of China's imports, even though the next two suppliers are not like-minded countries.[114] Mixtures of bismuth, of tungsten, and of vanadium [HS 382499] are included because even

TABLE 6.4 China's Vulnerability Interdependence in Critical Minerals (2024)

COUNTRY AND ITEM (HS CODE)	PERCENT DEPENDENCE (TRADE VALUE, USD)*	REPLACEMENT RATIO[†]	SUBSTITUTE SUPPLIERS[‡] (PERCENT CHINA DEPENDENCE)	DESCRIPTION
UNITED STATES Supported catalysts other than with nickel or precious metal or their compounds as the active substance (381519)	43.93 ($272,902,363)	0.98	Germany (17.9) Japan (10.4)	Used for organic synthesis or oxidation of methylene blue (copper-based catalyst); oxidation (cobalt-based catalyst)
UNITED STATES Nickel alloy, bars, rods and profiles (750512)	68.71 ($225,335,361)	0.70	Japan (7.93) Germany (5.99)	Used for steam turbines and aircraft gas turbines, and for construction
UNITED STATES Nickel articles thereof n.e.c. in item no. 7508.1 (750890)	47.03 ($142,279,620)	0.13	South Korea (8.16) Mexico (7.83)	Used for a wide range of semi-manufactured nickel products (e.g. nickel glands, collars, and plugs)
UNITED STATES Supported catalysts with nickel or nickel compounds as the active substance (381511)	44.39 ($75,474,503)	0.59	Denmark (13.36) Germany (12.75)	Used in the chemical industry (for hydrogenation reaction, reforming reaction, oxidation reaction, hydrocyanation reaction) and environmental protection (e.g., treatment of wastewater)

Country / Product (HS code)	Value	%	Top exporters	Use
SOUTH KOREA Zinc alloy, unwrought (790120)	34.96 ($48,818,325)	0.13	Japan (18.35) Australia (15.06)	Used in the auto industry (e.g., die-cast parts and fuel system components) and the aerospace industry (e.g., engine mounts, brackets, and fittings)
AUSTRALIA Mineral substances, n.e.c. in chapter 25 (including spodumene) (253090)§	62.10 ($3,229,183,817)	0.02	Zimbabwe (15.22) Brazil (5.32)	Used for lithium batteries
UNITED STATES Supported catalysts with precious metal or precious metal compounds as the active substance (could include platinum or palladium) (381512)	47.34 ($390,342,287)	0.35	Italy (17.43) Germany (12.91)	Used for hydrogen evolution reaction in fuel cells (platinum); hydrogenation process in the petroleum industry (palladium); and to produce ethylene (ruthenium)
SOUTH KOREA Salts of oxometallic or peroxometallic acids; n.e.c. in heading no. 2841 (e.g. Vanadates) (284190)	60.61 ($156,950,390)	0.52	Japan (28.43) Chile (5.06)	Used in the energy storage system (e.g., vanadium batteries); military vehicles and high-speed aircraft

(continued)

TABLE 6.4 (*continued*)

COUNTRY AND ITEM (HS CODE)	PERCENT DEPENDENCE (TRADE VALUE, USD)*	REPLACEMENT RATIO[†]	SUBSTITUTE SUPPLIERS[‡] (PERCENT CHINA DEPENDENCE)	DESCRIPTION
UNITED STATES Cobalt articles n.e.c. in heading no. 8105 (810590)	47.64 ($31,947,051)	0.19	Germany (13.66) United Kingdom (13.56)	Used for cobalt alloy rods (aerospace applications); cobalt-based wear-resistant coatings (industrial machinery); cobalt-free magnet production waste
JAPAN Chemical products, mixtures, and preparations; n.e.c. heading 3824 (e.g. mixtures of bismuth, mixture of tungsten, mixture of vanadium) (382499)[§]	25.99 ($1,774,896,067)	0.87	South Korea (16.22) United States (12.07)	Used in medication, cosmetics, industrial and laboratory chemicals, and metallurgical additives (mixtures of bismuth); vanadium electrolyte for vanadium redox flow batteries (mixtures of vanadium)
FRANCE Zirconium, articles, nesoi, containing less than 1 part hafnium to 500 parts zirconium by weight (810991)	99.64 ($18,458,631)	0.32	Netherlands (0.32) Germany (0.02)	Used for cladding for fuel rods inside nuclear reactors, ceramics, abrasives, lamp filaments, jet engines and space shuttle parts, dental and surgical implants

UNITED STATES Reaction initiators, reaction accelerators, and catalytic preparations, nesoi, consisting wholly of bismuth, of tungsten, or of vanadium (381590)§	25.48 ($108,806,523)	0.66	Japan (19.35) Germany (15.98)	Used for organic synthesis, environmental protection, aerospace (bismuth); hydration reaction, oxidation reaction, condensation reaction (tungsten); oxidation reaction, polymerization and wastewater treatment (vanadium)
JAPAN Polishes, creams, and similar preparations for glass or metal (340590)	35.01 ($209,205,000)	0.09	Taiwan (30.98) South Korea (17.77)	Used for polishing and cleaning metal surfaces (e.g., faucets and valves)
UNITED STATES Palladium, in semi-manufactured forms (711029)	54.74 ($11,781,350)	0.05	Taiwan (23.72) Japan (12.34)	Used in catalytic converters for gasoline-powered vehicles, electronic components, and jewelry

Source: Author's original table with data derived from UN Comtrade database at https://comtradeplus.un.org/.

* China's dependence on the source country for the good as a percentage of total imports of that good.

† Domestic production of the good is measured using reported Chinese exports of the good as the proxy variable. The replacement metric is the exports/imports ratio. A number greater than 1 suggests a strong capacity to replace a loss of imports with domestic sources by diverting exports to fill demand.

‡ China's dependence on the next largest source country(ies) for the good (after the primary source) as a percentage of China's total imports of that good.

§ Although this good does not meet the 50 percent high-dependence requirement, it is included because (1) trade value is significant and/or (2) the next two largest alternate suppliers are G7+IP2 countries.

though the first two suppliers (Japan and South Korea) do not total over 50 percent of China's dependence, the third supplier, the United States, is like-minded and, together with Japan and South Korea, takes the dependence metric over 50 percent. Reaction initiators involving bismuth, tungsten, or vanadium [HS 381590] are included for similar reasons, given the three like-minded suppliers, the United States, Japan, and Germany.

The analysis of these fourteen items offers several findings. If G7+IP-2 countries band together, they can issue credible collective economic deterrence signals to China to discourage economic bullying of others. Collective retaliation in critical minerals sectors could be used to deter further economic coercion beyond gallium, germanium, graphite, and other critical minerals, or it could be used to deter economic bullying in other commodity sectors.

One high-dependence critical mineral for China is nickel. G7+IP-2 countries have a relatively strong collective resilience capability over nickel compared to other critical minerals. As shown in table 6.4, three out of fourteen items listed are nickel-related, with the total value of these exports from G7+IP-2 countries to China exceeding $535 million. For instance, the United States, Japan, and Germany can leverage the supply of bars, rods, and profiles of nickel alloys [HS 750512], critical to the manufacturing of heat- and pressure-resistant steel in China. The three make up more than 82 percent of China's imports. Nickel alloys have many applications, ranging from aircraft components and engine parts (aerospace) to wind turbines and solar panels (renewable energy) to engine components (automotive) and implants and surgical equipment (medical). The United States and Germany can use their exports to China of nickel-containing supported catalysts [HS 381511], used for hydrogenation reaction, oxidation reaction, and environmental protection, totaling nearly 57.14 percent of China's global imports.[115] Similarly, the United States and South Korea can leverage their nickel article exports [HS 750890], used in a wide range of nickel-based products such as nickel glands and collars, comprising almost 55.19 percent of China's global imports.

China's trade vulnerability to nickel relates to its limited domestic production capacity. China is one of the world's largest consumers of nickel because of its use in the EV industry and stainless-steel production.[116] Yet China's nickel reserve constitutes only a small fraction (4.4 percent) of the world's total reserves, which are highly concentrated in Indonesia, Australia, Brazil, and Russia.[117] In 2023, China ranked seventh in global nickel production, with an output of 110,400 tons.[118] To support its high nickel consumption, China relies on imports of nickel ore and concentrates from the Philippines, Russia, and New Caledonia, and has invested in Indonesia's nickel industry.[119] Between 2014 and 2024, China reportedly invested more than $65 billion in Indonesia's nickel industry.[120]

Would China care about a collective resilience strategy that leveraged nickel to deter coercion? As table 6.4 shows, China's imports of all three nickel-related items have a replacement ratio less than 1. Nickel-based supported catalysts [HS 381511] have a replacement ratio of 0.59. Nickel bars, rods, and profiles [HS 750512] and nickel articles [HS 750890] have replacement ratios of 0.70 and 0.13, respectively. These low replacement ratios mean that it would be highly costly for China to offset a loss of imports of these items through domestic production. China's awareness of its trade vulnerability is evident in its efforts to diversify suppliers of nickel. As table 6.5 shows, China was trying to reduce imports of nickel powder and flake [HS 750400] and its dependence on G7+IP-2 countries between 2022 and 2024. Australia's share of China's total imports dropped from 72.77 percent in 2022 to 61.49 percent in 2023 and then to 5.09 percent in 2024. Russia replaced Australia as China's largest supplier in 2024, capturing 29.27 percent share of China's total imports, with a trade value over $29 million. However, even with bilateral cooperation in Putin's invasion of Ukraine, Sino-Russian relations are far from certain, and dependence on Russian sources could easily turn into vulnerabilities for China going forward. If Russian sources dry up for China, all of the other potential suppliers— the United Kingdom, the United States, Canada, Germany, and Australia—are G7+IP-2 countries.

Other high-dependence critical minerals for China are zirconium, zinc, cobalt, vanadium, and bismuth.[121] As table 6.4 shows, France, the Netherlands, and Germany collectively control nearly 100 percent of China's imports of zirconium articles [HS 810991], which are used in nuclear reactors (e.g., cladding for fuel rods inside nuclear reactors), ceramics, abrasives, lamp filaments, jet engines, space shuttle parts, and dental and surgical implants.[122] The replacement ratio of 0.32 shows that China has minimal domestic production to substitute for these zirconium article imports. Additionally, collective resilience partners' exports to China account for more than 68 percent of unwrought zinc alloys [HS 790120], 54 percent of miscellaneous chemical products (e.g. mixtures of bismuth, of tungsten, or of vanadium) [HS 382499], and 89 percent of salts of oxometallic or peroxometallic acids [HS 284190], with a total trade value of more than $4.0 billion. All three items also have low replacement ratios of 0.13 (for unwrought zinc alloys), 0.87 (for miscellaneous chemical products), and 0.52 (for salts of oxometallic or peroxometallic acids), meaning that these would be highly costly for China to replace. Among these items, South Korea alone accounts for almost 35 percent of China's imports of unwrought zinc alloys (trade value of $48 million), used in the production of gearboxes and door handles in the automotive industry, and 61 percent of salts of oxometallic or peroxometallic acids, such as vanadates (trade value of $156 million), which China needs for energy storage systems (particularly vanadium redox flow batteries).[123] Japan, South Korea, and the United States are

TABLE 6.5 China's Trade in Nickel Powder and Flake (HS 750400), 2022–2024

TRADE IN NICKEL POWDER AND FLAKE	2022	2023	2024
TOTAL IMPORT VALUE (QUANTITY)	$783,360,045 (30,689,229 kg)	$354,402,397 (13,527,406 kg)	$100,299,509 (4,014,318 kg)
TOTAL EXPORT VALUE (QUANTITY)	$136,859,264 (2,690,729 kg)	$93,598,131 (2,136,599 kg)	$124,137,336 (3,120,583 kg)
REPLACEMENT RATIO	0.17	0.13	1.24
CHINA'S TOP SIX SUPPLIERS, SHARE OF CHINA'S TOTAL IMPORTS (TRADE VALUE)	1. Australia 72.77% ($570,073,797)	1. Australia 61.49% ($217,906,901)	1. Russia 29.27% ($29,360,421)
	2. Canada 6.69% ($52,425,062)	2. Russia 11.77% ($41,695,699)	2. United Kingdom 22.99% ($23,063,604)
	3. United Kingdom 6.54% ($51,264,693)	3. United Kingdom 8.77% ($31,084,461)	3. United States 13.60% ($13,637,140)
	4. Russia 5.17% ($40,523,269)	4. Finland 6.27% ($22,234,171)	4. Canada 7.39% ($7,408,634)
	5. Finland 5.16% ($40,451,604)	5. Canada 5.34% ($18,938,685)	5. Germany 6.69% ($6,713,415)
	6. United States 1.56% ($12,204,706)	6. United States 2.28% ($8,066,594)	6. Australia 5.09% ($5,103,883)

Source: Authors' original table with data derived from UN Comtrade database at https://comtradeplus.un.org/.

major suppliers of miscellaneous chemical mixtures involving bismuth, tungsten, or vanadium to China, with a trade value of $3.7 billion. Despite China's advantage in cobalt-refining capacity, China's imports of cobalt articles [HS 810590] from the United States, Germany, and the United Kingdom constitute more than 74 percent of its total trade, and a low replacement ratio of 0.19 shows that China has little capacity to replace external dependence with domestic production. Some examples of cobalt articles include cobalt alloy rods for aerospace applications, cobalt-based wear-resistant coatings for industrial machinery, cobalt-free magnet production waste, cobalt-nickel alloy exhaust system components for automotive use, and cobalt-based battery recycling residue.[124]

Semi-manufactured palladium [HS 711029], used in catalytic converters for gasoline-powered vehicles, and polishing creams for glass or metal surfaces [HS 340590] are other items that collective resilience partners can leverage. Not only do these two distinct items have low replacement ratios of 0.05 and 0.09, respectively, but their major suppliers are also the United States, Japan, and South Korea. The United States and Japan together account for more than 67 percent of China's total palladium imports, with a trade value exceeding $14 million. Similarly, Japan and South Korea's exports to China account for more than 52 percent of the polishing cream, but with a total trade value exceeding $315 million.

Another high-dependence critical mineral for China is used in reaction and catalytic products. The United States is the primary exporter to China of three different types of supported catalysts: nickel or nickel compounds [HS 381511], precious metal or precious metal compounds [HS 381512], and others [HS 381519], with highly costly replacement ratios of 0.59, 0.35, and 0.98, respectively. Nickel-based catalysts are used in the chemical industry for hydrogenation reaction, reforming reaction, and oxidation reaction, and in the environmental protection field for the treatment of wastewater. Precious metal–based catalysts include platinum-based, used for hydrogen evolution reaction in fuel cells, and palladium- and ruthenium-based, used in the petroleum industry and the production of ethylene. Other catalysts include copper-based, used for organic synthesis or oxidation of methylene blue, and cobalt-based, used for oxidation.[125] As table 6.4 shows, the United States provides nearly 44 percent of China's imports of nickel-based supported catalysts, 47 percent of China's imports of metal-based supported catalysts, and *more than* nearly 44 percent of China's imports of other supported catalysts. Moreover, the top three suppliers of metal-based and non-nickel/metal-based supported catalysts to China are all G7+IP-2 countries. In the case of metal-based supported catalysts, the United States, Italy, and Germany account for more than 77 percent of China's total imports, with a total import value of more than $640 million. These Chinese dependencies translate to capabilities for G7+IP-2 countries to signal deterrence against further economic coercion.

Spodumene, classified under "Mineral substances, n.e.c. in chapter 25" [HS 253090] in table 6.4, is another critical mineral that could be leveraged by Australia for collective resilience. Australia is currently the largest producer of spodumene minerals in the world.[126] Spodumene is one of the major sources of lithium, a key component of lithium-ion batteries, making the spodumene mineral crucial to China's burgeoning EV battery industry.[127] Australia alone accounts for more than 62 percent of China's total global imports, with a trade value of $ 3.2 billion. If this were to be curtailed, China would likely look to the next two suppliers, Zimbabwe and Brazil, which are not G7+IP-2 countries, and therefore might not participate in a collective resilience strategy. China's lithium reserve accounts for nearly 11 percent of global reserves, two of the major global lithium extractive companies are Chinese-owned, and Chinese companies have actively invested in Latin America to secure a sustainable lithium supply.[128] Despite that, the replacement ratio of 0.02 shows China's significantly insufficient domestic production capacity to replace its imports of spodumene mineral.

China's awareness of its vulnerability in spodumene—which suggests susceptibility to collective resilience—is evident in its efforts to secure other sources. As shown in table 6.6, in 2022 China was more than 85 percent dependent on imports of lithium-containing minerals from Australia (trade value over $7.8 billion) and nearly 6.2 percent dependent on the United States (trade value over $566 million), adding up to more than 91 percent of China's total imports. The replacement ratio is 0.02, suggesting a lack of capacity to fill gaps with domestic production. The following year, China began to increase its imports from Brazil, as well as from Zimbabwe, previously the fourth-largest supplier but in second place in 2024, accounting for more than 15 percent of China's imports. While the total quantity of China's imports from Australia rose between 2022 and 2024, China has reduced its reliance on Australia: Australia's share of China's total imports dropped by nearly 24 percent from 2023 to 2024. Australia's exports of spodumene to China were almost thirteen times higher in value than those from Brazil and Zimbabwe in 2023, but only three times higher in 2024.

Countering China's weaponization of critical minerals will not be easy. It may prove more difficult than deterring or stopping China's weaponization of general merchandise goods because of the uneven global distribution of critical minerals and China's dominant position in the global supply chains. China is a leading producer of many critical minerals essential for key technologies and green energy transitions. Chinese companies continue to expand their overseas investments to secure a stable supply of these minerals. The country already holds a dominant position in refining and processing, creating potential choke points in the global supply chains.

Despite all these disadvantages and caveats, the world has a choice. Countries could accept that China's choking off the supply of gallium, germanium, graphite, and other medium and heavy REEs is simply the new reality of international trade and economic security and expect that similar sanctions will come in the future—or they can try to deter it from happening again. The key point to

TABLE 6.6 China's Trade in Spodumene (HS 253090), 2022–2024

TRADE IN SPODUMENE	2022	2023	2024
TOTAL IMPORT VALUE (QUANTITY)	$9,181,480,190 (4,290,269,463 kg)	$15,498,717,151 (6,547,106,154 kg)	$5,199,965,848 (8,168,639,874 kg)
TOTAL EXPORT VALUE (QUANTITY)	$180,641,837 (1,125,918,780 kg)	$144,516,816 (996,656,282 kg)	$124,594,404 (777,162,570 kg)
REPLACEMENT RATIO	0.019	0.009	0.024
CHINA'S TOP FIVE SUPPLIERS, SHARE OF CHINA'S TOTAL IMPORTS (TRADE VALUE)	1. Australia 85.02% ($7,805,748,579)	1. Australia 85.89% ($13,312,600,103)	1. Australia 62.10% ($3,229,183,817)
	2. United States 6.17% ($566,371,617)	2. Brazil 3.40% ($526,375,660)	2. Zimbabwe 15.22% ($791,287,762)
	3. Brazil 3.40% ($312,555,978)	3. Zimbabwe 3.33% ($515,500,280)	3. Brazil 5.32% ($276,867,418)
	4. Zimbabwe 1.47% ($134,949,954)	4. United States 1.89% ($293,206,952)	4. Nigeria 4.01% ($208,434,477)
	5. Nigeria 0.90% ($83,030,988)	5. Nigeria 1.88% ($292,596,903)	5. Canada 3.58% ($185,951,642)

Source: Authors' original table with data derived from UN Comtrade database at https://comtradeplus.un.org/.

remember about a collective resilience strategy in critical minerals is not to provoke a trade war with China in which every supplier escalates to cutting each other off. G7+IP-2 countries did not initiate critical minerals sanctions, and under collective deterrence, it will never act first. China initiated the actions, and it is the responsibility of others to stop it. Our analysis shows that even in this sector traditionally dominated by China, if a group can come together, they can credibly signal costs to China if it continues such pathologies.

CHAPTER 7

THE STAKES COULD NOT
BE HIGHER

L eading nation-state actors, through their statements and actions, often determine the direction of the international system. The prime example of this was the United States at the end of World War II when it led the creation of the General Agreement on Tariffs and Trade (GATT) and the liberal trading order based on nondiscrimination and the free flow of goods and services. Today this system is being disrupted by the weaponization of economic interdependence in which leading powers are undertaking a variety of practices that include protectionist tariffs, nontariff barriers, investment controls, and industrial policy. The United States is clearly one of the culprits effecting this change, particularly under the second Trump administration during which the former underwriters of the postwar free trade order launched an unprecedented campaign of tariff barriers against friends and foes alike. While the United States is arguably the most prominent offender at the time of this writing in the first half of 2025, China is the worst offender dating back for decades. Unlike others, China's weaponization of trade has no legal or normative basis, is informal and discriminatory in nature, and is noncompliant with WTO rules. These practices not only degrade trust in the global trade environment but also threaten the liberal political order. Through the use of economic coercion, in conjunction with disinformation narratives and BRI financing of projects in the Global South, China is building an illiberal political order by encouraging others to pursue myopic self-interest, fostering self-censorship against freedom, generating mercantilist behavior, and fomenting acquiescence to China's autocratic values.

The solution to this problem is not, as some hardliners on China like former UN ambassador and Republican presidential candidate Nikki Haley, Republican senators Tom Cotton and Josh Hawley, or (then) vice presidential candidate J. D. Vance would advocate, suspending permanent normal trade relations (PNTR) with China.[1] The goal is not to destroy the Chinese economy (and that of the world) by decoupling; instead, the goal is to stop a pathology in China's behavior. This pathology is the use of a blunt force tool in lieu of diplomacy to achieve its political goals. Given the success it has experienced with economic coercion in persuading others to concede to its demands on Taiwan, Hong Kong, and other parochial interests, China has resorted to this tool as a shortcut rather than investing time and energy in traditional foreign policy. What we have argued for in this book is a strategy that (1) assumes that trade with China is necessary, (2) assumes that decoupling from China is not possible, and (3) moves China away from behavior that is destructive for itself, its trading partners, and the world.

In this context, collective resilience may look to many like another brick in building a U.S. protectionist wall against China, already laid with investment controls, tariffs, blocked access to technology, and industrial policy. But its goal is not decoupling from China, starting a trade war with China, or doing damage to the Chinese economy. All three of these outcomes would be mutually destructive to all parties. Collective resilience is a theory and strategy designed to address the fundamental dilemma of how to find protection from China's weaponization of trade without having to decouple. This protection can be found only in multilaterally organizing because no country can deal with China's economic predation on its own. The motivating idea behind the initiative is the simple premise that all economic interdependence—even asymmetrical interdependence—works both ways. Collective resilience overturns Beijing's assumption that no country would dare countersanction it.

The strategy's credibility rests equally in the promise to retaliate in meaningful ways if faced with coercion and to refrain from retaliation when not prompted. Beijing can be assured that this is not a weapon to be used indiscriminately against it, but only as a corrective in response to economic predation. As the international relations scholar Thomas Christensen argues cogently, a China strategy may feature "sticks" to punish the deviant behavior, but "equally important are credible assurances that the threatened punishment will only be carried out if the prohibited behavior is adopted."[2] If there is no bullying, then there is no need for a collective retaliatory response. In this regard, it is like deterrence in the security realm, in that retaliation should never be used if deterrence is effective. A successful collective resilience strategy will result in a decrease in the weaponization of interdependence and a regaining of trust in liberal trade and political order. This final chapter looks at practical steps for building a collective resilience framework.

WORDS ARE POLICY

Implementing a strategy of collective resilience would start with an explicit acknowledgment and condemnation by policy leaders of economic coercion practices. At the highest levels of government, words are policy, because they set the direction for bureaucracies and require ministries and departments to come up with ways to fulfill the mandate.

Though coercion by China goes back almost three decades, only within the last few years have leaders in Europe, Asia, and America truly focused on the problem. Starting from about 2021, leading democracies have called on states to come together, not just to advocate multi-method de-risking measures but to organize actively to deter it. U.S. secretary of state Antony Blinken unambiguously urged this in March 2021 at the NATO summit:

> We've got to broaden our capacity to address threats in the economic, technological, and informational realms. *And we can't just play defense—we have to take an affirmative approach.* We've seen how Beijing and Moscow are increasingly using access to critical resources, markets, and technologies to pressure our allies and drive wedges between us. . . . When one of us is coerced, we should respond as allies and work together to reduce our vulnerability by ensuring our economies are more integrated with each other than they are with our principal competitors. That means teaming up to develop cutting-edge innovations; ensuring that our sensitive supply chains are resilient; setting the norms and standards that will govern emerging technologies; imposing costs on those who break the rules. History tells us that, when we do, more countries will opt for the open and secure spaces that we build together.[3]

It is noteworthy that such statements have been made in bilateral and multilateral forums that feature G7+IP-2 countries. UK foreign secretary Liz Truss's statements in January 2022 in Australia were among the first: "[China] is using its economic muscle to attempt to coerce democracies like Australia and Lithuania . . . we will stand up for our economic security. That means calling out China when it blocks products from Lithuania or imposes punitive tariffs on Australian barley and wine."[4]

The commitment to organize has also become a fixture of U.S. summits with key allies. The April 2023 joint statement between the United States and South Korea carried an exemplary statement that signaled a willingness to counter Chinese economic coercion: "[The two presidents] share deep concerns about and express opposition to harmful uses of economic influence, including economic coercion as well as use of opaque tools with respect to foreign firms, and will coop-erate with like-minded partners to counter economic coercion."[5]

Similarly, since the leaders' agreement to address economic coercion on May 23, 2022, the April 2024 joint statement between the United States and Japan explic-itly recognized ongoing bilateral and multilateral efforts to counter economic coercion. "[The United States and Japan] are cooperating to deter and address economic coercion, through our bilateral cooperation as well as through our work with like-minded partners including the G7 Coordination Platform on Economic Coercion."[6]

The May 2023 G7 summit in Hiroshima, which included Australia and South Korea as guests, carried a watershed Leaders' Statement dedicated specifically to fostering common cause on recognizing and countering economic coercion:

> The world has encountered a disturbing rise in incidents of economic coercion that seek to exploit economic vulnerabilities and dependencies and underline the foreign and domestic policies and positions of G7 members as well as partners around the world. We will work together to ensure that attempts to weaponize economic dependencies by forcing G7 members and partners including small economies to comply and conform will fail and face consequences. We express serious concern over economic coercion and call on all countries to refrain from its use, which not only undermines the functioning of and trust in the multilat-eral trading system, but also infringes upon the international order centered on respect for sovereignty and the rule of law, and ultimately undermines global security and stability.[7]

The July 2024 NATO Summit in Washington, DC, which also included Australia, South Korea, Japan, and New Zealand, carried a strong statement of intent regarding countering economic coercion: "We remain open to construc-tive engagement with the PRC, including to build reciprocal transparency with the view of safeguarding the Alliance's security interests. At the same time, we are boosting our shared awareness, enhancing our resilience and preparedness, and protecting against the PRC's coercive tactics and efforts to divide the Alliance."[8]

In the case of the European Union, China's economic coercion against Lithu-ania in late 2021 provided political momentum for a rethinking of economic secu-rity that was already underway.[9] The Lithuania case laid a path for deliberate support by EU members for the creation of the Anti-Coercion Instrument (ACI). In December 2021, the European Commission, European Council, and European Parliament issued a joint declaration recognizing the problem of economic coercion by third parties: "The Commission confirms its intention to further examine a possible instrument, which could be adopted in order to dissuade or offset coercive actions by third countries and which would allow the expeditious adoption of countermeasures triggered by such actions."[10] This was followed by the launch of the New Economic Security Strategy in June 2023 and the ACI in December of the same year.[11]

The statements cited are only examples of the movement toward collective resilience. They are significant because they not only call out the problem but also express a commitment to organize and counter the activity. They commit the wheels of government to churn out policy deliverables in accordance with the mandates of the leadership.

RESEARCH AND INTELLIGENCE

In this book, we have presented some original data on high-dependence items in the merchandise trade and critical mineral sectors that could be used in a collective resilience strategy. But this is only the beginning. This study cries out for a universal mapping of all high-dependence exports to the Chinese market. Other studies have singled out critical technologies that could be leveraged. A 2024 CSIS study, for example, identified advanced epoxy resins, high-precision bearings, heavy-duty gas turbines, and electron microscopes as critical trade choke points for China.[12] Another study found that key components and technologies of China's satellite industry come from the West.[13] The major shift to an industrial policy among G7+IP-2 countries to protect economic security has focused on removing any dependence on China for critical supply chains. Intelligence agencies need to be tasked with a parallel effort to map all of China's supply chain vulnerabilities to Western markets, as well as efforts by China to reduce those dependencies. For example, UN Comtrade data from 2022 to 2024 showed a decrease in the total trade value of high-dependence items from Australia (down 77.9 percent), the United States (down 52.5 percent), Germany (down 31.7 percent), New Zealand (down 23 percent) and Japan (down 13.2 percent). Is this a conscious strategy being pursued by Beijing to replace its high-dependence trade vulnerabilities on Western-oriented economies? Is China's identification of new markets for this trade deliberately outside of the collective resilience network? Countries with the most high-dependence goods like the United States and Japan, the G7+IP-2 members, or the Five Eyes partners (United States, UK, Canada, Australia, and New Zealand) could be tasked with monitoring trends in China's trade dependencies in addition to new practices of economic coercion.

In addition to the G7+IP-2, socializing a new norm of collective resilience should be undertaken in groupings like IPEF, the Quad, U.S.–Japan–South Korea trilaterals, Five Eyes, or other Indo-Pacific and Euro-Atlantic forums. Incentives to implement sanctions (e.g., when China is sanctioning another country in the group but not your own) would need to be established, the most important of which is to minimize the economic pain done to a country that participates in the strategy. One such inducement might be to invite members to sanction only a handful of select strategic high-dependence items with China, rather than everything on the high-dependence list. Another would be for the big powers to announce impact-mitigation contingency measures in advance for any country that participates in the strategy. The United States did this for Lithuania through a variety of supporting financial measures. In the aftermath of a successful Lithuania response, the United States created an eight-person team at the State Department known colloquially as "the firm," led by Melanie Hart, the China policy coordinator for Undersecretary for Economic Growth, Energy, and the Environment Jose Fernandez. "The firm" became the first line of response in a crisis because it was able to coordinate with other U.S. agencies and utilize "every tool that the U.S. government has" to respond to China. According to Fernandez, "the firm" was run like a "consulting firm," and it counted more than a dozen countries that reached out to them for help in dealing with China's economic coercion.[14] While the nature of their assistance is confidential, their service has been described as an ambulance service because it helps a country "get past that scary emergency time."[15]

REORIENTING BUREAUCRACIES

In what admittedly would be a massive undertaking, collective resilience countries need to create mechanisms for carrying out the strategy, as well as coordinate among the different branches of government. Interagency task forces at the working level (assistant secretary [U.S.]/director-general level) would need to involve all relevant agencies in executing a collective resilience strategy. This would be led by the executive branch/presidential office/prime minister's office and would include foreign ministry, commerce ministry, intelligence agencies, trade ministry, treasury ministry, export financing agencies, and aid agencies, among others. The purpose of the interagency group would be to coordinate internally and with other collective resilience members on intelligence collection, information sharing with private-sector actors, damage/impact assessment on targeted sectors, and development of policy tools. Notionally, as one recent study enumerates, these tools should include executive or legislative authorities for (1) funds appropriated for foreign assistance, export financing, and loans to those targeted by coercion; (2) an expedited process for export licensing and regulatory processes to promote increased trade with affected collective resilience partners; (3) provisions for greater market access for imports from partners subject to coercion; (4) provisions for increasing tariffs on offending countries; (5) incentives for the private sector to participate in collective deterrence measures, including compensatory mechanisms for lost Chinese business; (6) transparency requirements and penalties for any firms that backfill the curtailed supply of a high-dependence item to China.[16]

In the United States, for example, Section 301 of the 1974 Trade Act gives the United States Trade Representative (USTR) the authority to identify trade actions by others as unfair or discriminatory and on that basis take retaliatory actions, including the imposition of punitive sanctions. But the credibility of this tool has been tarnished by the Trump administration's unilateral use of Section 301 as a form of economic coercion against trading partners.

Since October 2021, some collective resilience tools have been established through bipartisan legislation in Congress. The Countering China Economic Coercion Act, introduced by Representatives Ami Bera (D-California) and Ann Wagner (R-Missouri) in 2021 (House Resolution 5580) and the Senate version authored by Senators Todd Young (R-Indiana) and Christopher Coons (D-Connecticut), was signed into law in December 2022 by President Biden as part of the National Defense Authorization Act (NDAA) for FY2023.[17] This legislation created a Countering Economic Coercion Task Force chaired by the NSC that was tasked with developing and implementing a comprehensive U.S. interagency strategy to respond to the PRC's economic coercion, monitor the impact on U.S. national interests, and share information with the private sector and U.S. allies and partners. The legislation also mandates an annual forecast of economic coercion tools the PRC could employ in the future, review of available counter-coercion tools the United States could employ, and report on an early warning system for vulnerabilities of U.S. allies and partners to Beijing's economic coercion.[18] The Countering Economic Coercion Task Force was formally established in the last month of the Biden presidency, in December 2024.[19]

In 2023, Representative Ami Bera, along with colleagues Gregory Meeks (D-New York) and Tom Cole (R-Oklahoma), introduced another piece of legislation, the Countering Economic Coercion Act of 2023 (supported by a Senate version sponsored by Senators Todd Young and Christopher Coons) that would provide the White House with additional authorities to support affected partners and allies facing Chinese economic coercion.[20] These new tools would include waiving requirements for export financing, decreasing duties on goods to make up for lost exports, expediting export licensing decisions and regulatory processes, and appropriating funds for foreign aid, export financing, and loans. The bill also calls for increasing duties on imports from the coercer. The Department of Commerce is endowed with the authority to execute export controls on goods. Moreover, this authority is construed broadly enough to fit with a collective resilience strategy: "to carry out the foreign policy of the United States, including the protection of human rights and the promotion of democracy."[21] Within the Commerce Department, actions would be carried out by the BIS, which administers laws and policies on the export of trade commodities and technology as related to the pursuit of national security objectives. Within the Treasury Department, the International Emergency Economic Powers Act (IEEPA) can be used to regulate dollar transactions globally to prevent target countries from trading in dollars. IEEPA could be used to compel other countries to comply with U.S. export controls, although the presidential use of this tool, too, has been challenged in the courts over the Trump administration's use of IEEPA for the blanket imposition of tariffs on all U.S. trading partners.[22]

For the United States, collective resilience would be most credible if it took the form of bipartisan legislation rather than an executive order, because this would signal consensus that outlasts any particular presidency. Thankfully, countering economic coercion has been a focus of concern on both sides of the aisle. This sends a message both to allied countries and to China that the strategy is not subject to the political whims of a change of administration. The opposition to trade liberalization by both Democrats and Republicans poses a problem for executing a collective resilience strategy because market access is arguably one element of how partners can help an afflicted country. In the U.S. case, investment or export financing might be offered in lieu of market access, or legislators might agree to temporary market access.

South Korea has taken its own share of actions. As noted in chapter 4, the government introduced three pieces of legislation in 2023 and 2024 that laid the legal basis for a supply chain committee and stabilization fund. Furthermore, the government demonstrated its continued commitment to this issue through the elevation of National Security Adviser Wang Yunjong (discussed in chapter 4) and the reorganization of the foreign ministry.[23] Since 2023, South Korea has inaugurated and actively participated in several bilaterals, trilaterals, and multilaterals with like-minded partners, including a new economic security dialogue with Australia, a new critical minerals trilateral with the United States and Mongolia, a new trilateral economic security dialogue with the United States and Japan, and a new technology trilateral with the United States and India, as well as holding the chairmanship of the Minerals Security Partnership from 2024 to 2025.[24]

Japan continued to implement, innovate, and expand its bureaucracy to deal with economic security. The Japanese Diet passed the Economic Security Clearance Law in May 2024 to create a security clearance system that would enable the government to classify information related to cutting-edge technologies and infrastructure.[25] In July 2024, METI reorganized the Trade and Economic Cooperation Bureau into the Trade and Economic Security Bureau and created a new Economic Security Policy Division to act as a control tower for coordinating METI's economic security measures.[26] That same month, Keitaro Ohno, a Diet member and the state minister for cabinet affairs on economic security, outlined some key policy instruments at Tokyo's disposal, including "strengthening economic intelligence capabilities, preventing technology outflows, strengthening the development of human capital, and building a foundation for private-public policies."[27] These tools would allow Japan to improve its "strategic autonomy" and "strategic indispensability," which are the defensive and offensive components of its economic security policy. In addition to improving its domestic economic security, Japan has also underscored its desire to increase cooperation with like-minded partners through initiatives such as stockpile coordination, production infrastructure development, and creation of a new global industrial structure.[28]

The EU's effort at collective resilience features the ACI, launched in December 2023, with a twenty-articles legal framework and decision-making procedures for EU members to investigate, adjudicate, and take actions (Regulation (EU) No. 2023/2675). It defines the trigger for counter-coercion as "a situation where a third country attempts to pressure the EU or a Member State into making a particular choice by applying, or threatening to apply, measures affecting trade or investment against the EU or a Member State. The [ACI] instrument can be triggered by a wide range of coercive practices."[29]

A determination is made by vote of the members, after which an attempt is made to resolve the issue through negotiation with the coercer. If diplomacy fails, the European Commission can impose countermeasures from a portfolio of ACI tools, including restrictions on trade and investment, restrictions on financial services and intellectual property rights, restrictions on tender for public procurement projects, broadened export controls, restrictions on FDI, and restricted access to EU banking, insurance, and capital markets.[30] The EU also stipulates a framework for requiring the offending country to compensate for damages to the targeted state. Some scholars have argued that the ACI is an innovation to traditional bureaucracy because it takes a foreign policy issue—economic security—and addresses it through trade policy. This both expedites and empowers action largely because it takes decisions on economic coercion away from EU's Common Foreign and Security Policy (CFSP), which requires unanimity of the European Council, and makes it a matter for Common Commercial Policy, which has a lower (majority) bar for action.[31]

As with the ACI, the threshold for what constitutes triggering behavior for counter-coercion would need to be established and coordinated among collective resilience partners and communicated clearly to China. European discussions around the ACI provide a good example.[32] At one end of the spectrum, states could enumerate a list of predefined actions that would constitute economic coercion and therefore trigger a collective response. This could be defined as new tariffs imposed by China for explicit nontrade reasons that are aimed at changing policies of the target state on Taiwan, Tibet, or any other non-trade-related issue. This could be expanded to include nontariff measures for coercive purposes like the arbitrary imposition of domestic regulations.

The limitation of such an approach is that it would not capture other, less visible, more informal forms of coercion such as social media boycott campaigns, the stoppage of sending Chinese tourists or students, or consumer boycotts.[33] Thus, at the other end of the spectrum, it would be a more flexible and conceptual definition of triggers that allows members to consider any suspicious behavior as potentially qualifying for a collective response. The aggrieved party would present the case that China is using economic pressure to infringe on sovereign policy choices by the government. In this case, triggers would be evaluated on a case-by-case basis. In order to prevent delays, it would be important for this adjudication to be streamlined. The EU process, for example, has created a "single point of contact" for application of the ACI and stipulates four months to determine an affirmative examination of a case.[34] In a significant departure from practice, the EU also requires only a majority vote rather than the customary unanimity of all twenty-seven members for action to be taken. This would allow maximum flexibility and could deter China's gray-zone tactics of devising new means of coercing outside a published list of triggers. Some combination of predefined triggers along with provision for ad hoc investigations (done in a prompt manner) would appear to make the most sense and offer the best deterrent.[35]

COLLECTIVE RESILIENCE AND DE-ESCALATION

The legal implications of collective resilience need to be investigated. Counter-coercion measures advocated in this book are admittedly drastic, and they will gain wider acceptance if compliant, or at least not inconsistent, with existing rules and norms. Most of the work on this aspect of the strategy has been in Europe. There are three strands. The first suggests that collective resilience, because it is in response to a violation of one party's sovereignty, would meet the exception in WTO rules on the grounds of threats to national security.[36] Article XXI(b) of the GATT stipulates that any party to the agreement may theoretically take actions that are inconsistent with WTO practice—such as tariffs, import quotas, or bans—that are "necessary for the protection of its essential security interests."[37] How "security interests" is interpreted by the WTO is unclear and thus far has been adjudicated in the context of a war, but it might be applicable to cases of acute economic coercion threatening the sovereign choices of others.[38]

The second strand of legal thought argues that if collective resilience is framed as a reciprocal action only to be executed in response to Chinese coercion, then the strategy might still be compliant with WTO signatory nondiscrimination obligations.[39] The WTO dispute settlement process allows for a temporary suspension of WTO obligations for a complainant "if, within 20 days after the expiry of a reasonable period of time, the parties have not agreed on satisfactory compensation."[40] The complainant may request permission from the Dispute Settlement Body (DSB) to take retaliatory measures such as trade sanctions, although the WTO considers this a last-resort mechanism only to be used in extreme cases.[41]

A third and extended strand of legal thought acknowledges that the WTO's dispute settlement mechanism is not well-suited to dealing with informal economic coercion (such as consumer boycotts, social media doxing, or arbitrary regulatory enforcement). But according to a recent European Council on Foreign Relations report, WTO law (*lex specialis*) is complementary to international law (*lex generalis*), so that behavior not covered by the WTO should be covered by international law.[42] This is especially the case if the purpose of economic coercion is to infringe on the sovereign choices of the target state. As Hackenbroich, one of the authors of the report, explains, the basis of the applicable international law goes back to articles approved by the United Nations General Assembly (UNGA) decades ago, including UNGA Resolution 2625, which outlaws the unilateral use of economic coercion to "compel another state to subordinate to it the exercise of its sovereign rights."[43] If such a violation of international law is established, then "according to Article 49 of the Articles on the Responsibility of States for Internationally Wrongful Acts (the articles), states may implement countermeasures in the case of a violation of international law to induce the author of the violation to comply with its obligations."[44] The report goes on to note that Article 48 allows for a collective countermeasure, "since it allows states other than the targeted state (probably the EU27 collectively) to take action to correct the internationally wrongful act if the obligation breached is owed to a group of states that includes the target."[45]

Finally, a credible strategy must have mechanisms for rescinding or undoing any collective counter-coercion actions. In order to demonstrate that the strategy is not about decoupling from China, escalating to a trade war, or damaging the Chinese economy, it must signal not only an "on" button, but also an "off" button once China ceases the offending behavior. This also presumes the ability of the countries involved to agree in advance on what the bar is for turning off counter-coercion measures. As European conversations on the ACI stipulate, de-escalation is an essential part of the strategy. It demonstrates that collective resilience really is a measure of last resort and that it can be dialed down in favor of dialogue and negotiation to address China's concerns.[46]

Thinking about how to de-escalate collective resilience is not just a hypothetical exercise, for two additional reasons. First, if there is identifiable coercion by China, the target state will want retaliatory action sooner rather than later and will be resistant to waiting for a protracted DSB process in the WTO. Collective resilience partners, too, will want to see prompt action to reinforce deterrence. Therefore, counter-coercion action may be taken immediately, but there must also be an ability to rescind the action once the dispute is resolved in the WTO or if the collective resilience partners adjudicate later that the aggrieved party does not have a legitimate case. Second, there is a very good chance that China will resist collective resilience and will initially test the system by going after the perceived weakest link in the coalition. This would require a forceful and united response, but it would also require an ability to stand down if or when China complies. As we have heard from many in Europe and Asia, collective resilience is a counter-coercion weapon that must be handled with great care in its execution. If done properly, it could restore trust and hope in the liberal trading order by ridding the world of economic predation, but it could also lay a path to mutual trade sanctions, destroying the remnants of whatever order existed. The responsibility will lie with coalition members to internalize that the most critical element of this strategy's success is not the deterrent threat, or even the follow-through on that threat with coordinated counter-coercion activity, but rather the ability to stop those activities to assure China of the status quo intentions of the coalition members. That is the only path to stability, not a full-blown trade war.

PEER COMPETITION IS NOT EASY

An opinion piece in the *Wall Street Journal* in early 2021 stated emphatically that the world cannot wait any longer to stop economic coercion: "It's time to tell the bullies that if they poke one of us in the eye, we'll all poke back."[47] While globalists agree with the sentiment, they might find a strategy of collective resilience anathema to the liberal order they are trying to protect. However, they must treat it as a peer competition strategy necessary to save that order. It has been more than three decades since the United States engaged in great power competition, and some may have forgotten that high-stakes competition against another great power is not pretty and sometimes dirty, as when the United States had to countenance illiberal practices at times to protect the Western order during the Cold War.[48] As anti–free trade as collective resilience may appear, it is not illegal according to Article 22 of the UN Responsibility of States for Internationally Wrongful Acts, which states that countermeasures to an internationally wrongful act is not itself wrongful.[49] Moreover, it is not meant to undermine the WTO framework. On the contrary, it addresses the weaponization of trade not covered by the WTO dispute mechanism. Hopefully, the threat of collective resilience will never have to be exercised; it should be framed as a contingency measure when all else has failed. The EU, for example, explicitly states that the use of the ACI is a last resort, not a first one.[50] In that sense, it is like deterrence in the security realm. It requires both the capabilities and the political will of all involved to signal to Beijing that it can no longer use economic coercion as a tool of diplomacy that threatens the liberal international order.

Undeniably, there is a cost to such a drastic policy measure. Notwithstanding Trump's tariff wars in 2025 (discussed below), proponents of collective resilience will be accused of leading advanced industrialized democracies down a dark path. But the alternative of doing nothing to combat coercion could be even darker. One scholar explained the choices well: "The damage the United States does to its values by engaging . . . in dubious behavior, is surely less than the damage that would be done if a hyperaggressive Russia or neo-totalitarian China spread its influence across Eurasia and beyond."[51] If there was an alternative policy to stop China's economic coercion that is less drastic, then by all means it should be tried.

Absent such an alternative, drastic times unfortunately call for drastic measures. Policy critics are fond of arguing that there is always a better policy available than the one tried and that United States and others must compete with China in a way that remains consistent with our values. But in the world of policy, rarely do we make choices between the good and the perfect. More often than not, our choices are between bad and even worse alternatives. Or as Hal Brands observes, "the United States should avoid the fallacy of the false alternative. It must evaluate choices, and partners, against the plausible possibilities, not against the utopian idea.... In a world of lousy options, the crucial question is often: Lousy compared with what?"[52]

It is in this spirit that governments and firms need to contemplate a world with collective resilience—not as a strategy to destroy the Chinese economy or to start a trade war but as a last-gasp, almost tragic, attempt to avoid a world in which rampant economic coercion leaves states with two choices: they can protect themselves by decoupling, by autarky, and with distrust, or they can submit to the exigencies of a new illiberal world order. Collective resilience offers a third way to restore trust and normalcy to the rules-based order. The ultimate measure of the strategy's success will be its never having to be used. The stakes could not be higher.

POSTSCRIPT

As we conclude this book's writing, a giant hole has been torn into the global trading system. The second Trump administration from February 2025 launched a tariff war against allies, partners, and competitors, the likes of which the world has not seen since the days of Smoot-Hawley. As one scholar noted, Trump's actions have been driven by a three-step logic: (1) the United States is victimized by the world; (2) the primary evidence of this is America's perennial trade deficits with the world; and (3) tariffs are the best instrument for rebalancing.[1] In February, the president announced 25 percent tariffs against Mexico and Canada and on "Liberation Day," April 2, 2025, he announced reciprocal tariffs, ranging from 10 percent to 49 percent, against seventy U.S. trading partners. At the time of this writing, U.S. tariffs against China, which were as high as 145 percent at one point, were temporarily suspended until early August 2025.[2] But the two global powers remain engaged in a tariff war at levels so historically high that they effectively are on a path to decoupling.

The observations in our book give the reader perspective on the significance of this moment, but Trump's behavior does not change our bottom-line analysis and prescriptions. The threat to the global order remains the weaponization of economic and trade interdependence, and if anything, the two economic hegemons, while competing, are also converging in their behavior. That is, the United States is behaving in ways that resemble China's naked and rogue economic coercion described in this book, and China is behaving more like the United States, shifting tactically in the ways it frames its exercise of economic power.

While the media describe Trump's trade wars as disruptive and predatory, this book tells us that not all his tariff actions meet the definition of economic coercion. Economic coercion, as mastered by China and now practiced by the United

States, refers to the weaponization of trade for nontrade and/or political purposes. Trump's tariffs against Mexico and Canada at the beginning of his second term meet this definition because those tariffs were meant to punish the two trading partners for their alleged failure to stop illegal migration and the export of fentanyl across the northern and southern borders into the United States. On Truth Social, Trump wrote, "We cannot allow this scourge to continue to harm the USA, and therefore, until it stops, or is seriously limited, the proposed TARIFFS scheduled to go into effect on MARCH FOURTH will, indeed, go into effect, as scheduled."[3] By contrast, Trump's April 2025 reciprocal tariffs, as coercive as they appear, are framed by Trump as long overdue retaliation for unfair trade practices. The president is fond of citing the relative average tariff rates of the United States as being unfavorably low compared with those of other trading partners. During his March 2025 Joint Address to Congress, Trump called out the European Union, China, Brazil, India, Mexico, and Canada for "tremendously higher tariffs," with India's auto tariffs being "higher than 100 percent," China's average tariff twice as much, and South Korea's average tariff "four times higher."[4] In this regard, the reciprocal tariffs are not coercion per se; rather, they are protectionist trade actions taken to compel a lowering of tariffs, the removal of nontariff barriers, or modification of other forms of perceived discrimination against U.S. products.

FOUR PAGES FROM THE CHINA PLAYBOOK

Nevertheless, the continued use of reciprocal tariffs—even for trade purposes—could over the long run have the same effect as economic coercion. Trump is pulling four pages from the China coercion playbook, as we understand it thus far. The first refers to the regular use of trade weaponization as a tool of diplomacy. The parallels are clear. When the president calls tariffs "the most beautiful word in the dictionary," or when he grants temporary exemptions from tariffs (implying that the United States can levy tariffs any time that Trump sees fit), he is effectively signaling that the lead power in the international system sees trade weaponization as a normal and routine tool of diplomacy.[5]

Page two of the playbook refers to the unapologetic nature of China's economic coercion practices. Beijing operates in a workmanlike and businesslike fashion: you offended us on Taiwan; therefore, we hit you with trade sanctions. In a similar vein, Trump does not acknowledge that some of his actions uproot global norms and violate trust in the trading order. He remains undeterred in continuing the practice. Not only is Trump unapologetic, but he also trumpets his economic coercion as U.S. victorious retribution on behalf of "America First" against decades of victimization by the world.

Page three of China's economic coercion playbook adopted by Trump leverages the asymmetry of dependence in the weaponization of trade. In chapter 3, we wrote about how China's confidence in its strategy stems from the size of its market—accounting in 2024, for example, for 27.98 percent of Australia's global trade, 20.75 percent of South Korea's, 20.12 percent of Japan's, and 11.18 percent of the United States', while these countries constitute an equal or smaller fraction of China's overall exports. Trump exhibits a parallel mentality in justifying his actions, essentially stating that his tariff strategy's success rests on the fact that America needs the world less than the world needs it. For example, the White House Fact Sheet on the Trump's tariffs brims with U.S. hubris, stating that while trade accounts for only 24 percent of U.S. GDP, it accounts for 67 percent of Canada's GDP, 73 percent of Mexico's GDP, and 37 percent of China's GDP.[6]

Finally, Trump's page four from China's economic coercion playbook is the execution of his strategy in a dyadic format. Again, as we observed in chapter 3, using economic coercion bilaterally allows the coercer maximal asymmetrical advantage and intimidation over any one target government or company. In announcing the reciprocal tariffs on the White House lawn in April 2025, readers may recall, the president brandished an oversize bulletin board enumerating the levies country by country.[7] In negotiating potential exemptions from the tariffs during the ninety-day suspension period announced on April 9, Trump also expressed a preference for cutting deals bilaterally rather than in groups in order to maximize leverage (at the time of this writing, bilateral deals have been made between the United States and the United Kingdom and between the United States and Vietnam, as well as an interim deal between the United States and China, with no outright exemptions given to any party).[8]

Just as the United States is behaving more like China, Beijing is taking a page from the American playbook of trade weaponization. What distinguished U.S. coercion, as we observed in chapter 3, was its juridical nature, usually backed by legislation, executive order, or a UN resolution, to demonstrate that the American actions had legitimacy rather than being rogue behavior based on naked self-interest. China has learned to frame its economic coercion similarly. We see this in particular with regard to recent actions on critical minerals. China's export controls on gallium, germanium, and graphite in July and October 2023 were effectively targeted at the United States in retaliation for the Biden administration's export controls on semiconductor chips, but Beijing framed these measures in terms of national security and nonproliferation. China's April 4, 2025 economic coercion on seven REEs—samarium, gadolinium, terbium, dysprosium, lutetium, scandium, and yttrium—targeted the United States in retaliation for Trump's reciprocal tariffs, but they were once again framed in terms of national security and nonproliferation and a change in domestic requirements for export licenses (even though this licensing system has not yet been set up).[9] This represents a more sophisticated form of exerting influence not unlike how the United States has operated.

TRUMP'S COLLECTIVE RESILIENCE AND AUTARKY?

Some may question whether Trump's tariff wars are truly akin to China's economic coercion because they are intended more as bargaining chips to create leverage in reducing unfair tariffs and nontariff barriers by trading partners. For example, only days after announcing the reciprocal tariffs in April 2025, Trump announced a three-month temporary suspension for allies and partners, and when that expired, he extended the pause until August for some countries.[10]

The answer to this question will depend on the nature and type of exemptions that the Trump administration ultimately negotiates. If the United States makes deals to level the playing field in terms of other countries' average tariff rates and nontariff barriers and then removes all of the April 2025 duties, this could be seen as a trade tactic, albeit an unconventional one, rather than a China-like weaponization of trade.

However, we doubt that this will be the outcome. Instead, Trump will continue to use tariffs as a coercive threat or tool to get what he wants. Moreover, in cutting deals to grant exemptions from U.S. tariffs, he may require that allies and partners raise their tariffs against China in an effort to create a global decoupling from the Chinese economy. This would almost certainly elicit retaliatory tariffs from Beijing. In April 2025, China threatened to do as much, raising tariffs on American goods to 125 percent and calling Trump's tariffs "a joke."[11] If the United States took such a path, it would nominally be supporting a freer and fairer trading order for the United States (vis-à-vis allies and partners) but would effectively be promoting a norm of predatory liberalism globally, with all countries living in fear of trade weaponization by the two economic hegemons in the system.

The irony of a strategy in which Trump dealt out tariff exemptions in return for allied concessions but also gained allied commitments to weaponize trade against China is that this would start to resemble the collective resilience strategy of our book. Trump could effectively build a coalition of countries to enact tariffs or export controls against China by leveraging the threat of U.S. tariffs against allies. Trump could even demand allied tariffs or export controls on those items enumerated in this book for which China displays high dependence and lacks easy trade diversification alternatives.

While such a path might ostensibly produce the effects of collective resilience, it would not fulfill the spirit and ultimate objective of the strategy. First, the goals of the strategy would be different. If Trump leveraged U.S. tariff exemptions in return for higher allied tariffs against China, this would be part and parcel of a strategy to decouple from China. The fact that Trump and his team have talked about the potential suspensions of tariffs to allies in the context of allies instituting new tariffs against China suggests that decoupling may be his goal. But a strategy of collective resilience is not about decoupling from China; it is about engaging in trade with China but deterring Beijing's ability to weaponize trade. Second, collective resilience seeks to preserve the global free trade order and to instill trust in that order against the scourge of economic coercion. Trump, on the other hand, does not seek to reinforce the existing order; instead, he seeks to blow it up and remove rules that previously tied down the United States. Third, the strategic objectives differ. Collective resilience leverages the threat of action in the multilateral space to elicit cooperation from China. As we have stated in this book, it is a deterrence strategy. Trump's purported use of collective tariffing against China is a punishment strategy aimed at undermining a great power competitor. Finally, collective resilience rests in part on the moral authority of like-minded and status quo countries to work together to deter a revisionist actor from undermining the world order. It will be harder to garner multilateral momentum for such a strategy if the United States is seen as part of the problem rather than part of the solution.

APPENDIX 1

China's Economic Coercion Against Private-Sector Companies, 1997–2025

YEAR	COUNTRY	COMPANY	TARGETED ACTION	CHINA'S COERCION
1997	United States	Disney	Film (*Kundun*) portrays Dalai Lama and Chinese takeover of Tibet	Ban on film and all business cooperation
1997	United States	MGM	Film (*Red Corner*) portrays Chinese judicial system as corrupt and stars Richard Gere	Ban on film and all business cooperation
1997	United States	Columbia Tristar Pictures	Film (*Seven Years in Tibet*) portrays Dalai Lama and Chinese takeover of Tibet	Ban on film and all business cooperation
2003	United States	Electronic Arts	Video game (*Command and Conquer*) portrays China in negative light	Product ban
2004	Japan	Nippon Paint	Humorous ad using Chinese dragons	Boycott
2004	Sweden	Paradox Entertainment	Video game (*Hearts of Iron*) portrays Manchuria, Tibet, Xinjiang as independent of China	Product ban
2004	United States	Nike	Humorous ad using Chinese dragons	Boycott, product ban

(*continued*)

YEAR	COUNTRY	COMPANY	TARGETED ACTION	CHINA'S COERCION
2004	United States	Sports Interactive	Video game (*Football Manager 2005*) classifies Taiwan, Hong Kong, Tibet as independent from China	Boycott, product ban
2008	France	Carrefour	Pro-Tibet demonstrators disrupt Olympic torch relay	Boycott, public backlash at store locations
2008	France	Citroen	Pro-Tibet demonstrators disrupt Olympic torch relay	Boycott of products
2008	France	Louis Vuitton	Accused of donating money to Dalai Lama	Boycott of products
2008	France	Peugeot	Pro-Tibet demonstrators disrupt Olympic torch relay	Boycott of products
2008	Italy	Fiat	Ad with Tibet and Richard Gere	Public backlash; Fiat apologizes
2008	United States	McDonald's	Pro-Tibet agitators disrupt Olympic torch relay	Public backlash, call for boycott
2008	United States	The Coca-Cola Company	Ad shows Buddhist monks on roller coaster	Accusation of suggesting Tibetan independence, boycott of products
2009	France	Airbus	France hosts Dalai Lama visit	Cancels Airbus plane contract
2009	United States	Facebook	Uyghur protestors use Facebook for communications for 2009 Ürümqi riots	Ban on Facebook for China users
2010	Japan	Nissan	Dispute over contested Senkaku/Diaoyu Islands	Export restrictions on rare earth elements, hurting car engine production

YEAR	COUNTRY	COMPANY	TARGETED ACTION	CHINA'S COERCION
2010	Japan	Toyota	Dispute over contested Senkaku/Diaoyu Islands	Export restrictions on rare earth elements, hurting car engine production
2010	Japan	Mitsubishi	Dispute over contested Senkaku/Diaoyu Islands	Export restrictions on rare earth elements, hurting car engine production
2010	Japan	Honda	Dispute over contested Senkaku/Diaoyu islands	Export restrictions on rare earth elements, hurting car engine production
2010	Japan	Mazda	Dispute over contested Senkaku/Diaoyu Islands	Export restrictions on rare earth elements, hurting car engine production
2011	United States	MGM	*Red Dawn* film portrays China as military enemy	Hard product ban imposed on MGM movies
2012	Japan	Honda	Japanese government buys contested Senkaku/Diaoyu Islands from private owner	Anti-Japan protests, boycott of Japanese goods
2012	Japan	Uniqlo	Japanese government buys contested Senkaku/Diaoyu Islands from private owner	Anti-Japan protests, boycott of Japanese goods
2012	Japan	Mazda	Japanese government buys contested Senkaku/Diaoyu Islands from private owner	Anti-Japan protests, boycott of Japanese goods
2012	Japan	Toyota	Japanese government buys contested Senkaku/Diaoyu Islands from private owner	Anti-Japan protests, boycott of Japanese goods

(continued)

YEAR	COUNTRY	COMPANY	TARGETED ACTION	CHINA'S COERCION
2012	Japan	ANA	Japanese government buys contested Senkaku/Diaoyu Islands from private owner	Anti-Japan protests, boycott of Japanese goods
2012	Japan	Canon	Japanese government buys contested Senkaku/Diaoyu Islands from private owner	Anti-Japan protests, boycott of Japanese goods
2012	Japan	Panasonic	Japanese government buys contested Senkaku/Diaoyu Islands from private owner	Anti-Japan protests, boycott of Japanese goods
2012	Japan	Japan Airlines	Japanese government buys contested Senkaku/Diaoyu Islands from private owner	Anti-Japan protests, boycott of Japanese goods
2012	Japan	Mitsubishi	Japanese government buys contested Senkaku/Diaoyu Islands from private owner	Anti-Japan protests, boycott of Japanese goods
2012	Japan	Nissan	Japanese government buys contested Senkaku/Diaoyu Islands from private owner	Anti-Japan protests, boycott of Japanese goods
2012	Japan	Shiseido Co.	Japanese government buys contested Senkaku/Diaoyu Islands from private owner	Anti-Japan protests, boycott of Japanese goods
2013	United States	Electronic Arts	Video game (*Battlefield: China Rising*) portrays an overthrowing of China	Ban on the video game and censorship of all related materials
2016	France	Lancome	Actress Denise Ho to perform in 2016 "Occupy Central" concert in Hong Kong	*Global Times* incites public backlash; Lancome cancels event

YEAR	COUNTRY	COMPANY	TARGETED ACTION	CHINA'S COERCION
2016	South Korea	JYP Entertainment	Taiwanese member of South Korean girl group (TWICE) holds up Taiwanese flag during TV show	Boycott, censorship, product ban
2016	South Korea	LG Electronics	Emplacement of missile defense THAAD battery in South Korea	PRC decertifies LG EV batteries for use in cars and ends supply contracts
2016	South Korea	Samsung SDI	Emplacement of missile defense THAAD battery in South Korea	PRC decertifies Samsung batteries for use in China; Samsung closes production lines in three Chinese cities
2016	South Korea	SK	Emplacement of missile defense THAAD battery in South Korea	PRC decertifies SK batteries for use in China
2016	United States	Apple	International tribunal rules in favor of Philippines over contested Spratly Islands	Netizens blame United States for ruling; online campaign to boycott new iPhone 7
2016	United States	K-Swiss	K-Swiss Korea ad makes fun of Chinese person	Netizen public backlash against K-Swiss
2016	United States	KFC	International tribunal rules in favor of Philippines over contested Spratly Islands	Netizens blame United States for ruling; online campaign to boycott KFC
2017	South Korea	Korean Air	Emplacement of missile defense THAAD battery in South Korea	Ban on group tours to Korea
2017	South Korea	Galleria Duty Free	Emplacement of missile defense THAAD battery in South Korea	Ban on group tours to Korea (70 percent of duty-free sales revenues)

(continued)

YEAR	COUNTRY	COMPANY	TARGETED ACTION	CHINA'S COERCION
2017	South Korea	Aekyung	Emplacement of missile defense THAAD battery in South Korea	PRC bans import of Aekyung products (and nineteen other Korean cosmetics)
2017	South Korea	Iaso	Emplacement of missile defense THAAD battery in South Korea	PRC bans import of Iaso products (and nineteen other Korean cosmetics)
2017	South Korea	CJ Lion	Emplacement of missile defense THAAD battery in South Korea	PRC bans import of CJ Lion (and nineteen other Korean cosmetics)
2017	South Korea	Daelim	Emplacement of missile defense THAAD battery in South Korea	PRC bans sale of Daelim toilets/ household goods
2017	South Korea	Dham:a	Emplacement of missile defense THAAD battery in South Korea	PRC bans import of Dham:a cosmetics (and nineteen other Korean cosmetics)
2017	South Korea	Kocostar	Emplacement of missile defense THAAD battery in South Korea	PRC bans import of Kocostar cosmetics (and nineteen other Korean cosmetics)
2017	South Korea	Rice Day	Emplacement of missile defense THAAD battery in South Korea	PRC bans import of Rice Day cosmetics (and nineteen other Korean cosmetics)
2017	South Korea	AmorePacific	Emplacement of missile defense THAAD battery in South Korea	PRC bans import of AmorePacific (and nineteen other Korean cosmetics)
2017	South Korea	Shinsegae	Emplacement of missile defense THAAD battery in South Korea	Ban on group tours to Korea (70 percent of duty-free sales revenues)
2017	South Korea	Hotel Shilla	Emplacement of missile defense THAAD battery in South Korea	Ban on group tours to Korea

YEAR	COUNTRY	COMPANY	TARGETED ACTION	CHINA'S COERCION
2017	South Korea	Shilla Duty Free	Emplacement of missile defense THAAD battery in South Korea	Ban on group tours to Korea (70 percent of duty-free sales revenues)
2017	South Korea	Lotte	Emplacement of missile defense THAAD battery in South Korea	Widespread boycott against Lotte products and services nationally; 112 stores shut down, $1.78 billion losses
2017	South Korea	Emart	Emplacement of missile defense THAAD battery in South Korea	Widespread boycott against Emart; closed all locations
2017	South Korea	Hyundai	Emplacement of missile defense THAAD battery in South Korea	Calls for boycott of products; vandalism
2017	South Korea	Kia Motors	Emplacement of missile defense THAAD battery in South Korea	Calls for boycott of products
2017	United States	Disney	Government critics use the name and image of Winnie-the-Pooh to make fun of Xi Jinping	Censors name and images of Winnie-the-Pooh on social media sites
2017	United States	LPGA	Emplacement of missile defense THAAD battery in South Korea	Chinese golfers' nonparticipation in Korean LPGA event
2017	United States	Victoria's Secret	Singer Katy Perry and some models make pro-Taiwan and racist comments	Denies visa entry for Shanghai show
2018	Australia	Qantas	Website fails to label Taiwan as part of China	PRC forces Qantas to label Taiwan as part of China
2018	Austria	Austrian Airlines	Website fails to properly label Hong Kong, Macau, or Taiwan as part of China	PRC forces airline to properly label them as part of China

(continued)

YEAR	COUNTRY	COMPANY	TARGETED ACTION	CHINA'S COERCION
2018	Belgium	Brussel Airlines	Website fails to properly label Hong Kong, Macau, or Taiwan as part of China	PRC forces airline to properly label them as part of China
2018	Brazil	LATAM Airlines Brasil	Website fails to properly label Hong Kong, Macau, or Taiwan as part of China	PRC forces airline to properly label them as part of China
2018	Canada	Alimentation Couche-Tard	Website fails to label Taiwan as part of China	PRC designates seventy-four global companies with incorrect references to Taiwan/Hong Kong/Macau as separate from China
2018	Canada	Air Canada	Website fails to label Taiwan or Hong Kong as part of China	PRC forces Air Canada to label Taiwan as part of China
2018	Canada	Manulife Financial	Website fails to label Taiwan, Hong Kong, or Macau as part of China	PRC designates seventy-four global companies with incorrect references to Taiwan/Hong Kong/Macau as separate from China
2018	Denmark	Maersk Group	Website fails to label Taiwan as part of China	PRC designates seventy-four global companies with incorrect references to Taiwan/Hong Kong/Macau as separate from China
2018	Denmark, Norway, Sweden	SAS Airlines	Website fails to properly label Hong Kong, Macau, or Taiwan as part of China	PRC forces airline to properly label them as part of China
2018	Finland	Finnair	Website fails to label Taiwan as part of China	State-issued threats

YEAR	COUNTRY	COMPANY	TARGETED ACTION	CHINA'S COERCION
2018	France	Danone	Website fails to label Hong Kong as part of China	PRC designates seventy-four global companies with incorrect references to Taiwan/Hong Kong/Macau as separate from China
2018	France	Air France	Website fails to label Taiwan or Hong Kong as part of China	PRC forces Air France to label Taiwan as part of China
2018	France	BNP Paribas	Website fails to label Taiwan or Hong Kong as part of China	PRC designates seventy-four global companies with incorrect references to Taiwan/Hong Kong/Macau as separate from China
2018	France	Dior	Website fails to label Taiwan or Hong Kong as part of China	PRC designates seventy-four global companies with incorrect references to Taiwan/Hong Kong/Macau as separate from China
2018	France	Saint-Gobain Group	Website fails to label Taiwan as part of China	PRC designates seventy-four global companies with incorrect references to Taiwan/Hong Kong/Macau as separate from China
2018	France	TotalEnergies SE	Website fails to label Taiwan as part of China	PRC designates seventy-four global companies with incorrect references to Taiwan/Hong Kong/Macau as separate from China

(*continued*)

YEAR	COUNTRY	COMPANY	TARGETED ACTION	CHINA'S COERCION
2018	Germany	Air Berlin	Website fails to properly label Hong Kong, Macau, or Taiwan as part of China	PRC forces airline to properly label them as part of China
2018	Germany	BASF	Website fails to label Taiwan or Hong Kong as part of China	PRC designates seventy-four global companies with incorrect references to Taiwan/Hong Kong/ Macau as separate from China
2018	Germany	Deutsche Bank	Website fails to label Hong Kong as part of China	PRC designates seventy-four global companies with incorrect references to Taiwan/Hong Kong/ Macau as separate from China
2018	Germany	SAP	Website fails to label Taiwan or Hong Kong as part of China	PRC designates seventy-four global companies with incorrect references to Taiwan/Hong Kong/ Macau as separate from China
2018	Germany	Siemens	Website fails to label Taiwan, Hong Kong, or Macau as part of China	PRC designates seventy-four global companies with incorrect references to Taiwan/Hong Kong/ Macau as separate from China
2018	Germany	Talanx	Website fails to label Taiwan or Hong Kong as part of China	PRC designates seventy-four global companies with incorrect references to Taiwan/Hong Kong/ Macau as separate from China

YEAR	COUNTRY	COMPANY	TARGETED ACTION	CHINA'S COERCION
2018	India	Air India	Website fails to label Taiwan as part of China	PRC threatens a fine and forces Air India to label Taiwan as Chinese Taipei
2018	Indonesia	Garuda Indonesia	Website fails to label Taiwan as part of China	PRC forces airline to label Taiwan as part of China
2018	Ireland	Accenture	Website fails to label Taiwan or Hong Kong as part of China	PRC designates seventy-four global companies with incorrect references to Taiwan/Hong Kong/Macau as separate from China
2018	Israel	El Al	Website fails to properly label Hong Kong, Macau, or Taiwan as part of China	PRC forces airline to properly label them as part of China
2018	Italy	Alitalia	Website fails to properly label Hong Kong, Macau, or Taiwan as part of China	PRC forces airline to properly label them as part of China
2018	Italy	Dolce & Gabbana	Advertisement interpreted as insulting China	Social media boycott, brand ambassadors terminate contracts; stores vandalized
2018	Italy	UniCredit SPA	Website fails to label Hong Kong as part of China	PRC designates seventy-four global companies with incorrect references to Taiwan/Hong Kong/Macau as separate from China
2018	Japan	ANA	Website fails to designate Taiwan as part of China	PRC forces ANA to label Taiwan as part of China

(*continued*)

YEAR	COUNTRY	COMPANY	TARGETED ACTION	CHINA'S COERCION
2018	Japan	Denso Co., Ltd.	Website fails to label Taiwan as part of China	PRC designates seventy-four global companies with incorrect references to Taiwan/Hong Kong/Macau as separate from China
2018	Japan	Fujitsu	Website fails to label Taiwan or Hong Kong as part of China	PRC designates seventy-four global companies with incorrect references to Taiwan/Hong Kong/Macau as separate from China
2018	Japan	Hitachi	Website fails to label Taiwan or Hong Kong as part of China	PRC designates seventy-four global companies with incorrect references to Taiwan/Hong Kong/Macau as separate from China
2018	Japan	Japan Airlines	Website lists Hong Kong and Taiwan as separate destinations from China	PRC forces JAL to label Taiwan as part of China
2018	Japan	Matsushita	Website fails to label Taiwan or Hong Kong as part of China	PRC designates seventy-four global companies with incorrect references to Taiwan/Hong Kong/Macau as separate from China
2018	Japan	Mitsubishi Electric Co., Ltd.	Website fails to label Taiwanor Hong Kong as part of China	PRC designates seventy-four global companies with incorrect references to Taiwan/Hong Kong/Macau as separate from China

YEAR	COUNTRY	COMPANY	TARGETED ACTION	CHINA'S COERCION
2018	Japan	Mitsubishi Heavy Industries Co., Ltd.	Website fails to label Taiwan as part of China	PRC designates seventy-four global companies with incorrect references to Taiwan/Hong Kong/ Macau as separate from China
2018	Japan	Mitsui & Co., Ltd.	Website fails to label Taiwan or Hong Kong as part of China	PRC designates seventy-four global companies with incorrect references to Taiwan/Hong Kong/ Macau as separate from China
2018	Japan	Muji	Products mislabel Taiwan and contested Senkaku/ Diaoyutai Islands	Fine, product removal
2018	Japan	NEC Corporation	Website fails to label Taiwan or Hong Kong as part of China	PRC designates seventy-four global companies with incorrect references to Taiwan/Hong Kong/ Macau as separate from China
2018	Japan	Sony	Website fails to label Taiwan or Hong Kong as part of China	PRC designates seventy-four global companies with incorrect references to Taiwan/Hong Kong/ Macau as separate from China
2018	Japan	Subaru	Website fails to label Taiwan as part of China	PRC designates seventy-four global companies with incorrect references to Taiwan/Hong Kong/ Macau as separate from China

(continued)

YEAR	COUNTRY	COMPANY	TARGETED ACTION	CHINA'S COERCION
2018	Japan	Sumitomo Corporation	Website fails to label Taiwan or Hong Kong as part of China	PRC designates seventy-four global companies with incorrect references to Taiwan/Hong Kong/Macau as separate from China
2018	Japan	Suzuki Motors	Website fails to label Taiwan or Hong Kong as part of China	PRC designates seventy-four global companies with incorrect references to Taiwan/Hong Kong/Macau as separate from China
2018	Japan	Toyota	Website fails to label Taiwan or Hong Kong as part of China	PRC designates seventy-four global companies with incorrect references to Taiwan/Hong Kong/Macau as separate from China
2018	Jordan	Royal Jordanian	Website fails to properly label Hong Kong, Macau, or Taiwan as part of China	PRC forces airline to properly label them as part of China
2018	Malaysia	AirAsia	Website fails to label Taiwan as part of China	PRC forces AirAsia to label Taiwan as part of China
2018	Malaysia	Malaysia Airlines	Website fails to label Taiwan as part of China	PRC forces airline to label Taiwan as part of China
2018	Mauritius	Air Mauritius	Website fails to properly label Hong Kong, Macau, or Taiwan as part of China	PRC forces airline to properly label them as part of China
2018	Mongolia	MIAT Mongolian Airlines	Website fails to properly label Hong Kong, Macau, or Taiwan as part of China	PRC forces airline to properly label them as part of China

YEAR	COUNTRY	COMPANY	TARGETED ACTION	CHINA'S COERCION
2018	Netherlands	Altice	Website fails to label Taiwan or Hong Kong as part of China	PRC designates seventy-four global companies with incorrect references to Taiwan/Hong Kong/Macau as separate from China
2018	Netherlands	Heineken Holdings	Website fails to label Taiwan or Hong Kong as part of China	PRC designates seventy-four global companies with incorrect references to Taiwan/Hong Kong/Macau as separate from China
2018	Netherlands	KLM	Website fails to properly label Hong Kong, Macau, or Taiwan as part of China	PRC forces airline to properly label them as part of China
2018	Netherlands	Rabobank	Website fails to label Hong Kong as part of China	PRC designates seventy-four global companies with incorrect references to Taiwan/Hong Kong/Macau as separate from China
2018	Netherlands	Randstad	Website fails to label Hong Kong as part of China	PRC designates seventy-four global companies with incorrect references to Taiwan/Hong Kong/Macau as separate from China
2018	Netherlands	Royal Dutch Shell	Website fails to label Hong Kong or Macau as part of China	PRC designates seventy-four global companies with incorrect references to Taiwan/Hong Kong/Macau as separate from China

(continued)

YEAR	COUNTRY	COMPANY	TARGETED ACTION	CHINA'S COERCION
2018	New Zealand	Air New Zealand	Website fails to properly label Hong Kong, Macau, or Taiwan as part of China	PRC forces airline to properly label them as part of China
2018	Philippines	Philippine Airlines	Website fails to label Taiwan as part of China	PRC forces airline to label Taiwan as part of China
2018	Philippines	Cebu Pacific Air	Website fails to label Taiwan or Hong Kong as part of China	PRC forces airline to label Taiwan and Hong Kong as part of China
2018	Qatar	Qatar Airways	Website fails to properly label Hong Kong, Macau, or Taiwan as part of China	PRC forces airline to properly label them as part of China
2018	Russia	Aeroflot	Website fails to properly label Hong Kong, Macau, or Taiwan as part of China	PRC forces airline to properly label them as part of China
2018	Russia	S7 Airlines	Website fails to properly label Hong Kong, Macau, or Taiwan as part of China	PRC forces airline to properly label them as part of China
2018	Saudi Arabia	SABIC	Website fails to label Taiwan as part of China	PRC designates seventy-four global companies with incorrect references to Taiwan/Hong Kong/Macau as separate from China
2018	Saudi Arabia	Saudia	Website fails to properly label Hong Kong, Macau, or Taiwan as part of China	PRC forces airline to properly label them as part of China
2018	Singapore	Singapore Airlines	Website fails to label Taiwan as part of China	PRC forces airline to label Taiwan as part of China

YEAR	COUNTRY	COMPANY	TARGETED ACTION	CHINA'S COERCION
2018	South Korea	Asiana Airlines	Website fails to label Taiwan as part of China	PRC forces airline to label Taiwan as part of China
2018	South Korea	Kia Motors	Website fails to label Taiwan or Hong Kong as part of China	PRC designates seventy-four global companies with incorrect references to Taiwan/Hong Kong/Macau as separate from China
2018	South Korea	LG Electronics	Website fails to label Taiwan or Hong Kong as part of China	PRC designates seventy-four global companies with incorrect references to Taiwan/Hong Kong/Macau as separate from China
2018	Spain	Iberia	Website fails to properly label Hong Kong, Macau, or Taiwan as part of China	PRC forces airline to properly label them as part of China
2018	Spain	Inditex Company	Website fails to label Taiwan as part of China	PRC designates seventy-four global companies with incorrect references to Taiwan/Hong Kong/Macau as separate from China
2018	Spain	Mapfre	Website fails to label Taiwan as part of China	PRC designates seventy-four global companies with incorrect references to Taiwan/Hong Kong/Macau as separate from China
2018	Spain	Zara (Inditex)	Website fails to designate Taiwan as part of China	Website change and public apology

(continued)

YEAR	COUNTRY	COMPANY	TARGETED ACTION	CHINA'S COERCION
2018	Sri Lanka	Sri Lankan Airlines	Website fails to properly label Hong Kong, Macau, or Taiwan as part of China	PRC forces airline to properly label them as part of China
2018	Sweden	H&M	Website fails to label Taiwan or Hong Kong as part of China	PRC designates seventy-four global companies with incorrect references to Taiwan/Hong Kong/Macau as separate from China
2018	Sweden	IKEA	Lists Taiwan as country of origin on products	Print and social media pressure campaign
2018	Switzerland	Glencore	Website fails to label Taiwan as part of China	PRC designates seventy-four global companies with incorrect references to Taiwan/Hong Kong/Macau as separate from China
2018	Switzerland	Global Blue	Lists Taiwan and Hong Kong as countries in refund system	Social media campaign calling for boycott
2018	Switzerland	Nestlé	Website fails to label Taiwan or Hong Kong as part of China	PRC designates seventy-four global companies with incorrect references to Taiwan/Hong Kong/Macau as separate from China
2018	Switzerland	ABB Group	Website fails to label Taiwan as part of China	PRC designates seventy-four global companies with incorrect references to Taiwan/Hong Kong/Macau as separate from China

YEAR	COUNTRY	COMPANY	TARGETED ACTION	CHINA'S COERCION
2018	Switzerland	Swiss International Air Lines	Website fails to properly label Hong Kong, Macau, or Taiwan as part of China	PRC forces airline to properly label them as part of China
2018	Switzerland	UBS	Website fails to label Taiwan or Hong Kong as part of China	PRC designates seventy-four global companies with incorrect references to Taiwan/Hong Kong/Macau as separate from China
2018	Taiwan	85°C Bakery Cafe	Hosted patronage of Taiwan president	Boycott of stores in China
2018	Thailand	Thai Airways	Website fails to properly label Hong Kong, Macau, or Taiwan as part of China	PRC forces airline to properly label them as part of China
2018	Turkey	Turkish Airlines	Website fails to properly label Hong Kong, Macau, or Taiwan as part of China	PRC forces airline to properly label them as part of China
2018	United Arab Emirates	Etihad Airways	Website fails to label Taiwan, Hong Kong, or Macau as part of China	PRC forces airline to label them as part of China
2018	United Arab Emirates	Emirates	Website fails to label Taiwan, Hong Kong, or Macau as part of China	PRC forces airline to label them as part of China
2018	United Kingdom	GlaxoSmithKline	Website fails to label Taiwan or Hong Kong as part of China	PRC designates seventy-four global companies with incorrect references to Taiwan/Hong Kong/Macau as separate from China

(continued)

YEAR	COUNTRY	COMPANY	TARGETED ACTION	CHINA'S COERCION
2018	United Kingdom	Unilever	Website fails to label Taiwan as part of China	PRC designates seventy-four global companies with incorrect references to Taiwan/Hong Kong/Macau as separate from China
2018	United Kingdom	AstraZeneca	Website fails to label Taiwan or Hong Kong as part of China	PRC designates seventy-four global companies with incorrect references to Taiwan/Hong Kong/Macau as separate from China
2018	United Kingdom	Barclays	Website fails to label Taiwan or Hong Kong as part of China	PRC designates seventy-four global companies with incorrect references to Taiwan/Hong Kong/Macau as separate from China
2018	United Kingdom	British Airways	Website fails to label Taiwan, Hong Kong, or Macau as part of China	PRC forces airline to label them as part of China
2018	United Kingdom	Prudential	Website fails to label Taiwan or Hong Kong as part of China	PRC designates seventy-four global companies with incorrect references to Taiwan/Hong Kong/Macau as separate from China
2018	United Kingdom and Australia	Rio Tinto Group	Website fails to label Taiwan as part of China	PRC designates seventy-four global companies with incorrect references to Taiwan/Hong Kong/Macau as separate from China

YEAR	COUNTRY	COMPANY	TARGETED ACTION	CHINA'S COERCION
2018	United States	Amazon	Website fails to label Taiwan, Hong Kong, or Macau as part of China	PRC designates seventy-four global companies with incorrect references to Taiwan/Hong Kong/ Macau as separate from China
2018	United States	FedEx	Website fails to label Taiwan or Hong Kong as part of China	PRC designates seventy-four global companies with incorrect references to Taiwan/Hong Kong/ Macau as separate from China
2018	United States	Hawaiian Airlines	Website fails to designate Taiwan as part of China	PRC forces Hawaiian Airlines (and more than forty others) to label Taiwan as part of China
2018	United States	3M	Website fails to label Taiwan as part of China	PRC designates seventy-four global companies with incorrect references to Taiwan/Hong Kong/ Macau as separate from China
2018	United States	ADM Company	Website fails to label Taiwan as part of China	PRC designates seventy-four global companies with incorrect references to Taiwan/Hong Kong/ Macau as separate from China
2018	United States	American Airlines	Website fails to label Taiwan as part of China	PRC forces airline to label Taiwan as part of China

(*continued*)

YEAR	COUNTRY	COMPANY	TARGETED ACTION	CHINA'S COERCION
2018	United States	Amgen	Website fails to label Taiwan or Hong Kong as part of China	PRC designates seventy-four global companies with incorrect references to Taiwan/Hong Kong/Macau as separate from China
2018	United States	Apple	Website fails to label Taiwan, Hong Kong, or Macau as part of China	PRC designates seventy-four global companies with incorrect references to Taiwan/Hong Kong/Macau as separate from China
2018	United States	Coach	T-shirt lists Taiwan and Hong Kong as separate entities from China	Boycott of products; Chinese brand ambassadors terminate contracts; Coach apologizes
2018	United States	Delta Air Lines	Website fails to designate Taiwan as part of China	PRC forces Delta to label Taiwan and Tibet as part of China
2018	United States	DuPont	Website fails to label Taiwan or Hong Kong as part of China	PRC designates seventy-four global companies with incorrect references to Taiwan/Hong Kong/Macau as separate from China
2018	United States	Exxon Mobil	Website fails to label Taiwan or Hong Kong as part of China	PRC designates seventy-four global companies with incorrect references to Taiwan/Hong Kong/Macau as separate from China

YEAR	COUNTRY	COMPANY	TARGETED ACTION	CHINA'S COERCION
2018	United States	Facebook	Website fails to label Taiwan as part of China	PRC designates seventy-four global companies with incorrect references to Taiwan/Hong Kong/ Macau as separate from China
2018	United States	GAP	T-shirt with a map of China that excludes Taiwan and Tibet	Public backlash; Gap apologizes and removes product
2018	United States	Goldman Sachs	Website fails to label Taiwan as part of China	PRC designates seventy-four global companies with incorrect references to Taiwan/Hong Kong/ Macau as separate from China
2018	United States	HP	Website fails to label Taiwan or Hong Kong as part of China	PRC designates seventy-four global companies with incorrect references to Taiwan/Hong Kong/ Macau as separate from China
2018	United States	HBO	John Oliver joke about Xi Jinping	HBO and John Oliver banned in China
2018	United States	Intel	Website fails to label Taiwan as part of China	PRC designates seventy-four global companies with incorrect references to Taiwan/Hong Kong/ Macau as separate from China
2018	United States	Marriott	Online survey labels Taiwan, Tibet, Hong Kong, and Macau as countries	PRC shuts down Marriott's Chinese website, demands apology

(continued)

YEAR	COUNTRY	COMPANY	TARGETED ACTION	CHINA'S COERCION
2018	United States	McDonald's	Website fails to label Taiwan or Hong Kong as part of China	PRC designates seventy-four global companies with incorrect references to Taiwan/Hong Kong/Macau as separate from China
2018	United States	Medtronic	Website fails to designate Taiwan as part of China	PRC orders Medtronic to change label and apologize
2018	United States	Merck	Website fails to label Taiwan or Hong Kong as part of China	PRC designates seventy-four global companies with incorrect references to Taiwan/Hong Kong/Macau as separate from China
2018	United States	MetLife	Website fails to label Hong Kong as part of China	PRC designates seventy-four global companies with incorrect references to Taiwan/Hong Kong/Macau as separate from China
2018	United States	Morgan Stanley	Website fails to label Taiwan or Hong Kong as part of China	PRC designates seventy-four global companies with incorrect references to Taiwan/Hong Kong/Macau as separate from China
2018	United States	Nike	Website fails to label Taiwan as part of China	PRC designates seventy-four global companies with incorrect references to Taiwan/Hong Kong/Macau as separate from China

YEAR	COUNTRY	COMPANY	TARGETED ACTION	CHINA'S COERCION
2018	United States	Oracle Corporation	Website fails to label Taiwan or Hong Kong as part of China	PRC designates seventy-four global companies with incorrect references to Taiwan/Hong Kong/Macau as separate from China
2018	United States	Procter & Gamble	Website fails to label Taiwan or Hong Kong as part of China	PRC designates seventy-four global companies with incorrect references to Taiwan/Hong Kong/Macau as separate from China
2018	United States	Progressive	Website fails to label Taiwan or Hong Kong as part of China	PRC designates seventy-four global companies with incorrect references to Taiwan/Hong Kong/Macau as separate from China
2018	United States	Raytheon	Website fails to label Taiwan or Hong Kong as part of China	PRC designates seventy-four global companies with incorrect references to Taiwan/Hong Kong/Macau as separate from China
2018	United States	Tesoro Company	Website fails to label Taiwan or Hong Kong as part of China	PRC designates seventy-four global companies with incorrect references to Taiwan/Hong Kong/Macau as separate from China

(*continued*)

YEAR	COUNTRY	COMPANY	TARGETED ACTION	CHINA'S COERCION
2018	United States	The Coca-Cola Company	Website fails to label Hong Kong as part of China	PRC designates seventy-four global companies with incorrect references to Taiwan/Hong Kong/Macau as separate from China
2018	United States	United Airlines	Website fails to label Taiwan or Hong Kong as part of China	PRC forces airline to label them as part of China
2018	United States	Walmart	Lists Taiwan as country of origin on products	Public backlash; Walmart apologizes
2018	United States	Walmart	Website fails to label Taiwan as part of China	PRC designates seventy-four global companies with incorrect references to Taiwan/Hong Kong/Macau as separate from China
2019	Australia	ANZ Banking Group	Website fails to label Taiwan as part of China	PRC designates ninety-two new global companies with incorrect references to Taiwan/Hong Kong/Macau as separate from China
2019	Australia	Westpac	Website fails to label Hong Kong as part of China	PRC designates ninety-two new global companies with incorrect references to Taiwan/Hong Kong/Macau as separate from China
2019	Austria	Swarovski Group	Website does not recognize Hong Kong as part of China	Public backlash, brand ambassador termination; company apology

YEAR	COUNTRY	COMPANY	TARGETED ACTION	CHINA'S COERCION
2019	Canada	Scotiabank	Website fails to label Hong Kong as part of China	PRC designates ninety-two new global companies with incorrect references to Taiwan/Hong Kong/Macau as separate from China
2019	Canada	Royal Bank of Canada	Website fails to label Hong Kong as part of China	PRC designates ninety-two new global companies with incorrect references to Taiwan/Hong Kong/Macau as separate from China
2019	France	Groupe BPCE	Website fails to label Taiwan or Hong Kong as part of China	PRC designates ninety-two new global companies with incorrect references to Taiwan/Hong Kong/Macau as separate from China
2019	France	Auchan	Website fails to label Taiwan as part of China	PRC designates ninety-two new global companies with incorrect references to Taiwan/Hong Kong/Macau as separate from China
2019	France	BNP Paribas	Employee posts pro–Hong Kong Facebook post	Viral backlash calling for boycott on social media; company apologizes
2019	France	Carrefour	Website fails to label Taiwan as part of China	PRC designates ninety-two new global companies with incorrect references to Taiwan/Hong Kong/Macau as separate from China

(continued)

YEAR	COUNTRY	COMPANY	TARGETED ACTION	CHINA'S COERCION
2019	France	Clarins	Firm stops ads on pro-Beijing TVB over Hong Kong	Netizen attacks and calls for boycott
2019	France	Crédit Agricole	Website fails to label Taiwan or Hong Kong as part of China	PRC designates ninety-two new global companies with incorrect references to Taiwan/Hong Kong/Macau as separate from China
2019	France	Dior	Employee training session uses map that does not include Taiwan as part of China	Map goes viral; boycotts; company apologizes
2019	France	EDF	Website fails to label Taiwan or Hong Kong as part of China	PRC designates ninety-two new global companies with incorrect references to Taiwan/Hong Kong/Macau as separate from China
2019	France	Engie Group	Website fails to label Taiwan or Hong Kong as part of China	PRC designates ninety-two new global companies with incorrect references to Taiwan/Hong Kong/Macau as separate from China
2019	France	Givenchy	T-shirt design does not recognize Hong Kong or Taiwan as part of China	Anti-Givenchy outrage goes viral; boycott, brand ambassador termination
2019	France	L'Oreal	Website fails to label Taiwan as part of China	PRC designates ninety-two new global companies with incorrect references to Taiwan/Hong Kong/Macau as separate from China

YEAR	COUNTRY	COMPANY	TARGETED ACTION	CHINA'S COERCION
2019	France	Renault	Website fails to label Taiwan as part of China	PRC designates ninety-two new global companies with incorrect references to Taiwan/ Hong Kong/Macau as separate from China
2019	France	Sanofi	Website fails to label Taiwan or Hong Kong as part of China	PRC designates ninety-two new global companies with incorrect references to Taiwan/ Hong Kong/Macau as separate from China
2019	France	Schneider Electric	Website fails to label Taiwan or Hong Kong as part of China	PRC designates ninety-two new global companies with incorrect references to Taiwan/ Hong Kong/Macau as separate from China
2019	France	Société Générale	Website fails to label Taiwan or Hong Kong as part of China	PRC designates ninety-two new global companies with incorrect references to Taiwan/ Hong Kong/Macau as separate from China
2019	France	Vinci	Website fails to label Taiwan or Hong Kong as part of China	PRC designates ninety-two new global companies with incorrect references to Taiwan/ Hong Kong/Macau as separate from China

(continued)

YEAR	COUNTRY	COMPANY	TARGETED ACTION	CHINA'S COERCION
2019	Germany	Allianz Insurance Group	Website fails to label Taiwan or Hong Kong as part of China	PRC designates ninety-two new global companies with incorrect references to Taiwan/Hong Kong/Macau as separate from China
2019	Germany	Bayer AG	Website fails to label Taiwan or Hong Kong as part of China	PRC designates ninety-two new global companies with incorrect references to Taiwan/Hong Kong/Macau as separate from China
2019	Germany	Boehringer Ingelheim	Website fails to label Taiwan or Hong Kong as part of China	PRC designates ninety-two new global companies with incorrect references to Taiwan/Hong Kong/Macau as separate from China
2019	Germany	Bosch Group	Website fails to label Taiwan, Hong Kong, or Macau as part of China	PRC designates ninety-two new global companies with incorrect references to Taiwan/Hong Kong/Macau as separate from China
2019	Germany	DZ Bank	Website fails to label Hong Kong as part of China	PRC designates ninety-two new global companies with incorrect references to Taiwan/Hong Kong/Macau as separate from China
2019	Germany	Continental	Website fails to label Taiwan as part of China	PRC designates ninety-two new global companies with incorrect references to Taiwan/Hong Kong/Macau as separate from China

YEAR	COUNTRY	COMPANY	TARGETED ACTION	CHINA'S COERCION
2019	Germany	Heraeus	Website fails to label Taiwan, Hong Kong as part of China	PRC designates ninety-two new global companies with incorrect references to Taiwan/Hong Kong/Macau as separate from China
2019	Germany	Leica	Advertisement glorifies Tiananmen Square protests	PRC blocks Leica from Weibo; public backlash
2019	Germany	Munich Re	Website fails to label Taiwan as part of China	PRC designates ninety-two new global companies with incorrect references to Taiwan/Hong Kong/Macau as separate from China
2019	Germany	Tempo	Firm stops ads on pro-Beijing TVB over Hong Kong	Netizen attacks and calls for boycott
2019	Germany	Siemens	References to Taiwan as independent country	Social media boycott, brand ambassadors terminate contracts, stores vandalized
2019	Germany	Volkswagen	Website fails to label Taiwan as part of China	PRC designates ninety-two new global companies with incorrect references to Taiwan/Hong Kong/Macau as separate from China
2019	India	State Bank of India	Website fails to label Hong Kong as part of China	PRC designates ninety-two new global companies with incorrect references to Taiwan/Hong Kong/Macau as separate from China

(continued)

YEAR	COUNTRY	COMPANY	TARGETED ACTION	CHINA'S COERCION
2019	Italy	Eni SpA	Website fails to label Taiwan as part of China	PRC designates ninety-two new global companies with incorrect references to Taiwan/Hong Kong/Macau as separate from China
2019	Italy	Valentino	Website does not recognize Hong Kong or Taiwan as part of China	Anti-Valentino boycott goes viral on Weibo
2019	Italy	Versace	T-shirt design does not recognize Hong Kong or Macau as part of China	Anti-Versace boycott goes viral, brand ambassador Yang Mi quits
2019	Japan	Bridgestone	Website fails to label Taiwan as part of China	PRC designates ninety-two new global companies with incorrect references to Taiwan/Hong Kong/Macau as separate from China
2019	Japan	Itochu Corporation	Website fails to label Taiwan as part of China	PRC designates ninety-two new global companies with incorrect references to Taiwan/Hong Kong/Macau as separate from China
2019	Japan	ASICS	Website does not recognize Hong Kong, Taiwan as part of China	Anti-ASICS boycott goes viral on Weibo
2019	Japan	Canon	Website fails to label Taiwan or Hong Kong as part of China	PRC designates ninety-two new global companies with incorrect references to Taiwan/Hong Kong/Macau as separate from China

YEAR	COUNTRY	COMPANY	TARGETED ACTION	CHINA'S COERCION
2019	Japan	Idemitsu Kosan	Website fails to label Taiwan as part of China	PRC designates ninety-two new global companies with incorrect references to Taiwan/Hong Kong/Macau as separate from China
2019	Japan	Japan Mitsubishi Heavy Industries Co., Ltd.	Website fails to label Taiwan or Hong Kong as part of China	PRC designates ninety-two new global companies with incorrect references to Taiwan/Hong Kong/Macau as separate from China
2019	Japan	JFE Holdings	Website fails to label Taiwan as part of China	PRC designates ninety-two new global companies with incorrect references to Taiwan/Hong Kong/Macau as separate from China
2019	Japan	JXTG Holdings Ltd.	Website fails to label Taiwan as part of China	PRC designates ninety-two new global companies with incorrect references to Taiwan/Hong Kong/Macau as separate from China
2019	Japan	KDDI Corporation	Website fails to label Taiwan or Hong Kong as part of China	PRC designates ninety-two new global companies with incorrect references to Taiwan/Hong Kong/Macau as separate from China

(continued)

YEAR	COUNTRY	COMPANY	TARGETED ACTION	CHINA'S COERCION
2019	Japan	Marubeni Corporation	Website fails to label Taiwan as part of China	PRC designates ninety-two new global companies with incorrect references to Taiwan/Hong Kong/Macau as separate from China
2019	Japan	Mitsubishi	Website fails to label Taiwan as part of China	PRC designates ninety-two new global companies with incorrect references to Taiwan/Hong Kong/Macau as separate from China
2019	Japan	Mitsubishi UFJ Financial Group	Website fails to label Taiwan or Hong Kong as part of China	PRC designates ninety-two new global companies with incorrect references to Taiwan/Hong Kong/Macau as separate from China
2019	Japan	MS&AD Insurance Group Holdings Limited	Website fails to label Taiwan, Hong Kong, or Macau as part of China	PRC designates ninety-two new global companies with incorrect references to Taiwan/Hong Kong/Macau as separate from China
2019	Japan	Nissan	Website fails to label Taiwan or Hong Kong as part of China	PRC designates ninety-two new global companies with incorrect references to Taiwan/Hong Kong/Macau as separate from China
2019	Japan	Pocari Sweat	Firm stops ads on pro-Beijing TVB over Hong Kong	Netizen attacks and calls for boycott; brand ambassadors terminate contracts

YEAR	COUNTRY	COMPANY	TARGETED ACTION	CHINA'S COERCION
2019	Japan	Sumitomo Electric Industries	Website fails to label Taiwan or Hong Kong as part of China	PRC designates ninety-two new global companies with incorrect references to Taiwan/Hong Kong/Macau as separate from China
2019	Japan	Toshiba	Website fails to label Taiwan or Hong Kong as part of China	PRC designates ninety-two new global companies with incorrect references to Taiwan/Hong Kong/Macau as separate from China
2019	Japan	Undercover	Company founder posts on Instagram supporting Hong Kong protestors	Protests on Instagram; pressure causes Nike to end design collaboration with firm
2019	Japan	Yoshinoya	Employee posts pro-Hong Kong Facebook post	Weibo boycott of Yoshinoya
2019	Luxembourg	ArcelorMittal	Website fails to label Taiwan as part of China	PRC designates ninety-two new global companies with incorrect references to Taiwan/Hong Kong/Macau as separate from China
2019	Netherlands	ING Group	Website fails to label Taiwan as part of China	PRC designates ninety-two new global companies with incorrect references to Taiwan/Hong Kong/Macau as separate from China
2019	Netherlands	KPMG	Ad supportive of Hong Kong protestors	Threats to KPMG from *Global Times* and Weibo

(continued)

YEAR	COUNTRY	COMPANY	TARGETED ACTION	CHINA'S COERCION
2019	Netherlands	LyondellBasell Industries	Website fails to label Taiwan as part of China	PRC designates ninety-two new global companies with incorrect references to Taiwan/Hong Kong/Macau as separate from China
2019	Netherlands	Philips	Website fails to label Taiwan as part of China	PRC designates ninety-two new global companies with incorrect references to Taiwan/Hong Kong/Macau as separate from China
2019	New Zealand	Air New Zealand	References to Taiwan as independent country	PRC refuses landing of flights in China; apology
2019	Singapore	Wilmar International	Website fails to label Taiwan as part of China	PRC designates ninety-two new global companies with incorrect references to Taiwan/Hong Kong/Macau as separate from China
2019	South Korea	Hanwha Group	Website fails to label Taiwan as part of China	PRC designates ninety-two new global companies with incorrect references to Taiwan/Hong Kong/Macau as separate from China
2019	South Korea	Hyundai	Website fails to label Taiwan as part of China	PRC designates ninety-two new global companies with incorrect references to Taiwan/Hong Kong/Macau as separate from China

YEAR	COUNTRY	COMPANY	TARGETED ACTION	CHINA'S COERCION
2019	South Korea	KB Financial Group	Website fails to label Hong Kong as part of China	PRC designates ninety-two new global companies with incorrect references to Taiwan/Hong Kong/ Macau as separate from China
2019	South Korea	Samsung Electronics	Website fails to label Taiwan or Hong Kong as part of China	PRC designates ninety-two new global companies with incorrect references to Taiwan/Hong Kong/ Macau as separate from China
2019	South Korea	Samsung Electronics	United States adds Huawei to banned entity list	PRC threatens Samsung with consequences for honoring U.S. ban
2019	South Korea	SK	United States adds Huawei to banned entity list	PRC threatens SK with consequences for honoring U.S. ban
2019	Spain	ACS	Website fails to label Hong Kong as part of China	PRC designates ninety-two new global companies with incorrect references to Taiwan/Hong Kong/ Macau as separate from China
2019	Spain	Repsol	Website fails to label Taiwan as part of China	PRC designates ninety-two new global companies with incorrect references to Taiwan/Hong Kong/ Macau as separate from China
2019	Spain	Zara (Inditex)	Stores open late; seen as pro–Hong Kong action	Viral backlash calling for boycott on social media; company apologizes

(continued)

YEAR	COUNTRY	COMPANY	TARGETED ACTION	CHINA'S COERCION
2019	Sweden	Ericsson	Website fails to label Taiwan or Hong Kong as part of China	PRC designates ninety-two new global companies with incorrect references to Taiwan/Hong Kong/Macau as separate from China
2019	Switzerland	Chubb Limited	Website fails to label Taiwan or Hong Kong as part of China	PRC designates ninety-two new global companies with incorrect references to Taiwan/Hong Kong/Macau as separate from China
2019	Switzerland	Credit Suisse	Website fails to label Taiwan as part of China	PRC designates ninety-two new global companies with incorrect references to Taiwan/Hong Kong/Macau as separate from China
2019	Switzerland	Novartis	Website fails to label Taiwan or Hong Kong as part of China	PRC designates ninety-two new global companies with incorrect references to Taiwan/Hong Kong/Macau as separate from China
2019	Switzerland	Roche Switzerland	Website fails to label Taiwan as part of China	PRC designates ninety-two new global companies with incorrect references to Taiwan/Hong Kong/Macau as separate from China
2019	Switzerland	Zurich Insurance Group	Website fails to label Taiwan or Hong Kong as part of China	PRC designates ninety-two new global companies with incorrect references to Taiwan/Hong Kong/Macau as separate from China

YEAR	COUNTRY	COMPANY	TARGETED ACTION	CHINA'S COERCION
2019	Taiwan	Gong Cha	Accused of advocating for Hong Kong	Public backlash, calls for boycott
2019	Taiwan	CoCo	Store receipt supporting Hong Kong goes viral	Calls for boycott; local store is closed
2019	Taiwan	Red Candle Games	Video game (*Devotion*) references Xi Jinping as Winnie-the-Pooh	Public boycott and removal of game from Chinese market
2019	Taiwan	Wu Pao Chun Bakery	Accused of advocating Taiwan independence	Boycott of stores in China
2019	Taiwan	Yi Fang Fruit Tea	Local branch closes in support of Hong Kong	Public backlash, calls for boycott
2019	United Kingdom	ARM	United States adds Huawei to banned entity list	PRC threatens consequences for honoring U.S. ban
2019	United Kingdom	BT Group	Website fails to label Hong Kong as part of China	PRC designates ninety-two new global companies with incorrect references to Taiwan/Hong Kong/Macau as separate from China
2019	United Kingdom	Centrica plc	Website fails to label Hong Kong as part of China	PRC designates ninety-two new global companies with incorrect references to Taiwan/Hong Kong/Macau as separate from China
2019	United Kingdom	Arsenal	Star player expresses support for Uyghurs	Arsenal games blocked on CCTV; player's social media account blocked in China

(*continued*)

YEAR	COUNTRY	COMPANY	TARGETED ACTION	CHINA'S COERCION
2019	United Kingdom	British American Tobacco plc	Website fails to label Taiwan or Hong Kong as part of China	PRC designates ninety-two new global companies with incorrect references to Taiwan/Hong Kong/Macau as separate from China
2019	United Kingdom	Compass Group plc	Website fails to label Taiwan or Hong Kong as part of China	PRC designates ninety-two new global companies with incorrect references to Taiwan/Hong Kong/Macau as separate from China
2019	United Kingdom	Deloitte	Newspaper ad supporting Hong Kong	*Global Times* and Weibo protest, call for firing; company apologizes
2019	United Kingdom	Ernst & Young (EY)	Newspaper ad supporting Hong Kong	*Global Times* and Weibo protest, call for firing; company apologizes
2019	United Kingdom	PwC	Newspaper ad supporting Hong Kong	*Global Times* and Weibo protest, call for firing; company apologizes
2019	United Kingdom	Tesco	Website fails to label Taiwan as part of China	PRC designates ninety-two new global companies with incorrect references to Taiwan/Hong Kong/Macau as separate from China
2019	United Kingdom	Vodafone Group	Website fails to label Taiwan or Hong Kong as part of China	PRC designates ninety-two new global companies with incorrect references to Taiwan/Hong Kong/Macau as separate from China

YEAR	COUNTRY	COMPANY	TARGETED ACTION	CHINA'S COERCION
2019	United Kingdom	Wizarding World	Harry Potter website does not recognize Taiwan as part of China	Public backlash calling for boycott of website and Harry Potter
2019	United States	NBA	Houston Rockets general manager tweets support for Hong Kong	Suspension of business ties, sanctions on NBA streaming and merchandise
2019	United States	Apple	United States adds Huawei to banned entity list	PRC threatens consequences for honoring U.S. ban
2019	United States	MAC Cosmetics	Advertisement does not recognize Taiwan as part of China	Incites netizen backlash; MAC apologizes and pulls down content
2019	United States	AbbVie	Website fails to label Taiwan or Hong Kong as part of China	PRC designates ninety-two new global companies with incorrect references to Taiwan/Hong Kong/Macau as separate from China
2019	United States	Aetna	Website fails to label Hong Kong as part of China	PRC designates ninety-two new global companies with incorrect references to Taiwan/Hong Kong/Macau as separate from China
2019	United States	American International Group	Website fails to label Taiwan, Hong Kong, or Macau as part of China	PRC designates ninety-two new global companies with incorrect references to Taiwan/Hong Kong/Macau as separate from China
2019	United States	Apple	Launches app that crowdsources police location in Hong Kong	State media criticize Apple, demands removal of app

(continued)

YEAR	COUNTRY	COMPANY	TARGETED ACTION	CHINA'S COERCION
2019	United States	Amazon	T-shirts selling on platform supporting Hong Kong	Viral protests and boycott; company apologizes
2019	United States	Blizzard Entertainment	Advertisement does not recognize Hong Kong as part of China	Viral backlash calling for boycott on social media; company apologizes
2019	United States	Bunge Global SA	Website fails to label Taiwan as part of China	PRC designates ninety-two new global companies with incorrect references to Taiwan/Hong Kong/Macau as separate from China
2019	United States	Calvin Klein	Website does not recognize Hong Kong as part of China	Viral protests and boycott, brand ambassador quits; company apologizes
2019	United States	CHS Inc.	Website fails to label Taiwan as part of China	PRC designates ninety-two new global companies with incorrect references to Taiwan/Hong Kong/Macau as separate from China
2019	United States	Cigna	Website fails to label Taiwan or Hong Kong as part of China	PRC designates ninety-two new global companies with incorrect references to Taiwan/Hong Kong/Macau as separate from China
2019	United States	Cisco	Website fails to label Taiwan or Hong Kong as part of China	PRC designates ninety-two new global companies with incorrect references to Taiwan/Hong Kong/Macau as separate from China

YEAR	COUNTRY	COMPANY	TARGETED ACTION	CHINA'S COERCION
2019	United States	Citigroup	Website fails to label Taiwan, Hong Kong, or Macau as part of China	PRC designates ninety-two new global companies with incorrect references to Taiwan/Hong Kong/Macau as separate from China
2019	United States	Comedy Central	South Park episode is critical of China	South Park banned from Chinese websites
2019	United States	Dell	United States adds Huawei to banned entity list	PRC threatens consequences for honoring U.S. ban
2019	United States	DXC Technology	Website fails to label Taiwan or Hong Kong as part of China	PRC designates ninety-two new global companies with incorrect references to Taiwan/Hong Kong/Macau as separate from China
2019	United States	FedEx	FedEx misroutes Huawei packages	PRC raid, investigation
2019	United States	FedEx	Sending packages to Hong Kong protestors	Local offices are raided and investigated
2019	United States	Fresh	Website does not recognize Hong Kong as part of China	Weibo online campaign to boycott; company apologizes
2019	United States	Gilead Sciences	Website fails to label Taiwan or Hong Kong as part of China	PRC designates ninety-two new global companies with incorrect references to Taiwan/Hong Kong/Macau as separate from China
2019	United States	Google	Publishes game supportive of Hong Kong protests	Public backlash; Google takes game down

(continued)

YEAR	COUNTRY	COMPANY	TARGETED ACTION	CHINA'S COERCION
2019	United States	Hewlett Packard Enterprise	Website fails to label Taiwan or Hong Kong as part of China	PRC designates ninety-two new global companies with incorrect references to Taiwan/Hong Kong/Macau as separate from China
2019	United States	IBM	Website fails to label Taiwan as part of China	PRC designates ninety-two new global companies with incorrect references to Taiwan/Hong Kong/Macau as separate from China
2019	United States	JPMorgan Chase & Co.	Website fails to label Taiwan or Hong Kong as part of China	PRC designates ninety-two new global companies with incorrect references to Taiwan/Hong Kong/Macau as separate from China
2019	United States	Lockheed Martin	Website fails to label Taiwan as part of China	PRC designates ninety-two new global companies with incorrect references to Taiwan/Hong Kong/Macau as separate from China
2019	United States	Lowe's Companies	Website fails to label Taiwan or Hong Kong as part of China	PRC designates ninety-two new global companies with incorrect references to Taiwan/Hong Kong/Macau as separate from China
2019	United States	Marvel	Film *Shang-Chi* portrays Chinese character as villain	Movie's release is blocked in China
2019	United States	McDonald's	Airs ad suggesting Taiwan as independent country	Weibo and WeChat boycotts of McDonalds; apology

YEAR	COUNTRY	COMPANY	TARGETED ACTION	CHINA'S COERCION
2019	United States	Microsoft	Website fails to label Taiwan as part of China	PRC designates ninety-two new global companies with incorrect references to Taiwan/Hong Kong/Macau as separate from China
2019	United States	Microsoft	United States adds Huawei to banned entity list	PRC threatens consequences for honoring U.S. ban
2019	United States	PepsiCo	Website fails to label Taiwan as part of China	PRC designates ninety-two new global companies with incorrect references to Taiwan/Hong Kong/Macau as separate from China
2019	United States	Pfizer	Website fails to label Taiwan or Hong Kong as part of China	PRC designates ninety-two new global companies with incorrect references to Taiwan/Hong Kong/Macau as separate from China
2019	United States	Philip Morris International	Website fails to label Taiwan or Hong Kong as part of China	PRC designates ninety-two new global companies with incorrect references to Taiwan/Hong Kong/Macau as separate from China
2019	United States	Prudential Financial	Website fails to label Taiwan or Hong Kong as part of China	PRC designates ninety-two new global companies with incorrect references to Taiwan/Hong Kong/Macau as separate from China

(continued)

YEAR	COUNTRY	COMPANY	TARGETED ACTION	CHINA'S COERCION
2019	United States	Refinitiv	Publicizes Western stories regarding thirtieth anniversary of Tiananmen Square	PRC cyber ministry suspends company
2019	United States	Sheraton Hotels and Resorts	The Sheraton resort in Stockholm hosts Taiwan national day celebration	Chinese embassy forces Sheraton to pull down venue
2019	United States	Sysco	Website fails to label Taiwan, Hong Kong, or Macau as part of China	PRC designates ninety-two new global companies with incorrect references to Taiwan/ Hong Kong/Macau as separate from China
2019	United States	Valve Corporation	Game ridicules Xi Jinping	Incites backlash; game removed from China market
2019	United States	Vans	Sneaker design contest features Hong Kong flag motif	Viral backlash calling for boycott on social media; company apologizes
2019	United States	Tech Data Corporation	Website fails to label Hong Kong as part of China	PRC designates ninety-two new global companies with incorrect references to Taiwan/ Hong Kong/Macau as separate from China
2019	United States	*Wall Street Journal*	Publishes article critical of Xi Jinping family	Foreign ministry denies reporter credentials, expelled from country
2019	United States	Tiffany & Co.	Advertisement suggests sympathy with Hong Kong protests	Viral backlash calling for boycott on social media; company apologizes

YEAR	COUNTRY	COMPANY	TARGETED ACTION	CHINA'S COERCION
2019	United States	Time Warner	Website fails to label Hong Kong as part of China	PRC designates ninety-two new global companies with incorrect references to Taiwan/Hong Kong/Macau as separate from China
2019	United States	Warner Bros. (Taiwan)	Releases movie critical of China-Taiwan	Product is banned in China
2019	United States	Walt Disney Company	Website fails to label Taiwan as part of China	PRC designates ninety-two new global companies with incorrect references to Taiwan/Hong Kong/Macau as separate from China
2019	United States	World Fuel Services	Website fails to label Taiwan or Hong Kong as part of China	PRC designates ninety-two new global companies with incorrect references to Taiwan/Hong Kong/Macau as separate from China
2020	Australia	Accolade Wines	Australian government calls for independent investigation into origins of COVID	PRC government places 170 percent tariff on Accolade wine
2020	Australia	Australian Vintage	Australian government calls for independent investigation into origins of COVID	PRC government places 160 percent tariff on Australian Vintage wine
2020	Australia	Badger's Brook Estate Wines	Australian government calls for independent investigation into origins of COVID	PRC government places major tariff on Australian wines
2020	Australia	Brown Brothers	Australian government calls for independent investigation into origins of COVID	PRC government places 160 percent tariff on Brown Brothers wine

(continued)

YEAR	COUNTRY	COMPANY	TARGETED ACTION	CHINA'S COERCION
2020	Australia	Casella Wines	Australian government calls for independent investigation into origins of COVID	PRC government places 170 percent tariff on Casella wine
2020	Australia	Randall Wine Group	Australian government calls for independent investigation into origins of COVID	PRC government places major tariff on Australian wines
2020	Australia	Treasury Wine Estates	Australian government calls for independent investigation into origins of COVID	PRC government places 175 percent tariff on Penfolds wine
2020	Canada	Lululemon	Instagram post critical of China and COVID	Viral backlash calling for boycott on social media; company apologizes, employee fired
2020	Czechia	Home Credit Group	Senate speaker Jaroslav Kubera plans trip to Taiwan	Chinese embassy (Prague) warns Czech companies will "suffer" if visit takes place
2020	Czechia	Petrof Pianos	Senate speaker Kubera plans trip to Taiwan	Chinese embassy (Prague) warns Czech companies will "suffer" if visit takes place; cancels piano orders
2020	Czechia	Skoda Auto	Senate speaker Kubera plans trip to Taiwan	Chinese embassy (Prague) warns Czech companies will "suffer" if visit takes place
2020	France	Champagne Deutz	Facebook posts critical of China and COVID	Viral backlash calling for boycott on social media; company apologizes
2020	Italy	Bottega Spa	Letter by owner surfaces blaming China for pandemic	Viral backlash calling for boycott on social media; company apologizes

YEAR	COUNTRY	COMPANY	TARGETED ACTION	CHINA'S COERCION
2020	Japan	Cover (Hololive)	Popular VTubers display Taiwan flag	Viral backlash calling for boycott on social media; VTubers suspended
2020	Japan	Nintendo	Releases game used as vehicle for Hong Kong protests	Government blocks online sale of game
2020	Poland	GOG Ltd	Releases game that ridicules Xi Jinping	Viral backlash calling for boycott on social media; game release canceled
2020	South Korea	Big Hit Entertainment	BTS makes statement praising U.S. and South Korean sacrifices in Korean War	Viral backlash calling for boycott on social media
2020	South Korea	SBS	Korean drama has scene suggesting Taiwan independence	Viral backlash calling for boycott on social media; show is censored in China
2020	Sweden	Ericsson	Bans Huawei technology from 5G network	Government restricts Ericsson share of China mobile market
2020	Thailand	GMM Grammy	Thai TV actor tweets support for Hong Kong	Viral backlash calling for boycott on social media
2020	United Kingdom	Nature	Attributes COVID origins to Wuhan, China	PRC government criticizes the journal; journal issues apology
2020	United Kingdom	Ndemic Creations	Releases video game about pandemic insulting to China	PRC cyber agency bans game in China
2020	United States	Amazon	T-shirts selling on platform critical of China and COVID	Viral backlash calling for boycott on social media

(*continued*)

YEAR	COUNTRY	COMPANY	TARGETED ACTION	CHINA'S COERCION
2020	United States	Boeing	Arms sales to Taiwan	Government sanctions companies and individuals
2020	United States	Burger King	Facebook posts critical of China and COVID	Viral backlash calling for boycott on social media
2020	United States	Lockheed Martin	Arms sales to Taiwan	Government sanctions companies and individuals
2020	United States	Raytheon	Arms sales to Taiwan	Government sanctions companies and individuals
2020	United States	*New York Times*	Trump limits number of journalists in the United States working for Chinese state media	Foreign ministry revokes press credentials for *New York Times*, *Wall Street Journal*, and *Washington Post*
2020	United States	*Wall Street Journal*	Publishes op-ed critical of China and COVID	Foreign ministry protests the article, revokes visas for three reporters
2020	United States	*Washington Post*	Trump limits number of journalists in the United States working for Chinese state media	Foreign ministry revokes press credentials for *New York Times*, *Wall Street Journal*, and *Washington Post*
2020	United States	*Time* magazine	Trump limits number of journalists in the United States working for Chinese state media	Foreign ministry revokes press credentials for U.S. journalists
2020	United States	Voice of America	Trump limits number of journalists in the United States working for Chinese state media	Foreign ministry revokes press credentials for U.S. journalists

YEAR	COUNTRY	COMPANY	TARGETED ACTION	CHINA'S COERCION
2020	United States	Zoom	Platform allows meetings/events related to Tiananmen remembrances	Government pressures Zoom to disable use, demands IP addresses; Zoom complies
2021	France	Lacoste	Announces will not source cotton from Xinjiang	Viral backlash calling for boycott on social media, brand ambassador quits
2021	Germany	Puma	Announces will not source cotton from Xinjiang	Viral backlash calling for boycott on social media, brand ambassador quits
2021	Germany	Adidas	Announces will not source cotton from Xinjiang	Viral backlash calling for boycott on social media, brand ambassador quits
2021	Germany	Continental	Lithuania hosts Taiwan representative office opening	China imposes secondary sanctions
2021	Germany	Hugo Boss	Announces will not source cotton from Xinjiang	Viral backlash calling for boycott on social media, brand ambassador quits
2021	Japan	Uniqlo	Announces will not source cotton from Xinjiang	Viral backlash calling for boycott on social media, brand ambassador quits
2021	Japan	ASICS	Announces will not source cotton from Xinjiang	Viral backlash calling for boycott on social media, brand ambassador quits
2021	Lithuania	MV Group Production	Lithuania hosts Taiwan representative office opening	China blocks import of products
2021	Lithuania	Thermo Fisher Scientific Baltics	Lithuania hosts Taiwan representative office opening	China blocks operations of company in China

(*continued*)

YEAR	COUNTRY	COMPANY	TARGETED ACTION	CHINA'S COERCION
2021	South Korea	Big Hit Entertainment	Company financial report mistakenly lists Tibet as part of India	Viral backlash calling for boycott on social media
2021	Spain	Zara (Inditex)	Announces will not source cotton from Xinjiang	Viral backlash calling for boycott on social media; withdraws announcement
2021	Sweden	H&M	Announces will not source cotton from Xinjiang	Viral backlash calling for boycott on social media; withdraws announcement
2021	Taiwan	Far Eastern Group	Makes political donations to DPP	China imposes fines and NTBs on operations in China
2021	United Kingdom	BBC	Revokes broadcast license for CCP-run CGTN	PRC bans BBC
2021	United Kingdom	Burberry	Announces will not source cotton from Xinjiang	Viral backlash calling for boycott on social media, brand ambassador quits
2021	United States	Intel	Announces will not source materials from Xinjiang	Viral backlash calling for boycott on social media, brand ambassador quits; apology
2021	United States	LinkedIn	Does not control content critical of China	Chinese regulators demand censorship; company complies
2021	United States	Tommy Hilfiger	Announces will not source cotton from Xinjiang	Viral backlash calling for boycott on social media, brand ambassador quits
2021	United States	Nike	Announces will not source cotton from Xinjiang	Viral backlash calling for boycott on social media, brand ambassador quits

YEAR	COUNTRY	COMPANY	TARGETED ACTION	CHINA'S COERCION
2021	United States	Kodak	Publishes photos on website critical of Xinjiang	Viral backlash calling for boycott on social media; Kodak apologizes, removes photos
2021	United States	Marvel	Academy Awardee director Chloe Zhao speaks negatively of China	Movie (*The Eternals*) is banned in China
2021	United States	New Balance	Announces will not source cotton from Xinjiang	Viral backlash calling for boycott on social media
2021	United States	Under Armour	Announces will not source cotton from Xinjiang	Viral backlash calling for boycott on social media
2021	United States	Sam's Club	Removes Xinjiang-sourced items from sale	Viral backlash calling for boycott on social media
2021	United States	Searchlight Pictures	Academy Awardee director Chloe Zhao speaks negatively of China	Movie (*Nomadland*) is banned in China; Zhao is censored
2021	United States	Calvin Klein	Announces will not source cotton from Xinjiang	Viral backlash calling for boycott on social media, brand ambassador quits
2021	United States	Converse	Announces will not source cotton from Xinjiang	Viral backlash calling for boycott on social media, brand ambassador quits
2022	Lithuania	Klassmann-Deilmann Lietuva	Lithuania hosts Taiwan representative office opening	China blocks import of products to China
2022	Taiwan	Kuang Ta Hsiang Foodstuffs Co.	Nancy Pelosi visits Taiwan	Chinese customs bans thousands of food imports from Taiwan

(continued)

YEAR	COUNTRY	COMPANY	TARGETED ACTION	CHINA'S COERCION
2022	Taiwan	Ve Wong	Nancy Pelosi visits Taiwan	Chinese customs bans thousands of food imports from Taiwan
2022	Taiwan	Vitalon	Nancy Pelosi visits Taiwan	Chinese customs bans more than a hundred beverage products from Taiwan
2022	Taiwan	Wei Lih Food	Nancy Pelosi visits Taiwan	Chinese customs bans thousands of food imports from Taiwan
2022	Taiwan	A.G.V. Products	Nancy Pelosi visits Taiwan	Chinese customs bans thousands of food imports from Taiwan
2022	Taiwan	Chi Mei	Nancy Pelosi visits Taiwan	Chinese customs bans thousands of food imports from Taiwan
2022	Taiwan	Chia Te Bakery	Nancy Pelosi visits Taiwan	Chinese customs bans thousands of food imports from Taiwan
2022	Taiwan	HeySong Corp.	Nancy Pelosi visits Taiwan	Chinese customs bans beer and distilled spirits from Taiwan
2022	Taiwan	Imei Foods Co.	Nancy Pelosi visits Taiwan	Chinese customs bans thousands of food imports from Taiwan
2022	Taiwan	Kavalan Whisky	Nancy Pelosi visits Taiwan	Chinese customs bans beer and distilled spirits from Taiwan
2022	Taiwan	Kinmen Kaoliang Liquor Inc.	Nancy Pelosi visits Taiwan	Chinese customs bans beer and distilled spirits from Taiwan
2022	Taiwan	King Car Group	Nancy Pelosi visits Taiwan	Chinese customs bans thousands of food imports from Taiwan
2022	Taiwan	Kuai Kuai Co.	Nancy Pelosi visits Taiwan	Chinese customs bans thousands of food imports from Taiwan

YEAR	COUNTRY	COMPANY	TARGETED ACTION	CHINA'S COERCION
2022	Taiwan	Kuo Yuan Ye Corp.	Nancy Pelosi visits Taiwan	Chinese customs bans thousands of food imports from Taiwan
2022	Taiwan	Legend Brewery	Nancy Pelosi visits Taiwan	Chinese customs bans beer and distilled spirits from Taiwan
2022	Taiwan	Nin Jiom Medicine	Nancy Pelosi visits Taiwan	Chinese customs bans more than a hundred beverage products from Taiwan
2022	Taiwan	Oceanic Beverage	Nancy Pelosi visits Taiwan	Chinese customs bans more than a hundred beverage products from Taiwan
2022	Taiwan	Taihu Brewing	Nancy Pelosi visits Taiwan	Chinese customs bans beer and distilled spirits from Taiwan
2022	Taiwan	Taisun Enterprise Co.	Nancy Pelosi visits Taiwan	Chinese customs bans more than a hundred beverage products from Taiwan
2022	Taiwan	Taiwan Tobacco & Liquor Corporation	Nancy Pelosi visits Taiwan	Chinese customs bans beer and distilled spirits from Taiwan
2022	Taiwan	Uni-President	Nancy Pelosi visits Taiwan	Chinese customs bans more than a hundred beverage products from Taiwan
2022	Taiwan	Wei Chuan Foods Corp.	Nancy Pelosi visits Taiwan	Chinese customs bans more than a hundred beverage products from Taiwan
2022	Taiwan	Win Shan International Co.	Nancy Pelosi visits Taiwan	Chinese customs bans thousands of food imports from Taiwan

(continued)

YEAR	COUNTRY	COMPANY	TARGETED ACTION	CHINA'S COERCION
2022	Taiwan	Yu Jan Shin	Nancy Pelosi visits Taiwan	Chinese customs bans thousands of food imports from Taiwan
2022	Taiwan	Yunshan Distillery	Nancy Pelosi visits Taiwan	Chinese customs bans beer and distilled spirits from Taiwan
2022	United States	Mars Wrigley	Ad for new Snickers bar refers to Taiwan as country	Viral backlash calling for boycott on social media; company apologizes
2022	United States	Sony Pictures	Releases Spiderman movie with Statue of Liberty scene	Movie is banned in China
2022	United States	Walmart	Removes Xinjiang-sourced items from sale	Viral backlash calling for boycott on social media
2023	Italy	Bulgari	Website lists Taiwan separately from China	Viral backlash calling for boycott on social media, brand ambassador quits; apology
2023	Japan	Kose Corp.	Japanese releases treated water from Fukushima plant	Viral backlash calling for boycott of Japan cosmetics on social media
2023	Japan	Pola Orbis Holdings Inc.	Japanese releases treated water from Fukushima plant	Viral backlash calling for boycott of Japan cosmetics on social media
2023	Japan	Shiseido Co.	Japanese releases treated water from Fukushima plant	Viral backlash calling for boycott of Japan cosmetics on social media
2023	United Kingdom	Altitude Film Distribution	Winnie-the-Pooh movie release in Hong Kong and Macau	Bans release in China

YEAR	COUNTRY	COMPANY	TARGETED ACTION	CHINA'S COERCION
2023	United States	Boeing	Arms sale to Taiwan	PRC foreign ministry sanctions Boeing CEO
2023	United States	Lockheed Martin	Arms sale to Taiwan	PRC foreign ministry sanctions Lockheed leadership
2023	United States	Micron	G7 Summit in Hiroshima is critical of China	PRC cyber agency imposes sanctions on Micron
2023	United States	Mintz Group	Conducts due diligence work regarding forced labor in Xinjiang	Offices are raided, employees arrested
2023	United States	Raytheon	Arms sale to Taiwan	PRC foreign ministry sanctions Raytheon leadership
2024	Taiwan	Evergreen Group	Failure to display Chinese national flag in hotel lobby	Viral backlash calling for boycott on social media; hotel apologizes, all flags removed
2024	United Kingdom	PwC	Failed due diligence on Evergrande	Suspended for six months, fined
2024	United States	BAE Systems Land and Armament	Arms sale to Taiwan	Freezes properties and assets in China, prohibits transactions
2024	United States	Alliant Techsystems Operation	Arms sale to Taiwan	Freezes properties and assets in China, prohibits transactions
2024	United States	AeroVironment	Arms sale to Taiwan	Freezes properties and assets in China, prohibits transactions
2024	United States	ViaSat	Arms sale to Taiwan	Freezes properties and assets in China, prohibits transactions
2024	United States	Data Link Solutions	Arms sale to Taiwan	Freezes properties and assets in China, prohibits transactions

(continued)

YEAR	COUNTRY	COMPANY	TARGETED ACTION	CHINA'S COERCION
2024	United States	General Atomics Aeronautical Systems	Arms sale to Taiwan	Bars imports, exports, and investments and bans senior leadership from visiting China
2024	United States	General Dynamics Land Systems	Arms sale to Taiwan	Bars imports, exports, and investments and bans senior leadership from visiting China
2024	United States	Boeing	Arms sale to Taiwan	Bars imports, exports, and investments and bans senior leadership from visiting China
2024	United States	Lockheed Martin Missiles and Fire Control	Arms sale to Taiwan	Adds to unreliable entity list; bars imports, exports, and investments and bans senior leadership from visiting China
2024	United States	Lockheed Martin Aeronautics	Arms sale to Taiwan	Adds to unreliable entity list; bars imports, exports, and investments and bans senior leadership from visiting China
2024	United States	Raytheon/ Lockheed Martin Javelin Joint Venture	Arms sale to Taiwan	Adds to unreliable entity list; bars imports, exports, and investments and bans senior leadership from visiting China
2024	United States	Raytheon Missile Systems	Arms sale to Taiwan	Adds to unreliable entity list; bars imports, exports, and investments and bans senior leadership from visiting China

YEAR	COUNTRY	COMPANY	TARGETED ACTION	CHINA'S COERCION
2024	United States	General Dynamics Ordnance and Tactical Systems	Arms sale to Taiwan	Adds to unreliable entity list; bars imports, exports, and investments and bans senior leadership from visiting China
2024	United States	General Dynamics Information Technology	Arms sale to Taiwan	Adds to unreliable entity list; bars imports, exports, and investments and bans senior leadership from visiting China
2024	United States	General Dynamics Mission Systems	Arms sale to Taiwan	Adds to unreliable entity list; bars imports, exports, and investments and bans senior leadership from visiting China
2024	United States	Inter-Coastal Electronics, System Studies & Simulation	Arms sale to Taiwan	Adds to unreliable entity list; bars imports, exports, and investments and bans senior leadership from visiting China
2024	United States	IronMountain Solutions	Arms sale to Taiwan	Adds to unreliable entity list; bars imports, exports, and investments and bans senior leadership from visiting China
2024	United States	Applied Technologies Group	Arms sale to Taiwan	Adds to unreliable entity list; bars imports, exports, and investments and bans senior leadership from visiting China

(continued)

YEAR	COUNTRY	COMPANY	TARGETED ACTION	CHINA'S COERCION
2024	United States	Axient	Arms sale to Taiwan	Adds to unreliable entity list; bars imports, exports, and investments and bans senior leadership from visiting China
2024	United States	Boeing Defense, Space & Security	Arms sale to Taiwan	Adds to unreliable entity list; bars imports, exports, and investments and bans senior leadership from visiting China
2024	United States	General Dynamics Land Systems	Arms sale to Taiwan	Adds to unreliable entity list; bars imports, exports, and investments and bans senior leadership from visiting China
2024	United States	General Atomics Aeronautical Systems	Arms sale to Taiwan	Adds to unreliable entity list; bars imports, exports, and investments and bans senior leadership from visiting China
2024	United States	Cubic Corporation	Arms sale to Taiwan	Bars imports, exports, and investments and bans senior leadership from visiting China
2024	United States	S3 Aerospace	Arms sale to Taiwan	Bars imports, exports, and investments and bans senior leadership from visiting China
2024	United States	TCOM Ltd Partnership	Arms sale to Taiwan	Bars imports, exports, and investments and bans senior leadership from visiting China
2024	United States	TextOre	Arms sale to Taiwan	Bars imports, exports, and investments and bans senior leadership from visiting China

YEAR	COUNTRY	COMPANY	TARGETED ACTION	CHINA'S COERCION
2024	United States	Planate Management Group	Arms sale to Taiwan	Bars imports, exports, and investments and bans senior leadership from visiting China
2024	United States	ACT1 Federal	Arms sale to Taiwan	Bars imports, exports, and investments and bans senior leadership from visiting China
2024	United States	Exovera	Arms sale to Taiwan	Bars imports, exports, and investments and bans senior leadership from visiting China
2024	United States	Sierra Nevada Corporation	Arms sale to Taiwan	Bars imports, exports, and investments and bans senior leadership from visiting China
2024	United States	Stick Rudder Enterprises LLC	Arms sale to Taiwan	Bars imports, exports, and investments and bans senior leadership from visiting China
2024	United States	PVH Corp.	Discrimination against Xinjiang-made products	Adds to unreliable entity list
2024	United States	Nvidia	Violation in 2019 acquisition of Mellanox Technologies and U.S. chip ban	Opens investigation
2025	United States	General Dynamics	Arms sale to Taiwan	Adds to export control list, bars from imports and exports of dual-use items
2025	United States	L3 Harris Technologies	Arms sale to Taiwan	Adds to export control list, bars from imports and exports of dual-use items

(*continued*)

YEAR	COUNTRY	COMPANY	TARGETED ACTION	CHINA'S COERCION
2025	United States	Intelligent Epitaxy Technology	Arms sale to Taiwan	Adds to export control list, bars from imports and exports of dual-use items
2025	United States	Clear Align LLC	Arms sale to Taiwan	Adds to export control list, bars from imports and exports of dual-use items
2025	United States	Boeing Defense, Space & Security	Arms sale to Taiwan	Adds to export control list, bars from imports and exports of dual-use items
2025	United States	Lockheed Martin Corporation	Arms sale to Taiwan	Adds to export control list, bars from imports and exports of dual-use items
2025	United States	Raytheon Missiles & Defense	Arms sale to Taiwan	Adds to export control list, bars from imports and exports of dual-use items
2025	United States	Lockheed Martin Missiles and Fire Control	Arms sale to Taiwan	Adds to export control list, bars from imports and exports of dual-use items
2025	United States	Lockheed Martin Aeronautics	Arms sale to Taiwan	Adds to export control list, bars from imports and exports of dual-use items
2025	United States	Raytheon/ Lockheed Martin Javelin Joint Venture	Arms sale to Taiwan	Adds to export control list, bars from imports and exports of dual-use items
2025	United States	Raytheon Missile Systems	Arms sale to Taiwan	Adds to export control list, bars from import/exports of dual-use items

YEAR	COUNTRY	COMPANY	TARGETED ACTION	CHINA'S COERCION
2025	United States	General Dynamics Ordnance and Tactical Systems	Arms sale to Taiwan	Adds to export control list and bars from imports and exports of dual-use items
2025	United States	General Dynamics Information Technology	Arms sale to Taiwan	Adds to export control list, bars from imports and exports of dual-use items
2025	United States	General Dynamics Mission Systems	Arms sale to Taiwan	Adds to export control list, bars from imports and exports of dual-use items
2025	United States	Inter-Coastal Electronics, System Studies & Simulation	Arms sale to Taiwan	Adds to export control list, bars from imports and exports of dual-use items
2025	United States	System Studies & Simulation	Arms sale to Taiwan	Adds to export control list, bars from imports and exports of dual-use items
2025	United States	IronMountain Solutions	Arms sale to Taiwan	Adds to export control list, bars from imports and exports of dual-use items
2025	United States	Applied Technologies Group	Arms sale to Taiwan	Adds to export control list, bars from imports and exports of dual-use items
2025	United States	Axient	Arms sale to Taiwan	Adds to export control list, bars from imports and exports of dual-use items
2025	United States	Lockheed Martin Missile System Integration Lab	Arms sale to Taiwan	Adds to export control list, bars from imports and exports of dual-use items

(continued)

YEAR	COUNTRY	COMPANY	TARGETED ACTION	CHINA'S COERCION
2025	United States	Lockheed Martin Advanced Technology Laboratories	Arms sale to Taiwan	Adds to export control list, bars from imports and exports of dual-use items
2025	United States	Lockheed Martin Ventures	Arms sale to Taiwan	Adds to export control list, bars from imports and exports of dual-use items
2025	United States	Anduril Industries	Arms sale to Taiwan	Adds to export control list, bars from imports and exports of dual-use items
2025	United States	Maritime Tactical Systems	Arms sale to Taiwan	Adds to export control list, bars from import and exports of dual-use items
2025	United States	Pacific Rim Defense	Arms sale to Taiwan	Adds to export control list, bars from imports and exports of dual-use items
2025	United States	AEVEX Aerospace	Arms sale to Taiwan	Adds to export control list, bars from imports and exports of dual-use items
2025	United States	LKD Aerospace	Arms sale to Taiwan	Adds to export control list, bars from imports and exports of dual-use items
2025	United States	Summit Technologies Inc.	Arms sale to Taiwan	Adds to export control list, bars from imports and exports of dual-use items
2025	United States	Lockheed Martin Missiles and Fire Control	Arms sale to Taiwan	Adds to unreliable entity list; bars imports, exports, and investments and bans senior leadership from visiting China

YEAR	COUNTRY	COMPANY	TARGETED ACTION	CHINA'S COERCION
2025	United States	Lockheed Martin Aeronautics	Arms sale to Taiwan	Adds to unreliable entity list; bars imports, exports, and investments and bans senior leadership from visiting China
2025	United States	Lockheed Martin Missile System Integration Lab	Arms sale to Taiwan	Adds to unreliable entity list; bars imports, exports, and investments and bans senior leadership from visiting China
2025	United States	Lockheed Martin Advanced Technology Laboratories	Arms sale to Taiwan	Adds to unreliable entity list; bars imports, exports, and investments and bans senior leadership from visiting China
2025	United States	Lockheed Martin Ventures	Arms sale to Taiwan	Adds to unreliable entity list; bars imports, exports, and investments and bans senior leadership from visiting China
2025	United States	Raytheon/ Lockheed Martin Javelin Joint Venture	Arms sale to Taiwan	Adds to unreliable entity list; bars imports, exports, and investments and bans senior leadership from visiting China
2025	United States	Raytheon Missile Systems	Arms sale to Taiwan	Adds to unreliable entity list; bars imports, exports, and investments and bans senior leadership from visiting China

(continued)

YEAR	COUNTRY	COMPANY	TARGETED ACTION	CHINA'S COERCION
2025	United States	General Dynamics Ordnance and Tactical Systems	Arms sale to Taiwan	Adds to unreliable entity list; bars imports, exports, and investments and bans senior leadership from visiting China
2025	United States	General Dynamics Information Technology	Arms sale to Taiwan	Adds to unreliable entity list; bars imports, exports, and investments and bans senior leadership from visiting China
2025	United States	General Dynamics Mission Systems	Arms sale to Taiwan	Adds to unreliable entity list; bars imports, exports, and investments and bans senior leadership from visiting China
2025	United States	PVH Corp.	Trump administration's tariffs against China	Adds to unreliable entity list
2025	United States	Illumina	Trump administration's tariffs against China	Adds to unreliable entity list
2025	United States	Google	Trump administration's tariffs against China	Antitrust probe
2025	United States	Intel	Trump administration's tariffs against China	Antitrust probe
2025	United States	Leidos	Trump administration's tariffs against China	Adds to export control list
2025	United States	Gibbs & Cox, Inc.	Trump administration's tariffs against China	Adds to export control list
2025	United States	IP Video Market Info, Inc.	Trump administration's tariffs against China	Adds to export control list
2025	United States	Skydio, Inc.	Trump administration's tariffs against China	Adds to export control list
2025	United States	Rapid Flight LLC	Trump administration's tariffs against China	Adds to export control list

YEAR	COUNTRY	COMPANY	TARGETED ACTION	CHINA'S COERCION
2025	United States	Red Six Solutions	Trump administration's tariffs against China	Adds to export control list
2025	United States	HavocAI	Trump administration's tariffs against China	Adds to export control list
2025	United States	Neros Technologies	Trump administration's tariffs against China	Adds to export control list
2025	United States	Sourcemap, Inc.	Trump administration's tariffs against China	Adds to export control list
2025	United States	Skydio, Inc.	Trump administration's tariffs against China	Adds to unreliable entity list; bars imports, exports, and investments
2025	United States	Rapid Flight LLC	Trump administration's tariffs against China	Adds to unreliable entity list; bars imports, exports, and investments
2025	United States	Insitu, Inc.	Trump administration's tariffs against China	Adds to unreliable entity list; bars imports, exports, and investments
2025	United States	Domo Tactical Communications	Trump administration's tariffs against China	Adds to unreliable entity list; bars imports, exports, and investments
2025	United States	SYNEXXUS, Inc.	Trump administration's tariffs against China	PRC adds company to unreliable entity list and bars imports, exports, and investments
2025	United States	BRINC Drones, Inc.	Trump administration's tariffs against China	Adds to unreliable entity list; bars imports, exports, and investments
2025	United States	Firestorm Labs, Inc.	Trump administration's tariffs against China	Adds to unreliable entity list; bars imports, exports, and investments

(continued)

YEAR	COUNTRY	COMPANY	TARGETED ACTION	CHINA'S COERCION
2025	United States	Kratos Unmanned Aerial Systems, Inc.	Trump administration's tariffs against China	Adds to unreliable entity list; bars imports, exports, and investments
2025	United States	Red Six Solutions	Trump administration's tariffs against China	Adds to unreliable entity list; bars imports, exports, and investments
2025	United States	Shield AI, Inc.	Trump administration's tariffs against China	Adds to export control list
2025	United States	HavocAI	Trump administration's tariffs against China	Adds to unreliable entity list; bars imports, exports, and investments
2025	United States	Neros Technologies	Trump administration's tariffs against China	Adds to unreliable entity list; bars imports, exports, and investments
2025	United States	Group W	Trump administration's tariffs against China	Adds to export control list
2025	United States	Aerkomm Inc.	Trump administration's tariffs against China	Adds to export control list
2025	United States	General Atomics Aeronautical Systems, Inc.	Trump administration's tariffs against China	Adds to export control list
2025	United States	General Dynamics Land Systems	Trump administration's tariffs against China	Adds to export control list
2025	United States	Aero Vironment	Trump administration's tariffs against China	Adds to export control list
2025	United States	TCOM, Limited Partnership	Trump administration's tariffs against China	Adds to unreliable entity list; bars imports, exports, and investments
2025	United States	Stick Rudder Enterprises LLC	Trump administration's tariffs against China	Adds to unreliable entity list; bars imports, exports, and investments

YEAR	COUNTRY	COMPANY	TARGETED ACTION	CHINA'S COERCION
2025	United States	Teledyne Brown Engineering, Inc.	Trump administration's tariffs against China	Adds to unreliable entity list; bars imports, exports, and investments
2025	United States	Huntington Ingalls Industries Inc.	Trump administration's tariffs against China	Adds to unreliable entity list; bars imports, exports, and investments
2025	United States	S3 AeroDefense	Trump administration's tariffs against China	Adds to unreliable entity list; bars imports, exports, and investments
2025	United States	Cubic Corporation	Trump administration's tariffs against China	Adds to unreliable entity list; bars imports, exports, and investments
2025	United States	TextOre	Trump administration's tariffs against China	Adds to unreliable entity list; bars imports, exports, and investments
2025	United States	ACT1 Federal	Trump administration's tariffs against China	Adds to unreliable entity list; bars imports, exports, and investments
2025	United States	Exovera	Trump administration's tariffs against China	Adds to unreliable entity list; bars imports, exports, and investments
2025	United States	Planate Management Group	Trump administration's tariffs against China	Adds to unreliable entity list; bars imports, exports, and investments
2025	United States	GHS Inc.	Trump administration's tariffs against China	Suspends imports of soybeans
2025	United States	Louis Dreyfus Company Grains Merchandising LLC	Trump administration's tariffs against China	Suspends imports of soybeans

(continued)

YEAR	COUNTRY	COMPANY	TARGETED ACTION	CHINA'S COERCION
2025	United States	EGT, LLC	Trump administration's tariffs against China	Suspends imports of soybeans
2025	United States	High Point Aerotechnologies	Trump administration's tariffs against China	Adds to export control list
2025	United States	Universal Logistics Holdings, Inc.	Trump administration's tariffs against China	Adds to export control list
2025	United States	Source Intelligence, Inc.	Trump administration's tariffs against China	Adds to export control list
2025	United States	Coalition for a Prosperous America	Trump administration's tariffs against China	Adds to export control list
2025	United States	Sierra Nevada Corporation	Trump administration's tariffs against China	Adds to export control list
2025	United States	Edge Autonomy Operations LLC	Trump administration's tariffs against China	Adds to export control list
2025	United States	Cyberlux Corporation	Trump administration's tariffs against China	Adds to export control list
2025	United States	Hudson Technologies Co.	Trump administration's tariffs against China	Adds to export control list
2025	United States	Saronic Technologies, Inc.	Trump administration's tariffs against China	Adds to export control list
2025	United States	Oceaneering International, Inc.	Trump administration's tariffs against China	Adds to export control list
2025	United States	Stick Rudder Enterprises LLC	Trump administration's tariffs against China	Adds to export control list
2025	United States	Cubic Corporation	Trump administration's tariffs against China	Adds to export control list
2025	United States	S3 AeroDefense	Trump administration's tariffs against China	Adds to export control list
2025	United States	TCOM, Limited Partnership	Trump administration's tariffs against China	Adds to export control list

YEAR	COUNTRY	COMPANY	TARGETED ACTION	CHINA'S COERCION
2025	United States	TextOre	Trump administration's tariffs against China	Adds to export control list
2025	United States	ACT1 Federal	Trump administration's tariffs against China	Adds to export control list
2025	United States	Shield AI, Inc.	Trump administration's tariffs against China	Adds to unreliable entity list; bars imports, exports, and investments
2025	United States	Sierra Nevada Corporation	Trump administration's tariffs against China	Adds to unreliable entity list; bars imports, exports, and investments
2025	United States	Cyberlux Corporation	Trump administration's tariffs against China	Adds to unreliable entity list; bars imports, exports, and investments
2025	United States	Edge Autonomy Operations LLC	Trump administration's tariffs against China	Adds to unreliable entity list; bars imports, exports, and investments
2025	United States	Group W	Trump administration's tariffs against China	Adds to unreliable entity list; bars imports, exports, and investments
2025	United States	Hudson Technologies Co.	Trump administration's tariffs against China	Adds to unreliable entity list; bars imports, exports, and investments
2025	United States	American Photonics	Trump administration's tariffs against China	Adds to export control list
2025	United States	Novotech, Inc.	Trump administration's tariffs against China	Adds to export control list
2025	United States	Echodyne	Trump administration's tariffs against China	Adds to export control list

(continued)

YEAR	COUNTRY	COMPANY	TARGETED ACTION	CHINA'S COERCION
2025	United States	Marvin Engineering Company, Inc.	Trump administration's tariffs against China	Adds to export control list
2025	United States	Exovera	Trump administration's tariffs against China	Adds to export control list
2025	United States	Teledyne Brown Engineering, Inc.	Trump administration's tariffs against China	Adds to export control list
2025	United States	BRINC Drones, Inc.	Trump administration's tariffs against China	Adds to export control list
2025	United States	SYNEXXUS, Inc.	Trump administration's tariffs against China	Adds to export control list
2025	United States	Firestorm Labs, Inc.	Trump administration's tariffs against China	Adds to export control list
2025	United States	Kratos Unmanned Aerial Systems, Inc.	Trump administration's tariffs against China	Adds to export control list
2025	United States	Domo Tactical Communications	Trump administration's tariffs against China	Adds to export control list
2025	United States	Insitu, Inc.	Trump administration's tariffs against China	Adds to export control list

Source: Original data compiled by authors.

APPENDIX 2

China's High-Dependence Trade with Eighteen Governments Targeted with Economic Coercion (Summary, 2024)

COERCED COUNTRY	CHINA'S TOTAL IMPORTS VALUE (USD)	>70 PERCENT DEPENDENCE		>80 PERCENT DEPENDENCE		>90 PERCENT DEPENDENCE	
		# OF ITEMS	VALUE (USD)	# OF ITEMS	VALUE (USD)	# OF ITEMS	VALUE (USD)
Japan	$156.24 bn	147	$9.44 bn	96	$6.54 bn	48	$4.61 bn
United States	$164.59 bn	132	$5.71 bn	102	$4.14 bn	73	$3.36 bn
Germany	$94.79 bn	95	$1.43 bn	56	$350.49 mn	33	$190.37 mn
South Korea	$181.50 bn	48	$8.57 bn	34	$5.06 bn	19	$4.23 bn
France	$35.16 bn	38	$2.61 bn	29	$2.30 bn	19	$1.31 bn
Canada	$46.56 bn	26	$5.45 bn	17	$3.57 bn	14	$3.56 bn
New Zealand	$12.42 bn	23	$5.34 bn	17	$3.59 bn	13	$2.96 bn

(continued)

COERCED COUNTRY	CHINA'S TOTAL IMPORTS VALUE (USD)	>70 PERCENT DEPENDENCE		>80 PERCENT DEPENDENCE		>90 PERCENT DEPENDENCE	
		# OF ITEMS	VALUE (USD)	# OF ITEMS	VALUE (USD)	# OF ITEMS	VALUE (USD)
Australia	$140.78 bn	22	$2.35 bn	14	$398.19 mn	12	$129.73 mn
Norway	$5.14 bn	16	$596.65 mn	12	$71.05 mn	9	$55.81 mn
United Kingdom	$19.57 bn	13	$412.54 mn	10	$409.01 mn	7	$17.21 mn
Mongolia	$13.73 bn	9	$474.17 mn	5	$282.11 mn	3	$250.31 mn
Philippines	$19.33 bn	9	$294.05 mn	6	$233.06 mn	6	$233.06 mn
Sweden	$8.81 bn	7	$321.84 mn	3	$48.31 mn	2	$16.69 mn
Czech Republic	$5.68 bn	4	$17.33 mn	3	$9.45 mn	1	$8.44 mn
Estonia	$335.25 mn	0	$0	0	$0	0	$0
Latvia	$285.81 mn	0	$0	0	$0	0	$0
Lithuania	$211.23 mn	0	$0	0	$0	0	$0
Palau	$3,576	0	$0	0	$0	0	$0
Total	**$905.19 bn**		**$43.06 bn**		**$27.03 bn**		**$20.94 bn**

Source: Authors' original table with data derived from UN Comtrade database at https://comtradeplus.un.org/.

APPENDIX 3

Itemized List of China's High-Dependence Goods by Country (for Eighteen Governments Targeted with Economic Coercion, 2024)

Ordered from 100 Percent to 70 Percent Dependence

HS CODE	PRODUCT DESCRIPTION	TRADE VALUE OF CHINA'S IMPORTS FROM JAPAN (USD)	TRADE VALUE OF CHINA'S IMPORTS FROM THE WORLD (USD)	JAPAN'S SHARE OF CHINA'S TOTAL IMPORTS (PERCENT)
870290	Buses	$27,461,996	$27,461,996	100.00
480550	Felt paper and paperboard rolls	$6,701,516	$6,701,516	100.00
284520	Boron enriched in boron-10 compounds	$6,511,600	$6,511,600	100.00
290348	HFC-365mfc and HFC-43-10mee	$407,250	$407,250	100.00
730520	Iron or steel (excluding cast iron): casing of a kind used in drilling for oil or gas (not seamless), having circular cross-sections, external diameter exceeds 406.4mm	$133,465	$133,465	100.00
860699	Railway cars	$125,388	$125,388	100.00

(continued)

**147 ITEMS FOR WHICH CHINA IS MORE THAN 70 PERCENT DEPENDENT ON JAPAN
(TOTAL VALUE = $9,447,462,727)**

HS CODE	PRODUCT DESCRIPTION	TRADE VALUE OF CHINA'S IMPORTS FROM JAPAN (USD)	TRADE VALUE OF CHINA'S IMPORTS FROM THE WORLD (USD)	JAPAN'S SHARE OF CHINA'S TOTAL IMPORTS (PERCENT)
600541	Warp knit fabrics: artificial fibers	$98,548	$98,548	100.00
845910	Way-type unit head machines, for drilling, boring, milling, threading, or tapping by removing metal	$41,353	$41,353	100.00
370253	Polychrome slide film: rolls	$25,875	$25,875	100.00
870110	Tractors: single axle	$7,605	$7,605	100.00
280620	Chlorosulphuric acid	$467	$467	100.00
300251	Cell cultures: cell therapy products	$450	$450	100.00
441891	Wood: bamboo joinery and carpentry	$121	$121	100.00
100821	Cereals: millet, seed	$10	$10	100.00
540500	Monofilament: strip	$14,982,494	$14,991,062	99.94
290242	Cyclic hydrocarbons: m-xylene	$15,279,136	$15,294,293	99.90
283711	Cyanides and cyanide oxides	$765,365	$766,449	99.86
721020	Flat-rolled, plated, or coated products	$211,838	$212,847	99.53
290612	Cyclohexanol, methylcyclohexanols	$265,177	$266,693	99.43
720838	Flat-rolled iron/nonalloy steel coils	$157,110,986	$158,458,113	99.15
870340	Hybrid electric vehicles	$3,951,111,137	$3,996,818,260	98.86

147 ITEMS FOR WHICH CHINA IS MORE THAN 70 PERCENT DEPENDENT ON JAPAN
(TOTAL VALUE = $9,447,462,727)

HS CODE	PRODUCT DESCRIPTION	TRADE VALUE OF CHINA'S IMPORTS FROM JAPAN (USD)	TRADE VALUE OF CHINA'S IMPORTS FROM THE WORLD (USD)	JAPAN'S SHARE OF CHINA'S TOTAL IMPORTS (PERCENT)
550640	Synthetic staple fibers of polypropylene, carded, combed, or otherwise processed for spinning	$34,421	$35,024	98.28
721011	Tin-coated flat-rolled steel, >/= 0.5mm	$390,036	$397,956	98.01
722720	Silico-manganese steel bars and rods	$18,800,362	$19,239,347	97.72
382768	Mixtures containing halogenated derivatives of methane, ethane, or propane: containing other HFCs but not containing CFCs or HCFCs	$195,478	$200,384	97.55
291714	Maleic anhydride	$2,308,843	$2,368,184	97.49
700530	Wired float glass sheets	$1,473,824	$1,513,023	97.41
291462	Quinones: coenzyme Q10	$7,121,963	$7,317,151	97.33
600543	Warp knit (including those made on galloon knitting machines) of artificial fibers, of yarns of different colors	$153,321	$158,207	96.91
440410	Coniferous wood: poles, stakes, etc.	$84,566	$87,830	96.28
580230	Tufted textile fabrics	$5,047,837	$5,243,156	96.27
580123	Cotton weft pile fabrics, NES	$3,502,872	$3,639,258	96.25
841911	Instantaneous gas water heaters	$36,924,949	$38,402,162	96.15

(continued)

147 ITEMS FOR WHICH CHINA IS MORE THAN 70 PERCENT DEPENDENT ON JAPAN
(TOTAL VALUE = $9,447,462,727)

HS CODE	PRODUCT DESCRIPTION	TRADE VALUE OF CHINA'S IMPORTS FROM JAPAN (USD)	TRADE VALUE OF CHINA'S IMPORTS FROM THE WORLD (USD)	JAPAN'S SHARE OF CHINA'S TOTAL IMPORTS (PERCENT)
700320	Cast glass sheets: wired	$182,209	$190,277	95.76
711100	Base metals: silver or gold clad	$10,531,169	$11,053,070	95.28
282810	Commercial calcium hypochlorite	$52,456	$55,543	94.44
610419	Women's or girls' suits, knitted or crocheted	$1,371	$1,461	93.84
870210	Public transport vehicles: diesel engine	$7,344,860	$7,850,033	93.56
480220	Paper and paperboard base	$3,609,598	$3,879,965	93.03
721430	Iron/nonalloy steel bars and rods	$251,984	$273,018	92.30
680911	Plaster, or plaster compositions: boards, sheets, panels, tiles, and similar articles, faced or reinforced with paper or paperboard only, not ornamented	$1,380,779	$1,508,846	91.51
720837	Iron or non-alloy steel: in coils, without patterns in relief, flat-rolled, of a width 600mm or more, hot-rolled, of a thickness of 4.75mm or more but not exceeding 10mm	$4,189,164	$4,586,253	91.34
441299	Plywood: n.e.c. in heading 4412, with both outer plies of coniferous wood	$173,327	$189,776	91.33
282890	Hypochlorites (excluding calcium)	$20,475,716	$22,419,332	91.33

147 ITEMS FOR WHICH CHINA IS MORE THAN 70 PERCENT DEPENDENT ON JAPAN (TOTAL VALUE = $9,447,462,727)

HS CODE	PRODUCT DESCRIPTION	TRADE VALUE OF CHINA'S IMPORTS FROM JAPAN (USD)	TRADE VALUE OF CHINA'S IMPORTS FROM THE WORLD (USD)	JAPAN'S SHARE OF CHINA'S TOTAL IMPORTS (PERCENT)
441873	Wood: assembled flooring panels, of bamboo or with at least the top layer (wear layer) of bamboo	$1,681	$1,841	91.31
10612	Live mammals, including whales, dolphins, porpoises, manatees, dugongs seals, sea lions, and walruses	$11,832,581	$12,983,298	91.14
720610	Iron or non-alloy steel: ingots (excluding iron of heading no. 7203)	$502,471	$554,918	90.55
844520	Textile spinning machinery	$293,648,772	$325,590,999	90.19
220600	Other fermented beverages (cider, perry)	$72,202,204	$80,320,763	89.89
853529	Automatic circuit breakers: 72.5kV or more	$15,173,701	$16,925,702	89.65
282540	Nickel oxides and hydroxides	$38,012,629	$42,775,753	88.86
290721	Resorcinol and salts	$9,542,114	$10,764,644	88.64
60230	Rhododendrons and azaleas	$2,601,974	$2,939,418	88.52
293919	Opium alkaloids	$21,770,221	$24,616,088	88.44
730120	Iron or steel: angles, shapes, and sections, welded	$6,506,370	$7,403,536	87.88
721491	Hot-rolled steel bars and rods	$5,199,894	$5,922,769	87.79
720852	Flat-rolled steel: hot-rolled, >/= 600mm	$73,115,669	$83,454,860	87.61
850750	Nickel-metal hydride accumulators	$65,940,209	$75,572,625	87.25

(continued)

147 ITEMS FOR WHICH CHINA IS MORE THAN 70 PERCENT DEPENDENT ON JAPAN
(TOTAL VALUE = $9,447,462,727)

HS CODE	PRODUCT DESCRIPTION	TRADE VALUE OF CHINA'S IMPORTS FROM JAPAN (USD)	TRADE VALUE OF CHINA'S IMPORTS FROM THE WORLD (USD)	JAPAN'S SHARE OF CHINA'S TOTAL IMPORTS (PERCENT)
600521	Warp knit (including those made on galloon knitting machines) of cotton, unbleached or bleached	$29,107	$33,423	87.09
720839	Hot-rolled steel: <3mm thick	$32,071,181	$36,986,974	86.71
920190	Harpsichords: other keyboard stringed instruments	$791,219	$917,479	86.24
280480	Arsenic	$855,184	$992,024	86.21
960810	Ballpoint pens	$81,208,841	$94,430,935	86.00
842959	Mechanical shovels, excavators, and shovel loaders	$6,583,821	$7,666,678	85.88
850133	DC motors/generators	$28,100,553	$32,741,491	85.83
290389	Halogenated cyclanic derivatives	$11,567,171	$13,489,499	85.75
551323	Dyed woven fabrics: <85% polyester	$3,612,589	$4,224,454	85.52
722880	Hollow drill bars and rods	$73,368	$86,046	85.27
911019	Rough watch movements	$871,181	$1,025,048	84.99
910819	Battery watch movements	$3,713,376	$4,372,731	84.92
400520	Rubber solutions: dispersions, unvulcanized	$20,270,494	$23,885,237	84.87
521059	Woven fabrics: <85% cotton, printed	$487,285	$574,767	84.78
370120	Unexposed instant print flat film	$34,714,449	$40,953,048	84.77
710610	Silver powder	$892,448,804	$1,053,723,192	84.69
821195	Base metal handle knives	$2,620,566	$3,102,789	84.46

147 ITEMS FOR WHICH CHINA IS MORE THAN 70 PERCENT DEPENDENT ON JAPAN
(TOTAL VALUE = $9,447,462,727)

HS CODE	PRODUCT DESCRIPTION	TRADE VALUE OF CHINA'S IMPORTS FROM JAPAN (USD)	TRADE VALUE OF CHINA'S IMPORTS FROM THE WORLD (USD)	JAPAN'S SHARE OF CHINA'S TOTAL IMPORTS (PERCENT)
330520	Hair preparations: for permanent waving or straightening	$2,610,486	$3,103,483	84.11
681591	Stone articles and articles containing magnesite, magnesia in the form of periclase, dolomite including in the form of dolime, or chromite	$1,142,156	$1,358,404	84.08
890120	Tankers	$20,411,360	$24,411,360	83.61
840721	Spark-ignition outboard motors	$154,536,893	$185,631,915	83.25
600624	Knitted or crocheted fabrics, of cotton, printed	$2,171,641	$2,612,222	83.13
842911	Bulldozers and angledozers: self-propelled, track laying	$60,818,733	$73,346,206	82.92
521051	Printed plain cotton weave	$2,717,610	$3,283,826	82.76
283311	Disodium sulfate	$1,983,530	$2,402,015	82.58
540120	Artificial filament sewing thread	$348,568	$423,216	82.36
911012	Incomplete watch movements	$3,012,624	$3,670,754	82.07
540339	Single artificial yarn	$33,209,902	$40,651,547	81.69
700521	Non-wire float glass sheets	$27,224,096	$33,394,007	81.52
290629	Alcohols: aromatic and derivatives, other than benzyl alcohol	$13,666,753	$16,831,934	81.20
910811	Battery watch movements	$121,127,726	$149,318,550	81.12

(continued)

147 ITEMS FOR WHICH CHINA IS MORE THAN 70 PERCENT DEPENDENT ON JAPAN (TOTAL VALUE = $9,447,462,727)

HS CODE	PRODUCT DESCRIPTION	TRADE VALUE OF CHINA'S IMPORTS FROM JAPAN (USD)	TRADE VALUE OF CHINA'S IMPORTS FROM THE WORLD (USD)	JAPAN'S SHARE OF CHINA'S TOTAL IMPORTS (PERCENT)
721391	Hot-rolled iron steel bars, <14mm	$34,887,698	$43,037,845	81.06
550630	Acrylic or modacrylic staple fibers	$438,941	$545,337	80.49
282010	Manganese dioxide	$3,108,611	$3,863,148	80.47
291469	Quinones: other than anthraquinone and coenzyme Q10 (ubidecarenone (INN))	$8,273,819	$10,282,341	80.47
960840	Pencils: propelling or sliding	$7,023,128	$8,743,656	80.32
700330	Glass: cast glass and rolled glass, profiles, not otherwise worked	$825,955	$1,028,402	80.31
551423	Dyed woven fabrics: <85% polyester	$1,120,673	$1,397,679	80.18
290378	Perhalogenated derivatives, other than those only with fluorine and chlorine	$5,024,817	$6,302,395	79.73
270740	Naphthalene	$4,906,192	$6,154,182	79.72
850640	Silver oxide primary batteries	$18,342,481	$23,125,360	79.32
481620	Self-copy paper	$341,968	$431,447	79.26
847629	Automatic beverage-vending machines	$6,207	$7,837	79.20
731419	Woven iron/steel products	$6,596,167	$8,376,342	78.75
290341	Trifluoromethane (HFC-23)	$1,833,134	$2,341,453	78.29

147 ITEMS FOR WHICH CHINA IS MORE THAN 70 PERCENT DEPENDENT ON JAPAN (TOTAL VALUE = $9,447,462,727)

HS CODE	PRODUCT DESCRIPTION	TRADE VALUE OF CHINA'S IMPORTS FROM JAPAN (USD)	TRADE VALUE OF CHINA'S IMPORTS FROM THE WORLD (USD)	JAPAN'S SHARE OF CHINA'S TOTAL IMPORTS (PERCENT)
722530	Flat rolled alloy steel	$214,054,771	$274,334,631	78.03
910890	Watch movements: complete and assembled, not automatic winding or electrically operated	$660,322	$846,832	77.98
392073	Plates, sheets, and film of cellulose acetate	$466,056,030	$598,070,381	77.93
550942	Synthetic staple fiber yarn (85%+)	$706,636	$908,026	77.82
960400	Hand sieves and hand riddles	$81,680	$105,214	77.63
960920	Pencil leads: black or colored	$2,995,288	$3,859,124	77.62
480990	Carbon paper and other copying or transfer papers, in rolls or sheets	$5,405,440	$6,970,565	77.55
842952	Mechanical shovels, excavators, and shovel loaders: with a 360-degree revolving super structure	$162,562,297	$210,108,011	77.37
741012	Copper foil	$202,555,244	$262,822,250	77.07
950440	Playing cards	$76,718,783	$99,981,393	76.73
540832	Dyed woven artificial filament fabrics	$31,342,834	$41,137,182	76.19
920110	Musical instruments: pianos, upright, including automatic pianos	$48,020,509	$63,481,950	75.64

(continued)

147 ITEMS FOR WHICH CHINA IS MORE THAN 70 PERCENT DEPENDENT ON JAPAN (TOTAL VALUE = $9,447,462,727)

HS CODE	PRODUCT DESCRIPTION	TRADE VALUE OF CHINA'S IMPORTS FROM JAPAN (USD)	TRADE VALUE OF CHINA'S IMPORTS FROM THE WORLD (USD)	JAPAN'S SHARE OF CHINA'S TOTAL IMPORTS (PERCENT)
690990	Ceramic wares: pots, jars, and similar articles used for the conveyance or packing of goods and ceramic troughs, tubs, and similar receptacles used in agriculture	$159,541	$211,230	75.53
960899	Duplicating stylos, pen-holders, pencil-holders, and similar holders, parts of the articles of heading 9608, including caps and clips	$20,473,079	$27,188,411	75.30
910812	Watch movements: complete and assembled, electrically operated, by means of solar cells, with opto-electronic display	$1,171,186	$1,562,111	74.97
847950	Industrial robots	$481,954,200	$644,723,789	74.75
950790	Fishing tackle	$20,707,594	$27,749,227	74.62
290349	Saturated fluorinated derivatives of acyclic hydrocarbons	$4,052,452	$5,440,348	74.49
252210	Quicklime: excluding calcium oxide and hydroxide of heading no. 2825	$299,473	$402,124	74.47
960860	Ballpoint pen refills	$16,633,562	$22,338,009	74.46
392071	Regenerated cellulose plastics: noncellular	$11,021,474	$14,856,070	74.19
911440	Clock/watch plates and bridges	$4,288,262	$5,801,800	73.91

147 ITEMS FOR WHICH CHINA IS MORE THAN 70 PERCENT DEPENDENT ON JAPAN (TOTAL VALUE = $9,447,462,727)

HS CODE	PRODUCT DESCRIPTION	TRADE VALUE OF CHINA'S IMPORTS FROM JAPAN (USD)	TRADE VALUE OF CHINA'S IMPORTS FROM THE WORLD (USD)	JAPAN'S SHARE OF CHINA'S TOTAL IMPORTS (PERCENT)
291090	Epoxides, epoxyalcohols	$39,852,738	$54,046,196	73.74
810820	Titanium: unwrought, powders	$12,127,724	$16,482,016	73.58
721410	Iron or non-alloy steel: bars and rods, forged, hot-rolled, hot-drawn, or hot-extruded, but including those twisted after rolling	$1,037,625	$1,411,167	73.53
731431	Iron or steel wire: grill, netting, and fencing, welded at the intersection, plated or coated with zinc	$1,017,670	$1,390,745	73.17
720449	Ferrous waste/scrap, NES	$10,092,600	$13,846,677	72.89
810199	Tungsten (wolfram): articles n.e.c. in heading no. 8101	$36,181,077	$49,709,112	72.79
721640	Iron/steel L or T sections	$31,446,779	$43,233,983	72.74
900661	Photographic flashlights: electronic	$314,982,266	$433,158,413	72.72
293311	Phenazone (antipyrin) derivatives	$482,550	$663,778	72.70
250590	Sands: natural (other than silica and quartz sands), whether or not colored (other than metal-bearing sands of chapter 26)	$13,141,679	$18,088,318	72.65
551110	Retail synthetic staple fiber yarn	$43,138	$59,489	72.51

(*continued*)

147 ITEMS FOR WHICH CHINA IS MORE THAN 70 PERCENT DEPENDENT ON JAPAN (TOTAL VALUE = $9,447,462,727)

HS CODE	PRODUCT DESCRIPTION	TRADE VALUE OF CHINA'S IMPORTS FROM JAPAN (USD)	TRADE VALUE OF CHINA'S IMPORTS FROM THE WORLD (USD)	JAPAN'S SHARE OF CHINA'S TOTAL IMPORTS (PERCENT)
731414	Stainless steel woven cloth	$92,824,279	$128,024,811	72.50
701919	Glass fibers: including glass wool, threads, and mats, other than mechanically or chemically bonded mats	$16,137,997	$22,313,643	72.32
370244	Photographic film: in rolls, sensitized, unexposed, without sprocket holes, of a width exceeding 105mm but not exceeding 610mm (other than of paper, paperboard, or textiles)	$82,776,428	$114,852,951	72.07
400249	Chloroprene rubber: primary forms	$50,764,611	$70,964,000	71.54
10619	Live mammals other than primates, whales, dolphins, porpoises, manatees, dugongs, seals, sea lions, walruses, camels, other camelids, rabbits, and hares	$10,238,581	$14,374,012	71.23
551341	Fabrics, woven: plain weave, printed, of polyester staple fibers, containing less than 85% by weight of such fibers, mixed mainly or solely with cotton, not exceeding 170g/m2	$145,759	$205,162	71.05
320650	Coloring matter: inorganic products of a kind used as luminophores	$33,467,253	$47,133,719	71.00
290722	Polyphenols: hydroquinone (quinol) and its salts	$24,258,010	$34,229,037	70.87

147 ITEMS FOR WHICH CHINA IS MORE THAN 70 PERCENT DEPENDENT ON JAPAN
(TOTAL VALUE = $9,447,462,727)

HS CODE	PRODUCT DESCRIPTION	TRADE VALUE OF CHINA'S IMPORTS FROM JAPAN (USD)	TRADE VALUE OF CHINA'S IMPORTS FROM THE WORLD (USD)	JAPAN'S SHARE OF CHINA'S TOTAL IMPORTS (PERCENT)
340391	Textile lubricants	$305,917,476	$433,054,679	70.64
720825	Iron or non-alloy steel: in coils, without patterns in relief, flat-rolled, of a width of 600mm or more, hot-rolled, pickled, of a thickness of 4.75mm or more	$15,380,116	$21,864,795	70.34
920991	Musical instruments: parts and accessories for pianos	$3,971,284	$5,650,015	70.29

132 ITEMS FOR WHICH CHINA IS MORE THAN 70 PERCENT DEPENDENT ON THE UNITED STATES
(TOTAL VALUE =$5,713,431,562)

HS CODE	PRODUCT DESCRIPTION	TRADE VALUE OF CHINA'S IMPORTS FROM THE UNITED STATES (USD)	TRADE VALUE OF CHINA'S IMPORTS FROM THE WORLD (USD)	U.S. SHARE OF CHINA'S TOTAL IMPORTS (PERCENT)
160232	Poultry meat preparations: fowls	$167,889,807	$167,889,807	100.00
880230	Airplanes and other aircraft, except unmanned: of an unladen weight exceeding 2000kg but not exceeding 15,000kg	$9,680,699	$9,680,699	100.00

(*continued*)

132 ITEMS FOR WHICH CHINA IS MORE THAN 70 PERCENT DEPENDENT ON THE UNITED STATES
(TOTAL VALUE =$5,713,431,562)

HS CODE	PRODUCT DESCRIPTION	TRADE VALUE OF CHINA'S IMPORTS FROM THE UNITED STATES (USD)	TRADE VALUE OF CHINA'S IMPORTS FROM THE WORLD (USD)	U.S. SHARE OF CHINA'S TOTAL IMPORTS (PERCENT)
360410	Fireworks	$5,251,907	$5,251,907	100.00
20621	Frozen bovine tongues	$2,819,215	$2,819,215	100.00
410330	Swine hides and skins	$1,846,057	$1,846,057	100.00
160231	Turkeys, prepared or preserved meat, or meat offal (excluding livers and homogenized preparations)	$1,055,473	$1,055,473	100.00
841121	Turbo-propellers: up to 1,100kW	$781,712	$781,712	100.00
840120	Isotopic separation machinery	$201,000	$201,000	100.00
730629	Iron or steel (excluding cast iron): casing and tubing of a kind used in drilling for oil and gas (other than stainless steel or seamless), n.e.c. in chapter 73	$111,929	$111,929	100.00
292217	Amino-alcohols: their ethers and esters	$44,748	$44,748	100.00
930621	Ammunition: shotgun cartridges	$40,462	$40,462	100.00
230210	Bran, sharps, and other residues of maize (corn)	$39,803	$39,803	100.00
381111	Antiknock preparations: based on lead compounds	$38,125	$38,125	100.00
20610	Fresh or chilled edible bovine offal	$12,741	$12,741	100.00

132 ITEMS FOR WHICH CHINA IS MORE THAN 70 PERCENT DEPENDENT ON THE UNITED STATES
(TOTAL VALUE =$5,713,431,562)

HS CODE	PRODUCT DESCRIPTION	TRADE VALUE OF CHINA'S IMPORTS FROM THE UNITED STATES (USD)	TRADE VALUE OF CHINA'S IMPORTS FROM THE WORLD (USD)	U.S. SHARE OF CHINA'S TOTAL IMPORTS (PERCENT)
360200	Explosives, prepared: other than propellent powders	$11,326	$11,326	100.00
292146	Aromatic amine-function compounds	$5,490	$5,490	100.00
292214	Dextropropoxyphene (INN) and its salts	$3,922	$3,922	100.00
284530	Lithium enriched in lithium-6	$3,823	$3,823	100.00
811251	Thallium and thallium articles	$3,034	$3,034	100.00
293295	Heterocyclic compounds: oxygen only	$2,451	$2,451	100.00
30469	Fish fillets: frozen, carp	$2,173	$2,173	100.00
292231	Amino-aldehydes, amino-ketones: salts	$875	$875	100.00
293491	Other heterocyclic compounds	$811	$811	100.00
293341	Quinoline or isoquinoline ring compounds	$767	$767	100.00
293010	Dithiocarbonates (xanthates)	$682	$682	100.00
293972	Vegetal alkaloids: cocaine and derivatives	$450	$450	100.00
293945	Ephedrine alkaloids and derivatives	$360	$360	100.00

(continued)

132 ITEMS FOR WHICH CHINA IS MORE THAN 70 PERCENT DEPENDENT
ON THE UNITED STATES
(TOTAL VALUE =$5,713,431,562)

HS CODE	PRODUCT DESCRIPTION	TRADE VALUE OF CHINA'S IMPORTS FROM THE UNITED STATES (USD)	TRADE VALUE OF CHINA'S IMPORTS FROM THE WORLD (USD)	U.S. SHARE OF CHINA'S TOTAL IMPORTS (PERCENT)
40811	Birds' eggs, yolks, dried, whether or not containing added sugar or other sweetening matter	$356	$356	100.00
300443	Medicaments: containing norephedrine	$294	$294	100.00
282911	Chlorates: of sodium	$202	$202	100.00
151521	Maize (corn) oil and its fractions, crude, not chemically modified	$193	$193	100.00
282919	Chlorates: other than sodium	$94	$94	100.00
293355	Pyrimidine or piperazine ring compounds	$85	$85	100.00
292411	Acyclic amides and carbamates: salts	$55	$55	100.00
30299	Fresh or chilled fish fins	$43	$43	100.00
10690	Live nonmammal animals, NES	$76,246	$76,324	99.90
690590	Ceramic chimney pots, cowls, chimney liners, architectural ornaments, and other constructional goods (excluding roofing tiles)	$1,353,963	$1,356,786	99.79
291212	Ethanal (acetaldehyde)	$68,401	$68,788	99.44
100710	Grain sorghum, seed	$20,163	$20,311	99.27

**132 ITEMS FOR WHICH CHINA IS MORE THAN 70 PERCENT DEPENDENT
ON THE UNITED STATES
(TOTAL VALUE =$5,713,431,562)**

HS CODE	PRODUCT DESCRIPTION	TRADE VALUE OF CHINA'S IMPORTS FROM THE UNITED STATES (USD)	TRADE VALUE OF CHINA'S IMPORTS FROM THE WORLD (USD)	U.S. SHARE OF CHINA'S TOTAL IMPORTS (PERCENT)
230330	Brewing/distilling dregs and waste	$65,703,906	$66,348,381	99.03
370191	Photographic plates	$26,447	$26,750	98.87
870451	Vehicles with engine types and weights	$8,799,813	$8,906,585	98.80
551349	Fabrics, woven: printed, containing less than 85% by weight of synthetic staple fibers (other than polyester, plain weave), mixed mainly or solely with cotton, not exceeding 170g/m2	$763	$773	98.71
811219	Beryllium and articles thereof: wrought other than waste and scrap	$1,003,733	$1,017,204	98.68
160249	Swine, meat or meat offal (including mixtures), prepared or preserved, n.e.c. in heading no. 1602	$44,879,849	$45,521,541	98.59
440794	Cherry wood	$103,449,895	$104,959,768	98.56
370254	Polychrome film: rolls, width exceeding 16mm but less than 35mm, length not exceeding 30m	$16,711,613	$16,955,669	98.56
120241	Raw groundnuts	$70,725,774	$71,829,505	98.46
290110	Acyclic hydrocarbons	$2,604,826,737	$2,653,916,152	98.15

(continued)

**132 ITEMS FOR WHICH CHINA IS MORE THAN 70 PERCENT DEPENDENT
ON THE UNITED STATES
(TOTAL VALUE =$5,713,431,562)**

HS CODE	PRODUCT DESCRIPTION	TRADE VALUE OF CHINA'S IMPORTS FROM THE UNITED STATES (USD)	TRADE VALUE OF CHINA'S IMPORTS FROM THE WORLD (USD)	U.S. SHARE OF CHINA'S TOTAL IMPORTS (PERCENT)
360360	Electric detonators	$804,633	$821,845	97.91
280519	Alkali or alkali-earth metals: other than sodium and calcium	$13,292,745	$13,694,229	97.07
282410	Lead: lead monoxide (litharge, massicot)	$4,934	$5,086	97.01
71040	Frozen sweet corn	$2,519,610	$2,610,835	96.51
290345	Saturated fluorinated acyclic hydrocarbons	$7,962,359	$8,290,767	96.04
290351	Unsaturated fluorinated acyclic hydrocarbons	$32,589,648	$33,995,444	95.86
841210	Reaction engines: not turbojets	$45,000	$47,090	95.56
291242	Ethylvanillin	$1,418,683	$1,485,945	95.47
121010	Hop cones	$16,644	$17,559	94.79
850231	Wind-powered electric generating sets	$7,392,300	$7,817,735	94.56
852842	Monitors: cathode-ray tube, capable of directly connecting to and designed for use with an automatic data processing machine of heading 84.71	$106,654	$112,865	94.50
710421	Stones: diamonds, unworked or simply sawn or roughly shaped	$9,240,579	$9,814,780	94.15
370256	Polychrome film: rolls, width exceeding 35mm	$473,944	$504,857	93.88

132 ITEMS FOR WHICH CHINA IS MORE THAN 70 PERCENT DEPENDENT ON THE UNITED STATES
(TOTAL VALUE =$5,713,431,562)

HS CODE	PRODUCT DESCRIPTION	TRADE VALUE OF CHINA'S IMPORTS FROM THE UNITED STATES (USD)	TRADE VALUE OF CHINA'S IMPORTS FROM THE WORLD (USD)	U.S. SHARE OF CHINA'S TOTAL IMPORTS (PERCENT)
540342	Cellulose yarn: multiple or cabled	$7,428,858	$7,937,149	93.60
961380	Lighters: NES	$35,079,987	$37,646,786	93.18
120924	Kentucky bluegrass seed	$20,308,770	$21,818,352	93.08
10511	Live fowls: Gallus domestic species	$48,940,063	$52,765,579	92.75
290329	Unsaturated chlorinated acyclic hydrocarbons	$1,982,322	$2,148,567	92.26
262190	Slag and ash: seaweed ash	$798,940	$868,963	91.94
51110	Bovine semen	$53,535,288	$58,231,943	91.93
310390	Fertilizers: mineral or chemical	$173,306	$188,900	91.74
80221	Hazelnuts in shell: fresh or dried	$9,882,884	$10,781,671	91.66
382212	Reagents for zika and other diseases transmitted by mosquitoes of the genus Aedes	$45,339	$49,625	91.36
300290	Toxins: microorganisms, non-yeast	$421,898	$467,970	90.15
280440	Oxygen	$1,774,114	$1,981,217	89.55
852849	Monitors: cathode-ray tube, n.e.c. in subheading 8528.42, whether or not color	$295,425	$331,406	89.14
293334	Unfused pyridine ring compounds	$6,821	$7,655	89.11

(continued)

132 ITEMS FOR WHICH CHINA IS MORE THAN 70 PERCENT DEPENDENT ON THE UNITED STATES
(TOTAL VALUE =$5,713,431,562)

HS CODE	PRODUCT DESCRIPTION	TRADE VALUE OF CHINA'S IMPORTS FROM THE UNITED STATES (USD)	TRADE VALUE OF CHINA'S IMPORTS FROM THE WORLD (USD)	U.S. SHARE OF CHINA'S TOTAL IMPORTS (PERCENT)
284011	Anhydrous disodium tetraborate	$16,921,907	$18,998,180	89.07
370255	Polychrome film: rolls, width exceeding 16mm but less than 35mm, length exceeding 30m	$15,698,726	$17,647,884	88.96
293353	Various barbiturates: salts	$1,866	$2,099	88.90
10649	Live insects (not bees)	$126,456	$142,746	88.59
850162	AC generators	$46,127,972	$52,794,057	87.37
850240	Electric rotary converters	$400,418	$459,159	87.21
380700	Wood tar: wood tar oils	$366,350	$420,438	87.14
30311	Frozen Pacific salmon: sockeye (red)	$9,801,630	$11,427,467	85.77
391211	Non-plasticized cellulose acetates	$207,245,157	$241,918,997	85.67
300650	Pharmaceutical goods: first aid boxes and kits	$3,421,689	$3,996,244	85.62
843320	Mowers: NES (including cutter bars)	$8,233,816	$9,638,980	85.42
292122	Amine compounds	$95,557,095	$112,332,826	85.07
870431	Gas trucks: for transporting goods	$189,683,993	$223,839,669	84.74
360690	Ferrocerium: pyrophoric alloys	$1,797,600	$2,124,957	84.59
300259	Cell cultures: not cell therapy	$26,258,964	$31,139,917	84.33

**132 ITEMS FOR WHICH CHINA IS MORE THAN 70 PERCENT DEPENDENT
ON THE UNITED STATES
(TOTAL VALUE =$5,713,431,562)**

HS CODE	PRODUCT DESCRIPTION	TRADE VALUE OF CHINA'S IMPORTS FROM THE UNITED STATES (USD)	TRADE VALUE OF CHINA'S IMPORTS FROM THE WORLD (USD)	U.S. SHARE OF CHINA'S TOTAL IMPORTS (PERCENT)
711510	Metal: catalysts in the form of wire cloth or grill, of platinum	$1,012	$1,217	83.16
540259	Single synthetic yarn	$12,055,951	$14,546,681	82.88
901420	Aeronautical/space instruments	$101,269,501	$122,775,300	82.48
370252	Polychrome film: rolls, width less than 16mm	$106,885	$129,608	82.47
871639	Goods transport trailers	$633,000	$770,118	82.20
900580	Monoculars: other optical telescopes and astronomical instruments, excluding instruments for radio astronomy	$7,563,397	$9,278,353	81.52
120923	Fescue seed: for sowing	$23,010,758	$28,232,837	81.50
271129	Petroleum gases and hydrocarbons	$778,169	$955,088	81.48
360610	Liquefied-gas fuel for lighters	$1,056,932	$1,298,187	81.42
854091	Cathode-ray tube parts	$700,954	$861,656	81.35
842449	Mechanical appliances: agricultural or horticultural sprayers: other than portable sprayers	$14,430,081	$17,839,888	80.89
370239	Unexposed photographic film: <105mm	$15,088	$19,012	79.36

(*continued*)

132 ITEMS FOR WHICH CHINA IS MORE THAN 70 PERCENT DEPENDENT ON THE UNITED STATES
(TOTAL VALUE =$5,713,431,562)

HS CODE	PRODUCT DESCRIPTION	TRADE VALUE OF CHINA'S IMPORTS FROM THE UNITED STATES (USD)	TRADE VALUE OF CHINA'S IMPORTS FROM THE WORLD (USD)	U.S. SHARE OF CHINA'S TOTAL IMPORTS (PERCENT)
870432	Vehicles: with only spark-ignition internal combustion piston engine, for transport of goods (of a g.v.w. exceeding 5 metric tons), n.e.c. in item no 8704.1	$9,086,568	$11,455,501	79.32
283620	Carbonates: disodium carbonate	$172,032,464	$218,453,738	78.75
630319	Curtain or bed valances, knitted or crocheted, of textile materials other than synthetic fibers	$331,699	$422,368	78.53
230110	Flours, meats, and pellets from meat/offal	$237,897,016	$304,345,716	78.17
200981	Juice: cranberry: Lingonberry, unfermented, not containing added spirit	$1,771,349	$2,293,197	77.24
350211	Albumins: egg albumin, dried	$75,968	$98,786	76.90
480452	Kraft paper and paperboard: uncoated, weight 225g/m2 or more, bleached uniformly throughout, more than 95% of total fiber content consists of chemically processed wood fibers, in rolls or sheets	$3,668,439	$4,772,692	76.86
491191	Printed matter: pictures, designs, photographs	$126,796,993	$165,484,510	76.62
540730	Fabrics, woven: from synthetic filament yarn, adhesive or thermal bonded	$247,756	$323,504	76.59

**132 ITEMS FOR WHICH CHINA IS MORE THAN 70 PERCENT DEPENDENT
ON THE UNITED STATES
(TOTAL VALUE =$5,713,431,562)**

HS CODE	PRODUCT DESCRIPTION	TRADE VALUE OF CHINA'S IMPORTS FROM THE UNITED STATES (USD)	TRADE VALUE OF CHINA'S IMPORTS FROM THE WORLD (USD)	U.S. SHARE OF CHINA'S TOTAL IMPORTS (PERCENT)
810430	Magnesium: raspings, turnings, powders	$59,395	$77,567	76.57
901814	Scintigraphic medical instruments	$91,876,205	$120,438,360	76.28
440791	Oak wood	$312,519,528	$414,080,593	75.47
300213	Blood products: immunological, not retail	$71,267,963	$94,563,560	75.37
811249	Rhenium and articles thereof: wrought, other than powders, waste, and scrap	$221,040	$295,108	74.90
970199	Artwork: other than paintings, drawings, pastels, mosaics, executed entirely by hand, other than drawings of heading no. 4906, of an age not exceeding 100 years	$2,088,422	$2,802,611	74.52
330124	Peppermint essential oils	$11,715,229	$15,748,811	74.39
300670	Gel preparations designed to be used in human or veterinary medicine as a lubricant for parts of the body for surgical operations or physical examinations or as a coupling agent between the body and medical instruments	$9,754,363	$13,151,583	74.17
291211	Acyclic aldehydes: methanal (formaldehyde)	$192,859	$260,129	74.14

(continued)

132 ITEMS FOR WHICH CHINA IS MORE THAN 70 PERCENT DEPENDENT ON THE UNITED STATES
(TOTAL VALUE =$5,713,431,562)

HS CODE	PRODUCT DESCRIPTION	TRADE VALUE OF CHINA'S IMPORTS FROM THE UNITED STATES (USD)	TRADE VALUE OF CHINA'S IMPORTS FROM THE WORLD (USD)	U.S. SHARE OF CHINA'S TOTAL IMPORTS (PERCENT)
30339	Frozen flat fish	$139,452,348	$188,481,462	73.99
690410	Ceramic building bricks	$1,536,123	$2,077,982	73.92
121490	Forage products	$354,489,657	$480,508,372	73.77
870460	Vehicles: with only electric motor for propulsion	$2,009,381	$2,765,904	72.65
284441	Tritium and its compounds: alloys, dispersions (including cermets), ceramic products, and mixtures containing tritium or its compounds	$1,534,824	$2,115,540	72.55
151550	Sesame oil and its fractions, whether or not refined, but not chemically modified	$4,013,640	$5,547,295	72.35
151229	Cottonseed oil and its fractions, other than crude, whether or not refined, but not chemically modified	$19,320	$26,732	72.27
281640	Oxides, hydroxides, and peroxides, of strontium or barium	$129,467	$179,525	72.12
293391	Heterocyclic compounds: various (INNs)	$20,969	$29,335	71.48
854079	Microwave tubes: not magnetrons	$11,239,023	$15,761,029	71.31

95 ITEMS FOR WHICH CHINA IS MORE THAN 70 PERCENT DEPENDENT ON GERMANY
(TOTAL VALUE = $1,430,635,581)

HS CODE	PRODUCT DESCRIPTION	TRADE VALUE OF CHINA'S IMPORTS FROM GERMANY (USD)	TRADE VALUE OF CHINA'S IMPORTS FROM THE WORLD (USD)	GERMANY'S SHARE OF CHINA'S TOTAL IMPORTS (PERCENT)
870510	Vehicles: crane lorries	$1,630,201	$1,630,201	100.00
841630	Mechanical stokers, mechanical grates, mechanical ash dischargers, and similar appliances	$181,081	$181,081	100.00
370241	Photographic film: for color photography (polychrome), in rolls, sensitized, unexposed, without sprocket holes, of a width exceeding 610mm and of a length exceeding 200m	$73,689	$73,689	100.00
860500	Passenger coaches, luggage vans, post office coaches, and other special purpose railway or tramway coaches, not self-propelled	$26,876	$26,876	100.00
847432	Mineral mixing machines	$19,121	$19,121	100.00
292011	Parathion (ISO) and parathion-methyl (ISO) (methyl-parathion)	$488	$488	100.00
240492	Nicotine products for transdermal application	$391	$391	100.00
100310	Barley, seed	$246	$246	100.00
290381	Cyclanic, cyclenic, cycloterpenic hydrocarbons derivatives	$205	$205	100.00

(continued)

95 ITEMS FOR WHICH CHINA IS MORE THAN 70 PERCENT DEPENDENT ON GERMANY
(TOTAL VALUE = $1,430,635,581)

HS CODE	PRODUCT DESCRIPTION	TRADE VALUE OF CHINA'S IMPORTS FROM GERMANY (USD)	TRADE VALUE OF CHINA'S IMPORTS FROM THE WORLD (USD)	GERMANY'S SHARE OF CHINA'S TOTAL IMPORTS (PERCENT)
292412	Fluoroacetamide (ISO), monocrotophos (ISO), and phosphamidon (ISO)	$141	$141	100.00
290911	Acyclic ethers: derivatives	$89	$89	100.00
470429	Bleached non-coniferous chemical wood pulp	$5,932,301	$5,938,896	99.89
310250	Sodium nitrate	$97,711	$97,868	99.84
560721	Twine: binder or baler twine, of sisal or other textile fibers of the genus agave	$385	$386	99.74
292244	Amino acids: tilidine and esters	$157,546	$159,048	99.06
730590	Iron or steel (excluding cast iron): tubes and pipes n.e.c. in heading no. 7305, having circular cross-sections, external diameter exceeds 406.4mm (not seamless)	$247,270	$249,643	99.05
290323	Tetrachloroethylene	$17,487,779	$17,746,795	98.54
847930	Machinery for wood or cork	$22,719,529	$23,108,172	98.32
950825	Amusement park rides and water park amusements: water rides	$6,220,069	$6,371,208	97.63
730810	Iron/steel structures: bridges	$3,624,737	$3,734,359	97.06
441840	Wood: shuttering for concrete constructional work	$19,077	$19,970	95.53

**95 ITEMS FOR WHICH CHINA IS MORE THAN 70 PERCENT DEPENDENT
ON GERMANY
(TOTAL VALUE = $1,430,635,581)**

HS CODE	PRODUCT DESCRIPTION	TRADE VALUE OF CHINA'S IMPORTS FROM GERMANY (USD)	TRADE VALUE OF CHINA'S IMPORTS FROM THE WORLD (USD)	GERMANY'S SHARE OF CHINA'S TOTAL IMPORTS (PERCENT)
293790	Hormones and related compounds	$29,692,730	$31,255,558	95.00
845522	Metal-rolling mills: cold	$37,344,293	$39,818,345	93.79
732429	Iron or steel baths, NES	$4,446,029	$4,751,449	93.57
282510	Hydrazine and hydroxylamine	$13,223,385	$14,200,480	93.12
810929	Zirconium powders: less hafnium	$3,470,867	$3,729,143	93.07
844120	Bag- and sack-making machines	$19,847,340	$21,442,689	92.56
290541	Alcohols: polyhydric, 2-ethyl-2- (hydroxymethyl) propane-1,3-diol (trimethylolpropane)	$1,024,973	$1,107,897	92.52
820713	Rock drilling or boring tools	$3,459,866	$3,767,979	91.82
910990	Clock movements: complete and assembled	$254,401	$277,362	91.72
870332	Vehicles with only compression-ignition internal combustion piston engine (diesel or semi-diesel), cylinder capacity over 1500 but not over 2500cc	$17,959,937	$19,763,043	90.88
151630	Microbial fats and oils and their fractions	$3,638	$4,005	90.84

(continued)

95 ITEMS FOR WHICH CHINA IS MORE THAN 70 PERCENT DEPENDENT ON GERMANY
(TOTAL VALUE = $1,430,635,581)

HS CODE	PRODUCT DESCRIPTION	TRADE VALUE OF CHINA'S IMPORTS FROM GERMANY (USD)	TRADE VALUE OF CHINA'S IMPORTS FROM THE WORLD (USD)	GERMANY'S SHARE OF CHINA'S TOTAL IMPORTS (PERCENT)
730230	Switchblades, crossing frogs	$1,208,789	$1,338,954	90.28
200560	Vegetable asparagus: preserved, not frozen	$425	$481	88.36
901540	Surveying equipment: photogrammetrical surveying instruments and appliances	$1,412,451	$1,602,153	88.16
843010	Pile drivers and pile extractors	$22,844,654	$25,962,000	87.99
292620	1-Cyanoguanidine (dicyanidiamide)	$3,491,449	$3,983,196	87.65
390529	Vinyl acetate copolymers: other than in aqueous dispersion, in primary forms	$7,092,986	$8,122,081	87.33
100510	Maize (corn) seed	$34,353,944	$39,420,884	87.15
760320	Lamellar aluminum powders	$8,779,147	$10,119,739	86.75
292019	Thiophosphoric esters and their salts: other than parathion (ISO) and parathion-methyl (ISO) (methyl-parathion)	$1,185,982	$1,373,980	86.32
481200	Paper pulp filter blocks, slabs	$10,383,334	$12,088,555	85.89
950822	Amusement park rides and water park amusements: carousels, swings, and roundabouts	$3,108,428	$3,658,026	84.98
382481	Oxirane-containing chemical products	$118,606	$139,713	84.89
842831	Continuous-action elevators/conveyors	$13,099,680	$15,452,645	84.77

95 ITEMS FOR WHICH CHINA IS MORE THAN 70 PERCENT DEPENDENT ON GERMANY
(TOTAL VALUE = $1,430,635,581)

HS CODE	PRODUCT DESCRIPTION	TRADE VALUE OF CHINA'S IMPORTS FROM GERMANY (USD)	TRADE VALUE OF CHINA'S IMPORTS FROM THE WORLD (USD)	GERMANY'S SHARE OF CHINA'S TOTAL IMPORTS (PERCENT)
860400	Railway or tramway maintenance or service vehicles: whether or not self-propelled (e.g., workshops, cranes, ballast tampers, track liners, testing coaches, and track inspection vehicles)	$13,417,932	$15,944,646	84.15
731442	Plastic-coated wire: grill, netting	$279,678	$334,059	83.72
420219	Trunks, suitcases, NES	$32,928,076	$39,390,205	83.59
871610	Housing or camping trailers	$435,804	$523,878	83.19
721661	Iron or non-alloy steel: angles, shapes, and sections, cold-formed or cold-finished, obtained from flat-rolled products	$395,074	$476,589	82.90
283522	Mono- or disodium phosphates	$2,228,412	$2,701,592	82.49
293154	Halogenated organophosphorus derivatives	$279	$340	82.06
843840	Machinery: industrial, brewery machinery	$1,112,364	$1,368,131	81.31
680919	Nonornamental plaster boards	$1,654,299	$2,049,895	80.70
380620	Rosin/resin acid salts	$1,391,888	$1,727,039	80.59
293625	Vitamins: vitamin B6 and its derivatives, unmixed	$402,934	$500,198	80.55

(continued)

95 ITEMS FOR WHICH CHINA IS MORE THAN 70 PERCENT DEPENDENT ON GERMANY
(TOTAL VALUE = $1,430,635,581)

HS CODE	PRODUCT DESCRIPTION	TRADE VALUE OF CHINA'S IMPORTS FROM GERMANY (USD)	TRADE VALUE OF CHINA'S IMPORTS FROM THE WORLD (USD)	GERMANY'S SHARE OF CHINA'S TOTAL IMPORTS (PERCENT)
292421	Cyclic amides: ureines, salts	$1,430,044	$1,799,684	79.46
847920	Machinery: for the extraction or preparation of animal or fixed vegetable or microbial fats or oils	$479,888	$604,261	79.42
731590	Chain parts, iron/steel, NES	$8,289,428	$10,461,016	79.24
731582	Welded iron/steel chains	$61,505,849	$77,676,795	79.18
701914	Glass fibers: including glass wool, mechanically bonded mats	$507,565	$641,292	79.15
846130	Broaching machines, working by removing metal, sintered metal carbides, or cermets	$22,902,939	$28,940,032	79.14
730422	Steel, stainless: seamless, drill pipe, of a kind used in drilling for oil or gas	$1,339,160	$1,696,315	78.95
283110	Sodium dithionites and sulphoxylates	$4,620,190	$5,881,612	78.55
293623	Vitamin B2: unmixed	$2,295,032	$2,929,688	78.34
700231	Fused quartz or silica tubes	$61,302,573	$78,779,103	77.82
40140	Milk and cream, not concentrated, not containing added sugar or other sweetening matter, of a fat content, by weight, exceeding 6% but not exceeding 10%	$56,243	$72,427	77.65
720810	Iron or steel: flat-rolled coils	$38,566	$49,695	77.61

95 ITEMS FOR WHICH CHINA IS MORE THAN 70 PERCENT DEPENDENT ON GERMANY
(TOTAL VALUE = $1,430,635,581)

HS CODE	PRODUCT DESCRIPTION	TRADE VALUE OF CHINA'S IMPORTS FROM GERMANY (USD)	TRADE VALUE OF CHINA'S IMPORTS FROM THE WORLD (USD)	GERMANY'S SHARE OF CHINA'S TOTAL IMPORTS (PERCENT)
830910	Stoppers: corks, of base metal	$173,964	$224,460	77.50
120910	Sugar beet seeds, of a kind used for sowing	$29,968,362	$39,047,971	76.75
711420	Gold/silver articles: wares and parts	$50,073	$65,634	76.29
843020	Snowplows and snowblowers	$3,260,420	$4,276,531	76.24
570232	Carpets and other textile floor coverings: woven (not tufted or flocked), of man-made textile materials, of pile construction, not made up	$837,042	$1,098,904	76.17
843353	Root/tuber harvesting machinery	$10,631,846	$14,046,435	75.69
71030	Frozen spinach	$11,186	$14,781	75.68
846310	Metalworking machine tools: no material removal	$25,413,013	$33,669,129	75.48
911090	Clocks: movements, whether complete, incomplete, assembled, or unassembled	$228,134	$302,752	75.35
110720	Roasted malt	$3,253,057	$4,342,225	74.92
392079	Plastics: plates, sheets, film, foil, and strip (not self-adhesive), of cellulose derivatives n.e.c. in heading no. 3920	$13,593,668	$18,176,532	74.79

(continued)

95 ITEMS FOR WHICH CHINA IS MORE THAN 70 PERCENT DEPENDENT ON GERMANY
(TOTAL VALUE = $1,430,635,581)

HS CODE	PRODUCT DESCRIPTION	TRADE VALUE OF CHINA'S IMPORTS FROM GERMANY (USD)	TRADE VALUE OF CHINA'S IMPORTS FROM THE WORLD (USD)	GERMANY'S SHARE OF CHINA'S TOTAL IMPORTS (PERCENT)
844313	Offset printing machinery	$444,424,041	$594,948,345	74.70
847910	Machinery for public works	$23,415,147	$31,433,515	74.49
441300	Densified wood: blocks, plates, strips	$27,128,423	$36,495,509	74.33
281217	Thionyl chloride	$3,334,656	$4,534,671	73.54
290391	Halogenated derivatives of aromatic hydrocarbons: chlorobenzene, o-dichlorobenzene, and p-dichlorobenzene	$255,933	$351,105	72.89
390519	Poly (vinyl acetate): primary forms	$2,862,995	$3,932,147	72.81
440500	Wood wool: wood flour	$1,557,143	$2,148,027	72.49
841382	Liquid elevators	$1,556,784	$2,155,677	72.22
847810	Machinery: for preparing or making up tobacco, n.e.c. in this chapter	$17,152,673	$23,921,713	71.70
843231	No-till seeders and planters	$13,212,772	$18,479,455	71.50
960830	Pens: fountain, stylograph, and other pens	$29,506,722	$41,338,589	71.38
700232	Glass tubes: unworked, specific expansion	$29,152,034	$41,006,079	71.09
293159	Halogenated organo-phosphorous derivatives: other halogenated organo-phosphorous derivatives	$1,541,639	$2,172,660	70.96
847730	Blow molding machine	$98,626,258	$139,463,646	70.72

95 ITEMS FOR WHICH CHINA IS MORE THAN 70 PERCENT DEPENDENT
ON GERMANY
(TOTAL VALUE = $1,430,635,581)

HS CODE	PRODUCT DESCRIPTION	TRADE VALUE OF CHINA'S IMPORTS FROM GERMANY (USD)	TRADE VALUE OF CHINA'S IMPORTS FROM THE WORLD (USD)	GERMANY'S SHARE OF CHINA'S TOTAL IMPORTS (PERCENT)
843351	Combine harvester-threshers	$103,780,452	$147,226,200	70.49
722410	Ingots, alloy steel	$30,446,661	$43,201,795	70.48

48 ITEMS FOR WHICH CHINA IS MORE THAN 70 PERCENT DEPENDENT
ON SOUTH KOREA
(TOTAL VALUE = $8,577,531,035)

HS CODE	PRODUCT DESCRIPTION	TRADE VALUE OF CHINA'S IMPORTS FROM SOUTH KOREA (USD)	TRADE VALUE OF CHINA'S IMPORTS FROM THE WORLD (USD)	SOUTH KOREA'S SHARE OF CHINA'S TOTAL IMPORTS (PERCENT)
30229	Fresh or chilled flat fish	$1,969,053	$1,969,053	100.00
30712	Frozen oysters: with or without shell	$784,529	$784,529	100.00
440692	Wood: railway or tramway sleepers (crossties), impregnated, non-coniferous	$53,044	$53,044	100.00
30241	Fresh or chilled herrings	$15,358	$15,358	100.00
410632	Tanned or crust hides and skins: of swine, without hair on, whether or not split, but not further prepared, in the dry state (crust)	$9,526	$9,526	100.00

(continued)

48 ITEMS FOR WHICH CHINA IS MORE THAN 70 PERCENT DEPENDENT ON SOUTH KOREA
(TOTAL VALUE = $8,577,531,035)

HS CODE	PRODUCT DESCRIPTION	TRADE VALUE OF CHINA'S IMPORTS FROM SOUTH KOREA (USD)	TRADE VALUE OF CHINA'S IMPORTS FROM THE WORLD (USD)	SOUTH KOREA'S SHARE OF CHINA'S TOTAL IMPORTS (PERCENT)
844621	Weaving machines (looms): for weaving fabrics of a width exceeding 30cm, shuttle type, power looms	$8,603	$8,603	100.00
880699	Unmanned aircraft: for other than remote-controlled flight and other than for carriage of passengers with a maximum takeoff weight of more than 150kg	$3,956	$3,956	100.00
30244	Fresh or chilled mackerel	$927	$927	100.00
160551	Prepared mollusks: oysters	$905	$905	100.00
810411	Magnesium: unwrought, containing at least 99.8% by weight of magnesium	$75,268	$75,278	99.99
551443	Printed woven fabrics	$1,546,236	$1,565,392	98.78
160552	Prepared mollusks: scallops	$269,606	$274,042	98.38
382211	Reagents for malaria	$400,296	$408,995	97.87
790310	Zinc dust	$8,132,536	$8,409,728	96.70
852412	OLED flat panel displays, without drivers or control circuits	$2,118,159,315	$2,253,161,932	94.01
284290	Other inorganic salts	$2,060,419,042	$2,199,699,231	93.67
290346	Saturated fluorinated acyclic hydrocarbons	$43,219,499	$46,263,186	93.42
911290	Clock case parts	$46,413	$49,955	92.91

48 ITEMS FOR WHICH CHINA IS MORE THAN 70 PERCENT DEPENDENT ON SOUTH KOREA
(TOTAL VALUE = $8,577,531,035)

HS CODE	PRODUCT DESCRIPTION	TRADE VALUE OF CHINA'S IMPORTS FROM SOUTH KOREA (USD)	TRADE VALUE OF CHINA'S IMPORTS FROM THE WORLD (USD)	SOUTH KOREA'S SHARE OF CHINA'S TOTAL IMPORTS (PERCENT)
310221	Fertilizers, mineral or chemical: nitrogenous, ammonium sulphate	$152,068	$165,381	91.95
280800	Nitric and sulphonitric acids	$26,927,923	$30,005,758	89.74
520419	Cotton sewing thread: <85% cotton	$138,944	$155,231	89.51
30344	Frozen bigeye tuna: excluding fillets	$297,859	$333,504	89.31
30345	Frozen bluefin tuna (no fillets)	$3,980,640	$4,488,998	88.68
292990	Nitrogen-function compounds: NES	$44,669,313	$51,350,433	86.99
847510	Machines for assembling electric or electronic lamps, tubes, valves, or flashbulbs in glass envelopes	$731,080	$841,589	86.87
282690	Fluorides: fluorosilicates, fluoroaluminates, and other complex fluorine salts, n.e.c. in heading no. 2826	$22,771,665	$26,433,500	86.15
292511	Saccharin and salts	$899,229	$1,046,265	85.95
283720	Complex cyanides	$6,537,300	$7,652,659	85.43
281520	Potassium hydroxide (caustic potash)	$17,412,937	$20,702,639	84.11
80241	Chestnuts: fresh/dried, in shell	$7,092,884	$8,520,050	83.25

(*continued*)

48 ITEMS FOR WHICH CHINA IS MORE THAN 70 PERCENT DEPENDENT ON SOUTH KOREA
(TOTAL VALUE = $8,577,531,035)

HS CODE	PRODUCT DESCRIPTION	TRADE VALUE OF CHINA'S IMPORTS FROM SOUTH KOREA (USD)	TRADE VALUE OF CHINA'S IMPORTS FROM THE WORLD (USD)	SOUTH KOREA'S SHARE OF CHINA'S TOTAL IMPORTS (PERCENT)
290123	Unsaturated acyclic hydrocarbons	$19,297,048	$23,384,722	82.52
290344	Pentafluoroethane (HFC-125), 1,1,1-trifluoroethane (HFC-143a), and 1,1,2-trifluoroethane (HFC-143)	$1,196,915	$1,489,727	80.34
901510	Range finders	$678,644,041	$844,915,385	80.32
730539	Iron or steel (excluding cast iron): tubes and pipes (other than line pipe or casing of a kind used for oil or gas pipelines), welded (not longitudinally welded), having circular cross-sections, external diameter exceeds 406.4mm (not seamless)	$1,119,996	$1,399,604	80.02
283719	Cyanides, cyanide oxides	$9,697,555	$12,154,847	79.78
400251	Acrylonitrile-butadiene rubber (NBR): primary forms	$106,583,920	$136,241,100	78.23
721070	Iron or non-alloy steel: flat-rolled, 600mm or more, painted, varnished, or coated with plastics	$89,810,301	$114,847,676	78.20

**48 ITEMS FOR WHICH CHINA IS MORE THAN 70 PERCENT DEPENDENT
ON SOUTH KOREA
(TOTAL VALUE = $8,577,531,035)**

HS CODE	PRODUCT DESCRIPTION	TRADE VALUE OF CHINA'S IMPORTS FROM SOUTH KOREA (USD)	TRADE VALUE OF CHINA'S IMPORTS FROM THE WORLD (USD)	SOUTH KOREA'S SHARE OF CHINA'S TOTAL IMPORTS (PERCENT)
283640	Potassium carbonates	$6,778,335	$8,698,016	77.93
720917	Cold-rolled steel: 0.5–1mm thick	$164,207,911	$211,455,682	77.66
290313	Saturated chlorinated hydrocarbons: chloroform	$761,106	$1,001,314	76.01
845510	Metal rolling tube mills	$6,572,928	$8,832,419	74.42
290122	Propylene, unsaturated	$1,295,108,795	$1,743,358,335	74.29
721699	Iron or non-alloy steel: angles, shapes, and sections, n.e.c. in heading no. 7216	$5,680,482	$7,799,047	72.84
721250	Flat rolled steel: <600mm width	$75,109,942	$103,739,926	72.40
700490	Drawn/blown glass sheets: non-tinted	$928,091,114	$1,295,433,364	71.64
841583	Air-conditioning machines: containing a motor driven fan, other than window or wall types, not incorporating a refrigerating unit	$9,787,532	$13,799,699	70.93
281219	Arsenic trichloride: chlorides, oxides	$30,637,868	$43,304,106	70.75
840810	Marine propulsion engines	$781,719,292	$1,116,118,666	70.04

(continued)

38 ITEMS FOR WHICH CHINA IS MORE THAN 70 PERCENT DEPENDENT ON FRANCE
(TOTAL VALUE = $2,618,002,507)

HS CODE	PRODUCT DESCRIPTION	TRADE VALUE OF CHINA'S IMPORTS FROM FRANCE (USD)	TRADE VALUE OF CHINA'S IMPORTS FROM THE WORLD (USD)	FRANCE'S SHARE OF CHINA'S TOTAL IMPORTS (PERCENT)
240391	Homogenized/reconstituted tobacco	$8,814,292	$8,814,292	100.00
10614	Live mammals: rabbits and hares	$1,139,688	$1,139,688	100.00
30222	Fresh or chilled plaice	$100,324	$100,324	100.00
30223	Fresh or chilled sole	$83,114	$83,114	100.00
730621	Steel, stainless: casing and tubing of a kind used in drilling for oil and gas, n.e.c. in chapter 73, welded (not seamless)	$40,700	$40,700	100.00
30253	Fresh or chilled coalfish	$10,112	$10,112	100.00
160241	Swine meat preparations hams and cuts	$9,758	$9,758	100.00
160220	Prepared or preserved liver of any animal (excluding homogenized preparations)	$1,807	$1,807	100.00
30453	Fish meat, excluding fillets, whether or not minced: fresh or chilled	$272	$272	100.00
293941	Alkaloids: ephedrine and their derivatives, salts thereof	$176	$176	100.00
280410	Hydrogen	$358,477	$358,484	100.00
40520	Dairy spreads	$39,542	$39,592	99.87
844811	Dobbies, Jacquards, card-reducing machines	$24,143,269	$24,204,345	99.75

38 ITEMS FOR WHICH CHINA IS MORE THAN 70 PERCENT DEPENDENT ON FRANCE
(TOTAL VALUE = $2,618,002,507)

HS CODE	PRODUCT DESCRIPTION	TRADE VALUE OF CHINA'S IMPORTS FROM FRANCE (USD)	TRADE VALUE OF CHINA'S IMPORTS FROM THE WORLD (USD)	FRANCE'S SHARE OF CHINA'S TOTAL IMPORTS (PERCENT)
810991	Zirconium: other forms, less hafnium	$18,458,631	$18,526,130	99.64
220820	Spirits	$1,223,858,496	$1,233,579,514	99.21
880100	Balloons, dirigibles, gliders, hang gliders	$222,037	$232,598	95.46
470421	Wood pulp: chemical wood pulp, sulphite (other than dissolving grades), semi-bleached or bleached, of coniferous wood	$22,833,336	$24,368,250	93.70
290543	Mannitol	$9,998,879	$10,955,809	91.27
200510	Homogenized preserved vegetables	$273,920	$302,627	90.51
292529	Imines and salts: non-chlordimeform	$213,582,286	$240,335,147	88.87
160530	Lobster, prepared or preserved	$164,975	$185,663	88.86
870192	Tractors: of an engine power exceeding 18kW but not exceeding 37kW	$1,522,665	$1,725,375	88.25
530121	Broken or scutched flax	$756,652,158	$870,641,586	86.91
732392	Household tables	$19,509,293	$22,494,323	86.73
970210	Engravings, prints, and lithographs: original of an age exceeding 100 years	$18,596	$21,533	86.36
550119	Fibers: synthetic filament tow, of nylon or other polyamides, of other than aramids	$606,151	$708,041	85.61

(continued)

38 ITEMS FOR WHICH CHINA IS MORE THAN 70 PERCENT DEPENDENT ON FRANCE
(TOTAL VALUE = $2,618,002,507)

HS CODE	PRODUCT DESCRIPTION	TRADE VALUE OF CHINA'S IMPORTS FROM FRANCE (USD)	TRADE VALUE OF CHINA'S IMPORTS FROM THE WORLD (USD)	FRANCE'S SHARE OF CHINA'S TOTAL IMPORTS (PERCENT)
821510	Tableware sets	$1,644,493	$1,924,723	85.44
151519	Linseed oil: refined, non-crude	$1,628,320	$1,985,346	82.02
160558	Snails, other than sea snails, prepared or preserved	$105,907	$131,457	80.56
970192	Mosaics: executed entirely by hand, other than drawings of heading no. 4906, of an age not exceeding 100 years	$1,200,000	$1,505,322	79.72
390450	Vinylidene chloride polymers	$26,030,212	$33,884,739	76.82
844512	Textile machinery: combing machines for preparing textile fibers	$1,639,103	$2,134,704	76.78
20321	Meat: of swine, carcasses and half-carcasses, frozen	$40,194	$52,947	75.91
480630	Paper: tracing papers, in rolls or sheets	$166,907	$222,789	74.92
90520	Vanilla, crushed or ground	$169,893	$229,508	74.02
621390	Non-cotton handkerchiefs: textile materials	$1,616,672	$2,251,040	71.82
293492	Heterocyclic compounds: other fentanyls n.e.c. in 2934, and their derivatives	$2,216	$3,127	70.87
851150	Generators n.e.c. in heading no. 8511, of a kind used for spark- or compression-ignition internal combustion engines	$281,315,636	$400,200,394	70.29

**26 ITEMS FOR WHICH CHINA IS MORE THAN 70 PERCENT DEPENDENT
ON CANADA
(TOTAL VALUE = $5,457,672,022)**

HS CODE	PRODUCT DESCRIPTION	TRADE VALUE OF CHINA'S IMPORTS FROM CANADA (USD)	TRADE VALUE OF CHINA'S IMPORTS FROM THE WORLD (USD)	CANADA'S SHARE OF CHINA'S TOTAL IMPORTS (PERCENT)
120510	Rape or colza seeds	$3,294,156,686	$3,294,156,850	100.00
100830	Cereals: canary seeds	$4,198,654	$4,198,654	100.00
300442	Medicaments: containing pseudoephedrine	$928	$928	100.00
150430	Marine mammal fats and oils	$292	$292	100.00
100210	Rye, seed	$220	$220	100.00
440713	Coniferous wood: S-P-F, sawn or chipped	$92,167,241	$92,204,140	99.96
30612	Frozen lobsters	$31,401,447	$31,458,447	99.82
360330	Percussion caps	$870,599	$872,316	99.80
30772	Frozen clams, cockles, ark shells	$69,340,049	$69,593,444	99.64
440714	Coniferous wood: hem-fir species	$61,866,957	$62,904,617	98.35
170220	Maple sugar and syrup	$2,273,132	$2,324,777	97.78
293336	Containing an unfused pyridine ring (whether or not hydrogenated) in the structure, 4-anilino-N-phenethylpiperidine (ANPP)	$9,132	$9,387	97.28
841122	Turbo-propellers: >1,100kW	$6,804,774	$7,057,191	96.42
160556	Prepared mollusks: clams, cockles, ark shells	$776,187	$825,970	93.97
120921	Lucerne (alfalfa) seeds	$8,439,692	$9,724,254	86.79

(continued)

26 ITEMS FOR WHICH CHINA IS MORE THAN 70 PERCENT DEPENDENT ON CANADA
(TOTAL VALUE = $5,457,672,022)

HS CODE	PRODUCT DESCRIPTION	TRADE VALUE OF CHINA'S IMPORTS FROM CANADA (USD)	TRADE VALUE OF CHINA'S IMPORTS FROM THE WORLD (USD)	CANADA'S SHARE OF CHINA'S TOTAL IMPORTS (PERCENT)
960110	Worked ivory items	$1,241,787	$1,458,777	85.13
100410	Cereals: oats	$4,313,507	$5,260,493	82.00
271410	Bituminous or oil shale and tar sands	$733	$919	79.76
30632	Lobsters, nonfrozen	$609,077,551	$771,396,769	78.96
470500	Semichemical wood pulp	$470,210,161	$612,161,478	76.81
230641	Oil cake: from rape/colza seed	$783,343,131	$1,040,925,730	75.25
30821	Live sea urchins: fresh/chilled	$1,872,254	$2,565,571	72.98
252930	Leucite: nepheline and nepheline syenite	$914,881	$1,270,102	72.03
30812	Frozen sea cucumbers	$11,699,413	$16,253,922	71.98
843330	Haymaking machinery	$2,670,373	$3,764,321	70.94
51000	Ambergris, castoreum, civet, musk, cantharides, bile (dried or not) glands, and other animal products, for pharmaceutical purposes	$22,241	$31,569	70.45

**23 ITEMS FOR WHICH CHINA IS MORE THAN 70 PERCENT DEPENDENT
ON NEW ZEALAND
(TOTAL VALUE = $5,347,529,586)**

HS CODE	PRODUCT DESCRIPTION	TRADE VALUE OF CHINA'S IMPORTS FROM NEW ZEALAND (USD)	TRADE VALUE OF CHINA'S IMPORTS FROM THE WORLD (USD)	NEW ZEALAND'S SHARE OF CHINA'S TOTAL IMPORTS (PERCENT)
30732	Frozen mussels	$21,417,925	$21,417,925	100.00
20890	Pigeon, game, or reindeer meat	$16,797,779	$16,797,779	100.00
440311	Coniferous wood: rough or treated	$6,818,891	$6,818,920	100.00
30739	Dried mollusks: mussels	$50,720	$50,720	100.00
30479	Frozen fish fillets (various families)	$799	$799	100.00
20622	Frozen bovine livers	$15,983	$16,160	98.90
81050	Fresh kiwifruit	$590,226,297	$598,376,593	98.64
30619	Frozen crustaceans: NES	$59,927,682	$60,936,857	98.34
410221	Sheep and lamb skin, without wool on	$273,928	$281,232	97.40
30731	Live mussels: fresh or chilled	$6,328,137	$6,617,770	95.62
40590	Dairy fats and oils (not butter)	$195,090,677	$208,455,499	93.59
30213	Fresh or chilled Pacific salmon	$16,249,152	$17,561,756	92.53
440321	Pinewood	$2,048,897,736	$2,219,204,321	92.33
20210	Frozen bovine carcasses: half carcasses	$390,412	$457,992	85.24
81120	Blackberries, raspberries	$6,497,433	$7,780,348	83.51
71021	Frozen peas: shelled or unshelled	$35,523,844	$43,902,901	80.91

(continued)

23 ITEMS FOR WHICH CHINA IS MORE THAN 70 PERCENT DEPENDENT ON NEW ZEALAND
(TOTAL VALUE = $5,347,529,586)

HS CODE	PRODUCT DESCRIPTION	TRADE VALUE OF CHINA'S IMPORTS FROM NEW ZEALAND (USD)	TRADE VALUE OF CHINA'S IMPORTS FROM THE WORLD (USD)	NEW ZEALAND'S SHARE OF CHINA'S TOTAL IMPORTS (PERCENT)
40510	Butter	$591,644,848	$737,431,199	80.23
20441	Frozen sheep carcasses	$90,034,164	$113,025,595	79.66
40221	Solid milk and cream	$1,287,144,337	$1,625,392,375	79.19
80810	Apples, fresh	$169,120,570	$217,848,599	77.63
350110	Casein	$111,596,470	$144,321,443	77.32
50790	Tortoiseshell/whalebone/whale	$58,270,649	$78,713,658	74.03
40900	Natural honey	$35,211,153	$48,297,196	72.91

22 ITEMS FOR WHICH CHINA IS MORE THAN 70 PERCENT DEPENDENT ON AUSTRALIA
(TOTAL VALUE = $2,357,003,034)

HS CODE	PRODUCT DESCRIPTION	TRADE VALUE OF CHINA'S IMPORTS FROM AUSTRALIA (USD)	TRADE VALUE OF CHINA'S IMPORTS FROM THE WORLD (USD)	AUSTRALIA'S SHARE OF CHINA'S TOTAL IMPORTS (PERCENT)
10221	Cattle: live, purebred breeding animals	$21,760,100	$21,760,100	100.00
20410	Sheep meat: fresh or chilled	$2,726,233	$2,726,233	100.00
30485	Frozen toothfish fillets	$500,798	$500,798	100.00

22 ITEMS FOR WHICH CHINA IS MORE THAN 70 PERCENT DEPENDENT ON AUSTRALIA
(TOTAL VALUE = $2,357,003,034)

HS CODE	PRODUCT DESCRIPTION	TRADE VALUE OF CHINA'S IMPORTS FROM AUSTRALIA (USD)	TRADE VALUE OF CHINA'S IMPORTS FROM THE WORLD (USD)	AUSTRALIA'S SHARE OF CHINA'S TOTAL IMPORTS (PERCENT)
711299	Waste and scrap of precious metals, including metal clad with precious metals	$115,500	$115,500	100.00
30346	Frozen southern bluefin tuna (not fillets)	$4,595,461	$4,595,863	99.99
10229	Cattle: live, other than purebred breeding animals	$63,368,452	$63,820,962	99.29
30236	Southern bluefin tuna: fresh/chilled	$1,624,752	$1,636,478	99.28
160557	Prepared mollusks: abalone	$2,579,321	$2,610,911	98.79
30239	Fresh or chilled tuna, excluding fillets	$977,788	$991,697	98.60
20450	Fresh, chilled, or frozen goat meat	$20,928,129	$21,239,567	98.53
110412	Rolled or flaked oats	$2,788,581	$2,851,142	97.81
150210	Tallow: not of heading 1503	$7,764,935	$8,163,673	95.12
120729	Oilseeds	$190,302,622	$216,000,349	88.10
20443	Frozen boned sheep meat	$78,165,455	$90,128,637	86.73
80212	Almonds, fresh or dried, shelled	$176,727,323	$221,426,147	79.81
110422	Worked oats: other, NES	$3,912,861	$4,936,363	79.27

(continued)

22 ITEMS FOR WHICH CHINA IS MORE THAN 70 PERCENT DEPENDENT ON AUSTRALIA
(TOTAL VALUE = $2,357,003,034)

HS CODE	PRODUCT DESCRIPTION	TRADE VALUE OF CHINA'S IMPORTS FROM AUSTRALIA (USD)	TRADE VALUE OF CHINA'S IMPORTS FROM THE WORLD (USD)	AUSTRALIA'S SHARE OF CHINA'S TOTAL IMPORTS (PERCENT)
510111	Greasy wool	$1,543,854,694	$1,948,894,578	79.22
190420	Unroasted cereal flakes or mixtures of unroasted cereal flakes and roasted cereal flakes or swelled cereals	$21,846,078	$28,748,298	75.99
510130	Carbonized wool: not carded	$1,749,503	$2,329,445	75.10
420600	Articles of gut (other than silkworm gut), of goldbeater's skin, of bladders, or of tendons	$315,923	$421,676	74.92
80211	Almonds, fresh or dried, in shell	$210,391,773	$287,648,930	73.14
81330	Dried apples	$6,752	$9,240	73.07

16 ITEMS FOR WHICH CHINA IS MORE THAN 70 PERCENT DEPENDENT ON NORWAY
(TOTAL VALUE = $596,650,834)

HS CODE	PRODUCT DESCRIPTION	TRADE VALUE OF CHINA'S IMPORTS FROM NORWAY (USD)	TRADE VALUE OF CHINA'S IMPORTS FROM THE WORLD (USD)	NORWAY'S SHARE OF CHINA'S TOTAL IMPORTS (PERCENT)
30211	Fresh or chilled trout	$1,033,446	$1,033,446	100.00
30442	Fish fillets: fresh or chilled, trout	$2,221	$2,221	100.00
30532	Fish fillets: dried, salted, or in brine, but not smoked	$20	$20	100.00
30543	Trout, includes fillets, smoked	$201,013	$201,857	99.58
30910	Fish flours: human consumption	$186,434	$189,756	98.25
681520	Peat: articles of peat n.e.c. or included	$106,049	$108,300	97.92
30365	Frozen coalfish	$53,139,004	$54,353,732	97.77
30634	Live fresh/chilled Norway lobsters	$648,732	$672,790	96.42
840220	Superheated water boilers	$494,331	$520,127	95.04
151610	Animal fats and oils and their fractions	$9,547,469	$10,836,452	88.11
30579	Fish: edible offal, other than shark fins, fish heads, tails, and maws	$5,484,492	$6,261,429	87.59
30251	Fresh/chilled cod (not fillets)	$207,903	$252,647	82.29
292429	Cyclic amides (including carbamates)	$388,946,033	$487,486,391	79.79
30441	Fresh/chilled salmon fillets	$18,894,287	$24,203,991	78.06
284442	Radioactive elements: various	$3,840,914	$4,963,511	77.38
30354	Frozen mackerel, excluding fillets	$113,918,486	$161,307,020	70.62

13 ITEMS FOR WHICH CHINA IS MORE THAN 70 PERCENT DEPENDENT ON THE UNITED KINGDOM
(TOTAL VALUE =$412,544,078)

HS CODE	PRODUCT DESCRIPTION	TRADE VALUE OF CHINA'S IMPORTS FROM THE UNITED KINGDOM (USD)	TRADE VALUE OF CHINA'S IMPORTS FROM THE WORLD (USD)	UNITED KINGDOM'S SHARE OF CHINA'S TOTAL IMPORTS (PERCENT)
860110	Rail locomotives: powered from an external source of electricity	$3,247,234	$3,247,234	100.00
382751	Mixtures of halogenated methane derivatives	$466,581	$466,581	100.00
382759	Halogenated methane, ethane, or propane mixtures	$38,187	$38,187	100.00
150500	Wool grease and fatty substances derived therefrom (including lanolin)	$13	$13	100.00
840731	Engines: reciprocating piston engines, of a kind used for the propulsion of vehicles of chapter 87, of a cylinder capacity not exceeding 50cc	$35,049	$36,549	95.90
293911	Alkaloids: opium and their derivatives, salts thereof	$13,391,449	$14,570,773	91.91
851920	Coin-operated sound recording apparatus	$33,446	$36,917	90.60
220830	Whiskies	$391,179,828	$451,434,570	86.65
293372	Lactams: clobazam, methyprylon	$407	$488	83.40
370296	Photographic film: b&w, rolls	$620,033	$769,961	80.53
851633	Hand-drying apparatus: electro-thermic	$95,271	$124,585	76.47

13 ITEMS FOR WHICH CHINA IS MORE THAN 70 PERCENT DEPENDENT ON THE UNITED KINGDOM
(TOTAL VALUE =$412,544,078)

HS CODE	PRODUCT DESCRIPTION	TRADE VALUE OF CHINA'S IMPORTS FROM THE UNITED KINGDOM (USD)	TRADE VALUE OF CHINA'S IMPORTS FROM THE WORLD (USD)	UNITED KINGDOM'S SHARE OF CHINA'S TOTAL IMPORTS (PERCENT)
580110	Fabrics: woven pile, of wool or fine animal hair, other than fabrics of heading no. 5802 or 5806	$3,409,217	$4,489,042	75.95
30541	Salmon, Pacific, Atlantic, and Danube, includes fillets, smoked	$27,363	$38,815	70.50

9 ITEMS FOR WHICH CHINA IS MORE THAN 70 PERCENT DEPENDENT ON MONGOLIA
(TOTAL VALUE = $474,174,554)

HS CODE	PRODUCT DESCRIPTION	TRADE VALUE OF CHINA'S IMPORTS FROM MONGOLIA (USD)	TRADE VALUE OF CHINA'S IMPORTS FROM THE WORLD (USD)	MONGOLIA'S SHARE OF CHINA'S TOTAL IMPORTS (PERCENT)
160290	Meat preparations	$57,470,828	$57,470,828	100.00
510219	Fine animal hair	$135,861,149	$144,133,489	94.26
20500	Meat: of horses, asses, etc.	$56,987,660	$62,454,289	91.25
80292	Pine nuts: fresh/dried, shelled	$25,802,811	$30,572,596	84.40
740312	Copper: refined, unwrought, wire-bars	$5,995,467	$7,410,521	80.90
252921	Fluorspar	$159,058,845	$199,252,626	79.83

(continued)

9 ITEMS FOR WHICH CHINA IS MORE THAN 70 PERCENT DEPENDENT ON MONGOLIA
(TOTAL VALUE = $474,174,554)

HS CODE	PRODUCT DESCRIPTION	TRADE VALUE OF CHINA'S IMPORTS FROM MONGOLIA (USD)	TRADE VALUE OF CHINA'S IMPORTS FROM THE WORLD (USD)	MONGOLIA'S SHARE OF CHINA'S TOTAL IMPORTS (PERCENT)
510510	Carded wool	$30,481	$40,080	76.05
510220	Hair: coarse animal hair, not carded or combed	$15,059,369	$19,995,516	75.31
160250	Bovine meat preparations	$17,907,944	$24,456,895	73.22

9 ITEMS FOR WHICH CHINA IS MORE THAN 70 PERCENT DEPENDENT ON THE PHILIPPINES
(TOTAL VALUE = $294,055,795)

HS CODE	PRODUCT DESCRIPTION	TRADE VALUE OF CHINA'S IMPORTS FROM THE PHILIPPINES (USD)	TRADE VALUE OF CHINA'S IMPORTS FROM THE WORLD (USD)	PHILIPPINES' SHARE OF CHINA'S TOTAL IMPORTS (PERCENT)
80720	Papaws (papayas): fresh	$1,858,688	$1,858,688	100.00
30729	Dried mollusks: scallops and others	$13,331	$13,331	100.00
30751	Octopus: live, fresh or chilled	$72	$72	100.00
80430	Pineapples	$198,918,517	$203,595,753	97.70
961310	Gas-fueled pocket lighters	$2,182,977	$2,241,521	97.39
852862	Projectors: for automatic data processing	$30,089,990	$32,019,969	93.97

**9 ITEMS FOR WHICH CHINA IS MORE THAN 70 PERCENT DEPENDENT
ON THE PHILIPPINES
(TOTAL VALUE = $294,055,795)**

HS CODE	PRODUCT DESCRIPTION	TRADE VALUE OF CHINA'S IMPORTS FROM THE PHILIPPINES (USD)	TRADE VALUE OF CHINA'S IMPORTS FROM THE WORLD (USD)	PHILIPPINES' SHARE OF CHINA'S TOTAL IMPORTS (PERCENT)
440721	Wood, tropical: sawn or chipped lengthwise, sliced, or peeled, whether or not planed, sanded, or finger-jointed, thicker than 6mm	$133,104	$172,841	77.01
440220	Wood: charcoal of nut or shell, whether or not agglomerated	$52,565,720	$70,462,827	74.60
170410	Chewing gum	$8,293,396	$11,315,008	73.30

**7 ITEMS FOR WHICH CHINA IS MORE THAN 70 PERCENT DEPENDENT ON SWEDEN
(TOTAL VALUE = $321,842,049)**

HS CODE	PRODUCT DESCRIPTION	TRADE VALUE OF CHINA'S IMPORTS FROM SWEDEN (USD)	TRADE VALUE OF CHINA'S IMPORTS FROM THE WORLD (USD)	SWEDEN'S SHARE OF CHINA'S TOTAL IMPORTS (PERCENT)
240491	Nicotine products for oral application	$1,062,005	$1,131,997	93.82
851411	Hot isostatic presses	$15,635,122	$17,274,249	90.51
843050	Mining machinery	$31,613,091	$38,000,053	83.19
481092	Multi-ply paper: kaolin coated	$264,344,377	$358,392,464	73.76

(continued)

7 ITEMS FOR WHICH CHINA IS MORE THAN 70 PERCENT DEPENDENT ON SWEDEN
(TOTAL VALUE = $321,842,049)

HS CODE	PRODUCT DESCRIPTION	TRADE VALUE OF CHINA'S IMPORTS FROM SWEDEN (USD)	TRADE VALUE OF CHINA'S IMPORTS FROM THE WORLD (USD)	SWEDEN'S SHARE OF CHINA'S TOTAL IMPORTS (PERCENT)
470693	Pulp: of fibrous cellulosic material, obtained by a combination of mechanical and chemical processes	$2,621,127	$3,622,609	72.35
843410	Milking machines	$4,951,239	$6,896,914	71.79
842111	Centrifuges: cream separators	$1,615,088	$2,284,952	70.68

4 ITEMS FOR WHICH CHINA IS MORE THAN 70 PERCENT DEPENDENT ON THE CZECH REPUBLIC
(TOTAL VALUE = $17,336,818)

HS CODE	PRODUCT DESCRIPTION	TRADE VALUE OF CHINA'S IMPORTS FROM THE CZECH REPUBLIC (USD)	TRADE VALUE OF CHINA'S IMPORTS FROM THE WORLD (USD)	CZECH REPUBLIC'S SHARE OF CHINA'S TOTAL IMPORTS (PERCENT)
293969	Rye ergot alkaloids: salts	$8,440,740	$8,855,378	95.32
370298	Photographic film: b&w, >35mm rolls	$400,847	$468,932	85.48
845612	Machine tools: for working any material by removal of material: operated by other light or photon beam processes (not laser)	$615,000	$765,961	80.29
860290	Non-diesel-electric rail locomotives	$7,880,231	$10,084,780	78.14

Source: Authors' original tables with data derived from UN Comtrade database at https://comtradeplus.un.org/.

Note: There are no items for which China is more than 70 percent dependent on Estonia, Latvia, Lithuania, or Palau.

APPENDIX 4

China's Vulnerability Interdependence (Expanded List, 2024)

Substitutability and Replacement Ratio

COUNTRY AND ITEM (HS CODE)	PERCENT CHINA DEPENDENCE (TRADE VALUE, USD)*	REPLACEMENT RATIO[†]	SUBSTITUTE SUPPLIERS[‡] (PERCENT CHINA DEPENDENCE)	DESCRIPTION
AUSTRALIA Iron ores and concentrates (260111)	61.45[§] ($79,510,063,078)	0.020	Brazil (22.12) South Africa (3.36)	Critical component for steel (pig iron)
AUSTRALIA Other mineral substances (253090)	62.10[§] ($3,229,183,817)	0.024	Zimbabwe (15.22) Brazil (5.32)	Natural minerals including spodumene, a critical component of lithium (used for lithium batteries)
AUSTRALIA Greasy wool (510111)	79.22 ($1,543,854,694)	0.000	South Africa (8.56) New Zealand (4.67)	Source of lanolin, a natural wax used in personal care products like lip balm, lotions, and creams

(continued)

COUNTRY AND ITEM (HS CODE)	PERCENT CHINA DEPENDENCE (TRADE VALUE, USD)*	REPLACEMENT RATIO†	SUBSTITUTE SUPPLIERS‡ (PERCENT CHINA DEPENDENCE)	DESCRIPTION
AUSTRALIA Oilseeds (120729)	88.10 ($190,302,622)	0.000	United States (11.90)	Used for extraction of vegetable oils used for cooking, industrial processes, and biofuel production
CANADA Rape or colza seeds (120510)	100 ($3,294,156,686)	0.000	N/A	Used for cooking oil (canola)
CANADA Cereals: wheat/meslin: durum wheat, non-seed (100119)	58.43§ ($855,522,112)	0.000	Australia (30.89) United States (10.00)	Used for food products and agriculture
CANADA Oil cake: from rape/colza seed (230641)	75.25 ($783,343,131)	0.002	UAE (17.33) Russia (4.77)	Used as animal feed
CANADA Lobsters, nonfrozen (030632)	78.96 ($609,077,551)	0.000	United States (20.69)	Luxury good
CANADA Semichemical wood pulp (470500)	76.81 ($470,210,161)	0.008	New Zealand (8.18) Sweden (5.49)	Used in the paper and packing industries

Product	Value	Number	Countries	Description
CANADA Coniferous wood: S-P-F, sawn or chipped (440713)	99.96 ($92,167,241)	0.038	Austria (0.03) Romania (0.01)	Used for wood framing in construction
CANADA Coniferous wood: Hem-fir species (440714)	98.35 ($61,866,957)	0.057	United States (1.64) Japan (0.01)	Used for wood framing in construction
CANADA Frozen lobsters (030612)	99.82 ($31,401,447)	0.033	United States (0.18)	Luxury good
CANADA Lucerne (alfalfa) seed (120921)	86.79 ($8,439,692)	0.009	Australia (7.86) France (4.79)	Crop grown for feeding livestock and soil improvement
FRANCE Spirits (220820)	99.21 ($1,223,858,496)	0.203	Spain (0.27) Taiwan (0.21)	Strong distilled liquor (brandy). Brandy is the largest imported spirit in China.
FRANCE Broken or scutched flax (530121)	86.91 ($756,652,158)	0.000	Egypt (6.11) Belgium (5.48)	Used for production of linen fabric and paper
FRANCE Perfumes (330300)	63.8§ ($636,303,705)	0.511	Italy (13.26) Spain (11.26)	Fragrance products like perfume and cologne
FRANCE Champagne and sparkling wine (220410)	69.16§ ($46,495,694)	0.051	Italy (22.61) Spain (4.62)	Luxury good

(continued)

COUNTRY AND ITEM (HS CODE)	PERCENT CHINA DEPENDENCE (TRADE VALUE, USD)*	REPLACEMENT RATIO[†]	SUBSTITUTE SUPPLIERS[‡] (PERCENT CHINA DEPENDENCE)	DESCRIPTION
FRANCE Homogenized/reconstituted tobacco (240391)	100.00 ($8,814,292)	0.000	N/A	Brown shredded innards used as filler in cigarettes
FRANCE Vinylidene chloride polymers (390450)	76.82 ($26,030,212)	0.702	Japan (22.84) Belgium (0.34%)	Makes plastics such as flexible films or wraps; also used in flame retardant coatings
GERMANY Offset printing machinery (844313)	74.70 ($444,424,041)	0.391	Japan (24.52)	Prints large quantity of items such as newspaper and magazines
GERMANY Gear machinery (846140)	64.48[§] ($351,044,084)	0.169	Switzerland (18.15) Japan (13.92)	Cuts, grinds, and finishes common gears: spur, helical, and bevel
GERMANY Fused quartz or silica tubes (700231)	77.82 ($61,302,573)	0.345	United States (11.16) Japan (5.95)	Used for semiconductor manufacturing, optical fibers, and laboratory equipment
GERMANY Ingots, alloy steel (722410)	70.48 ($30,446,661)	0.266	Malaysia (10.23) India (5.29)	Primary forms of alloy steel used in construction and shipbuilding
GERMANY Tetrachloroethylene (290323)	98.54 ($17,487,779)	0.929	Japan (1.46)	A chemical commonly used to dry-clean fabrics

Country / Product (code)		Value	Share	Importers (share)	Description
JAPAN	Hybrid electric vehicles (870340)	98.86 ($3,951,111,137)	1.154	United States (1.11) Republic of Korea (0.02)	Energy-efficient vehicles that use both an internal combustion engine and an electric motor for propulsion, such as the Toyota Prius
JAPAN	Industrial robots (847950)	74.75 ($481,954,200)	0.888	Germany (5.66) France (4.44)	Important to manufacturing and advanced industries
JAPAN	Silver powder (710610)	84.69 ($892,448,804)	0.005	United States (9.99) Taiwan (2.58)	Used in photovoltaic and electronic conductive paste needed for solar panels
JAPAN	Plates, sheets, and film of cellulose acetate (392073)	77.93 ($466,056,030)	0.140	Republic of Korea (10.27) Taiwan (6.19)	Used for packaging of food, beverages, and medical supplies and textile treatment
JAPAN	Textile lubricants (340391)	70.64 ($305,917,476)	0.160	Germany (16.55) Italy (3.72)	Used for treatment of textiles and leathers
JAPAN	Copper foil (741012)	77.07 ($202,555,244)	0.295	Germany (8.37) United States (6.84)	Used in construction to produce locks, wiring, doors, and electrical sockets
JAPAN	Staple fibers (550330)	62.68§ ($71,891,880)	0.149	Thailand (11.86) Turkey (8.98)	Of acrylic, modacrylic, and nylon; used in clothing
JAPAN	Opium alkaloids (293319)	88.44 ($21,770,221)	0.001	India (8.02) Italy (1.36)	Used in pharmaceuticals

(continued)

COUNTRY AND ITEM (HS CODE)	PERCENT CHINA DEPENDENCE (TRADE VALUE, USD)*	REPLACEMENT RATIO†	SUBSTITUTE SUPPLIERS‡ (PERCENT CHINA DEPENDENCE)	DESCRIPTION
MONGOLIA Fine animal hair (510219)	94.26 ($135,861,149)	0.031	Peru (3.53) Bolivia (0.73)	Used for clothing, textiles, and makeup brushes
MONGOLIA Fluorspar (252921)	79.83 ($159,058,845)	0.404	Thailand (4.85) Zambia (4.83)	Alternative to lithium-ion, commonly used in EV batteries
NEW ZEALAND Pinewood (440321)	92.33 ($2,048,897,736)	0.000	Poland (2.16) Australia (1.82)	Used for construction, furniture, and paper production
NEW ZEALAND Solid milk and cream (040221)	79.19 ($1,287,144,337)	0.038	Australia (12.69) Netherlands (4.73)	Milk powder or cream
NEW ZEALAND Butter (040510)	80.23 ($591,644,848)	0.016	France (8.64) Netherlands (3.38)	Food staple
NEW ZEALAND Fresh kiwifruit (081050)	98.64 ($590,226,297)	0.072	Italy (1.22) Greece (0.14)	Food staple
NEW ZEALAND Casein (350110)	77.32 ($111,596,470)	0.016	Ireland (9.27) France (4.22)	Used for cheese making and protein supplements
NORWAY Frozen coalfish (030365)	97.77 ($53,139,004)	0.000	Russia (1.87) Greenland (0.36)	Food staple

Country / Product (HS code)		Source countries	Description
PHILIPPINES Nickel ores and concentrates (260400)	59.91§ ($1,597,758,356) 0.000	Russia (12.03) Australia (6.05)	Essential element in the battery cathodes used in the electric vehicle industry
PHILIPPINES Pineapples (080430)	97.70 ($198,918,517) 0.116	Indonesia (1.44) Thailand (0.64)	Fresh or dried
SOUTH KOREA Other inorganic salts (284290)	93.67 ($2,060,419,042) 0.932	Japan (4.73) United States (0.42)	Salts used for various agricultural, industrial, and scientific applications, including fertilizers and glass
SOUTH KOREA OLED flat panel displays, without drivers or control circuits (852412)	94.01 ($2,118,159,31) 0.185	Japan (3.64) Taiwan (2.05)	Used for smartphones, televisions, monitors, laptops, and other electronic devices
SOUTH KOREA Ethylene, unsaturated (290121)	69.87§ ($1,383,967,103) 0.033	Japan (17.41) Oman (4.68)	Critical base product for petrochemicals
SOUTH KOREA Propylene, unsaturated (290122)	74.29 ($1,295,108,795) 0.044	Japan (18.3) Philippines (2.59)	Crucial building block for producing plastics and other chemicals
SOUTH KOREA Drawn/blown glass sheets: non-tinted (700490)	71.64 ($928,091,114) 0.269	Taiwan (19.49) Japan (6.96)	Used for buildings, mirrors, and windows

(continued)

COUNTRY AND ITEM (HS CODE)	PERCENT CHINA DEPENDENCE (TRADE VALUE, USD)*	REPLACEMENT RATIO†	SUBSTITUTE SUPPLIERS‡ (PERCENT CHINA DEPENDENCE)	DESCRIPTION
SOUTH KOREA Marine propulsion engines (840810)	70.04 ($781,719,292)	0.244	Japan (13.62) Germany (4.89)	Diesel or semi-diesel fuel ship propulsion engines that are more efficient
SOUTH KOREA Acrylonitrile-butadiene rubber (NBR): primary forms (400251)	78.23 ($106,583,920)	0.220	Malaysia (7.45) Japan (6.940)	Nitrile rubber, known for its resistance to oils and fuels, used to make disposable gloves, fuel hoses, sealants, and more
SWEDEN Hot isostatic presses (851411)	90.51 ($15,635,122)	0.001	United States (9.49)	Machinery critical for high-performance products such as aircraft parts, power generation turbine blades, and semiconductor materials
UNITED KINGDOM Whiskies (220830)	86.65 ($391,179,828)	0.153	Japan (6.71) United States (3.21)	Luxury good
UNITED STATES Turbojet turbine (841191)	62.81§ ($4,057,954,464)	0.341	France (8.36) Germany (6.44)	Gas turbine engine used in aircraft
UNITED STATES Acyclic hydrocarbons (290110)	98.15 ($2,604,826,737)	0.034	Spain (0.77) Japan (0.35)	Chemical compound used in lubricants and polyethylene (plastic bags)
UNITED STATES Turbojets (841112)	48.86§ ($2,179,113,096)	0.129	France (43.09) United Kingdom (7.65)	Gas turbine with a propelling nozzle used in aircraft

Country / Product (code)	Value		Top partners (%)	Description
UNITED STATES Grain sorghum (100790)	66.85§ ($1,733,210,890)	0.000	Australia (22.30) Argentina (10.81)	Used to produce traditional Chinese drink (*baijiu*)
UNITED STATES Pistachios (080251)	67.50§ ($578,239,257)	0.024	Iran (30.63) Australia (1.79)	Fresh or dried, shelled
UNITED STATES Forage products (121490)	73.77 ($354,489,657)	0.002	Australia (15.99) Spain (5.23)	Root vegetables, legumes, and plants used for animal feed
UNITED STATES Oak wood (440791)	75.47 ($312,519,528)	0.008	Russia (16.20) Canada (3.84)	Sawn/chipped, used for furniture, flooring, construction, and wine/whiskey barrels
UNITED STATES Flours, meats, and pellets from meat/offal (230110)	78.17 ($237,897,016)	0.000	Uruguay (7.42) Australia (7.02)	Used as animal feed or fertilizer
UNITED STATES Non-plasticized cellulose acetates (391211)	85.67 ($207,245,157)	0.258	Japan (14.27) Germany (0.06)	Processed for common synthetic plastics
UNITED STATES Cherry wood (440794)	98.56 ($103,449,895)	0.000	Canada (1.36) Taiwan (0.04)	Sawn/chipped, used for furniture, flooring, and construction
UNITED STATES Aeronautical/space instruments (901420)	82.48 ($101,269,501)	0.182	France (8.82) Taiwan (1.71)	Inertial navigation systems
UNITED STATES Amine compounds (292122)	85.07 ($95,557,095)	0.246	Germany (7.72) France (6.61)	Includes acyclic polyamines and HMDA that can be used for production of nylon 66 and as curing agent for epoxy resins

(*continued*)

COUNTRY AND ITEM (HS CODE)	PERCENT CHINA DEPENDENCE (TRADE VALUE, USD)*	REPLACEMENT RATIO[†]	SUBSTITUTE SUPPLIERS[‡] (PERCENT CHINA DEPENDENCE)	DESCRIPTION
UNITED STATES Scintigraphic medical instruments (901814)	76.28 ($91,876,205)	0.681	Israel (9.19) Germany (8.38)	Used in nuclear medicine for diagnostic imaging, including cancer detection
UNITED STATES Raw groundnuts (120241)	98.46 ($70,725,774)	0.521	Vietnam (1.54)	Peanuts used for snack foods, cooking, and oil production
UNITED STATES Gas turbines: power not exceeding 5MW (841181)	64.42[§] ($64,005,290)	0.380	France (21.67) Canada (4.53)	Engines used for power generation, mechanical drives, and cogeneration systems (heat and electricity)
UNITED STATES Bovine semen (051110)	91.93 ($53,535,288)	0.000	Germany (5.51) France (1.86)	Used for insemination of Chinese cattle
UNITED STATES Kentucky bluegrass seed (120924)	93.08 ($20,308,770)	0.000	Denmark (6.92)	Cool-season grass seed planted as turf in athletic fields

Source: Authors' original table with data derived from UN Comtrade database at https://comtradeplus.un.org/

* China's dependence on the source country for the good as a percentage of total imports of that good.

[†] Domestic production of the good is measured using reported Chinese exports of the good as the proxy variable. The replacement metric is the exports/imports ratio. A number greater than 1 suggests a strong capacity to replace a loss of imports with domestic sources by diverting exports to fill demand.

[‡] China's dependence on the next largest source country(ies) for the good (after the primary source) as a percentage of China's total imports of that good.

[§] Falls below 70 dependency, but included because (1) trade value is significant and/or (2) alternate supplier(s) is a coerced, like-minded country.

NOTES

PREFACE

1. Victor Cha, "How to Stop Chinese Coercion: The Case for Collective Resilience," *Foreign Affairs*, December 14, 2022, https://www.foreignaffairs.com/world/how-stop-china-coercion-collective-resilience-victor-cha; Victor Cha and Andy Lim, "Flagrant Foul: China's Predatory Liberalism and the NBA," *Washington Quarterly* 42, no. 4 (2019): 23–42.
2. Victor D. Cha, "Collective Resilience: Deterring China's Weaponization of Economic Interdependence," *International Security* 48, no. 1 (2023): 91–124.

1. WHAT DO PELOSI'S TAIWAN TRIP, BANCO DELTA ASIA, AND TRUMP'S MEXICO TARIFFS HAVE IN COMMON?

1. Karen Hao, "Nancy Pelosi Kicks Off Taiwan Visit Reaffirming U.S. Ties with the Island," *Wall Street Journal*, August 2, 2022, https://www.wsj.com/livecoverage/nancy-pelosi-taiwan-visit-china-us-tensions/card/nancy-pelosi-kicks-off-taiwan-visit-reaffirming-u-s-ties-with-the-island-iWvv9B4jVHenUIXagMr2; Jeanne Whalen and Cate Cadell, "Pelosi Dined with Taiwan Computer Chip Executives During Her Brief Visit," *Washington Post*, August 3, 2022, www.washingtonpost.com/technology/2022/08/03/pelosi-tsmc-meeting-lunch-semiconductors/.
2. Office of the President, Republic of China (Taiwan), "President Tsai Meets U.S. Delegation Led by House of Representatives Speaker Nancy Pelosi," August 3, 2022, https://english.president.gov.tw/NEWS/6292.
3. Chris Buckley, Keith Bradsher, and Tiffany May, "New Security Law Gives China Sweeping Powers Over Hong Kong," *New York Times*, June 29, 2020, https://www.nytimes.com/2020/06/29/world/asia/china-hong-kong-security-law-rules.html; Vivian Wang, "Chinese Military Drills Aim to Awe, Both Abroad and at Home," *New York Times*, August 6, 2022, www.nytimes.com/2022/08/06/world/asia/china-exercises-taiwan.html.
4. Laura He, "China Hits Taiwan with Trade Restrictions After Pelosi Visit," CNN, August 3, 2022, https://www.cnn.com/2022/08/03/economy/china-suspends-imports-taiwan-products-intl-hnk/; Ralph Jennings and Huifeng He, "China's Ban on Taiwan Imports Leaves Some Consumers Wondering Where to Get Their Food Fix," *South China Morning Post*, August 16, 2022,

https://www.scmp.com/economy/china-economy/article/3188938/chinas-ban-taiwan-imports
-leaves-some-consumers-wondering; Christian Shepherd and Pei-Lin Wu, "Their Fruit Forbidden in China, Taiwan's Pomelo Growers Feel Squeeze," *Washington Post*, August 29, 2022,
www.washingtonpost.com/world/2022/08/29/china-import-ban-taiwan-fruit-pomelo/.

5. Andrew Lee, "Mainland China Bans Taiwan Wax and Sugar Apple Imports as Cross-Strait Rela-
    tions Continue to Worsen," *South China Morning Post*, September 19, 2021, https://www.scmp.com
    /news/china/politics/article/3149339/mainland-china-bans-taiwan-wax-and-sugar-apple
    -imports-cross; Tim McDonald, "China and Taiwan Face Off in Pineapple War," *BBC*, March 19,
    2021, https://www.bbc.com/news/business-56353963; Amy Chang Chien, "First Pineapples, Now
    Fish: To Pressure Taiwan, China Flexes Economic Muscle," *New York Times*, June 22, 2022, https://
    www.nytimes.com/2022/06/22/business/china-taiwan-grouper-ban.html.

6. International Trade Administration, "Taiwan—Country Commercial Guide," January 10, 2024,
    https://www.trade.gov/country-commercial-guides/taiwan-market-overview.

7. Cissy Zhou and Thompson Chau, "China Bans Thousands of Taiwan Food Imports as Pelosi Trip
    Riles," *Nikkei Asia*, August 2, 2022, https://asia.nikkei.com/Politics/International-relations/US
    -China-tensions/China-bans-thousands-of-Taiwan-food-imports-as-Pelosi-trip-riles.

8. U.S. Department of State, "Joint Statement of the Fourth Round of the Six-Party Talks Beijing,
    September 19, 2005," September 19, 2005, https://2001-2009.state.gov/r/pa/prs/ps/2005/53490
    .htm.

9. Peter Van Ness, "Why the Six Party Talks Should Succeed," *Asian Perspective* 29, no. 2 (2005): 231–
    246; Gilbert Rozman, "The North Korean Nuclear Crisis and U.S. Strategy in Northeast Asia,"
    Asian Survey 47, no. 4 (2007): 601–621; Scott Snyder, "Six-Party Talks: 'Action for Action' and
    the Formalization of Regional Security Cooperation in Northeast Asia," *International Journal of
    Korean Unification Studies* 16, no. 1 (2007): 1–24; Shulong Chu and Xinzhu Lin, "The Six Party
    Talks: A Chinese Perspective," *Asian Perspective* 32, no. 4 (2008): 29–43; Chung-in Moon, "Diplo-
    macy of Defiance and Facilitation: The Six-Party Talks and the Roh Moo Hyun Government,"
    Asian Perspective 32, no. 4 (2008): 71–105.

10. Federal Register, "Finding That Banco Delta Asia SARL Is a Financial Institution of Primary
    Money Laundering Concern," September 20, 2005, https://www.federalregister.gov/documents
    /2005/09/20/05-18660/finding-that-banco-delta-asia-sarl-is-a-financial-institution-of-primary
    -money-laundering-concern.

11. U.S. Department of the Treasury, "Treasury Designates Banco Delta Asia as Primary Money Laun-
    dering Concern Under USA PATRIOT Act," September 15, 2005, https://home.treasury.gov
    /news/press-releases/js2720.

12. See chapters 9 and 10 in Juan Zarate, *Treasury's War: The Unleashing of a New Era of Financial
    Warfare* (New York: Public Affairs, 2013).

13. Victor D. Cha, *The Impossible State: North Korea, Past and Future* (New York: Harper Collins,
    2012), 264–267.

14. White House, "Fact Sheet: President Donald J. Trump Imposes Tariffs on Imports from Canada,
    Mexico, and China," February 1, 2025, https://www.whitehouse.gov/fact-sheets/2025/02/fact
    -sheet-president-donald-j-trump-imposes-tariffs-on-imports-from-canada-mexico-and-china/.

15. White House, "Fact Sheet: President Donald J. Trump Imposes Tariffs on Imports from Canada,
    Mexico, and China."

16. David Baldwin, "The Sanctions Debate and the Logic of Choice," *International Security* 24, no. 3
    (1999): 80–107.

17. Michael J. Mazarr, *Mastering the Gray Zone: Understanding a Changing Era of Conflict* (Wash-
    ington, DC: U.S. Army War College Press, 2015).

18. Victor D. Cha and Andy Lim, "Flagrant Foul: China's Predatory Liberalism and the NBA," *Wash-
    ington Quarterly* 42, no. 4 (2019): 23–42.

19. Anne-Marie Slaughter, "America's Edge: Power in the Networked Century," *Foreign Affairs* 88, no. 1 (2009): 94–113; Henry Farrell and Abraham Newman, "Weaponized Interdependence: How Global Economic Networks Shape State Coercion," *International Security* 44, no. 1 (2019): 42–79; Daniel W. Drezner, Henry Farrell, and Abraham Newman, eds., *The Uses and Abuses of Weaponized Interdependence* (Washington, DC: Brookings Institution Press, 2021); Margaret M. Pearson, Meg Rithmire, and Kellee S. Tsai, "China's Party-State Capitalism and International Backlash: From Interdependence to Insecurity," *International Security* 47, no. 2 (2022): 135–176; Henry Farrell and Abraham Newman, *Underground Empire: How America Weaponized the World Economy* (New York: Holt, 2023).

20. The first case in our database is from 1997 against Columbia Tristar, Disney, and MGM movie production companies. See appendix 1.

21. Article 5 of the North Atlantic Treaty provides that an attack on any one member will be considered an attack on all.

2. THE SOURCES OF PREDATORY LIBERALISM IN THE GLOBAL ECONOMY

1. See Albert O. Hirschman, *National Power and the Structure of Foreign Trade* (Berkeley: University of California Press, 1945); Johan Galtung, "On the Effect of International Economic Sanctions: With Examples from the Case of Rhodesia," *World Politics* 19, no. 3 (1967): 378–416; Robert A. Pape, "Why Economic Sanctions Do Not Work," *International Security* 22, no. 2 (1997): 90–136; Jean-Marc F. Blanchard and Norrin M. Ripsman, "Asking the Right Question: When Do Economic Sanctions Work Best?," *Security Studies* 9, no. 1 (1999): 219–253; Daniel W. Drezner, "Sanctions Sometimes Smart: Targeted Sanctions in Theory and Practice," *International Studies Review* 13, no. 1 (2011): 96–108; Risa A. Brooks, "Sanctions and Regime Type: What Works and When?," *Security Studies* 11, no. 4 (2002): 1–50; Irfan Nooruddin, "Modeling Selection Bias in Studies on Sanctions Efficacy," *International Interactions* 28, no. 1 (2002): 59–75; Gary Hufbauer et al., *Economic Sanctions Reconsidered*, 3rd ed. (Washington, DC: Peterson Institute for International Economics, 2007); Jonathan Kirshner, "The Microfoundations of Economic Sanctions," *Security Studies* 6, no. 3 (2007): 32–64; Elena V. McLean and Mitchell T. Radtke, "Political Relations, Leader Stability and Economic Coercion," *International Studies Quarterly* 62, no. 2 (2018): 357–370; Bryan R. Early and Menevis Cilizoglu, "Economic Sanctions in Flux: Enduring Challenges, New Policies, and Defining the Future Research Agenda," *International Studies Perspectives* 21, no. 4 (2020): 438–477.

2. Robert O. Keohane and Joseph S. Nye, *Power and Interdependence* (Cambridge, MA: Harvard University Press, 1972); David Baldwin, *Economic Statecraft* (Princeton, NJ: Princeton University Press, 1985).

3. Anne-Marie Slaughter, "America's Edge: Power in the Networked Century," *Foreign Affairs* 88, no. 1 (2009): 94–113; Henry Farrell and Abraham Newman, "Weaponized Interdependence: How Global Economic Networks Shape State Coercion," *International Security* 44, no. 1 (2019): 42–79; Daniel W. Drezner, Henry Farrell, and Abraham Newman, eds., *The Uses and Abuses of Weaponized Interdependence* (Washington, DC: Brookings Institution Press, 2021); Henry Farrell and Abraham Newman, *Underground Empire: How America Weaponized the World Economy* (New York: Holt, 2023).

4. Darren J. Lim and Victor Ferguson, "Informal Economic Sanctions: The Political Economy of Chinese Coercion During the THAAD Dispute," *Review of International Political Economy* 29, no. 5 (2022): 1525–1548.

5.   Michael Green et al., "Counter-Coercion Series: Scarborough Shoal Standoff," Center for Strategic and International Studies, May 22, 2017, https://amti.csis.org/counter-co-scarborough-standoff/.

6.   Jonathan Hackenbroich et al., "Defending Europe's Economic Sovereignty: New Ways to Resist Economic Coercion," European Council on Foreign Relations, October 20, 2020, https://ecfr.eu/publication/defending_europe_economic_sovereignty_new_ways_to_resist_economic_coercion/.

7.   For India, see Dan Strumpf and Shruti Srivastava, "What Trump's Reciprocal Tariffs Mean for India," Bloomberg, April 3, 2025, https://www.bloomberg.com/news/articles/2025-04-03/trump-tariffs-on-india-how-is-country-economy-impacted-what-is-modi-doing; for South Korea, see Eun-joong Kim and Su-hyeon Park, "Trump's Tariff Plan Built on Misleading Trade Deficit Math," *Chosun Daily*, April 3, 2025, https://www.chosun.com/english/national-en/2025/04/03/ZBTJFC6ZXFHLJPFS5RTMCORHCI/.

8.   Jonathan Hackenbroich and Pawel Zerka, "Measured Response: How to Design a European Instrument Against Economic Coercion," European Council on Foreign Relations, June 23, 2021, https://ecfr.eu/publication/measured-response-how-to-design-a-european-instrument-against-economic-coercion/.

9.   Farrell and Newman, *Underground Empire*, 55.

10.   Gregory Wischer, "The U.S. Military and NATO Face Serious Risks of Mineral Shortages," Carnegie Endowment for International Peace, February 12, 2024, https://carnegieendowment.org/2024/02/12/u.s.-military-and-nato-face-serious-risks-of-mineral-shortages-pub-91602.

11.   Katie Tarasov, "ASML Is the Only Company Making the $200 Million Machines Needed to Print Every Advanced Microchip. Here's an Inside Look," CNBC, March 23, 2022, www.cnbc.com/2022/03/23/inside-asml-the-company-advanced-chipmakers-use-for-euv-lithography.html.

12.   Arjun Kharpal, "Netherlands, Home to a Critical Chip Firm, Follows U.S. with Export Curbs on Semiconductor Tools," CNBC, June 30, 2023, https://www.cnbc.com/2023/06/30/netherlands-follows-us-with-semiconductor-export-restrictions-.html.

13.   Farrell and Newman, *Underground Empire*.

14.   Samuel M. Goodman, Dan Kim, and John VerWey, "The South Korea–Japan Trade Dispute in Context: Semiconductor Manufacturing, Chemicals, and Concentrated Supply Chains," Office of Industries Working Paper, U.S. International Trade Commission, October 2019, https://www.usitc.gov/publications/332/working_papers/the_south_korea-japan_trade_dispute_in_context_semiconductor_manufacturing_chemicals_and_concentrated_supply_chains.pdf.

15.   Kirshner, "The Microfoundations of Economic Sanctions."

16.   Slaughter, "America's Edge"; Farrell and Newman, *Underground Empire*.

17.   Mark Leonard, ed., *Connectivity Wars: Why Migration, Finance and Trade Are the Geo-Economic Battlegrounds of the Future* (London: European Council of Foreign Relations, 2016); Sophie Meunier and Kalypso Nicolaidis, "The Geopoliticization of European Trade and Investment Policy," *JCMS: Journal of Common Market Studies* 57 (2019): 103–113; Drezner, Farrell, and Newman, *The Uses and Abuses of Weaponized Interdependence*; Christian Freudlsperger and Sophie Meunier, "When Foreign Policy Becomes Trade Policy: The EU's Anti-Coercion Instrument," *JCMS: Journal of Common Market Studies* 62, no. 4 (2024): 1063–1079; Wolfgang Weiß, "The EU's Strategic Autonomy in Times of Politicisation of International Trade: The Future of Commission Accountability," *Global Policy* 14, no. S3 (2023): 1–11; Anna Herranz-Surrallés, Chad Damro, and Sandra Eckert, "The Geoeconomic Turn of the Single European Market? Conceptual Challenges and Empirical Trends," *JCMS: Journal of Common Market Studies* 62, no. 4 (2024): 919–937.

18.   Drezner, Farrell, and Newman, *The Uses and Abuses of Weaponized Interdependence*, 4; Peter Harrell and Elizabeth Rosenberg, "Economic Dominance, Financial Technology and the Future of U.S. Economic Coercion," Center for a New American Security, April 29, 2019, https://www.cnas

.org/publications/reports/economic-dominance-financial-technology-and-the-future-of-u-s
-economic-coercion; Juan Zarate, *Treasury's War: The Unleashing of a New Era of Financial Warfare* (New York: Public Affairs, 2013).

19. Farrell and Newman, *Underground Empire*.

20. Richard Haass, *Economic Sanctions and American Diplomacy* (New York: Council on Foreign Relations, 1998); A. Cooper Drury, "Sanctions as Coercive Diplomacy: The U.S. President's Decision to Initiate Economic Sanctions," *Political Research Quarterly* 54, no. 3 (2001): 485–508.

21. White House, "Fact Sheet: President Donald J. Trump Imposes Tariffs on Imports from Canada, Mexico, and China," February 1, 2025, https://www.whitehouse.gov/fact-sheets/2025/02/fact-sheet
-president-donald-j-trump-imposes-tariffs-on-imports-from-canada-mexico-and-china/.

22. Xiawen Chen and Roberto Javier Garcia, "Economic Sanctions and Trade Diplomacy: Sanction-Busting Strategies, Market Distortion, and Efficacy of China's Restrictions on Norwegian Salmon Imports," *China Information* 30, no. 1 (2016): 33.

23. U.S. Department of the Treasury, "Treasury Designates Banco Delta Asia as Primary Money Laundering Concern Under USA PATRIOT Act," September 15, 2005, https://home.treasury.gov
/news/press-releases/js2720.

24. White House, "Fact Sheet: President Donald J. Trump Imposes Tariffs on Imports from Canada, Mexico, and China."

25. State Sponsors of Terrorism legislation is designated pursuant to three laws: section 1754(c) of the National Defense Authorization Act for Fiscal Year 2019, section 40 of the Arms Export Control Act, and section 620A of the Foreign Assistance Act of 1961; see U.S. Department of State, "State Sponsors of Terrorism," www.state.gov/state-sponsors-of-terrorism/.

26. Michael Schuman, "Why Biden's Block on Chips to China Is a Big Deal," *Atlantic*, October 25, 2022, www.theatlantic.com/international/archive/2022/10/biden-export-control-microchips
-china/671848/.

27. This Korean case is fully elaborated in the next chapter. See Lim and Ferguson, "Informal Economic Sanctions."

28. Lim and Ferguson, "Informal Economic Sanctions," 1539.

29. Chen and Garcia, "Economic Sanctions and Trade Diplomacy," 38.

30. Qiang Su, "Rare Earth Will Not Be Used as Bargaining Chip: Wen," *China Daily*, October 8, 2010, www.chinadaily.com.cn/china/2010-10/08/content_11382162.htm; Reuters, "China Denies Banning Rare Earths Exports to Japan," September 23, 2010, www.reuters.com/article/world/us/china
-denies-banning-rare-earths-exports-to-japan-idUSTRE68M0PF/.

31. Eugene Gholz and Llewelyn Hughes, "Market Structure and Economic Sanctions: The 2010 Rare Earth Elements Episode as a Pathway Case of Market Adjustment," *Review of International Political Economy* 23, no. 3 (2019): 613–615.

32. "Premier: We All Know Why," *China Daily*, February 3, 2009, https://www.chinadaily.com.cn
/china/2009-02/03/content_7440286.htm; Tong Zhao, "Sanction Experience and Sanction Behavior: An Analysis of Chinese Perception and Behavior on Economic Sanctions," *Contemporary Politics* 16, no. 3 (2010): 274.

33. Bethany Allen, *Beijing Rules: How China Weaponized Its Economy to Confront the World* (New York: Harper, 2023), 6.

34. James Reilly, "China's Unilateral Sanctions," *Washington Quarterly* 35, no. 4 (2012): 124.

35. Allen, *Beijing Rules*, 7.

36. Allen, *Beijing Rules*, 6.

37. Chen and Garcia, "Economic Sanctions and Trade Diplomacy," 30.

38. Our definition is not dissimilar to those of William J. Norris, *Chinese Economic Statecraft: Commercial Actors, Grand Strategy, and State Control* (Ithaca, NY: Cornell University Press, 2016), 3–5; Lim and Ferguson, "Informal Economic Sanctions," 1538; Allen, *Beijing Rules*, xx.

39. Elizabeth Economy, *The World According to China* (Cambridge: Polity, 2022); Maria Repnikova, *Chinese Soft Power* (Cambridge: Cambridge University Press, 2022); Allen, *Beijing Rules*.

40. Michael Clarke, "The Belt and Road Initiative: China's New Grand Strategy?," *Asia Policy* 24 (2017): 71–79; Gerald M. Acosta, "China's One Road, One Belt Grand Strategy: Founded on the Weaponization of the Global Supply Chain," *Defense Transportation Journal* 76, no. 6 (2020): 17–22; Xue Gong, "China's Economic Statecraft: The Belt and Road in Southeast Asia and the Impact on the Indo-Pacific," *Security Challenges* 16, no. 3 (2020): 39–46; Matt Ferchen, "The Two Faces of the China Model: The BRI in Southeast Asia," in *Global Perspectives on China's Belt and Road Initiative: Asserting Agency Through Regional Connectivity*, ed. Florian Schneider, 245–264 (Amsterdam: Amsterdam University Press, 2021); Henryk Szadziewski, "A Search for Coherence: The Belt and Road Initiative in the Pacific Islands," in *The China Alternative: Changing Regional Order in the Pacific Islands*, ed. Graeme Smith and Terence Wesley-Smith, 283–318 (Sydney: Australian National University Press, 2021); Sophie Wintgens, "China's Footprint in Latin America," European Union Institute for Security Studies, September 2022, www.iss.europa.eu/sites/default /files/EUISSFiles/Brief_9_China%20in%20Latin%20America_web.pdf.

41. Daniel Kliman et al., "Dangerous Synergies: Countering Chinese and Russian Digital Influence Operations," Center for a New American Security, May 7, 2020, https://www.cnas.org/publications /reports/dangerous-synergies; Kechang Feng, " 'Rumor-Debunking' as a Propaganda and Censorship Strategy in China," in *Disinformation in the Global South*, ed. Herman Wasserman and Dani Madrid-Morales, 108–122 (New York: Wiley, 2022); Joshua Kurlantzick, *Beijing's Global Media Offensive: China's Uneven Campaign to Influence Asia and the World* (New York: Oxford University Press, 2022); Kenton Thibaut, "Chinese Discourse Power: Aspirations, Reality, and Ambitions in the Digital Domain," Atlantic Council, August 24, 2022, https://www.atlanticcouncil.org/in -depth-research-reports/report/chinese-discourse-power-ambitions-and-reality-in-the-digital -domain/; Vivien Marsh, Dani Madrid-Morales, and Chris Paterson, "Global Chinese Media and a Decade of Change," *International Communication Gazette* 85, no. 1 (2023): 3–14; Oxford Analytica, "Digital Controls Give China an Edge in South-East Asia," Expert Briefings, 2023; U.S. Department of State, "How the People's Republic of China Seeks to Reshape the Global Information Environment," September 28, 2023, https://2021-2025.state.gov/gec-special-report-how-the-peoples -republic-of-china-seeks-to-reshape-the-global-information-environment/.

42. For a full list, see Fergus Hunter et al., "Countering China's Coercive Diplomacy," Australian Strategic Policy Institute, February 22, 2023, https://www.aspi.org.au/report/countering-chinas -coercive-diplomacy.

43. Audrye Wong, "How Not to Win Allies and Influence Geopolitics," *Foreign Affairs*, April 20, 2021, www.foreignaffairs.com/articles/china/2021-04-20/how-not-win-allies-and-influence -geopolitics.

44. European Commission, "2022 State of the Union Address by President von der Leyen," September 14, 2022, https://ec.europa.eu/commission/presscorner/detail/ov/SPEECH_22_5493.

45. Andreas Fuchs and Nils-Hendrik Klann, "Paying a Visit: The Dalai Lama Effect on International Trade," Center for European Governance and Economic Development Research Paper 113 (2010).

46. Aya Adachi, Alexander Brown, and Max J. Zenglein, "Fasten Your Seatbelts: How to Manage China's Economic Coercion," Mercator Institute for China Studies, August 25, 2022, https://merics .org/en/report/fasten-your-seatbelts-how-manage-chinas-economic-coercion; Reilly, "China's Unilateral Sanctions," 123.

47. Reilly, "China's Unilateral Sanctions," 125.

48. Reilly, "China's Unilateral Sanctions," 129.

49. Brian Hioe, "China Slaps Export Bans on Taiwanese Goods—Again," *Diplomat*, December 16, 2022, https://thediplomat.com/2022/12/china-slaps-export-bans-on-taiwanese-goods-again/.

50. Matej Šimalčík and Adam Kalivoda, "Sister-City Relations and Identity Politics," *Diplomat*, February 25, 2020, https://thediplomat.com/2020/02/sister-city-relations-and-identity-politics-the-case-of-prague-beijing-taipei-and-shanghai/.

51. This quote is a play on a famous 1950s Chinese propaganda song eulogizing China's effort against the United States during the Korean War. The line was "When friends visit us, we welcome them with fine wine. When jackals or wolves come, we will face them with shotguns." A version of this was co-opted by Ambassador Gui, and also later by Defense Minister Li Shangfu at the 2023 Shangri-La Dialogue; see "How Sweden Copes with Chinese Bullying," *Economist*, February 20, 2020, www.economist.com/europe/2020/02/20/how-sweden-copes-with-chinese-bullying; Shangfu Li, "Remarks at the Fifth Plenary Session, 20th Asia Security Summit: The Shangri-La Dialogue," International Institute for Strategic Studies, June 4, 2023, https://www.iiss.org/globalassets/media-library---content--migration/files/shangri-la-dialogue/2023/final-transcripts/p-5/general-li-shangfu-state-councilor-minister-of-national-defense-china---as-delivered.pdf.

52. Andrew Tillett, "Australia Hits Back at China's 'Economic Coercion,'" *Australian Financial Review*, April 27, 2020, www.afr.com/politics/federal/payne-blasts-beijing-s-economic-coercion-over-virus-probe-push-20200427-p54nig.

53. Allen, *Beijing Rules*, 167.

54. Lim and Ferguson, "Informal Economic Sanctions," 1530.

55. Ben Blanchard and Yew Lun Tian, "Czech Senate Speaker Will Pay 'Heavy Price' for Taiwan Visit, China Says," Reuters, August 31, 2020, https://www.reuters.com/article/world/czech-senate-speaker-will-pay-heavy-price-for-taiwan-visit-china-says-idUSKBN25R02V/.

56. Yasufumi Saito et al., "China Canceled H&M. Every Other Brand Needs to Understand Why," Bloomberg, March 14, 2022, www.bloomberg.com/graphics/2022-china-canceled-hm/.

57. Raphael Satter and Nick Carey, "China Threatened to Harm Czech Companies Over Taiwan Visit—Letter," Reuters, February 19, 2020, www.reuters.com/article/business/china-threatened-to-harm-czech-companies-over-taiwan-visit-letter-idUSKBN20D1BB/.

58. Reilly, "China's Unilateral Sanctions," 126.

59. Toby Branigan, "Eighteen More Countries Refuse to Attend Nobel Peace Prize Ceremony," *Guardian*, December 7, 2010, https://www.theguardian.com/world/2010/dec/07/china-nobel-peace-prize-clowns; Reilly, "China's Unilateral Sanctions," 128

60. As reported in a speech by Wang Xiaolong cited in Stephen Wright, "China Warns New Zealand Against Squandering Trade Ties," *Wall Street Journal*, June 2, 2022, www.wsj.com/articles/china-warns-new-zealand-against-squandering-trade-relationship-11654147681.

61. Bonny Lin and Joel Wuthnow, "The Weakness Behind China's Strong Façade," *Foreign Affairs*, November 10, 2022, https://www.foreignaffairs.com/china/weakness-behind-china-strong-facade.

62. Ministry of Foreign Affairs, The People's Republic of China, "Full Text of President Xi Jinping's 2025 New Year Message," December 31, 2024, https://www.fmprc.gov.cn/mfa_eng/xw/zyxw/202412/t20241231_11524948.html.

63. Reilly, "China's Unilateral Sanctions," 122.

64. Reilly cites a series of works written in the 2000s showing China's study of economic coercion; see Reilly, "China's Unilateral Sanctions," 121–123.

65. Allen, *Beijing Rules*, 206.

66. Robert D. Atkinson, "The Case for a National Industrial Strategy to Counter China's Technological Rise," Information Technology and Innovation Foundation, April 13, 2020, https://itif.org/publications/2020/04/13/case-national-industrial-strategy-counter-chinas-technological-rise/.

67. Milton Friedman, "A Friedman Doctrine—The Social Responsibility of Business Is to Increase Its Profits," *New York Times*, September 13, 1970, https://www.nytimes.com/1970/09/13/archives/a-friedman-doctrine-the-social-responsibility-of-business-is-to.html.

68. Allen, *Beijing Rules*, 23.

69.   Allen, *Beijing Rules*, 206.

70.   "Clinton's Words on China: Trade Is the Smart Thing," *New York Times,* March 9, 2000, www
      .nytimes.com/2000/03/09/world/clinton-s-words-on-china-trade-is-the-smart-thing.html.

71.   Kurt M. Campbell and Ely Ratner, "The China Reckoning: How Beijing Defied American Expec-
      tations," *Foreign Affairs*, February 13, 2018, https://www.foreignaffairs.com/articles/china/2018
      -02-13/china-reckoning.

72.   Robert B. Zoellick, "Whither China: From Membership to Responsibility?," U.S. Department of
      State, September 21, 2005, https://2001-2009.state.gov/s/d/former/zoellick/rem/53682.htm.

73.   G. John Ikenberry, "The Rise of China and the Future of the West," *Foreign Affairs*, January 1,
      2008, https://www.foreignaffairs.com/articles/asia/2008-01-01/rise-china-and-future-west; World
      Bank, "Lifting 800 Million People Out of Poverty—New Report Looks at Lessons from China's
      Experience," April 1, 2022, www.worldbank.org/en/news/press-release/2022/04/01/lifting-800
      -million-people-out-of-poverty-new-report-looks-at-lessons-from-china-s-experience.

74.   Campbell and Ratner, "The China Reckoning."

3. CHINA'S ECONOMIC COERCION

1.   Xiawen Chen and Roberto Javier Garcia, "Economic Sanctions and Trade Diplomacy: Sanction-
     Busting Strategies, Market Distortion, and Efficacy of China's Restrictions on Norwegian Salmon
     Imports," *China Information* 30, no. 1 (2016): 35.

2.   The World Data Lab defines the "consumer class" as people spending at least $12 per day (mea-
     sured in 2017 purchasing power parity, or PPP). They estimate the world reached four billion con-
     sumers in June 2023. This means 22 percent of the world's consumers are Chinese. See Juan
     Caballero and Marco Fengler, "China and India: The Future of the Global Consumer Market,"
     Brookings Institution, April 14, 2023, https://www.brookings.edu/articles/china-and-india-the
     -future-of-the-global-consumer-market/; Wolfgang Fengler et al., "How the World Consumer Class
     Will Grow from 4 Billion to 5 Billion People by 2031," *Brookings Institution*, July 25, 2023, https://
     www.brookings.edu/articles/how-the-world-consumer-class-will-grow-from-4-billion-to-5
     -billion-people-by-2031/; World Data Lab, "China vs. India—Where Is the Momentum in Con-
     sumer Spending?," February 5, 2025, https://blog.worlddatalab.com/wdl/china-vs.-india-where-is
     -the-momentum-in-consumer-spending.

3.   Based on 2024 numbers for the United States, China as a share of U.S. total trade (11.18 percent)
     is now slightly less than the United States as a share of China's total trade (11.20 percent); these
     figures are from the UN Comtrade Database, https://comtradeplus.un.org/.

4.   Steven Lukes, *Power: A Radical View*, 2nd ed. (New York: Palgrave Macmillan, 2005).

5.   Fergus Hunter et al., "Countering China's Coercive Diplomacy," *Australian Strategic Policy Insti-
     tute*, February 22, 2023, https://www.aspi.org.au/report/countering-chinas-coercive-diplomacy, 2.

6.   Bethany Allen, *Beijing Rules: How China Weaponized Its Economy to Confront the World* (New
     York: Harper, 2023), 120.

7.   Charles Buckley, Keith Bradsher, and Tiffany May, "New Security Law Gives China Sweeping Pow-
     ers Over Hong Kong," *New York Times*, June 29, 2020, https://www.nytimes.com/2020/06/29
     /world/asia/china-hong-kong-security-law-rules.html; Office of Foreign Assets Control, "Hong
     Kong-Related Designations," U.S. Department of the Treasury, December 7, 2020, https://ofac
     .treasury.gov/recent-actions/20201207.

8.   VOA News, "China Scolds Germany Over Meeting with Hong Kong Activist," September 11, 2019,
     www.voanews.com/a/east-asia-pacific_china-scolds-germany-over-meeting-hong-kong-activist
     /6175623.html.

9. Reuters, "Brazil's Bolsonaro to Allow China's Huawei in 5G Auctions," January 16, 2021, www .reuters.com/article/us-brazil-huawei-tech/brazils-bolsonaro-to-allow-chinas-huawei-in-5g -auctions-newspaper-idUSKBN29L0JM/; Reuters, "Brazil Regulator Approves 5G Spectrum Auction Rules, No Huawei Ban," February 25, 2021, www.reuters.com/business/media-telecom /brazil-regulator-approves-5g-spectrum-auction-rules-no-huawei-ban-2021-02-26/.

10. Andreas Fuchs and Nils-Hendrik Klann, "Paying a Visit: The Dalai Lama Effect on International Trade," Center for European Governance and Economic Development Research Paper no. 113 (2010): 9.

11. James Reilly, "China's Unilateral Sanctions," *Washington Quarterly* 35, no. 4 (2012): 127.

12. Reilly, "China's Unilateral Sanctions," 128.

13. Michelle Toh and Anna Cooban, "Germany's Leader and Top CEOs Have Arrived in Beijing. They Need China More Than Ever," CNN, November 4, 2022, https://www.cnn.com/2022/11/03 /business/germany-china-olaf-scholz-visit-trade/index.html; Lily McElwee, "How Scholz's Unpopular Trip to Beijing Actually Served U.S. Interests," Center for Strategic and International Studies, November 7, 2022, https://www.csis.org/analysis/how-scholzs-unpopular-trip-beijing-actually -served-us-interests.

14. Elizabeth Paton, "Versace, Givenchy and Coach Apologize to China After T-Shirt Row," *New York Times*, August 12, 2019, www.nytimes.com/2019/08/12/fashion/china-donatella-versace-t-shirt .html.

15. William Zheng, "Chinese Internet Users Call for Boycott of BNP Paribas Over Worker's Support for Hong Kong Protest," *South China Morning Post*, September 18, 2019, www.scmp.com/news /china/politics/article/3027962/chinese-internet-users-call-boycott-bnp-paribas-over-workers.

16. Lisa Du et al., "How Keeping Quiet About Politics Helped Uniqlo Become China's Favorite Fashion Brand," Bloomberg, April 13, 2022, https://www.bloomberg.com/graphics/2022-uniqlo -china-politics/.

17. Guardian, "Gap Sorry for Selling T-Shirt with 'Incorrect' Map of China," May 14, 2019, www .theguardian.com/world/2018/may/15/gap-sorry-t-shirt-map-china.

18. Benjamin Haas, "Marriott Apologizes to China Over Tibet and Taiwan Error," *Guardian*, January 12, 2018, https://www.theguardian.com/world/2018/jan/12/marriott-apologises-to-china-over -tibet-and-taiwan-error.

19. Matt Glasby, "Bad Guys Changed from Chinese to North Korean in Red Dawn Remake at the Height of Hollywood Appeasing China in 2012—But It Still Flopped," *South China Morning Post*, September 2, 2022, https://www.scmp.com/lifestyle/entertainment/article/3190918/bad-guys -changed-chinese-north-korean-red-dawn-remake.

20. Bethany Allen, "China Is Censoring Hollywood's Imagination," Axios, September 1, 2020, www .axios.com/2020/09/01/china-censor-hollywood-films.

21. Daniel Barboza and Brooks Barnes, "How China Won the Keys to Disney's Magic Kingdom," *New York Times*, June 14, 2016, https://www.nytimes.com/2016/06/15/business/international/china -disney.html.

22. Eleanor Albert, "Which Countries Support the New Hong Kong National Security Law?" *Diplomat*, July 6, 2020, https://thediplomat.com/2020/07/which-countries-support-the-new-hong-kong -national-security-law/; Catherine Putz, "Which Countries Are for or Against China's Xinjiang Policies?" *Diplomat*, July 15, 2020. https://thediplomat.com/2020/10/2020-edition-which -countries-are-for-or-against-chinas-xinjiang-policies/.

23. Since 2016, ten countries have switched recognition from Taiwan to China: Burkina Faso, the Dominican Republic, El Salvador, Honduras, Kiribati, Nicaragua, Panama, Sao Tome and Principe, the Solomon Islands, and Nauru. See BBC, "Taiwan Loses Diplomatic Ally as Dominican Republic Switches Ties to China," May 1, 2018, https://www.bbc.com/news/world-asia-china -43958849; Bard Wilkinson, "Taiwan Slams China After Burkina Faso Cuts Ties," CNN, May 24,

2018, www.cnn.com/2018/05/24/asia/taiwan-china-burkina-faso-intl/index.html; Chris Horton, "El Salvador Recognizes China in Blow to Taiwan," *New York Times*, August 21, 2018, https://www .nytimes.com/2018/08/21/world/asia/taiwan-el-salvador-diplomatic-ties.html; Kate Lyons, "China Extends Influence in Pacific as Solomon Islands Break with Taiwan," *Guardian*, September 16, 2019, https://www.theguardian.com/world/2019/sep/16/china-extends-influence-in-pacific-as -solomon-islands-break-with-taiwan; Yimou Lee, "Taiwan Says China Lures Kiribati with Air- planes After Losing Another Ally," Reuters, September 20, 2019, https://www.reuters.com /article/idUSKBN1W50DH/; BBC, "Nicaragua Cuts Ties with Taiwan in Favour of Beijing," December 9, 2021, https://www.bbc.com/news/world-asia-59574532; Associated Press, "Hondu- ras Establishes Ties with China After Taiwan Break," March 26, 2023, https://apnews.com/article /china-honduras-diplomatic-ties-taiwan-bf5c143768814fb6f9f3beff34f611d7; Associated Press, "China Formally Restores Diplomatic Relations with Nauru After Pacific Island Nation Cut Tai- wan Ties," January 24, 2024, https://apnews.com/article/china-nauru-taiwan-diplomatic -recognition-23fd9cdd0210a2340b5ae2092d2a85d1.

24. As of June 2025, the twelve countries that maintain diplomatic ties with Taiwan are Marshall Islands, Republic of Palau, Tuvalu, Eswatini, Holy See, Belize, Republic of Guatemala, Haiti, Republic of Paraguay, St. Kitts and Nevis, Saint Lucia, and St. Vincent & the Grenadines. See Min- istry of Foreign Affairs, Republic of China (Taiwan). "Diplomatic Allies," https://en.mofa.gov.tw /AlliesIndex.aspx?n=1294&sms=1007.

25. Xinwei Huang, "Five Countries Demand Taiwan Rename Local Offices," CGTN, June 14, 2017, https://news.cgtn.com/news/3d6b6a4d3549444e/share_p.html; Stacy Hsu, "PNG Demands New Name for Taiwan Office," *Taipei Times*, June 2, 2018, https://www.taipeitimes.com/News/taiwan /archives/2018/06/02/2003694174; Demetri Sevastopulo and Kathrin Hille, "Washington Risks Beijing Ire Over Proposal to Rename Taiwan's US Office," *Financial Times*, September 10, 2021, www.ft.com/content/07810ece-b35b-47e7-a6d2-c876b7b40444.

26. Jake Chung, "Lithuania Plans to Open Office in Taiwan: Report," *Taipei Times*, March 4, 2021, https://www.taipeitimes.com/News/front/archives/2021/03/04/2003753209.

27. Ministry of Foreign Affairs, @MOFA_Taiwan, "We're proud to announce the planned establish- ment of The Taiwanese Representative Office in #Lithuania," X (formerly Twitter), July 19, 2021, 10:46 p.m., https://x.com/MOFA_Taiwan/status/1417314889236828165; Taiwan Today, "MOFA Announces Plans to Establish The Taiwanese Representative Office in Lithuania," New Southbound Policy Portal, July 21, 2021, https://nspp.mofa.gov.tw/nsppe/content_tt.php?unit=2&post=204651.

28. LRT, "China Slams Lithuania's Move to Build Ties with 'Taiwan Separatists,' " March 5, 2021, https://www.lrt.lt/en/news-in-english/19/1358551/china-slams-lithuania-s-move-to-build-ties -with-taiwan-separatists.

29. State Security Department of the Republic of Lithuania, "National Threat Assessment 2019," Feb- ruary 2019, www.vsd.lt/wp-content/uploads/2019/02/2019-Gresmes-internetui-EN.pdf.

30. Mindaugas Aušra, "Chinese Demonstration in Vilnius Unmasks Beijing's Reach Into Lithuania— LRT Investigation," LRT, October 9, 2019, www.lrt.lt/en/news-in-english/19/1104874/chinese -demonstration-in-vilnius-unmasks-beijing-s-reach-into-lithuania-lrt-investigation.

31. LRT, "Lithuania Hands Note to China Over Incident During Hong Kong Support Rally in Vil- nius," September 2, 2019, https://www.lrt.lt/naujienos/news-in-english/19/1093636/lithuania -hands-note-to-china-over-incident-during-hong-kong-support-rally-in-vilnius.

32. LRT, "Lithuanian President Doesn't Back Taiwan's WHO Membership—Aide," April 22, 2020, https://www.lrt.lt/en/news-in-english/19/1166291/lithuanian-president-doesn-t-back-taiwan-s -who-membership-aide.

33. LRT, "Calls to Support Taiwan 'Open Provocation,' Says China's Ambassador to Lithuania." April 30, 2020, https://www.lrt.lt/en/news-in-english/19/1169159/calls-to-support-taiwan-open -provocation-says-china-s-ambassador-to-lithuania.

34. Vaidotas Beniušis, "Lithuania's Support for Taiwan Draws Ire from Beijing," LRT, May 14, 2020, https://www.lrt.lt/en/news-in-english/19/1178311/lithuania-s-support-for-taiwan-draws-ire-from-beijing.

35. France 24, "Despite Praise for Covid19 Response, Taiwan Barred from WHO Assembly," May 18, 2020, https://www.france24.com/en/20200518-despite-praise-for-covid-19-response-taiwan-barred-from-who-assembly.

36. Euractiv, "Lithuania to Support 'Those Fighting for Freedom' in Taiwan," November 9, 2020, https://www.euractiv.com/section/politics/short_news/lithuania-to-support-those-fighting-for-freedom-in-taiwan/.

37. Konstantinas Andrijauskas, "An Analysis of China's Economic Coercion Against Lithuania," Council on Foreign Relations, May 12, 2022, www.cfr.org/blog/analysis-chinas-economic-coercion-against-lithuania.

38. Dominique Patton and Andrius Sytas, "China Suspends Lithuanian Beef, Dairy, Beer Imports as Taiwan Row Grows," Reuters, February 10, 2022, www.reuters.com/world/china/china-suspends-lithuanian-beef-imports-taiwan-row-grows-2022-02-10/.

39. Andrijauskas, "An Analysis of China's Economic Coercion Against Lithuania."

40. Matthew Reynolds and Matthew P. Goodman, "China's Economic Coercion: Lessons from Lithuania," Center for Strategic and International Studies, May 6, 2022, www.csis.org/analysis/chinas-economic-coercion-lessons-lithuania.

41. Vaida Kalinkaitė-Matuliauskienė, "German Investors in Lithuania Shy Away from Comments About Alleged Chinese Pressure," LRT, March 31, 2022, https://www.lrt.lt/en/news-in-english/19/1659484/german-investors-in-lithuania-refrain-from-comments-about-alleged-chinese-pressure.

42. Yew Lun Tian, "China Sanctions Lithuanian Deputy Minister for Taiwan Visit," Reuters, August 13, 2022, www.reuters.com/world/china-sanctions-lithuanian-deputy-minister-visiting-taiwan-2022-08-12/.

43. Patton and Sytas, "China Suspends Lithuanian Beef, Dairy, Beer Imports."

44. Benjamin David Baker, "Soul or Salmon: Norway's Chinese Dilemma," *Diplomat*, May 9, 2014, https://thediplomat.com/2014/05/soul-or-salmon-norways-chinese-dilemma/.

45. Chen and Garcia, "Economic Sanctions and Trade Diplomacy."

46. Mark Lewis, "Norway's Salmon Rots as China Takes Revenge for Dissident's Nobel Prize," *Independent*, October 6, 2011, https://www.independent.co.uk/news/world/europe/norway-s-salmon-rot-as-china-takes-revenge-for-dissident-s-nobel-prize-2366167.html; Chen and Garcia, "Economic Sanctions and Trade Diplomacy," 31.

47. Chen and Garcia, "Economic Sanctions and Trade Diplomacy," 31.

48. According to one study that extensively interviewed stakeholders in the dispute, Document 9 was meant to be nondiscriminatory in order to remain consistent with WTO rules, but 75 percent of the interviewees believed that the explicit purpose was to block only Norwegian salmon from China because of the Nobel prize. See Chen and Garcia, "Economic Sanctions and Trade Diplomacy," 38.

49. Chen and Garcia, "Economic Sanctions and Trade Diplomacy," 39.

50. Roberto Javier Garcia and Thi Ngan Giang Nguyen, "Market Integration Through Smuggling: China's Sanction on Norwegian Salmon," *Journal of Economic Integration* 38, no. 1 (2023): 93–114.

51. Echo Hwang and Isabella Steger, "Norway Wants China to Forget About the Human Rights Thing and Eat Salmon Instead," *Quartz*, June 14, 2017, https://qz.com/1000541/norway-wants-china-to-forget-about-the-human-rights-thing-and-eat-salmon-instead.

52. Sewell Chan, "Norway and China Restore Ties, 6 Years After Nobel Prize Dispute," *New York Times*, December 19, 2016, https://www.nytimes.com/2016/12/19/world/europe/china-norway-nobel-liu-xiaobo.html; Chen and Garcia, "Economic Sanctions and Trade Diplomacy," 19; Allen, *Beijing Rules*, 11.

53. Global Times, "Norway Understands Mutual Respect Six Years Later," December 20, 2016, https://www.globaltimes.cn/page/201612/1024603.shtml.

54. Adam Segal, "China-Philippines Hacking War: A Missed Opportunity for Beijing?," Council on Foreign Relations, May 10, 2012, www.cfr.org/blog/china-philippines-hacking-war-missed-opportunity-beijing.

55. Ketian Zhang, *China's Gambits—Explaining Chinese Coercion* (Cambridge: Cambridge University Press, 2024).

56. Michael Green et al., "Counter-Coercion Series: Scarborough Shoal Standoff," Center for Strategic and International Studies, May 22, 2017, https://amti.csis.org/counter-co-scarborough-standoff/.

57. BBC, "中国就黄岩岛指责菲律宾扩大事态" [China accused the Philippines of escalating tension in the Scarborough Shoal], May 8, 2012, https://www.bbc.com/zhongwen/simp/chinese_news/2012/05/120508_china_philippines.

58. Yunbi Zhang, "Protest Lodged at Harassment by Manila Ship," *China Daily*, April 12, 2012, https://usa.chinadaily.com.cn/china/2012-04/12/content_15026889.htm.

59. Qin Hong, "面对菲律宾，我们有足够手段" [Faced with the Philippines, we have adequate means], *Overseas Edition of People's Daily*, May 8, 2012, http://mil.news.sina.com.cn/2012-05-08/0718689884.html.

60. China Daily, "A Dangerous Delusion." May 10, 2012, https://www.china.org.cn/opinion/2012-05/10/content_25347880.htm.

61. BBC, "戴秉国：中国不会容忍菲律宾欺负" [Dai Bingguo: China will not tolerate bullying by the Philippines], May 16, 2012, https://www.bbc.com/zhongwen/simp/chinese_news/2012/05/120516_china_philippines.

62. Josephine Cuneta and James Hookway, "China Dispute Threatens Philippine Industries," *Wall Street Journal*, May 16, 2012, https://www.wsj.com/articles/SB100014240527023038796045774077730408858666.

63. John Hey, "China Gets Strict on Philippine Bananas," Asiafruit, March 9, 2012, https://www.fruitnet.com/asiafruit/china-gets-strict-on-philippine-bananas/13621.article.

64. Jane Perlez, "Dispute Between China and Philippines Over Island Becomes More Heated," *New York Times*, May 10, 2012, www.nytimes.com/2012/05/11/world/asia/china-philippines-dispute-over-island-gets-more-heated.html.

65. GMA News, "China's New Complaint About Bugs in PHL Fruits Puzzles Agriculture Exec," May 16, 2012, https://www.gmanetwork.com/news/money/content/258351/china-s-new-complaint-about-bugs-in-phl-fruits-puzzles-agriculture-exec/story/.

66. Andrew Higgins, "In Philippines, Banana Growers Feel Effect of South China Sea Dispute," *Washington Post*, June 10, 2012, https://www.washingtonpost.com/world/asia_pacific/in-philippines-banana-growers-feel-effect-of-south-china-sea-dispute/2012/06/10/gJQA47WVTV_story.html.

67. Kristine L. Alave, "DA Team to Go to China to Check on Stranded Banana Shipment," Inquirer.net, May 15, 2012, https://business.inquirer.net/59391/da-team-to-go-to-china-to-check-on-stranded-banana-shipment.

68. Xinhua, "China Maintains Quarantine on Philippines Fruit," *China Daily*, May 26, 2012, www.chinadaily.com.cn/business/2012-05/26/content_15392626.htm.

69. Agence France-Presse, "Philippine Banana Impounded Amid China Sea Spat," *Rappler*, May 12, 2012, www.rappler.com/business/5253-philippine-banana-impounded-amid-china-sea-spat/.

70. Cuneta and Hookway, "China Dispute Threatens Philippine Industries."

71. Food and Agriculture Organization, *Banana Market Review and Banana Statistics 2012–2013* (Rome: Food and Agriculture Organization of the United Nations, 2014).

72. Higgins, "In Philippines, Banana Growers Feel Effect of South China Sea Dispute."

73. Higgins, "In Philippines, Banana Growers Feel Effect of South China Sea Dispute."

74. Cuneta and Hookway, "China Dispute Threatens Philippine Industries."

75. Food and Agriculture Organization, *Banana Market Review 2022* (Rome: Food and Agriculture Organization of the United Nations, 2023).

76. Cliff Venzon, "China Uses Banana Diplomacy in Philippines to Edge Out Japan," *Nikkei Asia*, July 26, 2019, https://asia.nikkei.com/Politics/International-relations/China-uses-banana-diplomacy-in-Philippines-to-edge-out-Japan.

77. There is only one country from Africa (Mauritius) and one from South America on this list (Brazil).

78. Aya Adachi et al., "Dealing with China's Economic Coercion—The Case of Lithuania and Insights from East Asia and Australia," Mercator Institute for China Studies, December 20, 2021, https://merics.org/en/executive-memo/dealing-chinas-economic-coercion-case-lithuania-and-insights-east-asia-and-australia; Allen, *Beijing Rules*; Hunter et al., "Countering China's Coercive Diplomacy."

79. For Fortune 500 list (U.S. only), see Fortune, "Fortune 500," n.d. https://fortune.com/ranking/fortune500/; for Fortune Global 500 list, see Fortune, "Fortune Global 500," n.d. https://fortune.com/ranking/global500/.

80. Sean Gregory, " 'The Losses Have Already Been Substantial.' Adam Silver Addresses Fallout from the NBA China Controversy," *Time*, October 17, 2019, https://time.com/5703259/adam-silver-nba-china-time-100-health-summit/.

81. Kurt Badenhausen, "NBA Team Values 2018: Every Club Now Worth at Least $1 Billion," *Forbes*, February 7, 2018, https://www.forbes.com/sites/kurtbadenhausen/2018/02/07/nba-team-values-2018-every-club-now-worth-at-least-1-billion/?sh=483fce167155; James T. Areddy, "The NBA's New Normal in China," *Wall Street Journal*, October 25, 2019, www.wsj.com/articles/the-nbas-new-normal-in-china-11572017629; Bloomberg, "China's 500 Million NBA Fans Face Loyalty Test," October 9, 2019, https://www.bloomberg.com/news/articles/2019-10-09/china-s-500-million-nba-fans-face-loyalty-test-in-stand-off; Derek Wallbank and Alfred Cang, "How a Quickly-Deleted Tweet About China Got Pretty Much Everyone Mad at the NBA," *Time*, October 7, 2019, https://time.com/5694150/nba-china-hong-kong/.

82. Keith Nissen, "Global NBA basketball viewers, 2024," S&P Global, March 28, 2024, https://www.spglobal.com/market-intelligence/en/news-insights/research/global-nba-basketball-viewers-2024.

83. Chris Isidore, "The NBA Faces a No-Win Situation in China. Here's What It Stands to Lose," CNN, October 9, 2019, https://www.cnn.com/2019/10/08/business/daryl-morey-tweet-nba-china/index.html.

84. Mark Fainaru-Wada and Steve Fainaru, "ESPN Analysis: NBA Owners, Mum on China Relationship, Have More Than $10 Billion Invested There," ESPN, May 19, 2022, https://www.espn.com/nba/story/_/id/33938932/nba-owners-mum-china-relationship-more-10-billion-invested-there.

85. We counted a total of sixty-three current and former NBA players. The list is a combination of our original database in Victor D. Cha and Andy Lim, "Flagrant Foul: China's Predatory Liberalism and the NBA," *Washington Quarterly* 42, no. 4 (2019): 23–42; and Mike Fish and Michael A. Fletcher, "NBA Players Face Questions Over Shoe Deals with Chinese Companies Linked to Forced Labor," ESPN, January 28, 2022, https://www.espn.com/nba/story/_/id/33140405/nba-players-face-questions-shoe-deals-chinese-companies-linked-forced-labor.

86. Tweet from Williams, L. @TeamLou23: "That's your opinion. I like Peak. I'm my own boss over there. And I've made more in one season with them than 8 with Nike. Ha." X (formerly Twitter), January 21, 2017, 4:56 p.m., https://twitter.com/TeamLou23/status/822925786713915392.

87. ESPN, "Dwyane Wade Inks Lifetime Deal with Chinese Apparel Company Li-Ning," July 18, 2018, https://www.espn.com/nba/story/_/id/24130508/dwyane-wade-signs-life-deal-chinese-apparel

-company-li-ning; Brendan Dunne, "Dwyane Wade on LiNing, Way of Wade, Recruiting His Son, and Sneakers in China," Complex, November 10, 2021, https://www.complex.com/sneakers/a /brendan-dunne/dwyane-wade-li-ning-way-of-wade-zaire-china-sneakers; Rashad Grove, "Dwyane Wade's 'Statue' Sneakers Drop This Saturday," Sports Illustrated, October 28, 2024, https://www.si .com/fannation/sneakers/news/dwyane-wade-statue-sneakers-drop-this-saturday.

88. Global Times, "CBA, Sponsors Halt Cooperation with Houston Rockets After GM Tweets Supporting HK Riots," October 6, 2019, https://www.globaltimes.cn/content/1166090.shtml; Marc Stein, "China Conflict Mutes N.B.A.'s New-Season Buzz," New York Times, October 12, 2019, www.nytimes.com/2019/10/12/sports/basketball/nba-china-hong-kong.html.

89. Global Times, "CBA, Sponsors Halt Cooperation with Houston Rockets after GM Tweets Supporting HK Riots."

90. Global Times @globaltimesnews, X (formerly Twitter), October 8, 2019, 5:40 p.m., https://twitter .com/globaltimesnews/status/1181731004031148033.

91. ESPN, "Lakers' NBA Cares Event in Shanghai Canceled Amid China Rift," October 9, 2019, https://www.espn.com/nba/story/_/id/27803863/lakers-nba-cares-event-shanghaicanceled -amid-china-rift.

92. Jinshan Hong and Iain Marlow, "NBA Loses More Sponsors as China Flexes Economic Muscle," Bloomberg, October 8, 2019, https://www.bloomberg.com/news/articles/2019-10-09/china-flexes -economic-muscle-again-as-nba-loses-more-sponsors; Michelle Toh and Laura He, "All of the NBA's Official Chinese Partners Have Suspended Ties with the League," CNN Business, October 9, 2019, www.cnn.com/2019/10/09/business/nba-china-partners/index.html.

93. Shams Charania, "Charania: Inside What Went On Among Nets and Lakers Players on the Ground in China Amid the NBA China Conflict," The Athletic, October 14, 2019, https://theathletic .com/1281993/2019/10/14/charania-inside-what-went-on-among-netsand-lakers-players-on-the -ground-in-china-amid-the-nba-china-conflict/; Bill Oram, "Oram: What It Was Like to Cover the Lakers in China When the Media Was Shut Out," The Athletic, October 12, 2019, https:// theathletic.com/1288670/2019/10/12/oramwhat-it-was-like-to-cover-the-lakers-in-china-when -the-media-was-shut-out/.

94. ESPN, "Adam Silver Supports Free Speech Rights of Rockets GM Daryl Morey," October 7, 2019, https://www.espn.com/nba/story/_/id/27792662/adam-silver-supports-free-speech-rights -houston-rockets-gm-daryl-morey.

95. Nick Friedell @NickFriedell, "[Coach of the Golden State Warriors] Kerr also reiterated that the league has not told players or coaches what they can or cannot say in regard to the ongoing China situation," X (formerly Twitter), October 12, 2019, 5:30 p.m., https://twitter.com/NickFriedell /status/1183132785684316160. There were, however, reports of sports agents telling their clients not to speak about China issues; see Jabari Young, "Sports Agents Warn NBA Players to Avoid China Talk as Athletes, Executives Walk 'Fine Line,'" CNBC, October 10, 2019, https://www.cnbc.com /2019/10/10/sports-agents-warn-players-to-avoid-china-talk-as-nba-walks-fine-line.html.

96. James later clarified his comments with two tweets the same day. LeBron James @KingJames, "Let me clear up the confusion. I do not believe there was any consideration for the consequences and ramifications of the tweet. I'm not discussing the substance. Others can talk about that," X (formerly Twitter), October 14, 2019, 10:35 p.m., https://twitter.com/KingJames/status /1183934373671735296; Lebron James @KingJames, "My team and this league just went through a difficult week. I think people need to understand what a tweet or statement can do to others. And I believe nobody stopped and considered what would happen. Could have waited a week to send it," X (formerly Twitter), October 14, 2019, 10:36 p.m., https://twitter.com/KingJames/status /1183934569411530752. See Ohm Youngmisuk, "LeBron James: Daryl Morey Was 'Misinformed' Before Sending Tweet About China and Hong Kong," ESPN, October 14, 2019, www.espn.com /nba/story/_/id/27847951/daryl-morey-was-misinformed-sending-tweet-china-hong-kong.

97. Matt Eppers, "Rockets' James Harden on NBA China Dispute: 'I'm Staying Out of It,' " *USA Today*, October 13, 2019, https://www.usatoday.com/story/sports/nba/rockets/2019/10/13/james -harden-nba-china-dispute/3971503002/.

98. Paul Kasabian, "Warriors' Stephen Curry 'Not Sure' If He'll Go on Promotional China Trip in 2020," Bleacher Report, October 9, 2020, https://bleacherreport.com/articles/2857435-warriors -stephen-curry-not-sure-if-hell-go-on-promotional-china-trip-in-2020.

99. Tilman Fertitta @TilmanJFertitta, "Listen. . . . @dmorey does NOT speak for the @Houston-Rockets. Our presence in Tokyo is all about the promotion of the @NBA internationally and we are NOT a political organization. @espn, " X (formerly Twitter), October 4, 2019, 11:54 p.m., https://twitter.com/TilmanJFertitta/status/1180330287957495809.

100. Fish and Fletcher, "NBA Players Face Questions Over Shoe Deals."

101. Guardian, "China Drops Philadelphia 76ers Broadcasts as Hong Kong Row Continues," December 30, 2020, www.theguardian.com/sport/2020/dec/30/china-drops-76ers-broadcasts-daryl -morey; Raymond Zhong and Sopan Deb, "Celtics Games Are Pulled in China After Enes Kanter's Pro-Tibet Posts," *New York Times*, October 21, 2021, www.nytimes.com/2021/10/21/sports /basketball/celtics-kanter-china-tibet.html.

102. Toby Branigan, "Chinese Bloggers Claim Coca-Cola Backs Tibetans," *Guardian*, April 8, 2008, https://www.theguardian.com/world/2008/apr/09/china.tibet; Stephanie Clifford, "Olympic Protests Put Coca-Cola in a Quandary," *New York Times*, April 17, 2008, https://www.nytimes.com /2008/04/17/business/worldbusiness/17iht-coke.1.12085208.html.

103. Benjamin Haas, "Emirates Tells Cabin Crew to Swap Taiwanese Flag Pins for Chinese Ones," *Guardian*, May 31, 2017, https://www.theguardian.com/world/2017/may/31/emirates-taiwanese -chinese-flag-pins-one-china-policy; Vivienne Chow, "HBO's Site Remains Blocked in China but Its Shows Aren't," *Variety*, June 27, 2018, https://variety.com/2018/tv/news/john-oliver-hbo-china -game-of-thrones-website-1202859077/; Benjamin Haas, "China Bans Winnie-the-Pooh Films After Comparisons to President Xi," *Guardian*, August 6, 2018, https://www.theguardian.com /world/2018/aug/07/china-bans-winnie-the-pooh-film-to-stop-comparisons-to-president-xi.

104. Sui-Lee Wee, "Giving in to China, U.S. Airlines Drop Taiwan (in Name at Least)," *New York Times*, July 25, 2018, www.nytimes.com/2018/07/25/business/taiwan-american-airlines-china.html.

105. Wee, "Giving in to China."

106. Hamish Rutherford and John Anthony, "Air NZ Plane Forced to Turn Around After Airline Forgot to Remove Reference to Taiwan," Stuff, February 12, 2019, www.stuff.co.nz/business /110525974/air-nz-plane-forced-to-turn-around-after-airline-forgot-to-remove-reference-to -taiwan.

107. Sharon Waxman, "China Bans Work with Film Studios," *Washington Post*, November 1, 1997, www .washingtonpost.com/archive/lifestyle/1997/11/01/china-bans-work-with-film-studios/9f3a23e3 -4d83-4749-898c-bd1fef276f03/.

108. Jordan Ruimy, "Scorsese's 'Kundun' Banned by Disney, Much to China's Delight," World of Reel, November 10, 2023, www.worldofreel.com/blog/2023/11/10/rdep49sr2jiryudojiepyg34hqtha1.

109. Jane Li, "China Is Angry About Marvel's First Asian Superhero Movies," Quartz, July 23, 2019, https://qz.com/quartzy/1671394/china-is-angry-about-marvels-first-asian-superhero-movie.

110. Nicholas Yong, "China: Fans Rejoice as Marvel Films Return After Apparent Ban," BBC, January 17, 2023, https://www.bbc.com/news/world-asia-china-64300182.

111. Phoebe Zhang, "Chinese Netizens Boycott South Korean TV Show, 'Running Man,' " *South China Morning Post*, December 8, 2020, www.scmp.com/lifestyle/entertainment/article/3113196/chinese -netizens-boycott-south-korean-television-show.

112. Shen Lu and Ginger Adams Otis, "Snickers Maker Apologizes to China for Referring to Taiwan as Its Own Country," *Wall Street Journal*, August 5, 2022, https://www.wsj.com/articles/snickers -maker-apologizes-to-china-for-referring-to-taiwan-as-its-own-country-11659727945.

113. Zachary Evans, "Sony Refuses Chinese Demand to Delete Statue of Liberty from Latest Spider-man," *National Review*, May 2, 2022, https://www.nationalreview.com/news/sony-refuses-chinese-demand-to-delete-statue-of-liberty-from-latest-spider-man/.

114. Frank Bro, "Insulting China? No, Doctor Strange 2 is shaming US and Hollywood," *Global Times*, May 1, 2022, https://www.globaltimes.cn/page/202205/1260710.shtml.

115. Kira Bindrim, "Why 'Top Gun: Maverick' Has No Release Date in China," Quartz, July 20, 2022, https://qz.com/2170997/why-top-gun-maverick-has-no-release-date-in-china; Isaac Stone Fish, "Top Gun: Maverick Betrays Hollywood's Weakness in China," BBC, June 8, 2022, https://www.bbc.com/news/world-us-canada-61710500.

116. Ja-young Yoon, "China Bans Import of 19 Korean Cosmetics," *Korea Times*, January 10, 2017, www.koreatimes.co.kr/www/biz/2023/06/602_221794.html; Yonhap News Agency, "THAAD Row with China Costs S. Korea Dear: Report," September 15, 2017, https://en.yna.co.kr/view/AEN20170915008300320; Victoria Kim, "When China and U.S. Spar, It's South Korea That Gets Punched," *Los Angeles Times*, November 19, 2020, https://www.latimes.com/world-nation/story/2020-11-19/south-korea-china-beijing-economy-thaad-missile-interceptor; Darren J. Lim and Victor Ferguson, "Informal Economic Sanctions: The Political Economy of Chinese Coercion During the THAAD Dispute," *Review of International Political Economy* 29, no. 5 (2022): 1525–1548.

117. Ho-jung Won, "Duty Free Struggles as THAAD Crisis Persists," *Korea Herald*, September 1, 2017, https://www.koreaherald.com/view.php?ud=20170901000682; Kyung-Jin Shin, "Retaliation by Beijing Extends to Bidet Imports," *Joongang Ilbo*, January 19, 2017, https://koreajoongangdaily.joins.com/2017/01/19/economy/Retaliation-by-Beijing-extends-to-bidet-imports/3028897.html.

118. BBC, "Dior Apologizes for Using China Map Without Taiwan," October 17, 2019, https://www.bbc.com/news/business-50078886.

119. Allen, *Beijing Rules* 13.

120. Denise Tsang, "Uproar Against Firms Such as Pocari Sweat, Tempo, Yoshinoya, and Pizza Hut Show Brands Tread Dangerous Ground by Taking Sides on Hong Kong Extradition Protests, Say Marketing Experts," *South China Morning Post*, July 14, 2019, www.scmp.com/news/hong-kong/politics/article/3018539/uproar-against-firms-such-pocari-sweat-tempo-yoshinoya-and.

121. Iliana Magra and Christine Hauser, "Lululemon Fires Employee Over 'Bat Fried Rice' TShirt," *New York Times*, April 22, 2020, https://www.nytimes.com/2020/04/22/business/lululemon-bat-fried-rice-shirt-coronavirus.html.

122. Hsiao-hwa Hsia, Ray Chung, and Heung Yeung Lee, "Chinese Calls for Taiwan Hotel Boycott Part of Propaganda Machine," Radio Free Asia, August 19, 2024, https://www.rfa.org/english/news/china/china-paris-hotel-boycott-08192024133024.html.

123. Global Times, "Update: Evergreen Laurel Hotel's Apology Fails to Appease Angry Netizens Following Flag Controversy," August 15, 2024, https://www.globaltimes.cn/page/202408/1318119.shtml.

124. Mitch Philips, "Clubs Unlikely to Bite the Chinese Hand That Feeds," Reuters, December 16, 2019, www.reuters.com/article/uk-soccer-arsenal-china/clubs-unlikely-to-bite-the-chinese-hand-that-feeds-idUKKBN1YK26H/; Reuters, "Ozil Removed from Computer Game in China Over Uighur Comments," December 18, 2019, www.reuters.com/article/idUSKBN1YM23C/.

125. Michael Martina and Yew Lun Tian, "China Detains Staff, Raids Office of U.S. Due Diligence Firm Mintz Group," Reuters, March 24, 2023, https://www.reuters.com/world/us-due-diligence-firm-mintz-groups-beijing-office-raided-five-staff-detained-2023-03-24/.

126. Oscar Holland and Serenitie Wang. "Coach, Givenchy Joining Versace in Apologizing to Chinese Consumers Amid T-Shirt Outcry," CNN, August 13, 2019, https://edition.cnn.com/style/article/coach-givenchy-versace-t-shirt-controversy/index.html; Sue Ng and Huifeng He, "Versace and Coach Spark Outrage in China for Selling Shirts That List Hong Kong Without a Country," Goldthread, August 12, 2019, https://www.goldthread2.com/culture/versace-coach-china-hong-kong/article/3022467.

127. Associated Press, "Versace Apologizes in Flap Over T-Shirts Sold in China," August 11, 2019, https://apnews.com/general-news-movies-d4cd7b1c1ad34283b0e9bec39fcdaebc.

128. Oscar Holland, "Bulgari Apologizes for Taiwan Listing Amid Chinese Social Media Uproar," CNN, July 12, 2023, https://www.cnn.com/style/bulgari-china-apology-taiwan-listing/index.html.

129. BBC, "H&M: Fashion Giants Sees China Sales Slump After Xinjiang Boycott," July 2, 2021, https://www.bbc.com/news/business-57691415.

130. Rebecca Davis, "China Celebrities Stoke Nationalist Firestorm Against Foreign Brands Concerned by Xinjiang," *Variety*, March 26, 2021, https://variety.com/2021/film/news/china-celebrities-stoke-nationalist-backlash-against-xinjiang-criticism-1234938619/.

131. Keith Bradsher, "China to Investigate U.S. Retailer, Sending a Message Over Xinjiang," *New York Times*, September 24, 2024, https://www.nytimes.com/2024/09/24/business/china-xinjiang-calvin-klein-tommy-hilfiger.html.

132. Lester Ross and Kenneth Zhou, "MOFCOM Initiates Investigation into PVH Group Under China's Unreliable Entity List Regime," *WilmerHale*, October 14, 2024, https://www.wilmerhale.com/en/insights/client-alerts/20241014-mofcom-initiates-investigation-into-pvh-group-under-chinas-unreliable-entity-list-regime.

133. Gabrielle Fonrouge, "How Calvin Klein and Tommy Hilfiger Got Caught in Trump's Trade War with China," CNBC, February 6, 2025, https://www.cnbc.com/2025/02/06/calvin-klein-owner-pvh-blacklisted-in-china.html.

134. Meaghan Tobin et al., "China Opens Investigation Into Nvidia Over Potential Antitrust Violations," *New York Times*, December 9, 2024, https://www.nytimes.com/2024/12/09/technology/china-nvidia-investigation-antitrust-ai.html.

135. Mariko Oi, "Uniqlo Does Not Use Xinjiang Cotton, Boss Says," BBC, November 27, 2024, https://www.bbc.com/news/articles/c79zqdl7j2go.

136. David Keohane and Leo Lewis, "Fast Retailing Shares Fall Over Fears for Uniqlo Stores in China," *Financial Times*, December 2, 2024, https://www.ft.com/content/54c5650a-fc6a-4a8d-a20e-110c456d4a8f.

137. Chongjing Li and Winnie Hsu, "Controversial Fukushima Nuclear Waste Plan Spurs Chinese Boycott of Japanese Cosmetics," *Time*, June 23, 2023, https://time.com/6289566/chinese-boycott-japanese-cosmetics-nuclear-plant-water/.

138. France 24, "Anti-French Protests Sweep Across China," April 19, 2008, https://www.france24.com/en/20080419-anti-french-protests-sweep-across-china-china-france; Ben Blanchard, "Torch Protests Stir Strident Chinese Nationalism," Reuters, April 19, 2008, https://www.reuters.com/article/economy/torch-protests-stir-strident-chinese-nationalism-idUSPEK278227/.

139. Sales of Peugeot and Citroën cars were down 14.1 percent in 2008 compared to 2007; see James Prieger et al., "French Automobiles and the Chinese Boycotts of 2008: Politics Really Does Affect Commerce," Pepperdine University, School of Public Policy Working Papers no. 5 (2010), https://digitalcommons.pepperdine.edu/sppworkingpapers/5.

140. Seung-bum Kim and Seong-min Kim, "Chinese Boycott Takes Toll on Hyundai-Kia, Suppliers," *Chosun Daily*, July 4, 2017, https://www.chosun.com/english/industry-en/2017/07/04/ZVSX7FL3PJNMRRLXSBMLX5JC2M/; Lim and Ferguson, "Informal Economic Sanctions."

141. Bethany Allen provides an excellent discussion of these cases in chapter 5 of *Beijing Rules: How China Weaponized Its Economy to Confront the World*.

142. Reilly, "China's Unilateral Sanctions"; Bjørnar Sverdrup-Thygeson, "The Flexible Cost of Insulting China: Trade Politics and the 'Dalai Lama Effect,'" *Asian Perspective* 39, no. 1 (2015): 101–123; Audrye Wong, "How Not to Win Allies and Influence Geopolitics," *Foreign Affairs*, April 20, 2021, www.foreignaffairs.com/articles/china/2021-04-20/how-not-win-allies-and-influence-geopolitics; Derek Scissors, "Deterring Chinese Economic Coercion: Statement Before the House

Committee on Rules," American Enterprise Institute, May 10, 2023, www.aei.org/wp-content /uploads/2023/05/Derek-Scissors_Written-Testimony.pdf?x85095.

143. Emily Crane, "Kodak Bends to China by Deleting Instagram Post by French Photographer Who Called the Xinjiang Region—Where Beijing Is Accused of Human Rights Abuses—an 'Orwellian Dystopia,'" Daily Mail, July 21, 2021, https://www.dailymail.co.uk/news/article-9811531/Kodak -deletes-Instagram-post-calling-Chinas-Xinjiang-Orwellian-dystopia.html.

144. Chen and Garcia, "Economic Sanctions and Trade Diplomacy," 30.

145. Michael J. Mazarr, *Mastering the Gray Zone: Understanding a Changing Era of Conflict* (Washington, DC: US Army War College Press, 2015), https://press.armywarcollege.edu/monographs /428; Peter Layton, "China's Enduring Grey Zone Challenge," Air and Space Power Centre, 2021, https://airpower.airforce.gov.au/publications/chinas-enduring-grey-zone-challenge.

146. Elizabeth Economy, *The World According to China* (Cambridge: Polity, 2022); Allen, *Beijing Rules*, 166–168.

4. COLLECTIVE RESILIENCE

1. Urea is used in fertilizers and for emission control in diesel vehicles, which accounts for the vast majority of cargo trucks and buses in South Korea. See Steven Borowiec, "Urea Shortage Threatens to Paralyze South Korea's Economy," *Nikkei Asia*, November 17, 2021, https://asia.nikkei.com /Economy/Urea-shortage-threatens-to-paralyze-South-Korea-s-economy; Da-sol Kim and Byung-wook Kim, "Korea's Urea Crisis," *Korea Herald*, November 9, 2021, https://www.koreaherald .com/view.php?ud=20211109000809.

2. Chad P. Bown, "How COVID-19 Medical Supply Shortages Led to Extraordinary Trade and Industrial Policy," *Asian Economic Policy Review* 17, no. 1 (2022): 114–135.

3. Susan Helper and Evan Soltas, "Why the Pandemic Has Disrupted Supply Chains," White House, June 17, 2021, https://www.whitehouse.gov/cea/written-materials/2021/06/17/why-the-pandemic -has-disrupted-supply-chains/.

4. Daniel Howley, "These 169 Industries Are Being Hit by the Global Chip Shortage," Yahoo! Finance, April 25, 2021, https://finance.yahoo.com/news/these-industries-are-hit-hardest-by-the -global-chip-shortage-122854251.html; Ian King, Debby Wu, and Demetrios Pogkas, "How a Chip Shortage Snarled Everything from Phones to Cars," Bloomberg, March 29, 2021, https://www .bloomberg.com/graphics/2021-semiconductors-chips-shortage/.

5. Michael Wayland, "How Covid Led to a $60 Billion Global Chip Shortage for the Auto Industry," CNBC, February 11, 2021, www.cnbc.com/2021/02/11/how-covid-led-to-a-60-billion-global -chip-shortage-for-automakers.html; Michael Wayland, "Chip Shortage Expected to Cost Auto Industry $210 Billion in Revenue in 2021," CNBC, September 23, 2021, www.cnbc.com/2021/09 /23/chip-shortage-expected-to-cost-auto-industry-210-billion-in-2021.html.

6. Sean Tucker, "Average New Car Prices Sets Record," *Kelley Blue Book*, December 12, 2022, www .kbb.com/car-news/average-new-car-price-sets-record/; Jeanne Whalen, "In Detroit, the Chip Shortage Has Left the City Eerily Short of Cars," *Washington Post*, July 23, 2022, www .washingtonpost.com/technology/2022/07/23/chip-shortage-detroit-manufacturing/.

7. Mary Hui, "Japan's Global Rare Earths Quest Holds Lessons for the US and Europe," Quartz, April 23, 2021, https://qz.com/1998773/japans-rare-earths-strategy-has-lessons-for-us-europe/; Reuters, "Japan Passes Economic Security Bill to Guard Sensitive Technology," May 11, 2022, www .reuters.com/world/asia-pacific/japan-passes-economic-security-bill-guard-sensitive-technology -2022-05-11/.

8. Seok-min Oh, "S. Korea Launches 'Early Warning System' on Supply Chains of 4,000 Key Industry Items," Yonhap News Agency, November 26, 2021, https://en.yna.co.kr/view/AEN202111 26002700320.

9. Yonhap News Agency, "S. Korean Gov't Bolsters Supply Crunch Early Warning System Abroad," January 16, 2022, https://en.yna.co.kr/view/AEN20220116000800325.

10. Sung-hoon Kim and Minu Kim, "Korea's Yoon Gov't to Create Presidential Secretary for Economic Security Affairs," Pulse, April 22, 2022, https://pulsenews.co.kr/view.php?year=2022&no=358656.

11. Duk-kun Byun, "S. Korea, U.S. Hold Inaugural Economic Security Dialogue in Washington," Yonhap News Agency, July 8, 2022, https://en.yna.co.kr/view/AEN20220708000300325; Center for Strategic and International Studies, "Keynote Address by Wang Yunjong at ROK-U.S. Strategic Forum 2022," June 6, 2022, https://www.csis.org/analysis/keynote-address-wang-yunjong-rok-us -strategic-forum-2022; White House, "Readout of the Trilateral United States—Japan—Republic of Korea Economic Security Dialogue," February 28, 2023, https://bidenwhitehouse.archives.gov /briefing-room/statements-releases/2023/02/28/readout-of-the-trilateral-united-states-japan -republic-of-korea-economic-security-dialogue/.

12. Ji-hyoung Son, "Yoon Names New Security Office Deputy, Vice Foreign Minister," *Korea Herald*, January 10, 2024, www.koreaherald.com/view.php?ud=20240110000742.

13. See "Act on Special Measures for Strengthening the Competitiveness of Materials, Components, and Equipment Industries," Law No.19990, enacted January 9, 2024, effective July 10, 2024, www .motie.go.kr/kor/article/ATCL8764a1224/155118386/view; Ministry of Economy and Finance, "The Enactment of Framework Act on Supply Chain," December 27, 2023, https://english.moef .go.kr/pc/selectTbPressCenterDtl.do?boardCd=N0001&seq=5741; Seok-min Oh, "(LEAD) S. Korea Seeks to Cut Key Minerals Dependence on China to 50 Pct by 2030," Yonhap News Agency, February 27, 2023, https://en.yna.co.kr/view/AEN20230227003351320; Jennifer Ahn, "U.S.–South Korea Policy Coordination on Supply Chain Resiliency," Council on Foreign Relations, April 2, 2024, www.cfr.org/blog/us-south-korea-policy-coordination-supply-chain-resiliency; Ministry of Trade, Industry and Energy, "Special Act on National Resources Security," Law No. 20196, February 6, 2024, https://www.law.go.kr/lsInfoP.do?lsiSeq=259657&efYd=20250207#0000.

14. Ministry of Economy and Finance, "The 1st Supply Chain Stabilization Committee Meeting," June 27, 2024, https://english.moef.go.kr/pc/selectTbPressCenterDtl.do?boardCd=N0001&seq =5902.

15. Ministry of Economy and Finance, "The 1st Supply Chain Stabilization Committee Meeting."

16. Pablo Abril Marti and Mariusz Maciejewski, "The European Commission," European Parliament, April 2024, https://www.europarl.europa.eu/factsheets/en/sheet/25/the-european-commission.

17. European Commission, "European Industrial Strategy," n.d., https://commission.europa.eu /strategy-and-policy/priorities-2019-2024/europe-fit-digital-age/european-industrial-strategy _en.

18. European Commission, "In-Depth Reviews of Strategic Areas for Europe's Interests," n.d., https:// commission.europa.eu/strategy-and-policy/priorities-2019-2024/europe-fit-digital-age /european-industrial-strategy/depth-reviews-strategic-areas-europes-interests_en.

19. European Union, "European Chips Act," n.d., https://commission.europa.eu/strategy-and-policy /priorities-2019-2024/europe-fit-digital-age/european-chips-act_en.

20. European Commission, "European Chips Act: Commission Launches Pilot System to Monitor Semiconductor Supply Chain," May 10, 2023, https://digital-strategy.ec.europa.eu/en/news /european-chips-act-commission-launches-pilot-system-monitor-semiconductor-supply-chain; European Commission, "Joint Communication to the European Parliament, the European Council and the Council on European Economic Security," June 20, 2023, https://eur-lex.europa.eu /legal-content/EN/TXT/?uri=CELEX%3A52023JC0020&qid=1687525961309; European

Union, "Chips Joint Undertaking," n.d., https://european-union.europa.eu/institutions-law -budget/institutions-and-bodies/search-all-eu-institutions-and-bodies/chips-joint-undertaking _en.

21. European Commission, "Digital Sovereignty: European Chips Act Enters Into Force Today," September 21, 2023, https://ec.europa.eu/commission/presscorner/detail/en/ip_23_4518.

22. European Commission, "Commission Launches Chips Joint Undertaking Under the European Chips Act," November 30, 2023, https://ec.europa.eu/commission/presscorner/detail/en/ip_23 _6167.

23. European Commission, "2022 State of the Union Address by President von der Leyen," September 14, 2022, https://ec.europa.eu/commission/presscorner/detail/ov/SPEECH_22_5493.

24. European Commission, "Critical Raw Materials: Ensuring Secure and Sustainable Supply Chains for EU's Green and Digital Future," March 16, 2023. https://ec.europa.eu/commission/presscorner /detail/en/ip_23_1661.

25. European Commission, "Critical Raw Materials."

26. Eric Onstad and Yun Chee Foo, "EU to Set Up Central Buying Agency for Critical Minerals— Draft Law," Reuters, March 7, 2023, https://www.reuters.com/world/europe/eu-set-up-central -buying-agency-critical-minerals-draft-law-2023-03-07/.

27. European Commission, "New Tool to Enable EU to Withstand Economic Coercion Enters Into Force," December 27, 2023, https://ec.europa.eu/commission/presscorner/detail/en/ip_23_6804.

28. Dursun Peksen and Timothy M. Peterson, "Sanctions and Alternate Markets: How Trade and Alliances Affect the Onset of Economic Coercion," *Political Research Quarterly* 69, no. 1 (2016): 4–16.

29. For a concise description of China's obfuscation of information at the start of the pandemic, see Andrew Tillett and Phillip Coorey, "PM Wants Weapons Inspector–Like Powers for WHO," *Australian Financial Review*, April 22, 2020, www.afr.com/politics/federal/pm-wants-weapons -inspector-like-powers-for-world-health-organisation-20200422-p54m5x. See also Bethany Allen, *Beijing Rules: How China Weaponized Its Economy to Confront the World* (New York: Harper, 2023), 12–15.

30. Tariffs on barley began in May 2020; see Liangyue Cao and Jared Greenville, "Understanding How China's Tariff on Australian Barley Exports Will Affect the Agricultural Sector," Australian Government Department of Agriculture, Fisheries and Forestry, 2020, https://www.agriculture.gov .au/abares/research-topics/trade/understanding-chinas-tariff-on-australian-barley; Dan Conifer, "China Imposes 80pc Tariff on Australian Barley for Next Five Years Amid Global Push for Coronavirus Investigation," ABC News, May 18, 2020, https://www.abc.net.au/news/2020-05-18 /china-to-impose-tariffs-on-australian-barley/12261108. Import ban on beef began in May 2020; see Kirsty Needham and Colin Packham, "China Halts Beef Imports from Four Australian Firms as COVID-19 Spat Sours Trade," Reuters, May 12, 2020, https://www.reuters.com/article/world /china-halts-beef-imports-from-four-australian-firms-as-covid-19-spat-sours-trade -idUSKBN22O0FA/.

31. For numbers, see Meat & Livestock Australia, "State of the Industry Reports," October 18, 2023, https://www.mla.com.au/prices-markets/Trends-analysis/state-of-the-industry-reports/.

32. For China's tariffs on Australian goods, see Su-Lin Tan, "Explainer | What Happened Over the First Year of the China-Australia Trade Dispute?" *South China Morning Post*, October 28, 2020, www.scmp.com/economy/china-economy/article/3107228/china-australia-relations-what-has -happened-over-last-six. For data on Australian exports after Chinese actions, see Roland Rajah, "The Big Bark but Small Bite of China's Trade Coercion," Interpreter, April 8, 2021, www .lowyinstitute.org/the-interpreter/big-bark-small-bite-china-s-trade-coercion.

33. This is not to say that all wineries were able to withstand the sanctions; many indeed were shut down as a result of China's actions. See Allen, *Beijing Rules*, 15.

34. For a comprehensive look at how Australia responded to Chinese economic sanctions, see Richard McGregor, "Chinese Coercion, Australian Resilience," Lowy Institute, October 20, 2022, https://www.lowyinstitute.org/publications/chinese-coercion-australian-resilience#heading-6816; ABC News, "China's Appetite for Australian Barley Is Back, Three Years After Tariffs Halted the Near–$1 Billion Market," December 30, 2023, www.abc.net.au/news/2023-12-30/china-australian-barley-appetite-3-years-tariffs-halted-market/103274912; Minister for Foreign Affairs, "Resolution of Barley Dispute with China," August 5, 2023. https://www.foreignminister.gov.au/minister/penny-wong/media-release/resolution-barley-dispute-china.

35. Australian Government, "Barley—Diversifying at a Price Q2 2021," 2021, https://www.agriculture.gov.au/sites/default/files/documents/q2-barley-exports.pdf; McGregor, "Chinese Coercion, Australian Resilience."

36. Daniel Hurst, "How Much Is China's Trade War Really Costing Australia?" Guardian, October 27, 2020, https://www.theguardian.com/australia-news/2020/oct/28/how-much-is-chinas-trade-war-really-costing-australia; Josh Frydenberg, "Building Resilience and the Return of Strategic Competition, Melbourne," Ministers: Treasury Portfolio, September 6, 2021, https://ministers.treasury.gov.au/ministers/josh-frydenberg-2018/speeches/building-resilience-and-return-strategic-competition; Michael Smith, "China's Sanctions Against Australia Have Been a Spectacular Failure," *Australian Financial Review*, December 21, 2022, www.afr.com/world/asia/china-s-sanctions-against-australian-have-been-a-spectacular-failure-20221220-p5c7vl.

37. Ryan Woo, Albee Zhang, and Casey Hall, "China Lifts Tariffs on Australian Wine, Ends Three-Year Freeze in Trade," Reuters, April 2, 2024, www.reuters.com/markets/commodities/china-lifts-tariffs-australian-wine-ends-three-year-freeze-trade-2024-04-02/.

38. Eugene Gholz and Llewelyn Hughes, "Market Structure and Economic Sanctions: The 2010 Rare Earth Elements Episode as a Pathway Case of Market Adjustment," *Review of International Political Economy* 23, no. 3 (2019): 623–624.

39. Gholz and Hughes, "Market Structure and Economic Sanctions," 624–625.

40. Roni Dengler, "Global Trove of Rare Earth Metals Found in Japan's Deep Sea Mud," *Science*, April 13, 2018, https://www.science.org/content/article/global-trove-of-rare-earth-metals-found-japans-deep-sea-mud; Gholz and Hughes, "Market Structure and Economic Sanctions," 625; Mary Hui, "Japan Minted a New Economic Security Minister to Fix Supply Chain Disruptions," Quartz, October 8, 2021, https://qz.com/2070498/japan-has-a-new-economic-security-chief-to-secure-supply-chains/.

41. Andrius Sytas, "Lithuania to Get U.S. Trade Support as It Faces China Fury Over Taiwan," Reuters, November 19, 2021, www.reuters.com/business/lithuania-get-us-trade-support-it-faces-china-fury-over-taiwan-2021-11-19/; Jonas Deveikis, "China Sanctions vs Taiwan Investments—Lithuania's Central Bank Weighs Economic Impact," LRT, January 21, 2022, https://www.lrt.lt/en/news-in-english/19/1593215/china-sanctions-vs-taiwan-investments-lithuania-s-central-bank-weighs-economic-impact.

42. Center for Strategic and International Studies, "Economic Security: Perspectives from Seoul and Washington," February 23, 2023, YouTube video, 2:20:50–2:21:47, https://www.youtube.com/watch?v=AtqntHb5Iro.

43. Matt Atlas, "Komarek Buys Pianos Rejected by China Over Taiwan Row," *Prague Business Journal*, September 9, 2020, https://praguebusinessjournal.com/komarek-buys-pianos-rejected-by-china-over-taiwan-row/.

44. Jessie Yeung, "Prague's Tryst with Taipei Sees Shanghai Spurned in Sister City Love Triangle," CNN, January 15, 2020, www.cnn.com/2020/01/15/asia/prague-taiwan-china-intl-hnk-scli/index.html.

45. DW, "Czech Republic Delegation in Taiwan Draws Ire of China," August 31, 2020, https://www.dw.com/en/czech-china-taiwan/a-54764477.

46. DW, "'I Am Taiwanese': Top Czech Official Angers China in Taipei," September 1, 2020, https://www.dw.com/en/i-am-taiwanese-czech-official-angers-china-after-taipei-speech/a-54781326.

47. DW, "'I Am Taiwanese.'"

48. Yeping Yin, "Piano Firms Expect Hit After Czech Senate Speaker's Taiwan Visit," *Global Times*, September 7, 2020, www.globaltimes.cn/content/1200167.shtml.

49. Jake Chung, "Czech Magnate Buys Piano Order Canceled by PRC," *Taipei Times*, September 10, 2020, https://www.taipeitimes.com/News/front/archives/2020/09/10/2003743138/.

50. Atlas, "Komarek Buys Pianos Rejected by China Over Taiwan Row."

51. White House, "Fact Sheet: Quad Leaders' Summit," September 24, 2021, https://bidenwhitehouse.archives.gov/briefing-room/statements-releases/2021/09/24/fact-sheet-quad-leaders-summit/; White House, "Quad Joint Leaders' Statement," May 24, 2022, https://bidenwhitehouse.archives.gov/briefing-room/statements-releases/2022/05/24/quad-joint-leaders-statement/.

52. Shreya Upadhyay, "Covid-19 and Quad's 'Soft' Reorientation," *Research in Globalization* 3 (2021): 100069; N. D. Vivek, "The Quad: Can This Democratic Coalition Bolster Global Health Security?" *Diplomat*, March 2, 2024, https://thediplomat.com/2024/03/the-quad-can-this-democratic-coalition-bolster-global-health-security/.

53. White House, "Fact Sheet: Quad Leaders' Summit."

54. White House, "Fact Sheet: Quad Leaders' Summit."

55. The fourteen countries are Australia, Brunei Darussalam, Fiji, India, Indonesia, Japan, the Republic of Korea, Malaysia, New Zealand, the Philippines, Singapore, Thailand, the United States, and Vietnam. See White House, "Fact Sheet: In Asia, President Biden and a Dozen Indo-Pacific Partners Launch the Indo-Pacific Economic Framework for Prosperity" May 23, 2022, https://bidenwhitehouse.archives.gov/briefing-room/statements-releases/2022/05/23/fact-sheet-in-asia-president-biden-and-a-dozen-indo-pacific-partners-launch-the-indo-pacific-economic-framework-for-prosperity/.

56. U.S. Department of Commerce, "U.S. Department of Commerce Publishes Text of Landmark Indo-Pacific Economic Framework for Prosperity (IPEF) Supply Chain Agreement," September 7, 2023, https://www.commerce.gov/news/press-releases/2023/09/us-department-commerce-publishes-text-landmark-indo-pacific-economic.

57. U.S. Department of Commerce, "U.S. and IPEF Partners Establish Supply Chain Bodies and Convene First Virtual Meetings Under Landmark Supply Chain Agreement," July 30, 2024, www.commerce.gov/news/press-releases/2024/07/us-and-ipef-partners-establish-supply-chain-bodies-and-convene-first.

58. U.S. Department of Commerce, "U.S. Identifies Critical Sectors and Key Goods for Potential Cooperation Under the IPEF Supply Chain Agreement," August 23, 2024, www.commerce.gov/news/press-releases/2024/08/us-identifies-critical-sectors-and-key-goods-potential-cooperation.

59. David Lawder, "U.S.-Led Indo-Pacific Talks Produce Deal on Supply Chain Early Warnings," Reuters, May 27, 2023, https://www.reuters.com/markets/asia/us-led-indo-pacific-talks-produce-deal-supply-chain-early-warnings-2023-05-27/.

60. The initial member countries of this coalition are the United States, Australia, Canada, Finland, France, Germany, Japan, the Republic of Korea, Sweden, the United Kingdom, and the European Commission.

61. U.S. Department of State, "Minerals Security Partnership," June 14, 2022, www.state.gov/minerals-security-partnership/. See chapter 6 for more details on the MSP.

62. Youkyung Lee and Debby Wu, "US, Asian Partners Discussed Supply Chains in 'Chip 4' Talks," Bloomberg, February 26, 2023, https://www.bloomberg.com/news/articles/2023-02-26/us-asian-partners-discussed-chip-supply-chain-reports-say?leadSource=uverify%20wall.

63. Emily Benson, Japhet Quitzon, and William A. Reinsch, "Securing Semiconductor Supply Chains in the Indo-Pacific Economic Framework for Prosperity," Center for Strategic and International Studies, May 30, 2023, https://www.csis.org/analysis/securing-semiconductor-supply-chains-indo-pacific-economic-framework-prosperity.

64. Sarah Wu, "First US-Led 'Chip 4' Meeting Held, Featuring Taiwan," *Taipei Times*, October 1, 2022, www.taipeitimes.com/News/front/archives/2022/10/01/2003786225; Ben Blanchard, "Taiwan Says 'Fab 4' Chip Group Held First Senior Officials Meeting," Reuters, February 25, 2023, https://www.reuters.com/technology/taiwan-says-fab-4-chip-group-held-first-senior-officials-meeting-2023-02-25/.

65. Taipei Times, " 'Fab 4' Discuss Supply Chain Early Warning System," February 27, 2023, www.taipeitimes.com/News/front/archives/2023/02/27/2003795105.

66. Christian Davies, Jung-a Song, Kana Inagaki, and Richard Waters, "US Struggles to Mobilise Its East Asian 'Chip 4' Alliance," *Financial Times*, September 12, 2022, https://www.ft.com/content/98f22615-ee7e-4431-ab98-fb6e3f9de032.

67. Musha Research, "Japanese Stocks Outstandingly High, U.S.-China Confrontation and Super Weak Yen Turned the Tide." June 5, 2023. https://www.musha.co.jp/short_comment/detail/333?lang=en; Mireya Solís and Mathieu Duchâtel, "The Renaissance of the Japanese Semiconductor Industry," Brookings Institution, June 3, 2024, https://www.brookings.edu/articles/the-renaissance-of-the-japanese-semiconductor-industry/.

68. Jaemin Lee, "The U.S. and Its Allies Want to Bring the Entire Chip Supply Chain In-House—and That Could Create an OPEC-Style Cartel for the Digital Age," *Fortune*, March 28, 2024, https://fortune.com/asia/2024/03/28/chip-4-alliance-us-korea-japan-taiwan-semiconductors-china-opec-cartel-for-digital-age/.

69. Lee, "The U.S. and Its Allies Want to Bring the Entire Chip Supply Chain In-House."

70. Bureau of Industry and Security, "Commerce Implements New Export Controls on Advanced Computing and Semiconductor Manufacturing Items to the People's Republic of China (PRC)," October 7, 2022, https://www.bis.doc.gov/index.php/documents/about-bis/newsroom/press-releases/3158-2022-10-07-bis-press-release-advanced-computing-and-semiconductor-manufacturing-controls-final/file.

71. Bureau of Industry and Security, "Commerce Implements New Export Controls."

72. Jaewon Kim and Ting-Fang Cheng, "Samsung and SK Hynix Face China Dilemma from U.S. Export Controls," *Nikkei Asia*, October 25, 2022, https://asia.nikkei.com/Business/Tech/Semiconductors/Samsung-and-SK-Hynix-face-China-dilemma-from-U.S.-export-controls.

73. Gregory Allen, Emily Benson, and Margot Putnam, "Japan and the Netherlands Announce Plans for New Export Controls on Semiconductor Equipment," Center for Strategic and International Studies, April 10, 2023, https://www.csis.org/analysis/japan-and-netherlands-announce-plans-new-export-controls-semiconductor-equipment.

74. Ana Swanson, "Netherlands and Japan Said to Join U.S. in Curbing Chip Technology Sent to China," *New York Times*, January 30, 2023, www.nytimes.com/2023/01/28/business/economy/netherlands-japan-china-chips.html.

75. Annabelle Liang, "US-China Chip War: Japan Plans to Restrict Some Equipment Exports," BBC, March 31, 2023, https://www.bbc.com/news/business-65134017.

76. Tim Kelly and Miho Uranaka, "Japan Restricts Chipmaking Equipment Exports as It Aligns with US China Curbs," Reuters, March 31, 2023, https://www.reuters.com/technology/japan-restrict-chipmaking-equipment-exports-aligning-it-with-us-china-curbs-2023-03-31/.

77. Liang, "US-China Chip War."

78. Ting-fang Cheng and Lauly Li, "Netherlands' Chip Tool Export Controls Take Effect: 4 Things to Know," *Nikkei Asia*, August 31, 2023, https://asia.nikkei.com/Business/Tech/Semiconductors/Netherlands-chip-tool-export-controls-take-effect-4-things-to-know.

79. Cheng and Li, "Netherlands' Chip Tool Export Controls Take Effect."

80. Joyce Lee, "South Korean Firms Get Indefinite Waiver on U.S. Chip Gear Supplies to China," Reuters, October 9, 2023, https://www.reuters.com/technology/samsung-sk-hynix-wont-need -approvals-supply-us-chip-gear-china-yonhap-2023-10-09/.

81. White House, "President Biden Signs Executive Order on Addressing United States Investments in Certain National Security Technologies and Products in Countries of Concern," August 9, 2023, https://bidenwhitehouse.archives.gov/briefing-room/statements-releases/2023/08/09/president -biden-signs-executive-order-on-addressing-united-states-investments-in-certain-national -security-technologies-and-products-in-countries-of-concern/.

82. Cathleen Cimino-Issacs and Karen M. Sutter, "Regulation of U.S. Outbound Investment to China," Congressional Research Service, August 12, 2024, https://crsreports.congress.gov/product /pdf/IF/IF12629.

83. White House, "Fact Sheet: President Biden Issues Executive Order Addressing United States Investments in Certain National Security Technologies and Products in Countries of Concern; Treasury Department Issues Advance Notice of Proposed Rulemaking to Enhance Transparency and Clarity and Solicit Comments on Scope of New Program," August 9, 2023, https://home .treasury.gov/system/files/206/Outbound-Fact-Sheet.pdf.

84. White House, "President Biden Signs Executive Order on Addressing United States Investments."

85. White House, "America First Investment Policy," February 21, 2025, https://www.whitehouse.gov /presidential-actions/2025/02/america-first-investment-policy/.

86. European Commission, "Commission Proposes New Initiatives to Strengthen Economic Security," January 24, 2024, https://ec.europa.eu/commission/presscorner/detail/en/IP_24_363.

87. European Commission, "Commission Calls on Member States to Review Outbound Investments and Assess Risks to Economic Security," January 14, 2025, https://ec.europa.eu/commission /presscorner/detail/en/ip_25_261.

88. European Commission, "Commission Proposes New Initiatives to Strengthen Economic Security"; Horst Henschen, Ross Evans, Martin Juhasz, and Michelle Adam, "Outbound Investment Screening in the EU—A Major Step Forward?" Covington, February 14, 2024, https://www .covcompetition.com/2024/02/outbound-investment-screening-in-the-eu-a-major-step -forward/.

89. Allen, *Beijing Rules*, 38.

90. Allen, *Beijing Rules*, 38–39.

91. Former Trump administration White House official, personal interview, March 4, 2024.

92. White House, "Remarks by President Trump at APEC CEO Summit | Da Nang, Vietnam," November 10, 2017, https://trumpwhitehouse.archives.gov/briefings-statements/remarks-president -trump-apec-ceo-summit-da-nang-vietnam/.

93. White House, "Fact Sheet: President Biden Takes Action to Protect American Workers and Businesses from China's Unfair Trade Practices," May 14, 2024, https://bidenwhitehouse.archives.gov /briefing-room/statements-releases/2024/05/14/fact-sheet-president-biden-takes-action-to -protect-american-workers-and-businesses-from-chinas-unfair-trade-practices/.

94. White House, "Fact Sheet: President Donald J. Trump Imposes Tariffs on Imports from Canada, Mexico and China," February 1, 2025, https://www.whitehouse.gov/fact-sheets/2025/02/fact-sheet -president-donald-j-trump-imposes-tariffs-on-imports-from-canada-mexico-and-china/.

95. Glenn H. Snyder, *Deterrence and Defense: Toward a Theory of National Security* (Princeton, NJ: Princeton University Press, 1961); Robert J. Art, "To What Ends Military Power?" *International Security* 4, no. 4 (1980): 3–35.

96. Snyder, *Deterrence and Defense*; Alexander L. George and Richard Smoke, *Deterrence in American Foreign Policy: Theory and Practice* (New York: Columbia University Press, 1974); John L. Gaddis, *The Long Peace: Inquiries Into the History of the Cold War* (New York: Oxford University

Press, 1987); John L. Gaddis, *Strategies of Containment: A Critical Appraisal of Postwar American National Security Policy During the Cold War* (New York: Oxford University Press, 2023).

97. Art, "To What Ends Military Power?"

98. Byung-yeul Baek, "Gov't Criticized for Failing to Lower Dependence on China for Urea," *Korea Times*, December 5, 2023, https://www.koreatimes.co.kr/www/tech/2024/07/129_364527.html.

99. The term *collective resilience* first appeared in Eric Sayers and Brad Glosserman, "'Collective Resilience' Is the Way to Address the China Challenge," *Japan Times*, August 14, 2020, www.japantimes.co.jp/opinion/2020/08/14/commentary/world-commentary/collective-resilience-way-address-china-challenge/. Their formulation of a strategy differs from the one offered in this book, both empirically and theoretically. Bonnie Glaser has argued for a countersanction strategy by victims of Chinese coercion, but largely as a symbolic measure and embedded in a broader strategy of challenging Chinese actions in the WTO, among other steps. See Bonnie S. Glaser, "Time for Collective Pushback Against China's Economic Coercion," Center for Strategic and International Studies, January 13, 2021, https://www.csis.org/analysis/time-collective-pushback-against-chinas-economic-coercion. For later versions of the argument, see Aaron Friedberg, "Stopping the Next China Shock: A Collective Strategy for Countering Beijing's Mercantilism," *Foreign Affairs* 103, no. 5 (2024): 177–189.

100. White House, "Remarks by Vice President Al Gore," January 11, 1994, https://clintonwhitehouse6.archives.gov/1994/01/1994-01-11-remarks-by-vice-president-al-gore.html; Thomas Friedman, *The World Is Flat: A Brief History of the TwentyFirst Century* (New York: Farrar, Straus and Giroux, 2005).

101. Anne-Marie Slaughter, "America's Edge: Power in the Networked Century," *Foreign Affairs* 88, no. 1 (2009): 94–113; Henry Farrell and Abraham Newman, "Weaponized Interdependence: How Global Economic Networks Shape State Coercion," *International Security* 44, no. 1 (2019): 42–79; Daniel W. Drezner, Henry Farrell, and Abraham Newman, eds., *The Uses and Abuses of Weaponized Interdependence* (Washington, DC: Brookings Institution Press, 2021); Henry Farrell and Abraham Newman, *Underground Empire: How America Weaponized the World Economy* (New York: Holt, 2023).

102. See UN Comtrade Database, https://comtradeplus.un.org/.

103. Robert O. Keohane and Joseph S. Nye, *Power and Interdependence* (Cambridge, MA: Harvard University Press, 1972).

104. Glaser, "Time for Collective Pushback."

105. Daniel W. Drezner, "The Uses and Abuses of Weaponized Interdependence in 2021," *Washington Post*, March 2, 2021, https://www.washingtonpost.com/outlook/2021/03/02/uses-abuses-weaponized-interdependence-2021/.

106. Trade with these four countries totaled $1,537,754,756,074, which constituted 24.95 percent of China's global trade in 2024.

107. This list excludes Taiwan, as well as countries in which specific firms, but not the government, have been targeted by China. In that case, the number would balloon to forty-one countries. (Private-sector cases were dealt with separately in chapter 3.)

108. Jessica L. Weeks, "Autocratic Audience Costs: Regime Type and Signaling Resolve," *International Organization* 62, no. 1 (2008): 35–64; Jonathan N. Brown and Anthony S. Marcum, "Avoiding Audience Costs: Domestic Political Accountability and Concessions in Crisis Diplomacy," *Security Studies* 20, no. 2 (2011): 141–170.

109. Dursun Peksen and Timothy M. Peterson, "Sanctions and Alternate Markets: How Trade and Alliances Affect the Onset of Economic Coercion," *Political Research Quarterly* 69, no. 1 (2016): 4–16.

110. Spodumene is classified as part of "other mineral substances" (HS 253090).

111. China exports about 1 percent of its spodumene; it exports none of its nickel ores and concentrates.

112. Niccolo Conte, "Ranked: The World's Biggest Steel Producers, by Country," Visual Capitalist, May 19, 2023, https://www.visualcapitalist.com/biggest-steel-producers-country/.

113. According to UN Comtrade data, China imported about 731 million tons of iron ore from Australia in 2023, dwarfing the 245 million tons it imported from Brazil. For more on China's demand for iron ore, see Brian Peach and Su-Lin Tan, "Explainer | How Iron Ore Is Powering China's Infrastructure Boom, and Why Securing New Sources Is So Vitally Important," *South China Morning Post*, February 14, 2021, www.scmp.com/economy/china-economy/article/3120761/how-iron-ore-powering-chinas-infrastructure-boom-and-why.

114. Ben Westcott, "Iron Ore Is Saving Australia's Trade with China. How Long Can It Last?" CNN, May 6, 2021, www.cnn.com/2021/05/05/economy/australia-china-iron-ore-trade-intl-hnk/index.html.

115. Bovine semen is used for artificial insemination of Chinese cattle.

116. Rob Atkinson, "How Innovative Is China in the Robotics Industry?," Information Technology & Innovation Foundation, March 11, 2024, https://itif.org/publications/2024/03/11/how-innovative-is-china-in-the-robotics-industry/.

5. RESILIENCE AND THE GROUP OF SEVEN (G7)

1. Robert O. Keohane, *After Hegemony: Cooperation and Discord in the World Political Economy* (Princeton, NJ: Princeton University Press, 1984); Robert Axelrod and Robert O. Keohane, "Achieving Cooperation Under Anarchy: Strategies and Institutions," *World Politics* 38, no. 1 (1985): 226–254; Kenneth A. Oye, *Cooperation Under Anarchy* (Princeton, NJ: Princeton University Press, 1986); Edward D. Mansfield, Helen V. Milner, and B. Peter Rosendorff, "Why Democracies Cooperate More: Electoral Control and International Trade Agreements," *International Organization* 56, no. 3 (2002): 477–513.

2. Robert Axelrod and William D. Hamilton, "The Evolution of Cooperation," *Science* 211, no. 4489 (1981): 1390–1396; Robert O. Keohane, "Reciprocity in International Relations," *International Organization* 40, no. 1 (Winter 1986): 1–27.

3. G. John Ikenberry, "The G-7 Becomes a Power Player," *Foreign Policy*, August 31, 2023.

4. G. John Ikenberry, *A World Safe for Democracy: Liberal Internationalism and the Crises of Global Order* (New Haven, CT: Yale University Press, 2020).

5. Derek Scissors, "Deterring Chinese Economic Coercion," American Enterprise Institute, May 10, 2023, https://www.aei.org/wp-content/uploads/2023/05/Derek-Scissors_Written-Testimony.pdf?x85095.

6. Andrius Sytas and John O'Donnell, "German Big Business Piles Pressure on Lithuania in China Row," Reuters, January 21, 2022, https://www.reuters.com/world/europe/german-big-business-piles-pressure-lithuania-china-row-2022-01-21/; Bethany Allen, *Beijing Rules: How China Weaponized Its Economy to Confront the World* (New York: Harper, 2023), 228.

7. Allen, *Beijing Rules*, 225–226.

8. Bjørnar Sverdrup-Thygeson, "The Flexible Cost of Insulting China: Trade Politics and the 'Dalai Lama Effect.'" *Asian Perspective* 39, no. 1 (2015): 101–123.

9. Aya Adachi, Alexander Brown, and Max J. Zenglein, "Fasten Your Seatbelts: How to Manage China's Economic Coercion," Mercator Institute for China Studies, August 25, 2022, https://merics.org/en/report/fasten-your-seatbelts-how-manage-chinas-economic-coercion.

10. Darren J. Lim and Victor A. Ferguson, "Informal Economic Sanctions: The Political Economy of Chinese Coercion During the THAAD Dispute," *Review of International Political Economy* 29, no. 5 (2022): 1533.

11. Scissors, "Deterring Chinese Economic Coercion."

12. Scissors, "Deterring Chinese Economic Coercion."

13. Ben Murphy, "Chokepoints: China's Self-Identified Strategic Technology Import Dependencies," Center for Security and Emerging Technology, May 2022, https://cset.georgetown.edu/publication /chokepoints/, 11–14.

14. China's self-reported exports, using the UN Comtrade database, is the most immediately accurate and measurable way to assess domestic production. There are other measures, using a variety of other sources, but this is the most consistent and accurate across the array of items being measured for this study.

15. G7 Italia, "About the G7," n.d., https://www.g7italy.it/en/about-g7/.

16. European Council, "2021 G7 Leaders' Communiqué: Our Shared Agenda for Global Action to Build Back Better," June 13, 2021, www.consilium.europa.eu/en/press/press-releases/2021/06/13 /2021-g7-leaders-communique/; Prime Minister of Canada, "G7 Leaders' Communiqué," June 28, 2022, www.pm.gc.ca/en/news/statements/2022/06/28/g7-leaders-communique; Ministry of Foreign Affairs of Japan, "G7 Hiroshima Leaders' Communiqué," May 20, 2023, https://www.mofa .go.jp/policy/economy/summit/hiroshima23/documents/pdf/Leaders_Communique_01_en .pdf?v20231006; G7 Italia, "Apulia G7 Leaders' Communiqué," June 14, 2024, www.g7italy.it/wp -content/uploads/Apulia-G7-Leaders-Communique.pdf; "G7 Hiroshima Leaders' Communiqué," May 20, 2023, https://www.mofa.go.jp/policy/economy/summit/hiroshima23/documents/pdf /Leaders_Communique_01_en.pdf?v20231006.

17. Ikenberry, "The G-7 Becomes a Power Player"; Andrea Kendall-Taylor and Richard Fontaine, "The Axis of Upheaval: How America's Adversaries Are Uniting to Overturn the Global Order," *Foreign Affairs*, April 23, 2024, www.foreignaffairs.com/china/axis-upheaval-russia-iran-north-korea -taylor-fontaine.

18. The nine issues are Indo-Pacific security; economic resilience and security; food security; digital competitiveness; climate change; Ukraine; global economy, finance, and sustainable development; disarmament and nonproliferation; and labor. For the CSIS report, see John J. Hamre, Victor Cha, Emily Benson, Max Bergmann, Erin L. Murphy, and Caitlin Welsh, " 'Bending' the Architecture: Reimagining the G7," Center for Strategic and International Studies, June 12, 2024, https://www .csis.org/analysis/bending-architecture-reimagining-g7, 4.

19. In 2024, the BRICS expanded to BRICS+, which includes Egypt, Ethiopia, Iran, Saudi Arabia, and the United Arab Emirates, with plans to add additional members, including Malaysia and Thailand. See European Parliament, "Expansion of BRICS: A Quest for Greater Global Influence?," March 15, 2024, www.europarl.europa.eu/thinktank/en/document/EPRS_BRI(2024) 760368; Alexander Gabuev and Oliver Stuenkel, "The Battle for the BRICS," *Foreign Affairs*, September 24, 2024, https://www.foreignaffairs.com/russia/battle-brics; Steward Patrick, "BRICS Expansion, the G20, and the Future of World Order," Carnegie Endowment for International Peace, October 9, 2024, https://carnegieendowment.org/research/2024/10/brics-summit -emerging-middle-powers-g7-g20?lang=en.

20. Ikenberry, "The G-7 Becomes a Power Player"; Hamre et al., " 'Bending' the Architecture."

21. White House, "G7 Leaders' Statement on Economic Resilience and Economic Security," May 20, 2023, https://bidenwhitehouse.archives.gov/briefing-room/statements-releases/2023/05/20/g7 -leaders-statement-on-economic-resilience-and-economic-security/.

22. Minister for Trade and Tourism, "Australia Joins Global Minerals Security Partnership," July 12, 2022, www.trademinister.gov.au/minister/don-farrell/media-release/australia-joins-global -minerals-security-partnership.

23. Richard McGregor, "Chinese Coercion, Australian Resilience," Lowy Institute, October 20, 2022, www.lowyinstitute.org/publications/chinese-coercion-australian-resilience#heading-6816.

24. Australian Government—Defence, "Australia-Republic of Korea 2+2 Joint Statement," May 1, 2024, www.minister.defence.gov.au/statements/2024-05-01/australia-republic-korea-22-joint -statement.

25. The group of eighteen governments directly coerced by China registered six less items (589) valued at $43.06 billion (70 percent China dependency) than the G7 + IP-2 group's 595 items valued at $37.05 billion.

26. White House, "G7 Leaders' Statement on Economic Resilience and Economic Security."

6. COLLECTIVE RESILIENCE IN CRITICAL MINERALS

1. Federal Register, "A Federal Strategy to Ensure Secure and Reliable Supplies of Critical Minerals," *Federal Register* 82, no. 246 (2017): 60835–60837, www.federalregister.gov/documents/2017/12/26/2017-27899/a-federal-strategy-to-ensure-secure-and-reliable-supplies-of-critical-minerals.

2. The critical minerals list is required by law to be updated at least every three years, under Section 7002 ("Mineral Security"), Title VII ("Critical Minerals") of the Energy Act of 2020 (Public Law 116–260, December 27, 2020, 116th Congress). For the 2018 critical minerals list, see Department of the Interior, "Final List of Critical Minerals 2018," *Federal Register* 83, no. 97 (2018): 23295–23296, https://www.federalregister.gov/documents/2018/05/18/2018-10667/final-list-of-critical-minerals-2018.

3. United States Geological Survey, "U.S. Geological Survey Releases 2022 List of Critical Minerals," February 22, 2022, www.usgs.gov/news/national-news-release/us-geological-survey-releases-2022-list-critical-minerals.

4. The rare earth element (REE) group typically comprise seventeen elements: lanthanum (La), cerium (Ce), praseodymium (Pr), neodymium (Nd), promethium (Pm), samarium (Sm), europium (Eu), gadolinium (Gd), terbium (Tb), dysprosium (Dy), holmium (Ho), erbium (Er), thulium (Tm), ytterbium (Yb), and lutetium (Lu); some countries also include yttrium (Y) and scandium (Sc). Some countries include certain REEs in their lists of critical minerals. South Korea lists five REEs; the EU lists ten HREEs (heavy rare earth elements) and five LREEs (light rare earth elements). See U.S. Geological Survey, *The Rare-Earth Elements—Vital to Modern Technologies and Lifestyles* (Reston, VA: U.S. Geological Survey, 2014), doi:10.3133/fs20143078; Milan Grohol and Constanze Veeh, *Study on the Critical Raw Materials for the EU 2023* (European Union, 2023), https://data.europa.eu/doi/10.2873/725585. Platinum group metals (PGMs) include ruthenium (Ru), rhodium (Rh), palladium (Pd), osmium (Os), iridium (Ir), and platinum (Pt). South Korea and the EU do not include all six PGMs in their lists of critical minerals/materials. South Korea lists two (Pt and Pd), while the EU lists five (all six metals except Os). For Japan's critical minerals list, see the first footnote in Ministry of Economy, Trade and Industry [Japan], *Jūyō kōbutsu ni kakaru antei kyōkyū kakuho o hakaru tame no torikumi hōshin* 重要鉱物に係る安定供給確保を図るための取組方針 [Measures to secure a stable supply of critical minerals], 2023, https://www.meti.go.jp/policy/economy/economic_security/metal/torikumihoshin.pdf; Jane Nakano, *The Geopolitics of Critical Minerals Supply Chains* (Washington, DC: Center for Strategic and International Studies, 2021), 20, https://www.csis.org/analysis/geopolitics-critical-minerals-supply-chains.

5. Ministry of Trade, Industry and Energy [South Korea], *Cheomdansan-eob geullobeol gang-gug doyag-eul wihan haegsimgwangmul hwagbojeonlyag* 첨단산업 글로벌 강국 도약을 위한 핵심광물 확보전략 [Strategy for securing critical minerals to become a global leader in advanced industries], 2023, https://www.motie.go.kr/kor/article/ATCL3f49a5a8c/166862/view.

6. Department of Industry, Science and Resources, "Australia's Critical Minerals List and Strategic Materials List," February 20, 2024, https://www.industry.gov.au/publications/australias-critical-minerals-list-and-strategic-materials-list.

7. European Commission, "RMIS—Raw Materials Information System," https://rmis.jrc.ec.europa.eu/eu-critical-raw-materials.

8. For more analysis on the implications of these export controls, see Christopher Cytera, "Gallium, Germanium, and China—The Minerals Inflaming the Global Chip War," Center for European Policy Analysis, August 8, 2023, https://cepa.org/article/china-gallium-and-germanium-the-minerals-inflaming-the-global-chip-war/; John Seaman, "China's Weaponization of Gallium and Germanium: The Pitfalls of Leveraging Chokepoints," French Institute of International Relations, 2023, https://www.ifri.org/en/memos/chinas-weaponization-gallium-and-germanium-pitfalls-leveraging-chokepoints; and Zeyi Yang, "China Just Fought Back in the Semiconductor Exports War. Here's What You Need to Know," *MIT Technology Review*, July 10, 2023, www.technologyreview.com/2023/07/10/1076025/china-export-control-semiconductor-material/.

9. Cytera, "Gallium, Germanium, and China."

10. Cytera, "Gallium, Germanium, and China."

11. Cytera, "Gallium, Germanium, and China."

12. United States Geological Survey, "U.S. Geological Survey Releases 2022 List of Critical Minerals"; Siyi Liu and Dominique Patton, "China, World's Top Graphite Producer, Tightens Exports of Key Battery Material," Reuters, October 20, 2023, www.reuters.com/world/china/china-require-export-permits-some-graphite-products-dec-1-2023-10-20/.

13. Shunsuke Tabeta, "China Bans Exports of Rare-Earth Magnet Technologies," *Nikkei Asia*, December 21, 2023, https://asia.nikkei.com/Economy/Trade/China-bans-exports-of-rare-earth-magnet-technologies.

14. Ryan Woo, "China Issues Rare Earth Regulations to Further Protect Domestic Supply," Reuters, June 29, 2024, https://www.reuters.com/markets/commodities/china-issues-rare-earth-regulations-further-protect-domestic-supply-2024-06-29/.

15. Reuters, "China to Limit Antimony Exports in Latest Critical Mineral Curbs," August 15, 2024, https://www.reuters.com/world/china/china-limit-antimony-exports-latest-critical-mineral-curbs-2024-08-15/.

16. Juliana Liu, "China Proposes Fresh Export Curbs on EV Technology," CNN, January 3, 2025, https://www.cnn.com/2025/01/03/tech/china-ev-tech-export-controls-intl-hnk/index.html; Reuters, "China Expands Key Mineral Export Controls After US Imposes Tariffs," February 4, 2025, https://www.reuters.com/world/china/china-expands-critical-mineral-export-controls-after-us-imposes-tariffs-2025-02-04/.

17. Exiger, "China Announces Export Controls on Five Critical Minerals," February 12, 2025, https://www.exiger.com/perspectives/critical-minerals-export-controls/#:~:text=China's%20new%20export%20controls%20require,90%25%20of%20the%20world's%20mining.

18. Ministry of Commerce, People's Republic of China, "MOFCOM Regular Press Conference," July 6, 2023, https://english.mofcom.gov.cn/News/PressConference/art/2023/art_36fb2d80e4b445389bb8fc83e2b3c4e.html; Ministry of Commerce, People's Republic of China, "MOFCOM Regular Press Conference," October 26, 2023, https://english.mofcom.gov.cn/News/PressConference/art/2023/art_6fc7603ef80f4c819b79dba5baac76f6.html.

19. Gracelin Baskaran and Meredith Schwartz, "The Consequences of China's New Rare Earths Export Restrictions," Center for Strategic and International Studies, April 14, 2025, https://www.csis.org/analysis/consequences-chinas-new-rare-earths-export-restrictions

20. Keith Bradsher, "China Halts Critical Exports as Trade War Intensifies," *New York Times*, April 13, 2025, https://www.nytimes.com/2025/04/13/business/china-rare-earths-exports.html.

21. Keith Bradsher, "Amid Tension, China Blocks Vital Exports to Japan," *New York Times*, September 22, 2010, www.nytimes.com/2010/09/23/business/global/23rare.html; Keith Bradsher, "China Restarts Rare Earth Shipments to Japan," *New York Times*, November 19, 2010, www.nytimes.com/2010/11/20/business/global/20rare.html.

22. Keith Bradsher, "China's Supply of Minerals for iPhones and Missiles Could Be a Risky Trade Weapon," *New York Times*, May 23, 2019, www.nytimes.com/2019/05/23/business/china-us-trade

-war-rare-earths.html; Keith Johnson and Elias Groll, "China Raises Threat of Rare-Earths Cut-off to U.S.," *Foreign Policy*, May 21, 2019, https://foreignpolicy.com/2019/05/21/china-raises-threat-of-rare-earth-mineral-cutoff-to-us/.

23.   Bradsher, "China's Supply of Minerals for iPhones."

24.   Przemyslaw Kowalski and Clarisse Legendre, "Raw Materials Critical for the Green Transition: Production, International Trade and Export Restrictions," *OECD Trade Policy Papers*, no. 269 (2023): 41–43. Also see Harry Dempsey, "China Leads Rise in Export Restrictions on Critical Minerals, OECD Says," *Financial Times*, April 11, 2023, https://www.ft.com/content/198b6824-21d6-4633-9a97-00164d23c13f.

25.   International Energy Agency, "Prohibition of the Export of Nickel Ore," December 12, 2023, https://www.iea.org/policies/16084-prohibition-of-the-export-of-nickel-ore.

26.   Norman Goh, "Malaysia to Allow Exports of Processed Rare Earths: Minister," *Nikkei Asia*, October 24, 2023, https://asia.nikkei.com/Economy/Trade/Malaysia-to-allow-exports-of-processed-rare-earths-minister.

27.   Minderjeet Kaur and Ili Shazwani, "Malaysia's Govt Counters Potential Chinese Pressure with Proposed Ban on Rare-Earth Exports," *Benar News*, September 11, 2023, https://www.benarnews.org/english/news/malaysian/malaysia-rare-earth-ban-china-09112023142437.html.

28.   OECD, "OECD Inventory of Export Restrictions on Industrial Raw Materials 2024," September 16, 2024, https://www.oecd.org/en/publications/oecd-inventory-of-export-restrictions-on-industrial-raw-materials-2024_5e46bb20-en/full-report.html.

29.   Reed Blakemore, "What to Make of China's Latest Restrictions on Critical Mineral Exports," Atlantic Council, October 26, 2023, www.atlanticcouncil.org/blogs/new-atlanticist/what-to-make-of-chinas-latest-restrictions-on-critical-mineral-exports/; Sarah Godek, "Why China's Export Controls on Germanium and Gallium May Not Be Effective," Stimson Center, July 19, 2023, https://www.stimson.org/2023/why-chinas-export-controls-on-germanium-and-gallium-may-not-be-effective/; Arjun Kharpal, "What Are Gallium and Germanium? China Curbs Exports of Metals Critical to Chips and Other Tech," CNBC, July 4, 2023, https://www.cnbc.com/2023/07/04/what-are-gallium-and-germanium-china-curbs-exports-of-metals-for-tech.html.

30.   Idrees Ali, Phil Stewart, and Valerie Insinna, "Pentagon Has Strategic Germanium Stockpile but No Gallium Reserves," Reuters, July 6, 2023, https://www.reuters.com/markets/commodities/pentagon-has-strategic-germanium-stockpile-no-gallium-reserves-2023-07-06/.

31.   Ross L. Manley, Elisa Alonso, and Nedal T. Nassar, "A Model to Assess Industry Vulnerability to Disruptions in Mineral Commodity Supplies," *Resources Policy* 78 (2022): 5, https://doi.org/10.1016/j.resourpol.2022.102889; also cited in Matthew P. Funaiole, Brian Hart, and Aidan Powers-Riggs, "Mineral Monopoly: China's Control Over Gallium Is a National Security Threat," Center for Strategic and International Studies, July 18, 2023, https://features.csis.org/hiddenreach/china-critical-mineral-gallium/.

32.   Hannah Miao and Rebecca Feng, "China Flexes Chokehold on Rare-Earth Magnets as Exports Plunged in May," *Wall Street Journal*, June 19, 2025, https://www.wsj.com/world/china/china-flexes-chokehold-on-rare-earth-magnets-as-exports-plunge-in-may-c1adac50.

33.   White House, "Fact Sheet: President Donald J. Trump Secures a Historic Trade Win for the United States," May 12, 2025, https://www.whitehouse.gov/fact-sheets/2025/05/fact-sheet-president-donald-j-trump-secures-a-historic-trade-win-for-the-united-states/.

34.   Nectar Gan, "China Isn't Getting Rid of Its Controls Over Rare Earths, Despite Trade Truce with US," CNN, May 20, 2025, https://www.cnn.com/2025/05/20/business/china-rare-earth-export-controls-analysis-intl-hnk.

35.   Kylie Atwood, Kevin Liptak, and Phil Mattingly, "Trump Administration Took Action Against China due to Frustration on Trade Talks, Officials Say," CNN, May 30, 2025, https://www.cnn.com/2025/05/29/politics/us-china-trade-talk-frustration.

36. Bonnie Glaser and Abigail Wulf, "China's Role in Critical Mineral Supply Chains," German Marshall Fund, August 2, 2023, https://www.gmfus.org/news/chinas-role-critical-mineral-supply-chains#:~:text=China%20dominates%20global%20critical%20mineral,and%2085%25%20of%20processing%20capacity.

37. U.S. Geological Survey, *Mineral Commodity Summaries 2025*, 2025, https://pubs.usgs.gov/periodicals/mcs2024/mcs2024.pdf, 145.

38. U.S. Geological Survey, *Mineral Commodity Summaries 2025*, 145.

39. Glaser and Wulf, "China's Role in Critical Mineral Supply Chains."

40. International Energy Agency, "Geographical Distribution of Refined Material Production for Key Energy Transition Minerals in the Base Case, 2023–2040," May 2, 2024, https://www.iea.org/data-and-statistics/charts/geographical-distribution-of-refined-material-production-for-key-energy-transition-minerals-in-the-base-case-2023-2040-2.

41. See table 5 in U.S. Geological Survey, *Mineral Commodity Summaries 2025*, 23.

42. International Energy Agency, *Global Critical Minerals Outlook 2024*, 2024, https://iea.blob.core.windows.net/assets/ee01701d-1d5c-4ba8-9df6-abeeac9de99a/GlobalCriticalMineralsOutlook2024.pdf, 41, 42.

43. White House, "Fact Sheet: Biden-Harris Administration Announces Supply Chain Disruptions Task Force to Address Short-Term Supply Chain Discontinuities," June 8, 2021, https://bidenwhitehouse.archives.gov/briefing-room/statements-releases/2021/06/08/fact-sheet-biden-harris-administration-announces-supply-chain-disruptions-task-force-to-address-short-term-supply-chain-discontinuities/; Tabeta, "China Bans Exports of Rare-Earth Magnet Technologies"; Yeon-gyu Kim, *Gananhan migug buyuhan jung-gug* 가난한 미국 부유한 중국 [Poor America rich China]. (Seoul, South Korea: 라의 눈 [Eye of Ra], 2022), 342–343, 401.

44. S&P Global Market Intelligence, "China Outbound Mining Investment," 2021, https://pages.marketintelligence.spglobal.com/rs/565-BDO-100/images/china-outbound-mining-investment-infographic-150421.pdf.

45. S&P Global Market Intelligence, "China Outbound Mining Investment."

46. S&P Global Market Intelligence, "China Outbound Mining Investment."

47. Christoph Nedopil Wang, "China Belt and Road Initiative (BRI) Investment Report 2023 H1," Green Finance and Development Center, August 1, 2023, https://greenfdc.org/china-belt-and-road-initiative-bri-investment-report-2023-h1/; Polly Bindman, "Weekly Data: China Seeks to Extend Its Critical Minerals Dominance with Overseas Investment Surge," Energy Monitor, August 21, 2023, https://www.energymonitor.ai/industry/weekly-data-china-seeks-to-extend-its-critical-minerals-dominance-with-overseas-investment-surge/.

48. Bindman, "Weekly Data."

49. Bindman, "Weekly Data." Also see Harry Dempsey and Joseph Cotterill, "How China Is Winning the Race for Africa's Lithium," *Financial Times*, April 3, 2023, https://www.ft.com/content/02d6f35d-e646-40f7-894c-ffcc6acd9b25?shareType=nongif; tables 1 and 5 in Charles Chang et al., "China's Global Reach Grows Behind Critical Minerals," S&P Global, August 2023, https://www.spglobal.com/content/dam/spglobal/corporate/en/images/general/special-editorial/083123-china-s-global-reach-grows-behind-critical-minerals.pdf.

50. Federal Register, "A Federal Strategy to Ensure."

51. Federal Register, "A Federal Strategy to Ensure."

52. Federal Register, "Addressing the Threat to the Domestic Supply Chain from Reliance on Critical Minerals from Foreign Adversaries and Supporting the Domestic Mining and Processing Industries," *Federal Register* 85, no. 193 (2020): 62539–62544, www.federalregister.gov/documents/2020/10/05/2020-22064/addressing-the-threat-to-the-domestic-supply-chain-from-reliance-on-critical-minerals-from-foreign.

53. Federal Register, "Addressing the Threat to the Domestic Supply Chain."

54. Federal Register, "America's Supply Chains," *Federal Register* 86, no. 38 (2021): 11849–11854, https://www.federalregister.gov/documents/2021/03/01/2021-04280/americas-supply-chains;   White House, "Fact Sheet: Securing a Made in America Supply Chain for Critical Minerals," February 22, 2022, https://bidenwhitehouse.archives.gov/briefing-room/statements-releases/2022/02/22/fact-sheet-securing-a-made-in-america-supply-chain-for-critical-minerals/.

55. White House, "Fact Sheet: Securing a Made in America Supply Chain."

56. For a list of critical minerals projects in 2023, see U.S. Geological Survey, *Mineral Commodity Summaries 2024*, 18–19; Congress.gov, "H.R.3684—Infrastructure Investment and Jobs Act," November 15, 2021, https://www.congress.gov/bill/117th-congress/house-bill/3684.

57. U.S. Department of Defense, "Defense Production Act Title III Presidential Determination for Critical Materials in Large-Capacity Batteries," April 5, 2022, https://www.defense.gov/News/Releases/Release/Article/2989973/defense-production-act-title-iii-presidential-determination-for-critical-materi/#:~:text=The%20United%20States%20depends%20on,used%20in%20large%2Dcapacity%20batteries.

58. Congress.gov, "H.R.5376—Inflation Reduction Act of 2022," August 16, 2022, https://www.congress.gov/bill/117th-congress/house-bill/5376/text; U.S. Department of the Treasury, "Treasury Releases Proposed Guidance on New Clean Vehicle Credit to Lower Costs for Consumers, Build U.S. Industrial Base, Strengthen Supply Chains," March 31, 2023, https://home.treasury.gov/news/press-releases/jy1379; Ryan Costello, "Republicans Must Fix, Not Repeal, the Inflation Reduction Act," *The Hill*, August 14, 2024, https://thehill.com/opinion/4826275-ira-china-dispute-clean-energy/.

59. Office of the United States Trade Representative, "United States and Japan Sign Critical Minerals Agreement," March 28, 2023, https://ustr.gov/about-us/policy-offices/press-office/press-releases/2023/march/united-states-and-japan-sign-critical-minerals-agreement; Prime Minister of Australia, "Australia–United States Climate, Critical Minerals and Clean Energy Transformation Compact," May 20, 2023, https://www.pm.gov.au/media/australia-united-states-climate-critical-minerals-and-clean-energy-transformation-compact; U.S. Department of State, "Inaugural C5+1 Critical Minerals Dialogue Among the United States and Kazakhstan, the Kyrgyz Republic, Tajikistan, Turkmenistan, and Uzbekistan," February 9, 2024, https://2021-2025.state.gov/inaugural-c51-critical-minerals-dialogue-among-the-united-states-and-kazakhstan-the-kyrgyz-republic-tajikistan-turkmenistan-and-uzbekistan/.

60. White House, "Fact Sheet: The Trilateral Leaders' Summit at Camp David," August 18, 2023, https://bidenwhitehouse.archives.gov/briefing-room/statements-releases/2023/08/18/fact-sheet-the-trilateral-leaders-summit-at-camp-david/.

61. For more details, see U.S. Department of State, "Minerals Security Partnership," https://www.state.gov/minerals-security-partnership/#Projects.

62. U.S. Department of State, "Joint Statement of the Minerals Security Partnership," March 4, 2024, https://2021-2025.state.gov/joint-statement-of-the-minerals-security-partnership/.

63. U.S. Department of State, "Joint Statement of the Minerals Security Partnership."

64. Nakano, *The Geopolitics of Critical Minerals Supply Chains.*

65. Nakano, *The Geopolitics of Critical Minerals Supply Chains*, 20.

66. Nakano, *The Geopolitics of Critical Minerals Supply Chains*, 20.

67. Yen Nee Lee, "A Massive, 'Semi-Infinite' Trove of Rare-Earth Metals Has Been Found in Japan," CNBC, April 12, 2018, https://www.cnbc.com/video/2018/04/12/a-massive-trove-of-rare-earth-metals-has-been-found-in-japan.html.

68. Tatsuya Terazawa, "Chairman's Message: The Rare Earths Embargo of 2010 and Its Lessons," Institute of Energy Economics, Japan, October 2023, https://eneken.ieej.or.jp/en/chairmans-message/chairmans-message_202310.html#:~:text=The%20rare%20earths%20embargo%20by,and%20stockpiling%20can%20be%20effective.

69. Peter Smith, Jonathan Soble, and Leslie Hook, "Japan Secures Rare Earths Deal with Australia," *Financial Times*, November 23, 2010, https://www.ft.com/content/63a18538-f773-11df-8b42 -00144feab49a.

70. Smith, Soble, and Hook, "Japan Secures Rare Earths Deal with Australia."

71. "Sojitz and JOGMEC Enter Into Definitive Agreements with Lynas Including Availability Agreement to Secure Supply of Rare Earths Products to Japanese Market," Japan Organization for Metals and Energy Security, March 30, 2011, https://www.jogmec.go.jp/english/news/release /release0069.html.https://www.jogmec.go.jp/english/news/release/release0069.html.

72. Tom Parker, "Japan: Australia's Key Rare Earths Partner," Australian Resources & Investment, March 9, 2023, https://www.australianresourcesandinvestment.com.au/2023/03/09/japan -australias-key-rare-earths-partner/.

73. Nakano, *The Geopolitics of Critical Minerals Supply Chains*, 21. Also see Tatsuya Terazawa, "How Japan Solved Its Rare Earth Minerals Dependency Issue," World Economic Forum, October 13, 2023, https://www.weforum.org/agenda/2023/10/japan-rare-earth-minerals/; Ryosuke Hanafusa, "Japan to Pour Investment Into Non-China Rare-Earth Projects," *Nikkei Asia*, February 15, 2020, https://asia.nikkei.com/Politics/International-relations/Japan-to-pour-investment-into-non -China-rare-earth-projects.

74. Ministry of Economy, Trade and Industry [Japan], "Japan's New International Resource Strategy to Secure Rare Metals," September 30, 2020, https://www.enecho.meti.go.jp/en/category/special /article/detail_158.html.

75. Nakano, *The Geopolitics of Critical Minerals Supply Chains*, 20.

76. Prime Minister's Office of Japan, "Partnership Between Japan's Ministry of Economy, Trade and Industry and Australia's Department of Industry, Science and Resources and Department of Foreign Affairs and Trade Concerning Critical Minerals," https://japan.kantei.go.jp/content /000116662.pdf.

77. Prime Minister's Office of Japan, "Partnership Between Japan's Ministry of Economy."

78. Mamoru Tsuge and Shoya Okinaga, "Japan Takes First Stake in Heavy Rare Earths to Reduce China Reliance," *Nikkei Asia*, March 9, 2023, https://asia.nikkei.com/Spotlight/Supply-Chain /Japan-takes-first-stake-in-heavy-rare-earths-to-reduce-China-reliance.

79. White House, "G7 Hiroshima Leaders' Communiqué," May 20, 2023, https://bidenwhitehouse .archives.gov/briefing-room/statements-releases/2023/05/20/g7-hiroshima-leaders -communique/.

80. G7 Ministers' Meeting on Climate, Energy and Environment, "Five-Point Plan for Critical Minerals Security," 2023, https://www.meti.go.jp/information/g7hirosima/energy/pdf/Annex005 .pdf.

81. Oh Seok-min, "(LEAD) S. Korea Seeks to Cut Key Minerals Dependence on China to 50 Pct by 2030," Yonhap News Agency, February 27, 2023, https://en.yna.co.kr/view/AEN20230227003351320.

82. Kim Ju-yeon, "Korea's Reliance on China for Minerals Grows Despite U.S. Warnings," *Korea JoongAng Daily*, October 20, 2023, https://koreajoongangdaily.joins.com/news/2023-10-15/business /industry/Koreas-reliance-on-China-for-minerals-grows-despite-US-warnings/1889533.

83. Oh Seok-min, "(LEAD) S. Korea Seeks to Cut Key Minerals Dependence."

84. Oh Seok-min, "(LEAD) S. Korea Seeks to Cut Key Minerals Dependence"; Ministry of Trade, Industry and Energy [South Korea], "Strategy for Securing Critical Minerals."

85. Ministry of Trade, Industry and Energy [South Korea], "Strategy for Securing Critical Minerals."

86. Ministry of Trade, Industry and Energy [South Korea], "Strategy for Securing Critical Minerals."

87. Ministry of Economy and Finance [South Korea], "The 1st Supply Chain Stabilization Committee Meeting," June 27, 2024, https://english.moef.go.kr/pc/selectTbPressCenterDtl.do?boardCd =N0001&seq=5902; Ministry of Economy and Finance [South Korea], *Gong-geubmang anjeonghwa chujinjeonlyag*공급망 안정화 추진전략 [Supply chain stabilization strategy], June 27, 2024,

https://www.moef.go.kr/nw/nes/detailNesDtaView.do?menuNo=4010100&searchNttId1
=MOSF_000000000069481&searchBbsId1=MOSFBBS_000000000028.

88. Kim Seung Yeon, "S. Korea, Mongolia Launch Cooperation Ministry of Economy and Finance Held the First Supply Chain Committee Meeting in June 202 for Rare Metals Supply," Yonhap News Agency, November 20, 2023, https://en.yna.co.kr/view/AEN20231119002100315; KoreaPro, "South Korea–Mongolia Launch Rare Metals Cooperation Amid Geopolitical Risks," November 21, 2023, https://koreapro.org/2023/11/south-korea-mongolia-launch-rare-metals-cooperation-amid-geopolitical-risks/.

89. U.S. Department of State, "Inaugural U.S.-Mongolia-ROK Critical Minerals Dialogue Held in Ulaanbaatar," June 27, 2023, https://2021-2025.state.gov/inaugural-u-s-mongolia-rok-critical-minerals-dialogue-held-in-ulaanbaatar/.

90. Oh Seok-min, "S. Korea, Vietnam Agree to Boost Cooperation on Critical Minerals," Yonhap News Agency, December 7, 2023, https://en.yna.co.kr/view/AEN20231207005400320.

91. Shin Hyonhee, "South Korea, Africa Leaders Pledge Deeper Ties, Critical Mineral Development," Reuters, June 4, 2024, https://www.reuters.com/world/asia-pacific/south-koreas-yoon-calls-greater-cooperation-with-africa-minerals-trade-2024-06-04/.

92. Kim Eun-jung "(News Focus) Yoon Focuses on Critical Minerals During Central Asia Trip," Yonhap News Agency, June 15, 2024, https://en.yna.co.kr/view/AEN20240614008900315?section=search.

93. Kotaro Hosokawa, "Lithium Supply: Posco to Build $830m Plant in Argentina," Nikkei Asia, December 18, 2021, https://asia.nikkei.com/Business/Materials/Lithium-supply-Posco-to-build-830m-plant-in-Argentina.

94. Gabriel Araujo, "South Korea's Posco to Invest $4 Bln in Lithium Project in Argentina," Reuters, March 21, 2022, https://www.reuters.com/world/americas/south-koreas-posco-invest-4-bln-lithium-project-argentina-2022-03-21/.

95. Dae-Woon Cha, "Baeteoliyong lityum-heug-yeonseo huitolyukkaji . . . haegsimgwangmul 'taljung-gug' sidong" 배터리용 리튬.흑연서 희토류까지... 핵심광물 '탈중국' 시동 [From lithium and graphite for batteries to rare earths . . . The shift away from China for key minerals begins], Yonhap News Agency, March 13, 2024, https://www.yna.co.kr/view/AKR20240312125500003?input=1195m.

96. Cha, "From Lithium and Graphite for Batteries to Rare Earths."

97. Cha, "From Lithium and Graphite for Batteries to Rare Earths."

98. Cha, "From Lithium and Graphite for Batteries to Rare Earths."

99. Junnosuke Kobara, "South Korea, Japan to Help Crisis-Proof Indo-Pacific Supply Chain," Nikkei Asia, July 31, 2024, https://asia.nikkei.com/Spotlight/Supply-Chain/South-Korea-Japan-to-help-crisis-proof-Indo-Pacific-supply-chain.

100. Australian Trade and Investment Commission, "A Dependable Critical Minerals Partner," n.d., https://international.austrade.gov.au/en/do-business-with-australia/sectors/energy-and-resources/critical-minerals#:~:text=Australia%20is%20a%20secure%2C%20reliable,1%20lithium%20producer.

101. White House, "Australia–United States Climate, Critical Minerals and Clean Energy Transformation Compact," May 20, 2023, https://bidenwhitehouse.archives.gov/briefing-room/statements-releases/2023/05/20/australia-united-states-climate-critical-minerals-and-clean-energy-transformation-compact/.

102. Phil Mercer, "Australia Unveils $1.25 Billion Critical Minerals Plan," Voice of America, October 26, 2023, https://www.voanews.com/a/australia-unveils-1-25-billion-critical-minerals-plan/7327227.html.

103. International Energy Agency, "Australia-India Critical Minerals Investment Partnership," December 11, 2023, https://www.iea.org/policies/17873-australia-india-critical-minerals-investment-partnership; Minister for Resources [Australia], "Milestone in India and Australia Critical Minerals Investment Partnership," March 10, 2023, https://www.minister.industry.gov.au/ministers/king/media-releases/milestone-india-and-australia-critical-minerals-investment-partnership.

104. Zongyuan Zoe Liu, "How to Secure Critical Minerals for Clean Energy Without Alienating China," Council on Foreign Relations, May 25, 2023, https://www.cfr.org/blog/how-secure-critical-minerals-clean-energy-without-alienating-china.

105. Australian Department of Foreign Affairs and Trade, "Joint Statement on the Supply Chain Resilience Initiative by Australian, Indian and Japanese Trade Ministers," March 15, 2022, https://www.dfat.gov.au/news/media-release/joint-statement-supply-chain-resilience-initiative-australian-indian-and-japanese-trade-ministers-0.

106. Yukihiro Sakaguchi, "Quad to Discuss Joint Investments in Chips, Critical Minerals," *Nikkei Asia*, May 20, 2023, https://asia.nikkei.com/Spotlight/Supply-Chain/Quad-to-discuss-joint-investments-in-chips-critical-minerals.

107. "Quad Countries Agree to Diversify Critical Mineral Supplies Amid China Concerns," *Guardian*, July 2, 2025, https://www.theguardian.com/world/2025/jul/02/quad-countries-agree-to-diversify-critical-mineral-supplies-amid-china-concerns.

108. CNBC, "Australia Orders Chinese Investors to Sell Down Stake in Rare Earths Miner," June 3, 2024, www.cnbc.com/2024/06/03/australia-orders-chinese-investors-to-sell-down-stake-in-rare-earths-miner.html; Elouise Fowler, "China-Linked Investors Forced to Offload Northern Minerals Shares," *Financial Review*, June 4, 2024, www.afr.com/companies/mining/chinese-linked-investors-forced-to-offload-northern-minerals-shares-20240603-p5jips.

109. Fowler, "China-Linked Investors Forced to Offload Northern Minerals Shares."

110. CNBC, "Australia Orders Chinese Investors to Sell Down Stake"; Ben Westcott, "Australia Knocks Back China-Linked Investment in Rare Earths," *Bloomberg*, March 1, 2023, https://www.bloomberg.com/news/articles/2023-03-01/australia-knocks-back-china-linked-investment-in-rare-earths.

111. In the previous chapters, we used a 70 percent threshold to measure high-dependence items. However, this threshold is difficult to apply to the critical minerals trade because (1) critical minerals are unevenly distributed based on national endowments and (2) China holds a dominant position in the critical minerals supply chain. For these reasons, we adjusted the threshold for high-dependence items to greater than 50 percent when combining the dependency rate of two major suppliers, which are G7+IP2 countries in this case.

112. The replacement metric is the quotient of exports over imports (explained in chapter 5).

113. See International Trade Administration, "Draft List of Critical Supply Chains," n.d., https://www.trade.gov/data-visualization/draft-list-critical-supply-chains.

114. HS Code 253090 is classified as "Mineral substances; n.e.c. in chapter 25."

115. Alfa Chemistry, "Nickel Catalyst," www.alfachemic.com/catalysts/products/nickel-catalysts.html.

116. Stella Nolan, "Nickel: Driving the Future of EV Battery Technology Globally," *EV Magazine*, October 25, 2024, https://evmagazine.com/technology/nickel-driving-the-future-of-ev-battery-technology-globally; Wen Bo, "China's Demand for Nickel Puts Pressure on Environment," China Development Brief, May 6, 2023, https://chinadevelopmentbrief.org/reports/chinas-demand-for-nickel-puts-pressure-on-environment/.

117. Bo, "China's Demand for Nickel Puts Pressure on Environment."

118. Smruthi Nadig, "Top Ten Nickel-Producing Countries in 2023," Mining Technology, March 25, 2024, https://www.mining-technology.com/features/top-ten-nickel-producing-countries-in-2023/?cf-view.

119. Peter S. Goodman, "China's Nickel Plants in Indonesia Created Needed Jobs, and Pollution," *New York Times*, August 18, 2023, https://www.nytimes.com/2023/08/18/business/indonesia-nickel-sulawesi-china.html.

120. Michelle Anindya, "Indonesia, Home to the World's Largest Nickel Reserves, Struggles to Achieve Its EV Dreams," Rest of World, February 3, 2025, https://restofworld.org/2025/indonesia-ev-nickel-ban-global-investors/.

121. HS Code 284190 is "Salts of oxometallic or peroxometallic acids; n.e.c. in heading no. 2841." We use the six-digit HS code to be consistent with the UN Comtrade data, but the critical mineral that meets the collective resilience criteria is vanadate (eight-digit HTS code 28419010), which is

a subcategory item under "Other salts of oxometallic or peroxometallic acids." Similarly, this approach applies to Zinc sulfide (HTS code 28309010), cobalt articles (HTS code 81059000), and mixtures of bismuth (HTS code 38249931).

122. Artem Vlasov, "Five Interesting Facts to Know About Zirconium," International Atomic Energy Agency, February 1, 2023, https://www.iaea.org/newscenter/news/five-interesting-facts-to-know-about-zirconium.

123. Jessica Long and Jingtai Lun, "Vanadium Redox Flow Batteries: A New Direction for China's Energy Storage?," Fastmarkets, November 22, 2022, https://www.fastmarkets.com/insights/vanadium-redox-flow-batteries-a-new-direction-for-chinas-energy-storage/; Liqiang Mai, Lin Xu, and Wei Chen, *Vanadate-Based Nanomaterials for Electrochemical Energy Storage* (Switzerland: Springer Cham, 2023), 177–219; China Energy Storage Alliance, "China's First Vanadium Battery Industry–Specific Policy Issued," May 16, 2024, https://en.cnesa.org/new-blog/2024/5/16/chinas-first-vanadium-battery-industry-specific-policy-issued; National Mining Association, "Energy Fuels: Strengthening our Military Through Vanadium," December 2, 2019, https://nma.org/2019/12/02/energy-fuels-strengthening-our-military-through-vanadium/.

124. This list of cobalt article examples comes from the European Customs portal. See European Customs Portal, "HS Code 81059000—Cobalt articles not elsewhere specified," https://www.tariffnumber.com/2024/81059000#google_vignette.

125. Alfa Chemistry, "Nickel Catalyst"; Stanford Advanced Materials, "Precious Metal Catalysts for the Petroleum Sector," December 27, 2023, www.samaterials.com/precious-metal-catalysts-for-the-petroleum-sector.html; Matumuene Joe Ndolomingo, Ndzondelelo Bingwa and Reinout Meijboom, "Review of Supported Metal Nanoparticles: Synthesis Methodologies, Advantages and Application as Catalysts," *Journal of Materials Science* 55 (2020): 6195–6241.

126. Sergey Alyabyev, Murray Edstein, Aleksandra Krauze, and Mads Yde Jensen, "Australia's Potential in the Lithium Market," McKinsey & Company, June 9, 2023, www.mckinsey.com/industries/metals-and-mining/our-insights/australias-potential-in-the-lithium-market.

127. Alyabyev, Edstein, Krauze, and Jensen, "Australia's Potential in the Lithium Market"; Lithium for Future Technology, "Global Lithium Deposit Map," November 2021, https://lithiumfuture.org/map.html.

128. Julia Gerlo and Marius Troost, "The Foreign Financiers of Argentina's Lithium Rush: Export Credit Agencies' Support for Lithium Mining," Both Ends & FARN, October 2023, www.bothends.org/uploaded_files/document/The_foreign_financiers_of_Argentina_s_lithium_rush.pdf, 13.

7. THE STAKES COULD NOT BE HIGHER

1. Tom Cotton, "Cotton, Colleagues Introduce Bill to End China's Permanent Normal Trade Status," January 26, 2023, www.cotton.senate.gov/news/press-releases/cotton-colleagues-introduce-bill-to-end-chinas-permanent-normal-trade-status; Josh Hawley, "Hawley Announces First Bill in Worker's Agenda to Rebuild America: Ending Normal Trade Relations with China Act," March 20, 2023, www.hawley.senate.gov/hawley-announces-first-bill-workers-agenda-rebuild-america-ending-normal-trade-relations-china-act/; Seth McLaughlin, "Nikki Haley Calls for Ending Normal Trade Relations with China," *Washington Times*, June 27, 2023, www.washingtontimes.com/news/2023/jun/27/nikki-haley-calls-ending-normal-trade-relations-ch/.

2. Thomas J. Christensen, "Mutually Assured Disruption: Globalization, Security, and the Dangers of Decoupling," *World Politics* 75, no. 5 (2023): 1–18.

3. U.S. Department of State, "Reaffirming and Reimagining America's Alliances," March 24, 2021, https://2021-2025.state.gov/reaffirming-and-reimagining-americas-alliances/ (emphasis added).

4.   Government of the United Kingdom, "Foreign Secretary Liz Truss' Speech to the Lowy Institute," January 21, 2022, www.gov.uk/government/speeches/foreign-secretarys-speech-to-the-lowy -institute.

5.   White House, "Leaders' Joint Statement in Commemoration of the 70th Anniversary of the Alliance Between the United States of America and the Republic of Korea," April 26, 2023, https:// bidenwhitehouse.archives.gov/briefing-room/statements-releases/2023/04/26/leaders-joint -statement-in-commemoration-of-the-70th-anniversary-of-the-alliance-between-the-united -states-of-america-and-the-republic-of-korea/.

6.   White House, "United States–Japan Joint Leaders' Statement," April 10, 2024, https:// bidenwhitehouse.archives.gov/briefing-room/statements-releases/2024/04/10/united-states -japan-joint-leaders-statement/.

7.   White House, "G7 Leaders' Statement on Economic Resilience and Economic Security," May 20, 2023, https://bidenwhitehouse.archives.gov/briefing-room/statements-releases/2023/05/20/g7 -leaders-statement-on-economic-resilience-and-economic-security/.

8.   North Atlantic Treaty Organization, "Washington Summit Declaration," July 10, 2024, https:// www.nato.int/cps/cn/natohq/official_texts_227678.htm.

9.   Christian Freudlsperger and Sophie Meunier, "When Foreign Policy Becomes Trade Policy: The EU's Anti-Coercion Instrument," *JCMS: Journal of Common Market Studies* 62, no. 4 (2024): 1063–1079.

10.   European Union, "Joint Declaration of the Commission, the Council and the European Parliament on an Instrument to Deter and Counteract Coercive Actions by Third Countries," December 2, 2021, https://eur-lex.europa.eu/legal-content/EN/TXT/?uri=uriserv%3AOJ.C_ .2021.049.01.0001.01.ENG&toc=OJ%3AC%3A2021%3A049%3ATOC.

11.   European Commission, "Joint Communication to the European Parliament, the European Council and the Council on European Economic Security," June 20, 2023, https://eur-lex.europa .eu/legal-content/EN/TXT/?uri=CELEX%3A52023JC0020&qid=1687525961309.

12.   Ben Murphy, "Chokepoints: China's Self-Identified Strategic Technology Import Dependencies," Center for Security and Emerging Technologies, May 2022, https://cset.georgetown.edu /publication/chokepoints/; Cynthia Cook et al., "Expanding the Tool Kit to Counter China's Economic Coercion," Center for Strategic and International Studies, May 6, 2024. https://www.csis .org/analysis/expanding-tool-kit-counter-chinas-economic-coercion.

13.   David Lague, "Special Report: In Satellite Tech Race, China Hitched a Ride from Europe," Reuters, December 22, 2013, https://www.reuters.com/article/world/special-report-in-satellite-tech-race -china-hitched-a-ride-from-europe-idUSBRE9BL0CA/.

14.   Didi Tang, "China Has Threatened Trade with Some Countries After Feuds. They're Calling 'the Firm' for Help," Associated Press, May 27, 2024, https://apnews.com/article/china-trade-economic -firm-state-department-42655e067386a20b22f1317ce298f334.

15.   Tang, "China Has Threatened Trade."

16.   Cook et al., "Expanding the Tool Kit," 30.

17.   Congress.gov, "H.R.5580—Countering China Economic Coercion Act," October 15, 2021, https:// www.congress.gov/bill/117th-congress/house-bill/5580/text; Congress.gov, "S.4514—Countering Economic Coercion Act of 2022," July 13, 2022, https://www.congress.gov/bill/117th-congress /senate-bill/4514/text. On Chinese economic coercion in the FY 2023 NDAA, see Section 5514 in Congress.gov, "H.R. 7776—James M. Inhofe National Defense Authorization Act for Fiscal Year 2023," December 23, 2022, https://www.congress.gov/bill/117th-congress/house-bill/7776 /text.

18.   Emily Benson, "What Are the Trade Contours of the European Union's Anti-Coercion Instrument," Center for Strategic and International Studies, April 21, 2022, www.csis.org/analysis/what -are-trade-contours-european-unions-anti-coercion-instrument; Office of the Law Revision

Counsel of the United States House of Representatives, "22 USC 3362: Task Force to Counter Economic Coercion by the People's Republic of China," https://uscode.house.gov/view.xhtml?req=granuleid:USC-prelim-title22-section3362&num=0&edition=prelim#:~:text=Not%20later%20than%20180%20days,the%20%22Task%20Force%22).

19.   White House, "Memorandum on the Establishment of the Countering Economic Coercion Task Force," December 12, 2024, https://bidenwhitehouse.archives.gov/briefing-room/presidential-actions/2024/12/12/memorandum-on-the-establishment-of-the-countering-economic-coercion-task-force/.

20.   Ami Bera, "Bera Introduces Bill to Counter Chinese Economic Coercion," February 23, 2023, https://bera.house.gov/news/documentsingle.aspx?DocumentID=400046.

21.   Cook et al., "Expanding the Tool Kit," 29.

22.   For a good discussion of these statutory authorities, see Cook et al., "Expanding the Tool Kit," 14–15.

23.   Da-gyum Ji, "Foreign Ministry to Disband Peninsula Peace Bureau Amid NK Threats," *Korea Herald*, March 7, 2024, www.koreaherald.com/view.php?ud=20240307050829.

24.   U.S. Department of State, "Inaugural U.S.-Mongolia-ROK Critical Minerals Dialogue Held in Ulaanbaatar," June 27, 2023, https://2021-2025.state.gov/inaugural-u-s-mongolia-rok-critical-minerals-dialogue-held-in-ulaanbaatar/; White House, "G7 Leaders' Statement on Economic Resilience and Economic Security"; Han-joo Kim, "(LEAD) S. Korea, Australia to Launch 'Economic Security Dialogue,'" Yonhap News Agency, July 30, 2024, https://en.yna.co.kr/view/AEN20240730006651315; Ministry of Foreign Affairs, "Korea Assumes Chairmanship of Minerals Security Partnership (MSP)," June 27, 2024, https://overseas.mofa.go.kr/eng/brd/m_5676/view.do?seq=322611; U.S. Mission Korea, "Readout of the United States–India–Republic of Korea Trilateral Technology Dialogue," U.S. Embassy & Consulate in the Republic of Korea, March 13, 2024, https://kr.usembassy.gov/031324-readout-of-the-united-states-india-republic-of-korea-trilateral-technology-dialogue/.

25.   Kyodo News, "Japan's Diet Enacts Law to Create Economic Security Clearance System," May 10, 2024, https://english.kyodonews.net/news/2024/05/6d180e81198e-japans-diet-enacts-law-to-create-economic-security-clearance-system.html?phrase=kyoto&words=#google_vignette.

26.   Ministry of Economy, Trade and Industry, "As a Review of the Organization, METI Revises the Ordinance on the Organization of the Ministry of Economy, Trade and Industry," June 25, 2024, www.meti.go.jp/english/press/2024/0625_001.html.

27.   William Chou, "Japan's Strategy for Economic Security: An Interview with Deputy LDP Secretary-General Keitaro Ohno," Hudson Institute, July 23, 2024, https://www.hudson.org/economics/japans-strategy-economic-security-interview-deputy-ldp-secretary-general-keitaro-ohno.

28.   Chou, "Japan's Strategy for Economic Security."

29.   European Commission, "New Tool to Enable EU to Withstand Economic Coercion Enters Into Force," December 27, 2023, https://ec.europa.eu/commission/presscorner/detail/en/ip_23_6804.

30.   Benson, "What Are the Trade Contours"; Kim B. Olsen and Claudia Schmucker, "The EU's New Anti-Coercion Instrument Will Be a Success If It Isn't Used," *Internationale Politik Quarterly*, January 10, 2024, https://ip-quarterly.com/en/eus-new-anti-coercion-instrument-will-be-success-if-it-isnt-used.

31.   Freudlsperger and Meunier, "When Foreign Policy Becomes Trade Policy."

32.   Jonathan Hackenbroich and Pawel Zerka, "Measured Response: How to Design a European Instrument Against Economic Coercion," European Council on Foreign Relations, June 23, 2021, https://ecfr.eu/publication/measured-response-how-to-design-a-european-instrument-against-economic-coercion/.

33.   For example, China's economic coercion against the NBA involved no formal tariff. It took nonformal measures such as removing Houston Rockets merchandise from online sales. Its stoppage

of Philippine banana imports was executed informally with instructions delivered verbally to leave the imported produce on the docks to rot. China's ban on group tours to South Korea on the occasion of the Pyeongchang 2018 Winter Olympics was also done informally with no explicit sanction.

34. European Union, "Questions & Answers Regarding Anti-Coercion Instrument," https://policy.trade.ec.europa.eu/enforcement-and-protection/protecting-against-coercion/qa-regarding-anti-coercion-instrument_en; European Union, "Anti-Coercion Instrument," https://trade.ec.europa.eu/access-to-markets/en/content/anti-coercion-instrument.

35. Hackenbroich and Zerka, "Measured Response."

36. Ivo H. Daalder and Anders Fogh Rasmussen, "Memo on an 'Economic Article 5' to Counter Authoritarian Coercion," Chicago Council on Global Affairs, June 9, 2022, https://globalaffairs.org/research/policy-brief/memo-economic-article-5-counter-authoritarian-coercion.

37. World Trade Organization, "Article XXI: Security Exceptions," www.wto.org/english/res_e/booksp_e/gatt_ai_e/art21_e.pdf.

38. William Reinsch, "The WTO's First Ruling on National Security: What Does It Mean for the United States?," Center for Strategic and International Studies, April 5, 2019, www.csis.org/analysis/wtos-first-ruling-national-security-what-does-it-mean-united-states.

39. A requirement for WTO compliance might be that collective resilience would have to be informal rather than formal. The authors thank Christina Davis for raising this point.

40. World Trade Organization, "The Process—Stages in a Typical WTO Dispute Settlement Case," www.wto.org/english/tratop_e/dispu_e/disp_settlement_cbt_e/c6s1op1_e.htm.

41. World Trade Organization, "The Process."

42. Jonathan Hackenbroich et al., "Defending Europe's Economic Sovereignty: New Ways to Resist Economic Coercion," European Council on Foreign Relations, October 20, 2020, https://ecfr.eu/publication/defending_europe_economic_sovereignty_new_ways_to_resist_economic_coercion/. To address some of the WTO's shortcomings, the European Union created the Multi-Party Interim Appeal Arbitration Arrangement (MPIA) with WTO members to support arbitration among the members themselves. But this body has also been incapable of dealing with China's economic coercion, even though China is a member. Of the thirteen total cases listed on their website in February 2025, six involved China; two are ongoing, and four were "finalized without MPIA appeal, withdrawn, lapsed or settled." See Geneva Trade Platform, "MultiParty Interim Appeal Arbitration Arrangement (MPIA)," https://wtoplurilaterals.info/plural_initiative/the-mpia/.

43. Hackenbroich et al., "Defending Europe's Economic Sovereignty." For a dissenting opinion, see Kornel Olsthoorn, "The EU's Anti-Coercion Instrument: A Return of Unlawful Unilateral Trade Countermeasures in Disguise?," Legal Issues of Economic Integration 51, no. 1 (2024): 47–86.

44. Hackenbroich et al., "Defending Europe's Economic Sovereignty." Also see Article 13 in European Union, "Regulation (EU) 2023/2675 of the European Parliament and of the Council of 22 November 2023 on the Protection of the Union and its Member States from Economic Coercion by Third Countries," https://eur-lex.europa.eu/legal-content/EN/TXT/?uri=celex%3A32023R2675. For Articles on the Responsibility of States for Internationally Wrongful Acts (ARSIWA), see United Nations, "Responsibility of States for Internationally Wrongful Acts," https://legal.un.org/ilc/texts/instruments/english/draft_articles/9_6_2001.pdf.

45. Hackenbroich et al., "Defending Europe's Economic Sovereignty." Also see Articles 13–16 in European Union, "Regulation (EU) 2023/2675 of the European Parliament."

46. Hackenbroich and Zerka, "Measured Response." Also see Article 12 in European Union, "Regulation (EU) 2023/2675 of the European Parliament."

47. Jonas Parello-Plesner, "An 'Economic Article Five' to Counter China," Wall Street Journal, February 11, 2021, www.wsj.com/articles/an-economic-article-5-to-counter-china-11613084046.

48. Daniel W. Drezner, "The Uses and Abuses of Weaponized Interdependence in 2021," *Washington Post*, March 2, 2021, www.washingtonpost.com/outlook/2021/03/02/uses-abuses-weaponized -interdependence-2021/.

49. United Nations, "Responsibility of States for Internationally Wrongful Acts."

50. See Article 8 in European Union, "Regulation (EU) 2023/2675 of the European Parliament."

51. Hal Brands, "The Age of Amorality: Can America Save the Liberal Order Through Illiberal Means?," *Foreign Affairs* 103, no. 2 (2024): 113, https://www.foreignaffairs.com/united-states/age -amorality-liberal-brands.

52. Brands, "The Age of Amorality," 115.

POSTSCRIPT

1. See William Alan Reinsch in Victor D. Cha, Kristi Govella, and William Alan Reinsch, "Korea, Japan, and the Tariff War," *CSIS The Impossible State*, Podcast audio, April 21, 2025, https://www .csis.org/podcasts/impossible-state/korea-japan-and-tariff-war.

2. White House, "Fact Sheet: President Donald J. Trump Secures a Historic Trade Win for the United States," May 12, 2025, https://www.whitehouse.gov/fact-sheets/2025/05/fact-sheet-president -donald-j-trump-secures-a-historic-trade-win-for-the-united-states/.

3. Max Zahn, "What to Know as Tariffs Go Into Effect on Mexico, Canada, China," ABC News, March 4, 2025, https://abcnews.go.com/Business/tariffs-effect/story?id=119380711.

4. White House, "Remarks by President Trump in Joint Address to Congress," March 4, 2025, https:// www.whitehouse.gov/remarks/2025/03/remarks-by-president-trump-in-joint-address-to -congress/.

5. John McCormick, "Trump Calls Tariffs the 'Most Beautiful Word,'" *Wall Street Journal*, October 17, 2024, https://www.wsj.com/livecoverage/harris-trump-election-10-16-2024/card/trump -calls-tariffs-the-most-beautiful-word--YMVPAupw4EjBRp6yobOy.

6. White House, "Fact Sheet: President Donald J. Trump Imposes Tariffs on Imports from Canada, Mexico and China," February 1, 2025. https://www.whitehouse.gov/fact-sheets/2025/02/fact-sheet -president-donald-j-trump-imposes-tariffs-on-imports-from-canada-mexico-and-china/.

7. Alexandra Hutzler, "Trump Rolls Out Sweeping Tariffs as He Deems Deficits a 'National Emergency,'" ABC News, April 2, 2025, https://abcnews.go.com/Politics/trumps-liberation-day-arrives -gambles-big-risky-tariff/story?id=120382209.

8. Elisabeth Buchwald and Kevin Liptak, "Trump Announces 90-day Pause on 'Reciprocal' Tariffs with Exception of China," CNN, April 9, 2025, https://www.cnn.com/2025/04/09/business /reciprocal-tariff-pause-trump/index.html.

9. See Gracelin Baskaran and Meredith Schwartz, "The Consequences of China's New Rare Earths Export Restrictions," April 14, 2025. https://www.csis.org/analysis/consequences-chinas-new-rare -earths-export-restrictions; Joseph Sopcisak, "China Imposes Export Controls on Medium and Heavy Rare Earth Materials," Holland & Knight, April 4, 2024, https://www.hklaw.com/en /insights/publications/2025/04/china-imposes-export-controls-on-medium-and-heavy-rare -earth-materials.

10. Buchwald and Liptak, "Trump Announces 90-day Pause."

11. Alexandra Stevenson, "China Raises Tariffs on U.S. Imports to 125%, Calling Trump's Policies a 'Joke,'" *New York Times*, April 11, 2025, https://www.nytimes.com/2025/04/11/business/china -tariffs-125.html.

BIBLIOGRAPHY

ABC News. "China's Appetite for Australian Barley Is Back, Three Years After Tariffs Halted the Near-$1 Billion Market." December 30, 2023. www.abc.net.au/news/2023-12-30/china-australian-barley-appetite-3-years-tariffs-halted-market/103274912.

Acosta, Gerald M. "China's One Road, One Belt Grand Strategy: Founded on the Weaponization of the Global Supply Chain." *Defense Transportation Journal* 76, no. 6 (2020): 17–22.

Adachi, Aya, Alexander Brown, Francesca Ghiretti, Mikko Huotari, Jan Weidenfield, and Max J. Zenglein. "Dealing with China's Economic Coercion—The Case of Lithuania and Insights from East Asia and Australia." Mercator Institute for China Studies, December 20, 2021. https://merics.org/en/executive-memo/dealing-chinas-economic-coercion-case-lithuania-and-insights-east-asia-and-australia.

Adachi, Aya, Alexander Brown, and Max J. Zenglein. "Fasten Your Seatbelts: How to Manage China's Economic Coercion." Mercator Institute for China Studies, August 22, 2022. https://merics.org/en/report/fasten-your-seatbelts-how-manage-chinas-economic-coercion.

Agence France-Presse. "Philippine Banana Impounded Amid China Sea Spat." Rappler, May 12, 2012. www.rappler.com/business/5253-philippine-banana-impounded-amid-china-sea-spat/.

Ahn, Jennifer. "U.S.-South Korea Policy Coordination on Supply Chain Resiliency." Council on Foreign Relations, April 2, 2024. www.cfr.org/blog/us-south-korea-policy-coordination-supply-chain-resiliency.

Alave, Kristine L. "DA Team to Go to China to Check on Stranded Banana Shipment." Inquirer.net, May 15, 2012. https://business.inquirer.net/59391/da-team-to-go-to-china-to-check-on-stranded-banana-shipment.

Albert, Eleanor. "Which Countries Support the New Hong Kong National Security Law?" *Diplomat*, July 6, 2020. https://thediplomat.com/2020/07/which-countries-support-the-new-hong-kong-national-security-law/.

Alfa Chemistry. "Nickel Catalyst." n.d. www.alfachemic.com/catalysts/products/nickel-catalysts.html.

Allen, Bethany. *Beijing Rules: How China Weaponized Its Economy to Confront the World*. New York: Harper, 2023.

——. "China Is Censoring Hollywood's Imagination." Axios, September 1, 2020. www.axios.com/2020/09/01/china-censor-hollywood-films.

Allen, Gregory, Emily Benson, and Margot Putnam. "Japan and the Netherlands Announce Plans for New Export Controls on Semiconductor Equipment." Center for Strategic and International Studies,

April 10, 2023. https://www.csis.org/analysis/japan-and-netherlands-announce-plans-new-export -controls-semiconductor-equipment.

Alyabyev, Sergey, Murray Edstein, Aleksandra Krauze, and Mads Yde Jensen. *Australia's Potential in the Lithium Market*. McKinsey & Company, June 9, 2023. www.mckinsey.com/industries/metals-and -mining/our-insights/australias-potential-in-the-lithium-market.

Andrijauskas, Konstantinas. "An Analysis of China's Economic Coercion Against Lithuania." Council on Foreign Relations, May 12, 2022. www.cfr.org/blog/analysis-chinas-economic-coercion-against -lithuania.

Anindya, Michelle. "Indonesia, Home to the World's Largest Nickel Reserves, Struggles to Achieve Its EV Dreams." Rest of World, February 3, 2025. https://restofworld.org/2025/indonesia-ev-nickel-ban-global -investors/.

Areddy, James T. "The NBA's New Normal in China." *Wall Street Journal*, October 25, 2019. www.wsj .com/articles/the-nbas-new-normal-in-china-11572017629.

Art, Robert J. "To What Ends Military Power?" *International Security* 4, no. 4 (1980): 3–35.

Associated Press. "China Formally Restores Diplomatic Relations with Nauru After Pacific Island Nation Cut Taiwan Ties." January 24, 2024. https://apnews.com/article/china-nauru-taiwan-diplomatic -recognition-23fd9cdd0210a2340b5ae2092d2a85d1.

——. "Honduras Establishes Ties with China After Taiwan Break." March 26, 2023. https://apnews.com /article/china-honduras-diplomatic-ties-taiwan-bf5c143768814fb6f9f3beff34f611d7.

——. "Versace Apologizes in Flap over T-Shirts Sold in China." August 11, 2019. https://apnews.com /general-news-movies-d4cd7b1c1ad34283b0e9bec39fcdaebc.

Atkinson, Robert D. "The Case for a National Industrial Strategy to Counter China's Technological Rise." Information Technology & Innovation Foundation, April 13, 2020. https://itif.org/publications/2020 /04/13/case-national-industrial-strategy-counter-chinas-technological-rise/.

——. "How Innovative Is China in the Robotics Industry?" Information Technology & Innovation Foundation, March 11, 2024. https://itif.org/publications/2024/03/11/how-innovative-is-china-in-the -robotics-industry/.

Atlas, Matt. "Komarek Buys Pianos Rejected by China Over Taiwan Row." *Prague Business Journal*, September 9, 2020. https://praguebusinessjournal.com/komarek-buys-pianos-rejected-by-china-over -taiwan-row/.

Atwood, Kylie, Kevin Liptak, and Phil Mattingly. "Trump Administration Took Action Against China due to Frustration on Trade Talks, Officials Say." CNN, May 30, 2025. https://www.cnn.com/2025 /05/29/politics/us-china-trade-talk-frustration.

Aušra, Mindaugas. "Chinese Demonstration in Vilnius Unmasks Beijing's Reach into Lithuania—LRT Investigation." Lithuanian Radio and Television, October 9, 2019. www.lrt.lt/en/news-in-english/19 /1104874/chinese-demonstration-in-vilnius-unmasks-beijing-s-reach-into-lithuania-lrt -investigation.

Australian Department of Foreign Affairs and Trade. "Joint Statement on the Supply Chain Resilience Initiative by Australian, Indian, and Japanese Trade Ministers." March 15, 2022. www.dfat.gov.au/news /media-release/joint-statement-supply-chain-resilience-initiative-australian-indian-and-japanese -trade-ministers-0.

Australian Government. "Barley—Diversifying at a Price Q2 2021." 2021. https://www.agriculture.gov.au /sites/default/files/documents/q2-barley-exports.pdf.

Australian Government—Defence. "Australia–Republic of Korea 2+2 Joint Statement." May 1, 2024. https://www.minister.defence.gov.au/statements/2024-05-01/australia-republic-korea-22-joint -statement.

Australian Trade and Investment Commission, "A Dependable Critical Minerals Partner." n.d. https:// international.austrade.gov.au/en/do-business-with-australia/sectors/energy-and-resources/critical -minerals.

Axelrod, Robert. *The Evolution of Cooperation*. New York: Basic Books, 1984.

Axelrod, Robert, and William D. Hamilton. "The Evolution of Cooperation." *Science* 211, no. 4489 (1981): 1390–1396.

Axelrod, Robert, and Robert O. Keohane. "Achieving Cooperation Under Anarchy: Strategies and Institutions." *World Politics* 38, no. 1 (1985): 226–254.

Badenhausen, Kurt. "NBA Team Values 2018: Every Club Now Worth at Least $1 Billion." *Forbes*, February 7, 2018. https://www.forbes.com/sites/kurtbadenhausen/2018/02/07/nba-team-values-2018-every-club-now-worth-at-least-1-billion/?sh=483fce167155.

Baek, Byung-yeul. "Gov't Criticized for Failing to Lower Dependence on China for Urea." *Korea Times*, December 5, 2023. https://www.koreatimes.co.kr/www/tech/2024/07/129_364527.html.

Baker, Benjamin David. "Soul or Salmon: Norway's Chinese Dilemma." *Diplomat*, May 9, 2014. https://thediplomat.com/2014/05/soul-or-salmon-norways-chinese-dilemma/.

Baldwin, David. *Economic Statecraft*. Princeton, NJ: Princeton University Press, 1985.

——. "Interdependence and Power: A Conceptual Analysis." *International Organization* 30, no. 4 (1984): 471–506.

——. "The Sanctions Debate and the Logic of Choice." *International Security* 24, no. 3 (1999): 80–107.

Bantock, Jack. "NBA Commissioner Adam Silver Says League Lost 'Hundreds of Millions of Dollars' Due to China Fallout, Touches on Brittney Griner Situation." CNN, June 3, 2022. https://www.cnn.com/2022/06/03/sport/adam-silver-nba-china-brittney-griner-spt-intl/.

Barboza, Daniel, and Brooks Barnes. "How China Won the Keys to Disney's Magic Kingdom." *New York Times*, June 14, 2016. https://www.nytimes.com/2016/06/15/business/international/china-disney.html.

Baskaran, Gracelin, and Meredith Schwartz. "China Imposes Its Most Stringent Critical Minerals Export Restrictions Yet Amidst Escalating U.S.-China Tech War." Center for Strategic and International Studies, December 4, 2024. https://www.csis.org/analysis/china-imposes-its-most-stringent-critical-minerals-export-restrictions-yet-amidst.

——. "The Consequences of China's New Rare Earths Export Restrictions." Center for Strategic and International Studies, April 14, 2025. https://www.csis.org/analysis/consequences-chinas-new-rare-earths-export-restrictions.

BBC. 中国就黄岩岛指责菲律宾扩大事态" [China accused the Philippines of escalating tension in the Scarborough Shoal]. May 8, 2012. https://www.bbc.com/zhongwen/simp/chinese_news/2012/05/120508_china_philippines.

——. "戴秉国：中国不会容忍菲律宾欺负" [Dai Bingguo: China will not tolerate bullying by the Philippines]. May 16, 2012. https://www.bbc.com/zhongwen/simp/chinese_news/2012/05/120516_china_philippines.

——. "Dior Apologizes for Using China Map without Taiwan." October 17, 2019. https://www.bbc.com/news/business-50078886.

——. "H&M: Fashion Giants Sees China Sales Slump After Xinjiang Boycott." July 2, 2021. https://www.bbc.com/news/business-57691415.

——. "Nicaragua Cuts Ties with Taiwan in Favour of Beijing." December 9, 2021. https://www.bbc.com/news/world-asia-59574532.

——. "Taiwan Loses Diplomatic Ally as Dominican Republic Switches Ties to China." May 1, 2018. https://www.bbc.com/news/world-asia-china-43958849.

Beniušis, Vaidotas. "Lithuania's Support for Taiwan Draws Ire from Beijing." Lithuanian Radio and Television, May 14, 2020. https://www.lrt.lt/en/news-in-english/19/1178311/lithuania-s-support-for-taiwan-draws-ire-from-beijing.

Benson, Emily. "What Are the Trade Contours of the European Union's Anti-Coercion Instrument?" *Center for Strategic and International Studies*, April 21, 2022. https://www.csis.org/analysis/what-are-trade-contours-european-unions-anti-coercion-instrument.

Benson, Emily, and Thibault Denamiel. "China's New Graphite Restrictions." Center for Strategic and International Studies, October 23, 2023. https://www.csis.org/analysis/chinas-new-graphite-restrictions.

Benson, Emily, Japhet Quitzon, and William A. Reinsch. "Securing Semiconductor Supply Chains in the Indo-Pacific Economic Framework for Prosperity." Center for Strategic and International Studies, May 30, 2023. https://www.csis.org/analysis/securing-semiconductor-supply-chains-indo-pacific -economic-framework-prosperity.

Bera, Ami. "Bera Introduces Bill to Counter Chinese Economic Coercion." U.S. Representative Ami Bera, February 23, 2023. https://bera.house.gov/news/documentsingle.aspx?DocumentID=400046.

Bindman, Polly. "Weekly Data: China Seeks to Extend Its Critical Minerals Dominance with Overseas Investment Surge." Energy Monitor, August 21, 2023. https://www.energymonitor.ai/industry/weekly -data-china-seeks-to-extend-its-critical-minerals-dominance-with-overseas-investment-surge.

Bindrim, Kira. "Why 'Top Gun: Maverick' Has No Release Date in China." Quartz, July 20, 2022. https://qz.com/2170997/why-top-gun-maverick-has-no-release-date-in-china.

Blakemore, Reed. "What to Make of China's Latest Restrictions on Critical Mineral Exports." Atlantic Council, October 26, 2023. https://www.atlanticcouncil.org/blogs/new-atlanticist/what-to-make-of -chinas-latest-restrictions-on-critical-mineral-exports/.

Blanchard, Ben. "Taiwan Says 'Fab 4' Chip Group Held First Senior Officials Meeting." Reuters, February 25, 2023. https://www.reuters.com/technology/taiwan-says-fab-4-chip-group-held-first-senior -officials-meeting-2023-02-25/.

——. "Torch Protests Stir Strident Chinese Nationalism." Reuters, April 19, 2008. https://www.reuters .com/article/economy/torch-protests-stir-strident-chinese-nationalism-idUSPEK278227/.

Blanchard, Ben, and Yew Lun Tian. "Czech Senate Speaker Will Pay 'Heavy Price' for Taiwan Visit, China Says." Reuters, August 31, 2020. https://www.reuters.com/article/world/czech-senate-speaker-will-pay -heavy-price-for-taiwan-visit-china-says-idUSKBN25R02V/.

Blanchard, Jean-Marc F., and Norrin. M. Ripsman. "Asking the Right Question: When Do Economic Sanctions Work Best?" *Security Studies* 9, no. 1 (1999): 219–253.

Bloomberg. "China's 500 Million NBA Fans Face Loyalty Test." October 9, 2019. https://www.bloomberg .com/news/articles/2019-10-09/china-s-500-million-nba-fans-face-loyalty-test-in-standoff.

Bloomberg News. "How Keeping Quiet About Politics Helped Uniqlo Become China's Favorite Fashion Brand." Bloomberg, April 13, 2022. https://www.bloomberg.com/graphics/2022-uniqlo-china-politics/.

Bo, Wen. "China's Demand for Nickel Puts Pressure on Environment." China Development Brief, May 6, 2023. https://chinadevelopmentbrief.org/reports/chinas-demand-for-nickel-puts-pressure-on -environment/.

Borowiec, Steven. "Urea Shortage Threatens to Paralyze South Korea's Economy." *Nikkei Asia*, November 17, 2021. https://asia.nikkei.com/Economy/Urea-shortage-threatens-to-paralyze-South-Korea-s -economy.

Bown, Chad P. "How COVID-19 Medical Supply Shortages Led to Extraordinary Trade and Industrial Policy." *Asian Economic Policy Review* 17, no. 1 (2022): 114–135.

Bradsher, Keith. "Amid Tension, China Blocks Vital Exports to Japan." *New York Times*, September 22, 2010. https://www.nytimes.com/2010/09/23/business/global/23rare.html.

——. "China Halts Critical Exports as Trade War Intensifies," *New York Times*, April 13, 2025. https:// www.nytimes.com/2025/04/13/business/china-rare-earths-exports.html.

——. "China Restarts Rare Earth Shipments to Japan." *New York Times*, November 19, 2010. https://www .nytimes.com/2010/11/20/business/global/20rare.html.

——. "China's Supply of Minerals for iPhones and Missiles Could Be a Risky Trade Weapon." *New York Times*, May 23, 2019. https://www.nytimes.com/2019/05/23/business/china-us-trade-war-rare-earths .html.

——. "China to Investigate U.S. Retailer, Sending a Message Over Xinjiang," *New York Times*, September 24, 2024. https://www.nytimes.com/2024/09/24/business/china-xinjiang-calvin-klein-tommy -hilfiger.html.

Brands, Hal. "The Age of Amorality: Can America Save the Liberal Order Through Illiberal Means?" *Foreign Affairs* 103, no. 2 (2024).

Branigan, Toby. "Chinese Bloggers Claim CocaCola Backs Tibetans." *Guardian*, April 8, 2008. https://www.theguardian.com/world/2008/apr/09/china.tibet.

——. "Eighteen More Countries Refuse to Attend Nobel Peace Prize Ceremony." *Guardian*, December 7, 2010. https://www.theguardian.com/world/2010/dec/07/china-nobel-peace-prize-clowns.

Bro, Frank. "Insulting China? No, Doctor Strange 2 Is Shaming US and Hollywood." *Global Times*, May 1, 2022. https://www.globaltimes.cn/page/202205/1260710.shtml.

Brooks, Risa A. "Sanctions and Regime Type: What Works and When?" *Security Studies* 11, no. 4 (2002): 1–50.

Brown, Jonathan N., and Anthony S. Marcum. "Avoiding Audience Costs: Domestic Political Accountability and Concessions in Crisis Diplomacy." *Security Studies* 20, no. 2 (2011): 141–170.

Buchwald, Elisabeth, and Kevin Liptak. "Trump Announces 90-day Pause on 'Reciprocal' Tariffs with Exception of China." CNN, April 9, 2025. https://www.cnn.com/2025/04/09/business/reciprocal-tariff-pause-trump/index.html.

Buckley, Charles, Kenneth Bradsher, and Tiffany May. "New Security Law Gives China Sweeping Powers Over Hong Kong." *New York Times*, June 29, 2020. https://www.nytimes.com/2020/06/29/world/asia/china-hong-kong-security-law-rules.html.

Buckley, Chris, Amy Chang Chien, Eric Schmitt and David E. Sanger. "Chinese Missiles Strike Seas Off Taiwan, and Some Land Near Japan." *New York Times*, August 3, 2022. https://www.nytimes.com/2022/08/03/world/asia/taiwan-china-military-exercises.html.

Bureau of Industry and Security. "Commerce Implements New Export Controls on Advanced Computing and Semiconductor Manufacturing Items to the People's Republic of China (PRC)." October 7, 2022. https://www.bis.doc.gov/index.php/documents/about-bis/newsroom/press-releases/3158-2022-10-07-bis-press-release-advanced-computing-and-semiconductor-manufacturing-controls-final/file.

Byun, Duk-kun. "S. Korea, U.S. Hold Inaugural Economic Security Dialogue in Washington." Yonhap News Agency, July 8, 2022. https://en.yna.co.kr/view/AEN20220708000300325.

Caballero, Juan, and Marco Fengler. "China and India: The Future of the Global Consumer Market." Brookings Institution, April 14, 2023. https://www.brookings.edu/articles/china-and-india-the-future-of-the-global-consumer-market/.

Campbell, Kurt M., and Ely Ratner. "The China Reckoning: How Beijing Defied American Expectations." *Foreign Affairs* 97, no. 2 (2018): 60–70. https://www.foreignaffairs.com/articles/china/2018-02-13/china-reckoning.

Cao, Liangyue, and Jared Greenville. "Understanding How China's Tariff on Australian Barley Exports Will Affect the Agricultural Sector." Australian Government Department of Agriculture, Fisheries and Forestry, 2020. https://www.agriculture.gov.au/abares/research-topics/trade/understanding-chinas-tariff-on-australian-barley.

Cebu News. 2012. "Chinese Agencies Suspend Phl Tours." May 11, 2012. https://www.philstar.com/cebu-news/2012/05/11/805553/chinese-agencies-suspend-phl-tours.

Center for Strategic and International Studies. "Economic Security: Perspectives from Seoul and Washington." February 23, 2023. YouTube video, 2:20:50–2:21:47. https://www.youtube.com/watch?v=AtqntHb5Iro.

——. "Keynote Address by Wang Yunjong at ROK-U.S. Strategic Forum 2022." June 6, 2022. https://www.csis.org/analysis/keynote-address-wang-yunjong-rok-us-strategic-forum-2022.

Cha, Dae-Woon. "Baeteoliyong lityum·heug-yeonseo huitolyukkaji . . . haegsimgwangmul 'taljung-gug' sidong" 배터리용 리튬·흑연서 회토류까지... 핵심광물 '탈중국' 시동 [From lithium and graphite for batteries to rare earths . . . The shift away from China for key minerals begins]. Yonhap News Agency, March 13, 2024. https://www.yna.co.kr/view/AKR20240312125500003?input=1195m.

Cha, Victor D. "Collective Resilience: Deterring China's Weaponization of Economic Interdependence." *International Security* 48, no. 1 (2023): 91–124.

——. "How to Stop Chinese Coercion: The Case for Collective Resilience." *Foreign Affairs* 102, no. 1 (2023). https://www.foreignaffairs.com/world/how-stop-china-coercion-collective-resilience-victor-cha.

——. *The Impossible State: North Korea, Past and Future.* New York: HarperCollins, 2012.

Cha, Victor D., Kristi Govella, and William Alan Reinsch. "Korea, Japan, and the Tariff War." *CSIS The Impossible State*, Podcast audio, April 21, 2025. https://www.csis.org/podcasts/impossible-state/korea-japan-and-tariff-war.

Cha, Victor D., and Andy Lim. "Flagrant Foul: China's Predatory Liberalism and the NBA." *Washington Quarterly* 42, no. 4 (2019): 23–42.

Chan, Sewell. "Norway and China Restore Ties, 6 Years After Nobel Prize Dispute." *New York Times*, December 19, 2016. https://www.nytimes.com/2016/12/19/world/europe/china-norway-nobel-liu-xiaobo.html.

Chang, Charles, Diego Ocampo, Claire Yuan, Annie Ao, Stephen Chan, and Avery Chen. "China's Global Reach Grows Behind Critical Minerals." S&P Global, August 2023. https://www.spglobal.com/content/dam/spglobal/corporate/en/images/general/special-editorial/082423-china-s-global-reach-grows-behind-critical-minerals.pdf.

Charania, Shams. "Charania: Inside What Went On Among Nets and Lakers Players on the Ground in China Amid the NBA China Conflict." *Athletic*, October 14, 2019. https://theathletic.com/1281993/2019/10/14/charania-inside-what-went-on-among-netsand-lakers-players-on-the-ground-in-china-amid-the-nba-china-conflict/.

Chen, Xiawen, and Roberto Javier Garcia. "Economic Sanctions and Trade Diplomacy: Sanction-Busting Strategies, Market Distortion, and Efficacy of China's Restrictions on Norwegian Salmon Imports." *China Information* 30, no. 1 (2016): 29–57.

Cheng, Ting-fang, and Lauly Li. "Netherlands' Chip Tool Export Controls Take Effect: 4 Things to Know." *Nikkei Asia*, August 31, 2023. https://asia.nikkei.com/Business/Tech/Semiconductors/Netherlands-chip-tool-export-controls-take-effect-4-things-to-know.

Chien, Amy Chang. "First Pineapples, Now Fish: To Pressure Taiwan, China Flexes Economic Muscle." *New York Times*, June 22, 2022. https://www.nytimes.com/2022/06/22/business/china-taiwan-grouper-ban.html.

China Daily. "A Dangerous Delusion." May 10, 2012. https://www.china.org.cn/opinion/2012-05/10/content_25347880.htm.

——. "Premier: We All Know Why." February 3, 2009. https://www.chinadaily.com.cn/china/2009-02/03/content_7440286.htm.

China Energy Storage Alliance. "China's First Vanadium Battery Industry-Specific Policy Issued." May 16, 2024. https://en.cnesa.org/new-blog/2024/5/16/chinas-first-vanadium-battery-industry-specific-policy-issued.

Chou, Cybil. "Taiwan Visit Shows Czech Republic Can Resist China Retaliation." *Nikkei Asia*, September 7, 2020. https://asia.nikkei.com/Politics/International-relations/Taiwan-visit-shows-Czech-Republic-can-resist-China-retaliation.

Chou, William. "Japan's Strategy for Economic Security: An Interview with Deputy LDP Secretary-General Keitaro Ohno." Hudson Institute, July 23, 2024. https://www.hudson.org/economics/japans-strategy-economic-security-interview-deputy-ldp-secretary-general-keitaro-ohno.

Chow, Vivienne. "HBO's Site Remains Blocked in China but Its Shows Aren't." *Variety*, June 27, 2018. https://variety.com/2018/tv/news/john-oliver-hbo-china-game-of-thrones-website-1202859077/.

Christensen, Thomas J. "Mutually Assured Disruption: Globalization, Security, and the Dangers of Decoupling." *World Politics* 75, no. 5 (2023): 1–18.

Chu, Mei Mei, and Nigel Hunt. "China's Probes on EU Products Following EV Tariffs." Reuters, August 21, 2024. https://www.reuters.com/business/chinas-potential-probes-eu-firms-following-ev-tariffs-2024-06-14/.

Chu, Shulong, and Xinzhu Lin. "The Six Party Talks: A Chinese Perspective." *Asian Perspective* 32, no. 4 (2008): 29–43.

Chung, Jake. "Czech Magnate Buys Piano Order Canceled by PRC." *Taipei Times*, September 10, 2020. https://www.taipeitimes.com/News/front/archives/2020/09/10/2003743138/.

——. "Lithuania Plans to Open Office in Taiwan: Report." *Taipei Times*, March 4, 2021. https://www.taipeitimes.com/News/front/archives/2021/03/04/2003753209.

Cimino-Issacs, Cathleen, and Karen M. Sutter. "Regulation of U.S. Outbound Investment to China." Congressional Research Service, August 12, 2024. https://crsreports.congress.gov/product/pdf/IF/IF12629.

Clarke, Michael. "The Belt and Road Initiative: China's New Grand Strategy?" *Asia Policy* 24 (2017): 71–79.

Clifford, Stephanie. "Olympic Protests Put CocaCola in a Quandary." *New York Times*, April 17, 2008. https://www.nytimes.com/2008/04/17/business/worldbusiness/17iht-coke.1.12085208.html.

CNBC. "Australia Orders Chinese Investors to Sell Down Stake in Rare Earths Miner." CNBC, June 3, 2024. https://www.cnbc.com/2024/06/03/australia-orders-chinese-investors-to-sell-down-stake-in-rare-earths-miner.html.

Congress.gov. "H.R.3684—Infrastructure Investment and Jobs Act." November 15, 2021. https://www.congress.gov/bill/117th-congress/house-bill/3684.

——. "H.R.5376—Inflation Reduction Act of 2022." August 16, 2022. https://www.congress.gov/bill/117th-congress/house-bill/5376/text.

——. "H.R.5580—Countering China Economic Coercion Act." October 15, 2021. https://www.congress.gov/bill/117th-congress/house-bill/5580/text.

——. "H.R. 7776—James M. Inhofe National Defense Authorization Act for Fiscal Year 2023." December 23, 2022. https://www.congress.gov/bill/117th-congress/house-bill/7776/text.

——. "S.4514—Countering Economic Coercion Act of 2022." July 13, 2022. https://www.congress.gov/bill/117th-congress/senate-bill/4514/text.

Conifer, Dan. "China Imposes 80pc Tariff on Australian Barley for Next Five Years Amid Global Push for Coronavirus Investigation." ABC News, May 18, 2020. https://www.abc.net.au/news/2020-05-18/china-to-impose-tariffs-on-australian-barley/12261108.

Conte, Niccolo. "Ranked: The World's Biggest Steel Producers, by Country." Visual Capitalist, May 19, 2023. https://www.visualcapitalist.com/biggest-steel-producers-country/.

Cook, Cynthia, Gregory Sanders, Alexander Holderness, John Schaus, Nicholas Velazquez, Audrey Aldisert, Henry H. Carroll, and Emily Hardesty. "Expanding the Tool Kit to Counter China's Economic Coercion." Center for Strategic and International Studies, May 6, 2024. https://www.csis.org/analysis/expanding-tool-kit-counter-chinas-economic-coercion.

Costello, Ryan. "Republicans Must Fix, Not Repeal, the Inflation Reduction Act." *The Hill*, August 14, 2024. https://thehill.com/opinion/4826275-ira-china-dispute-clean-energy/.

Cotton, Tom. "Cotton, Colleagues Introduce Bill to End China's Permanent Normal Trade Status." Tom Cotton, January 26, 2023. https://www.cotton.senate.gov/news/press-releases/cotton-colleagues-introduce-bill-to-end-chinas-permanent-normal-trade-status.

Crane, Emily. "Kodak Bends to China by Deleting Instagram Post by French Photographer Who Called the Xinjiang Region—Where Beijing Is Accused of Human Rights Abuses—an 'Orwellian Dystopia.'" *Daily Mail*, July 21, 2021. https://www.dailymail.co.uk/news/article-9811531/Kodak-deletes-Instagram-post-calling-Chinas-Xinjiang-Orwellian-dystopia.html.

Cuneta, Josephine, and James Hookway. "China Dispute Threatens Philippine Industries." *Wall Street Journal*, May 16, 2012. https://www.wsj.com/articles/SB10001424052702303879604577407730408858666.

Cytera, Christopher. "Gallium, Germanium, and China—The Minerals Inflaming the Global Chip War." Center for European Policy Analysis, August 8, 2023. https://cepa.org/article/china-gallium-and-germanium-the-minerals-inflaming-the-global-chip-war/.

Davies, Christian, Jung-a Song, Kana Inagaki, and Richard Waters. "US Struggles to Mobilise Its East Asian 'Chip 4' Alliance." *Financial Times*, September 12, 2022. https://www.ft.com/content/98f22615-ee7e-4431-ab98-fb6e3f9de032.

Davis, Rebecca. "China Celebrities Stoke Nationalist Firestorm Against Foreign Brands Concerned by Xinjiang." *Variety*, March 26, 2021. https://variety.com/2021/film/news/china-celebrities-stoke-nationalist-backlash-against-xinjiang-criticism-1234938619/.

Dempsey, Harry. "China Leads Rise in Export Restrictions on Critical Minerals, OECD Says." *Financial Times*, April 11, 2023. https://www.ft.com/content/198b6824-21d6-4633-9a97-00164d23c13f.

Dempsey, Harry, and Joseph Cotterill. "How China Is Winning the Race for Africa's Lithium." *Financial Times*, April 3, 2023. https://www.ft.com/content/02d6f35d-e646-40f7-894c-ffcc6acd9b25?shareType=nongift.

Dengler, Roni. "Global Trove of Rare Earth Metals Found in Japan's Deep-Sea Mud." *Science*, April 13, 2018. https://www.science.org/content/article/global-trove-rare-earth-metals-found-japans-deep-sea-mud.

Department of Industry, Science and Resources. "Australia's Critical Minerals List and Strategic Materials List." Australian Government, February 20, 2024. https://www.industry.gov.au/publications/australias-critical-minerals-list-and-strategic-materials-list.

Deveikis, Jonas. "China Sanctions vs Taiwan Investments—Lithuania's Central Bank Weighs Economic Impact." LRT, January 21, 2022. https://www.lrt.lt/en/news-in-english/19/1593215/china-sanctions-vs-taiwan-investments-lithuania-s-central-bank-weighs-economic-impact.

Drezner, Daniel W. "Sanctions Sometimes Smart: Targeted Sanctions in Theory and Practice." *International Studies Review* 13, no. 1 (2011): 96–108.

——. "The Uses and Abuses of Weaponized Interdependence in 2021." *Washington Post*, March 2, 2021. https://www.washingtonpost.com/outlook/2021/03/02/uses-abuses-weaponized-interdependence-2021/.

Drezner, Daniel W., Henry Farrell, and Abraham Newman, eds. *The Uses and Abuses of Weaponized Interdependence*. Washington, DC: Brookings Institution Press, 2021.

Drury, A. Cooper. "Sanctions as Coercive Diplomacy: The U.S. President's Decision to Initiate Economic Sanctions." *Political Research Quarterly* 54, no. 3 (2001): 485–508.

Dunne, Brendan. "Dwyane Wade on Li-Ning, Way of Wade, Recruiting His Son, and Sneakers in China." Complex, November 10, 2021. https://www.complex.com/sneakers/a/brendan-dunne/dwyane-wade-li-ning-way-of-wade-zaire-china-sneakers.

DW. "Czech Republic Delegation in Taiwan Draws Ire of China." August 31, 2020. https://www.dw.com/en/czech-china-taiwan/a-54764477.

——. "'I Am Taiwanese:' Top Czech Official Angers China in Taipei." September 1, 2020. https://www.dw.com/en/i-am-taiwanese-czech-official-angers-china-after-taipei-speech/a-54781326.

Early, Bryan R., and Menevis Cilizoglu. "Economic Sanctions in Flux: Enduring Challenges, New Policies, and Defining the Future Research Agenda." *International Studies Perspectives* 21, no. 4 (2020): 438–477.

Economist. "How Sweden Copes with Chinese Bullying." February 20, 2020. www.economist.com/europe/2020/02/20/how-sweden-copes-with-chinese-bullying.

Economy, Elizabeth. *The World According to China*. Cambridge: Polity, 2022.

——. "Xi Jinping's New World Order." *Foreign Affairs* 101, no. 1 (2022). https://www.foreignaffairs.com/china/xi-jinpings-new-world-order.

Emont, Jon. "China Tightens Critical-Mineral Export Controls." *Wall Street Journal*, February 4, 2025. https://www.wsj.com/livecoverage/trump-tariffs-us-trade-stock-market-02-04-2025/card/china-restricts-exports-of-critical-minerals-in-retaliatory-move-e8omEEQJLU911Z1jt4gT.

Eppers, Matt. "Rockets' James Harden on NBAChina Dispute: 'I'm Staying Out of It.'" *USA Today*, October 13, 2019. https://www.usatoday.com/story/sports/nba/rockets/2019/10/13/james-harden-nba-china-dispute/3971503002/.

ESPN. "Adam Silver Supports Free Speech Rights of Rockets GM Daryl Morey." October 7, 2019. https://www.espn.com/nba/story/_/id/27792662/adam-silver-supports-free-speech-rights-houston-rockets-gm-daryl-morey.

——. "Dwyane Wade Inks Lifetime Deal with Chinese Apparel Company LiNing." July 18, 2018. https://www.espn.com/nba/story/_/id/24130508/dwyane-wade-signs-life-deal-chinese-apparel-company-li-ning.

——. "Lakers' NBA Cares Event in Shanghai Canceled Amid China Rift." October 9, 2019. https://www.espn.com/nba/story/_/id/27803863/lakers-nba-cares-event-shanghaicanceled-amid-china-rift.

——. "NBA, China's Tencent Extend Partnership 5 Years." July 28, 2019. https://www.espn.com/nba/story/_/id/27277771/nba-china-tencent-extend-partnership-5-years.

Euractiv. "Lithuania to Support 'Those Fighting for Freedom' in Taiwan." November 9, 2020. https://www.euractiv.com/section/china/news/lithuania-to-support-those-fighting-for-freedom-in-taiwan/.

European Commission. "2022 State of the Union Address by President von der Leyen." September 14, 2022. https://ec.europa.eu/commission/presscorner/detail/ov/SPEECH_22_5493.

——. "Commission Calls on Member States to Review Outbound Investments and Assess Risks to Economic Security." January 14, 2025. Updated January 15, 2025. https://ec.europa.eu/commission/presscorner/detail/en/ip_25_261.

——. "Commission Launches Chips Joint Undertaking Under the European Chips Act." November 30, 2023. https://ec.europa.eu/commission/presscorner/detail/en/ip_23_6167.

——. "Commission Proposes New Initiatives to Strengthen Economic Security." January 24, 2024. https://ec.europa.eu/commission/presscorner/detail/en/IP_24_363.

——. "Critical Raw Materials: Ensuring Secure and Sustainable Supply Chains for EU's Green and Digital Future." March 16, 2023. https://ec.europa.eu/commission/presscorner/detail/en/ip_23_1661.

——. "Digital Sovereignty: European Chips Act Enters Into Force Today." September 21, 2023. https://ec.europa.eu/commission/presscorner/detail/en/ip_23_4518.

——. "European Chips Act: Commission Launches Pilot System to Monitor Semiconductor Supply Chain." May 10, 2023. https://digital-strategy.ec.europa.eu/en/news/european-chips-act-commission-launches-pilot-system-monitor-semiconductor-supply-chain.

——. "European Industrial Strategy." n.d. https://commission.europa.eu/strategy-and-policy/priorities-2019-2024/europe-fit-digital-age/european-industrial-strategy_en.

——. "In-Depth Reviews of Strategic Areas for Europe's Interests." n.d. https://commission.europa.eu/strategy-and-policy/priorities-2019-2024/europe-fit-digital-age/european-industrial-strategy/depth-reviews-strategic-areas-europes-interests_en.

——. "Joint Communication to the European Parliament, the European Council and the Council on European Economic Security." June 20, 2023. https://eur-lex.europa.eu/legal-content/EN/TXT/?uri=CELEX%3A52023JC0020&qid=1687525961309.

——. "New Tool to Enable EU to Withstand Economic Coercion Enters Into Force." December 27, 2023. https://ec.europa.eu/commission/presscorner/detail/en/ip_23_6804.

——. "Questions and Answers on the European Critical Raw Materials Act." March 16, 2023. https://ec.europa.eu/commission/presscorner/detail/en/qanda_23_1662.

——. "RMIS—Raw Materials Information System." n.d. https://rmis.jrc.ec.europa.eu/eu-critical-raw-materials.

——. "Statement by Executive VicePresident Valdis Dombrovskis on Launch of Case at World Trade Organization." January 27, 2022. https://ec.europa.eu/commission/presscorner/detail/en/statement_22_7976.

European Council. "2021 G7 Leaders' Communiqué: Our Shared Agenda for Global Action to Build Back Better." June 13, 2021. https://www.consilium.europa.eu/en/press/press-releases/2021/06/13/2021-g7-leaders-communique/.

European Customs Portal. "HS Code 81059000—Cobalt Articles Not Elsewhere Specified." 2024. https://www.tariffnumber.com/2024/81059000#google_vignette.

European Parliament. "Expansion of BRICS: A Quest for Greater Global Influence?" March 15, 2024. https://www.europarl.europa.eu/thinktank/en/document/EPRS_BRI(2024)760368.

European Union. "AntiCoercion Instrument." n.d. https://trade.ec.europa.eu/access-to-markets/en/content/anti-coercion-instrument.

——. "Chips Joint Undertaking." n.d. https://european-union.europa.eu/institutions-law-budget/institutions-and-bodies/search-all-eu-institutions-and-bodies/chips-joint-undertaking_en.

——. "European Chips Act." n.d. https://commission.europa.eu/strategy-and-policy/priorities-2019-2024/europe-fit-digital-age/european-chips-act_en.

——. "Joint Declaration of the Commission, the Council and the European Parliament on an Instrument to Deter and Counteract Coercive Actions by Third Countries." Document 32021C0212(01), 2021. https://eur-lex.europa.eu/legal-content/EN/TXT/?uri=uriserv%3AOJ.C_.2021.049.01.0001.01.ENG&toc=OJ%3AC%3A2021%3A049%3ATOC.

——. "Questions & Answers Regarding AntiCoercion Instrument." n.d. https://policy.trade.ec.europa.eu/enforcement-and-protection/protecting-against-coercion/qa-regarding-anti-coercion-instrument_en.

——. Regulation (EU) 2023/2675 of the European Parliament and of the Council of 22 November 2023 on the Protection of the Union and its Member States from Economic Coercion by Third Countries. https://eur-lex.europa.eu/eli/reg/2023/2675/oj/eng.

Evans, Zachary. "Sony Refuses Chinese Demand to Delete Statue of Liberty from Latest Spiderman." *National Review*, May 2, 2022. https://www.nationalreview.com/news/sony-refuses-chinese-demand-to-delete-statue-of-liberty-from-latest-spider-man/.

Exiger. "China Announces Export Controls on Five Critical Minerals." February 12, 2025. https://www.exiger.com/perspectives/critical-minerals-export-controls/#:~:text=China's%20new%20export%20controls%20require,90%25%20of%20the%20world's%20mining.

Fainaru-Wada, Mark, and Steve Fainaru. "ESPN Analysis: NBA Owners, Mum on China Relationship, Have More Than $10 Billion Invested There." ESPN, May 19, 2022. https://www.espn.com/nba/story/_/id/33938932/nba-owners-mum-china-relationship-more-10-billion-invested-there.

Farrell, Henry, and Abraham Newman. *Underground Empire: How America Weaponized the World Economy*. New York: Holt, 2023.

——. "Weaponized Interdependence: How Global Economic Networks Shape State Coercion." *International Security* 44, no. 1 (2019): 42–79.

Federal Register. "Addressing the Threat to the Domestic Supply Chain from Reliance on Critical Minerals from Foreign Adversaries and Supporting the Domestic Mining and Processing Industries." October 5, 2020. https://www.federalregister.gov/documents/2020/10/05/2020-22064/addressing-the-threat-to-the-domestic-supply-chain-from-reliance-on-critical-minerals-from-foreign.

——. "America's Supply Chains." February 24, 2021. https://www.federalregister.gov/documents/2021/03/01/2021-04280/americas-supply-chains.

——. "A Federal Strategy to Ensure Secure and Reliable Supplies of Critical Minerals." December 20, 2017. https://www.federalregister.gov/documents/2017/12/26/2017-27899/a-federal-strategy-to-ensure-secure-and-reliable-supplies-of-critical-minerals.

——. "Finding That Banco Delta Asia SARL Is a Financial Institution of Primary Money Laundering Concern." September 20, 2005. https://www.federalregister.gov/documents/2005/09/20/05-18660/finding-that-banco-delta-asia-sarl-is-a-financial-institution-of-primary-money-laundering-concern.

Feng, Kechang. "'Rumor Debunking' as a Propaganda and Censorship Strategy in China." In *Disinformation in the Global South*, ed. Herman Wasserman and Dani Madrid-Morales, 108–122. New York: Wiley, 2022.

Fengler, Wolfgang, Homi Kharas, Juan Caballero, and Luis Simoes. "How the World Consumer Class Will Grow from 4 Billion to 5 Billion People by 2031." Brookings Institution, July 25, 2023. https://www.brookings.edu/articles/how-the-world-consumer-class-will-grow-from-4-billion-to-5-billion-people-by-2031/.

Ferchen, Matt. "The Two Faces of the China Model: The BRI in Southeast Asia." In *Global Perspectives on China's Belt and Road Initiative: Asserting Agency through Regional Connectivity*, ed. Florian Schneider, 245–264. Amsterdam: Amsterdam University Press, 2021.

Fish, Isaac Stone. "Top Gun: Maverick Betrays Hollywood's Weakness in China." BBC, June 8, 2022. https://www.bbc.com/news/world-us-canada-61710500.

Fish, Mike, and Michael A. Fletcher. "NBA Players Face Questions Over Shoe Deals with Chinese Companies Linked to Forced Labor." ESPN, January 28, 2022. https://www.espn.com/nba/story/_/id/33140405/nba-players-face-questions-shoe-deals-chinese-companies-linked-forced-labor.

Food and Agriculture Organization. *Banana Market Review and Banana Statistics 2012–2013*. Rome: Food and Agriculture Organization of the United Nations, 2014.

——. *Banana Market Review 2022*. Rome: Food and Agriculture Organization of the United Nations, 2023.

Fonrouge, Gabrielle. "How Calvin Klein and Tommy Hilfiger Got Caught in Trump's Trade War with China." CNBC, February 6, 2025. https://www.cnbc.com/2025/02/06/calvin-klein-owner-pvh-blacklisted-in-china.html.

Ford, Alessandro. "China Hits Back at Electric Vehicle Tariffs with Probe Into EU Dairy." Politico, August 21, 2024. https://www.politico.eu/article/china-hits-back-at-electric-vehicle-tariffs-with-probe-into-eu-dairy/.

Fortune. "Fortune 500." n.d. https://fortune.com/ranking/fortune500/.

——. "Fortune Global 500." n.d. https://fortune.com/ranking/global500/.

Fowler, Elouise. "China Linked Investors Forced to Offload Northern Minerals Shares." *Financial Review*, June 4, 2024. https://www.afr.com/companies/mining/chinese-linked-investors-forced-to-offload-northern-minerals-shares-20240603-p5jips.

France 24. "Anti-French Protests Sweep Across China." April 19, 2008. https://www.france24.com/en/20080419-anti-french-protests-sweep-across-china-china-france.

——. "Despite Praise for Covid19 Response, Taiwan Barred from WHO Assembly." May 18, 2020. https://www.france24.com/en/20200518-despite-praise-for-covid-19-response-taiwan-barred-from-who-assembly.

Freudlsperger, Christian, and Sophie Meunier. "When Foreign Policy Becomes Trade Policy: The EU's Anti-Coercion Instrument." *JCMS: Journal of Common Market Studies* 62, no. 4 (2024): 1063–1079.

Friedberg, Aaron. "Stopping the Next China Shock." *Foreign Affairs* 103, no. 5 (2024): 177–189. https://www.foreignaffairs.com/china/stopping-next-china-shock-friedberg.

Friedman, Milton. "A Friedman Doctrine—The Social Responsibility of Business Is to Increase Its Profits." *New York Times*, September 13, 1970. https://www.nytimes.com/1970/09/13/archives/a-friedman-doctrine-the-social-responsibility-of-business-is-to.html.

Friedman, Thomas. *The World Is Flat: A Brief History of the Twenty-First Century*. New York: Farrar, Straus and Giroux, 2005.

Frydenberg, Josh. "Building Resilience and the Return of Strategic Competition, Melbourne." Ministers: Treasury Portfolio, September 6, 2021. https://web.archive.org/web/20250324072450/https://ministers.treasury.gov.au/ministers/josh-frydenberg-2018/speeches/building-resilience-and-return-strategic-competition.

Fuchs, Andreas, and Nils-Hendrik Klann. "Paying a Visit: The Dalai Lama Effect on International Trade." Center for European Governance and Economic Development Research Paper no. 113 (2010).

Funaiole, Matthew P., Brian Hart, and Aidan Powers-Riggs. "Mineral Monopoly: China's Control Over Gallium Is a National Security Threat." Center for Strategic and International Studies, July 18, 2023. https://features.csis.org/hiddenreach/china-critical-mineral-gallium/.

G7 Italia. "About the G7." n.d. https://www.g7italy.it/en/about-g7/.

——. "Apulia G7 Leaders' Communiqué." June 14, 2024. https://www.g7italy.it/wp-content/uploads/Apulia-G7-Leaders-Communique.pdf.

G7 Ministers' Meeting on Climate, Energy and Environment. "Five-Point Plan for Critical Minerals Security." 2023. https://www.meti.go.jp/information/g7hirosima/energy/pdf/Annex005.pdf.

Gabuev, Alexander, and Oliver Stuenkel. "The Battle for the BRICS." *Foreign Affairs*, published online September 24, 2024. https://www.foreignaffairs.com/russia/battle-brics.

Gaddis, John L. *The Long Peace: Inquiries Into the History of the Cold War.* New York: Oxford University Press, 1987.

——. *Strategies of Containment: A Critical Appraisal of Postwar American National Security Policy During the Cold War.* New York: Oxford University Press, 2023.

Galtung, Johan. "On the Effect of International Economic Sanctions: With Examples from the Case of Rhodesia." *World Politics* 19, no. 3 (1967): 378–416.

Gan, Nectar, "China Isn't Getting Rid of Its Controls over Rare Earths, Despite Trade Truce with US." CNN, May 20, 2025. https://www.cnn.com/2025/05/20/business/china-rare-earth-export-controls-analysis-intl-hnk.

Garcia, Roberto Javier, and Thi Ngan Giang Nguyen. "Market Integration Through Smuggling: China's Sanction on Norwegian Salmon." *Journal of Economic Integration* 38, no. 1 (2023): 93–114.

Geneva Trade Platform. "MultiParty Interim Appeal Arbitration Arrangement (MPIA)." https://wtoplurilaterals.info/plural_initiative/the-mpia/.

George, Alexander L., and Richard Smoke. *Deterrence in American Foreign Policy: Theory and Practice.* New York: Columbia University Press, 1974.

Gerlo, Julia, and Marius Troost. "The Foreign Financiers of Argentina's Lithium Rush: Export Credit Agencies' Support for Lithium Mining." Both Ends & FARN, October 2023. https://www.bothends.org/uploaded_files/document/The_foreign_financiers_of_Argentina_s_lithium_rush.pdf.

Gholz, Eugene, and Llewelyn Hughes. "Market Structure and Economic Sanctions: The 2010 Rare Earth Elements Episode as a Pathway Case of Market Adjustment." *Review of International Political Economy* 23, no. 3 (2019): 611–634.

Glasby, Matt. "Bad Guys Changed from Chinese to North Korean in Red Dawn Remake at the Height of Hollywood Appeasing China in 2012—But It Still Flopped." *South China Morning Post*, September 2, 2022. https://www.scmp.com/lifestyle/entertainment/article/3190918/bad-guys-changed-chinese-north-korean-red-dawn-remake.

Glaser, Bonnie S. "Time for Collective Pushback Against China's Economic Coercion." Center for Strategic and International Studies, January 13, 2021. https://www.csis.org/analysis/time-collective-pushback-against-chinas-economic-coercion.

Glaser, Bonnie S., and Abigail Wulf. "China's Role in Critical Mineral Supply Chains." German Marshall Fund, August 2, 2023. https://www.gmfus.org/news/chinas-role-critical-mineral-supply-chains.

Global Times. "CBA, Sponsors Halt Cooperation with Houston Rockets After GM Tweets Supporting HK Riots." October 6, 2019. https://www.globaltimes.cn/content/1166090.shtml.

——. "Norway Understands Mutual Respect Six Years Later." December 20, 2016. https://www.globaltimes.cn/page/201612/1024603.shtml.

——. "Update: Evergreen Laurel Hotel's Apology Fails to Appease Angry Netizens Following Flag Controversy." August 15, 2024. https://www.globaltimes.cn/page/202408/1318119.shtml.

Global Times @globaltimesnews. "Freedom of Speech Is Never Free. The #NBA Incident with China Might Help the Western World to at Least Pay Attention to What and How Chinese Ordinary People, Including Basketball Fans, Feel About #HK Riots and Why They Are Offended." X (formerly Twitter), October 8, 2019, 5:40 pm. https://twitter.com/globaltimesnews/status/1181731004031148033.

GMA News. "China's New Complaint About Bugs in PHL Fruits Puzzles Agriculture Exec." May 16, 2012. https://www.gmanetwork.com/news/money/content/258351/china-s-new-complaint-about-bugs-in-phl-fruits-puzzles-agriculture-exec/story/.

Godek, Sarah. "Why China's Export Controls on Germanium and Gallium May Not Be Effective." Stimson, July 19, 2023. https://www.stimson.org/2023/why-chinas-export-controls-on-germanium-and-gallium-may-not-be-effective/.

Goh, Norman. "Malaysia to Allow Exports of Processed Rare Earths: Minister." *Nikkei Asia*, October 24, 2023. https://asia.nikkei.com/Economy/Trade/Malaysia-to-allow-exports-of-processed-rare-earths-minister.

Gong, Xue. "China's Economic Statecraft: The Belt and Road in Southeast Asia and the Impact on the Indo-Pacific." *Security Challenges* 16, no. 3 (2020): 39–46.

Goodman, Peter S. "China's Nickel Plants in Indonesia Created Needed Jobs, and Pollution." *New York Times*, April 18, 2023. https://www.nytimes.com/2023/08/18/business/indonesia-nickel-sulawesi-china.html.

Goodman, Samuel M., Dan Kim, and John VerWey. "The South Korea–Japan Trade Dispute in Context: Semiconductor Manufacturing, Chemicals, and Concentrated Supply Chains." Office of Industries Working Paper, U.S. International Trade Commission, October 2019. https://www.usitc.gov/publications/332/working_papers/the_south_korea-japan_trade_dispute_in_context_semiconductor_manufacturing_chemicals_and_concentrated_supply_chains.pdf.

Government of the United Kingdom. "Foreign Secretary Liz Truss' Speech to the Lowy Institute." January 21, 2022. https://www.gov.uk/government/speeches/foreign-secretarys-speech-to-the-lowy-institute.

Green, Michael, Kathleen Hicks, Zack Cooper, John Schaus, and Jake Douglas. "Counter-Coercion Series: Scarborough Shoal Standoff." Center for Strategic and International Studies, May 22, 2017. https://amti.csis.org/counter-co-scarborough-standoff/.

Gregory, Sean. " 'The Losses Have Already Been Substantial.' Adam Silver Addresses Fallout from the NBAChina Controversy." *Time*, October 17, 2019. https://time.com/5703259/adam-silver-nba-china-time-100-health-summit/.

Grohol, Milan, and Constanze Veeh. *Study on the Critical Raw Materials for the EU 2023*. European Union, 2023. https://data.europa.eu/doi/10.2873/725585.

Grove, Rashad. "Dwyane Wade's 'Statue' Sneakers Drop This Saturday." *Sports Illustrated*, October 28, 2024. https://www.si.com/fannation/sneakers/news/dwyane-wade-statue-sneakers-drop-this-saturday.

Guardian. "China Drops Philadelphia 76ers Broadcasts as Hong Kong Row Continues." December 30, 2020. www.theguardian.com/sport/2020/dec/30/china-drops-76ers-broadcasts-daryl-morey.

——. "Gap Sorry for Selling T-Shirt with 'Incorrect' Map of China." May 14, 2019. www.theguardian.com/world/2018/may/15/gap-sorry-t-shirt-map-china.

——. "Quad countries agree to diversify critical mineral supplies amid China concerns." July 2, 2025. https://www.theguardian.com/world/2025/jul/02/quad-countries-agree-to-diversify-critical-mineral-supplies-amid-china-concerns.

Haas, Benjamin. "Emirates Tells Cabin Crew to Swap Taiwanese Flag Pins for Chinese Ones." *Guardian*, May 31, 2017. https://www.theguardian.com/world/2017/may/31/emirates-taiwanese-chinese-flag-pins-one-china-policy.

——. "Marriott Apologizes to China Over Tibet and Taiwan Error." *Guardian*, January 12, 2018. https://www.theguardian.com/world/2018/jan/12/marriott-apologises-to-china-over-tibet-and-taiwan-error.

Haass, Richard. *Economic Sanctions and American Diplomacy*. New York: Council on Foreign Relations, 1998.

Hackenbroich, Jonathan, and Pawel Zerka. "Measured Response: How to Design a European Instrument Against Economic Coercion." European Council on Foreign Relations, June 23, 2021. https://ecfr.eu/publication/measured-response-how-to-design-a-european-instrument-against-economic-coercion/.

Hackenbroich, Jonathan, Janka Oertel, Philipp Sander, and Pawel Zerka. "Defending Europe's Economic Sovereignty: New Ways to Resist Economic Coercion." European Council on Foreign Relations,

October 20, 2020. https://ecfr.eu/publication/defending_europe_economic_sovereignty_new_ways
_to_resist_economic_coercion/.

Hamre, John J., Victor Cha, Emily Benson, Max Bergmann, Erin L. Murphy, and Caitlin Welsh. "'Bending' the Architecture: Reimagining the G7." Center for Strategic and International Studies, June 12,
2024. https://www.csis.org/analysis/bending-architecture-reimagining-g7.

Hanafusa, Ryosuke. "Japan to Pour Investment Into Non-China Rare Earth Projects." *Nikkei Asia*, February 15, 2020. https://asia.nikkei.com/Politics/International-relations/Japan-to-pour-investment-into
-non-China-rare-earth-projects.

Hao, Karen. "Nancy Pelosi Kicks Off Taiwan Visit Reaffirming U.S. Ties with the Island." *Wall Street
Journal*, August 2, 2022. https://www.wsj.com/livecoverage/nancy-pelosi-taiwan-visit-china-us
-tensions/card/nancy-pelosi-kicks-off-taiwan-visit-reaffirming-u-s-ties-with-the-island
-iWvv9B4jVHenUIXagMr2.

Harrell, Peter, and Elizabeth Rosenberg. "Economic Dominance, Financial Technology and the Future
of U.S. Economic Coercion." Center for a New American Security, April 29, 2019. https://www.cnas
.org/publications/reports/economic-dominance-financial-technology-and-the-future-of-u-s
-economic-coercion.

Hawley, Josh. "Hawley Announces First Bill in Worker's Agenda to Rebuild America: Ending Normal
Trade Relations with China Act." March 20, 2023. https://www.hawley.senate.gov/hawley-announces
-first-bill-workers-agenda-rebuild-america-ending-normal-trade-relations-china-act/.

He, Laura. "China Hits Taiwan with Trade Restrictions After Pelosi Visit." CNN, August 3, 2022. https://
www.cnn.com/2022/08/03/economy/china-suspends-imports-taiwan-products-intl-hnk/.

Helper, Susan, and Evan Soltas. "Why the Pandemic Has Disrupted Supply Chains." The White House,
June 17, 2021. https://bidenwhitehouse.archives.gov/cea/written-materials/2021/06/17/why-the
-pandemic-has-disrupted-supply-chains/.

Henschen, Horst, Ross Evans, Martin Juhasz, and Michelle Adam. "Outbound Investment Screening in
the EU—A Major Step Forward?" Covington, February 14, 2024. https://www.covcompetition.com
/2024/02/outbound-investment-screening-in-the-eu-a-major-step-forward/.

Herranz-Surrallés, Anna, Chad Damro, and Sandra Eckert. "The Geoeconomic Turn of the Single European Market? Conceptual Challenges and Empirical Trends." *JCMS: Journal of Common Market
Studies* 62, no. 4 (2024): 919–937.

Hey, John. "China Gets Strict on Philippine Bananas." Asiafruit, March 9, 2012. https://www.fruitnet.com
/asiafruit/china-gets-strict-on-philippine-bananas/13621.article.

Higgins, Andrew. "In Philippines, Banana Growers Feel Effect of South China Sea Dispute." *Washington
Post*, June 10, 2012. https://www.washingtonpost.com/world/asia_pacific/in-philippines-banana
-growers-feel-effect-of-south-china-sea-dispute/2012/06/10/gJQA47WVTV_story.html.

Hioe, Brian. "China Slaps Export Bans on Taiwanese Goods—Again." *Diplomat*, December 16, 2022.
https://thediplomat.com/2022/12/china-slaps-export-bans-on-taiwanese-goods-again/.

Hirschman, Albert O. *Exit, Voice, and Loyalty*. Cambridge, MA: Harvard University Press, 1970.

——. *National Power and the Structure of Foreign Trade*. Berkeley: University of California Press, 1945.

Holland, Oscar. "Bulgari Apologizes for Taiwan Listing Amid Chinese Social Media Uproar." CNN,
July 12, 2023. https://www.cnn.com/style/bulgari-china-apology-taiwan-listing/index.html.

Holland, Oscar, and Serenitie Wang. "Coach, Givenchy Joining Versace in Apologizing to Chinese Consumers Amid T-Shirt Outcry." CNN, August 13, 2019. https://edition.cnn.com/style/article/coach
-givenchy-versace-t-shirt-controversy/index.html.

Hong, Jinshan, and Iain Marlow. "NBA Loses More Sponsors as China Flexes Economic Muscle." Bloomberg, October 8, 2019. https://www.bloomberg.com/news/articles/2019-10-09/china-flexes
-economic-muscle-again-as-nba-loses-more-sponsors.

Hong, Qin. "面对菲律宾，我们有足够手段" [Faced with the Philippines, we have adequate means]. *Overseas Edition of People's Daily*, May 8, 2012. http://mil.news.sina.com.cn/2012-05-08/0718689884.html.

Horton, Chris. "El Salvador Recognizes China in Blow to Taiwan." *New York Times*, August 21, 2018. https://www.nytimes.com/2018/08/21/world/asia/taiwan-el-salvador-diplomatic-ties.html.

Hosokawa, Kotaro. "Lithium Supply: Posco to Build $830m Plant in Argentina." *Nikkei Asia*, December 18, 2021. https://asia.nikkei.com/Business/Materials/Lithium-supply-Posco-to-build-830m-plant-in -Argentina.

Howley, Daniel. "These 169 Industries Are Being Hit by the Global Chip Shortage." Yahoo! Finance, April 25, 2021. https://finance.yahoo.com/news/these-industries-are-hit-hardest-by-the-global-chip -shortage-122854251.html.

Hsia, Hsiao-hwa, Ray Chung, and Heung Yeung Lee. "Chinese Calls for Taiwan Hotel Boycott Part of Propaganda Machine." Radio Free Asia, August 19, 2024. https://www.rfa.org/english/news/china /china-paris-hotel-boycott-08192024133024.html.

Hsu, Stacy. "PNG Demands New Name for Taiwan Office." *Taipei Times*, June 2, 2018. https://www .taipeitimes.com/News/taiwan/archives/2018/06/02/2003694174.

Huang, Xinwei. "Five Countries Demand Taiwan Rename Local Offices." CGTN, June 14, 2017. https:// news.cgtn.com/news/3d6b6a4d3549444e/share_p.html.

Hufbauer, Gary, Jeffrey J. Schott, Kimberly Ann Elliott, and Barbara Oegg. *Economic Sanctions Reconsidered*. 3rd ed. Washington, DC: Peterson Institute for International Economics, 2007.

Hui, Mary. "Japan Minted a New Economic Security Minister to Fix Supply Chain Disruptions." Quartz, October 8, 2021. https://qz.com/2070498/japan-has-a-new-economic-security-chief-to-secure-supply -chains/.

——. "Japan's Global Rare Earths Quest Holds Lessons for the US and Europe." Quartz, April 23, 2021. https://qz.com/1998773/japans-rare-earths-strategy-has-lessons-for-us-europe/.

Hunter, Fergus, Daria Impiombato, Yvonne Lau, Adam Triggs, Albert Zhang, and Urmika Deb. "Countering China's Coercive Diplomacy." Australian Strategic Policy Institute, February 22, 2023. https:// www.aspi.org.au/report/countering-chinas-coercive-diplomacy.

Hurst, Daniel. "How Much Is China's Trade War Really Costing Australia?" *Guardian*, October 27, 2020. https://www.theguardian.com/australia-news/2020/oct/28/how-much-is-chinas-trade-war-really -costing-australia.

Hutzler, Alexandra. "Trump Rolls Out Sweeping Tariffs as He Deems Deficits a 'National Emergency.'" ABC News, April 2, 2025. https://abcnews.go.com/Politics/trumps-liberation-day-arrives-gambles-big -risky-tariff/story?id=120382209.

Hwang, Echo, and Isabella Steger. "Norway Wants China to Forget About the Human Rights Thing and Eat Salmon Instead." Quartz, June 14, 2017. https://qz.com/1000541/norway-wants-china-to-forget -about-the-human-rights-thing-and-eat-salmon-instead.

Ikenberry, G. John. "The G7 'Club of Democracies' Becomes a Power Player." *Foreign Policy*, August 31, 2023. https://foreignpolicy.com/2023/08/31/g7-geopolitics-alliance-west-democracies-us-europe-japan -free-world-liberal-order/.

——. "The Rise of China and the Future of the West." *Foreign Affairs* 87, no. 1 (2008): 23–37. https://www .foreignaffairs.com/articles/asia/2008-01-01/rise-china-and-future-west.

——. *A World Safe for Democracy: Liberal Internationalism and the Crises of Global Order*. New Haven, CT: Yale University Press, 2023.

Inquirer.net. "PH Bananas Rotting in Chinese Ports." May 12, 2012. https://newsinfo.inquirer.net/191951 /ph-bananas-rotting-in-chinese-ports.

International Energy Agency. "Australia-India Critical Minerals Investment Partnership." December 11, 2023. https://www.iea.org/policies/17873-australia-india-critical-minerals-investment-partnership.

——. "Geographical Distribution of Refined Material Production for Key Energy Transition Minerals in the Base Case, 2023–2040." May 13, 2024. https://www.iea.org/data-and-statistics/charts/geographical -distribution-of-refined-material-production-for-key-energy-transition-minerals-in-the-base-case -2023-2040-2.

——. *Global Critical Minerals Outlook 2024*. May 2024, https://iea.blob.core.windows.net/assets/ee01701d
-1d5c-4ba8-9df6-abeeac9de99a/GlobalCriticalMineralsOutlook2024.pdf.

——. "Prohibition of the Export of Nickel Ore." December 12, 2023. https://www.iea.org/policies/16084
-prohibition-of-the-export-of-nickel-ore.

International Trade Administration. "Draft List of Critical Supply Chains." n.d. https://www.trade.gov
/data-visualization/draft-list-critical-supply-chains.

——. "Taiwan—Country Commercial Guide." January 10, 2024. https://www.trade.gov/country
-commercial-guides/taiwan-market-overview.

Isidore, Chris. "The NBA Faces a No-Win Situation in China. Here's What It Stands to Lose." CNN,
October 9, 2019. https://www.cnn.com/2019/10/08/business/daryl-morey-tweet-nba-china/index
.html.

Japan Organization for Metals and Energy Security. "Sojitz and JOGMEC Enter Into Definitive Agreements with Lynas Including Availability Agreement to Secure Supply of Rare Earths Products to Japanese Market." March 30, 2011. https://www.jogmec.go.jp/english/news/release/release0069.html.

Jennings, Ralph, and Huifeng He. "China's Ban on Taiwan Imports Leaves Some Consumers Wondering
Where to Get Their Food Fix." *South China Morning Post*, August 16, 2022. https://www.scmp.com
/economy/china-economy/article/3188938/chinas-ban-taiwan-imports-leaves-some-consumers
-wondering.

Ji, Dagyum. "Foreign Ministry to Disband Peninsula Peace Bureau Amid NK Threats." *Korea Herald*,
March 7, 2024. https://www.koreaherald.com/view.php?ud=20240307050829.

Johnson, Keith, and Elias Groll. "China Raises Threat of Rare Earths Cutoff to U.S." *Foreign Policy*, May 21,
2019. https://foreignpolicy.com/2019/05/21/china-raises-threat-of-rare-earth-mineral-cutoff-to-us/.

Kalinkaitė-Matuliauskienė, Vaida. "German Investors in Lithuania Shy Away from Comments about
Alleged Chinese Pressure." Lithuanian Radio and Television, March 31, 2022. https://www.lrt.lt/en
/news-in-english/19/1659484/german-investors-in-lithuania-refrain-from-comments-about-alleged
-chinese-pressure.

Kasabian, Paul. "Warriors' Stephen Curry 'Not Sure' If He'll Go on Promotional China Trip in 2020."
Bleacher Report, October 9, 2020. https://bleacherreport.com/articles/2857435-warriors-stephen-curry
-not-sure-if-hell-go-on-promotional-china-trip-in-2020.

Kaur, Minderjeet, and Ili Shazwani. "Malaysia's Govt Counters Potential Chinese Pressure with Proposed
Ban on RareEarth Exports." *Benar News*, September 11, 2023. https://www.benarnews.org/english
/news/malaysian/malaysia-rare-earth-ban-china-09112023142437.html.

Kelly, Tim, and Miho Uranaka. "Japan Restricts Chipmaking Equipment Exports as It Aligns with US
China Curbs." Reuters, March 31, 2023. https://www.reuters.com/technology/japan-restrict
-chipmaking-equipment-exports-aligning-it-with-us-china-curbs-2023-03-31/.

Kendall-Taylor, Andrea, and Richard Fontaine. "The Axis of Upheaval: How America's Adversaries Are
Uniting to Overturn the Global Order." *Foreign Affairs* 103, no. 3 (2024). https://www.foreignaffairs
.com/china/axis-upheaval-russia-iran-north-korea-taylor-fontaine.

Keohane, David, and Leo Lewis. "Fast Retailing Shares Fall Over Fears for Uniqlo Stores in China." *Financial Times*, December 2, 2024. https://www.ft.com/content/54c5650a-fc6a-4a8d-a20e-110c456d4a8f.

Keohane, Robert O. *After Hegemony: Cooperation and Discord in the World Political Economy*. Princeton,
NJ: Princeton University Press, 1984.

——. "Reciprocity in International Relations." *International Organization* 40, no. 1 (1986): 1–27.

Keohane, Robert O., and Joseph S. Nye. *Power and Interdependence*. Cambridge, MA: Harvard University Press, 1972.

Kharpal, Arjun. "Netherlands, Home to a Critical Chip Firm, Follows U.S. with Export Curbs on Semiconductor Tools." CNBC, June 30, 2022. https://www.cnbc.com/2023/06/30/netherlands-follows-us
-with-semiconductor-export-restrictions-.html.

——. "What Are Gallium and Germanium? China Curbs Exports of Metals Critical to Chips and Other Tech." CNBC, July 4, 2023. https://www.cnbc.com/2023/07/04/what-are-gallium-and-germanium -china-curbs-exports-of-metals-for-tech.html.

Kim, Da-sol, and Byung-wook Kim. "Korea's Urea Crisis." *Korea Herald*, November 9, 2021. https://www .koreaherald.com/view.php?ud=20211109000809.

Kim, Eun-joong, and Su-hyeon Park. "Trump's Tariff Plan Built on Misleading Trade Deficit Math." *Chosun Daily*, April 3, 2025.

Kim, Eun-jung. "(News Focus) Yoon Focuses on Critical Minerals During Central Asia Trip." Yonhap News Agency, June 15, 2024. https://en.yna.co.kr/view/AEN20240614008900315.

Kim, Han-joo. "(LEAD) S. Korea, Australia to Launch 'Economic Security Dialogue.'" Yonhap News Agency, July 30, 2024. https://en.yna.co.kr/view/AEN20240730006651315.

Kim, Ju-yeon. "Korea's Reliance on China for Minerals Grows Despite U.S. Warnings." *Korea JoongAng Daily*, October 20, 2023. https://koreajoongangdaily.joins.com/news/2023-10-15/business/industry /Koreas-reliance-on-China-for-minerals-grows-despite-US-warnings/1889533.

Kim, Jaewon, and Ting-Fang Cheng. "Samsung and SK Hynix Face China Dilemma from U.S. Export Controls." *Nikkei Asia*, October 25, 2022. https://asia.nikkei.com/Business/Tech/Semiconductors /Samsung-and-SK-Hynix-face-China-dilemma-from-U.S.-export-controls.

Kim, Sung-hoon, and Minu Kim. "Korea's Yoon Gov't to Create Presidential Secretary for Economic Security Affairs." Pulse, April 22, 2022. https://pulsenews.co.kr/view.php?year=2022&no=358656.

Kim, Seung-bum, and Seong-min Kim. "Chinese Boycott Takes Toll on Hyundai-Kia, Suppliers." *Chosun Daily*, July 4, 2017. https://www.chosun.com/english/industry-en/2017/07/04/ZVSX7FL3PJN MRRLXSBMLX5JC2M/.

Kim, Seung-yeon. "S. Korea, Mongolia Launch Cooperation Committee for Rare Metals Supply." Yonhap News Agency, November 20, 2023. https://en.yna.co.kr/view/AEN20231119002100315.

Kim, Victoria. "When China and U.S. Spar, It's South Korea That Gets Punched." *Los Angeles Times*, November 19, 2020. https://www.latimes.com/world-nation/story/2020-11-19/south-korea-china -beijing-economy-thaad-missile-interceptor.

Kim, Yeon-gyu. *Gananhan migug buyuhan jung-gug*가난한 미국 부유한 중국 [Poor America rich China]. Seoul, South Korea: 라의 눈 (Eye of Ra), 2022.

King, Ian, Debby Wu, and Demetrios Pogkas. "How a Chip Shortage Snarled Everything from Phones to Cars." Bloomberg, March 29, 2021. https://www.bloomberg.com/graphics/2021-semiconductors-chips -shortage/.

Kirshner, Jonathan. "The Microfoundations of Economic Sanctions." *Security Studies* 6, no. 3 (2007): 32–64.

Kliman, Daniel, Andrea Kendall-Taylor, Kristine Lee, Joshua Fitt, and Carisa Nietsche. "Dangerous Synergies: Countering Chinese and Russian Digital Influence Operations." Center for a New American Security, May 7, 2020. https://www.cnas.org/publications/reports/dangerous-synergies.

Kobara, Junnosuke. "South Korea, Japan to Help Crisis-Proof Indo-Pacific Supply Chain." *Nikkei Asia*, July 31, 2024. https://asia.nikkei.com/Spotlight/Supply-Chain/South-Korea-Japan-to-help-crisis-proof -Indo-Pacific-supply-chain.

Kokas, Aynne. *Hollywood Made in China*. Berkeley: University of California Press, 2017.

KoreaPro. "South Korea–Mongolia Launch Rare Metals Cooperation Amid Geopolitical Risks." November 21, 2023. https://koreapro.org/2023/11/south-korea-mongolia-launch-rare-metals-cooperation -amid-geopolitical-risks/.

Kowalski, Przemyslaw, and Clarisse Legendre. "Raw Materials Critical for the Green Transition: Production, International Trade and Export Restrictions." *OECD Trade Policy Papers*, no. 269 (2023): 41–43.

Kurlantzick, Joshua. *Beijing's Global Media Offensive: China's Uneven Campaign to Influence Asia and the World*. New York: Oxford University Press, 2022.

Kyodo News. "Japan's Diet Enacts Law to Create Economic Security Clearance System." May 10, 2024. https://english.kyodonews.net/news/2024/05/6d180e81198e-japans-diet-enacts-law-to-create-economic-security-clearance-system.html?phrase=kyoto&words=#google_vignette.

Lague, David. "Special Report: In Satellite Tech Race, China Hitched a Ride from Europe." Reuters, December 22, 2013. https://www.reuters.com/article/world/special-report-in-satellite-tech-race-china-hitched-a-ride-from-europe-idUSBRE9BL0CA/.

Lawder, David. "U.S.-Led Indo-Pacific Talks Produce Deal on Supply Chain Early Warnings." Reuters, May 27, 2023. https://www.reuters.com/markets/asia/us-led-indo-pacific-talks-produce-deal-supply-chain-early-warnings-2023-05-27/.

Layton, Peter. "China's Enduring Grey Zone Challenge." Air and Space Power Centre, 2021. https://airpower.airforce.gov.au/publications/chinas-enduring-grey-zone-challenge.

LeBron James @KingJames. "Let Me Clear Up the Confusion. I Do Not Believe There Was Any Consideration for the Consequences and Ramifications of the Tweet. I'm Not Discussing the Substance. Others Can Talk About That." X (formerly Twitter), October 14, 2019, 10:35 pm. https://twitter.com/KingJames/status/1183934373671735296.

——. "My Team and This League Just Went Through a Difficult Week. I Think People Need to Understand What a Tweet or Statement Can Do to Others. And I Believe Nobody Stopped and Considered What Would Happen. Could Have Waited a Week to Send It." X (formerly Twitter), October 14, 2019, 10:36 pm. https://twitter.com/KingJames/status/1183934569411530752.

Lee, Andrew. "Mainland China Bans Taiwan Wax and Sugar Apple Imports as Cross-Strait Relations Continue to Worsen." South China Morning Post, September 19, 2021. https://www.scmp.com/news/china/politics/article/3149339/mainland-china-bans-taiwan-wax-and-sugar-apple-imports-cross.

Lee, Jaemin. "The U.S. and Its Allies Want to Bring the Entire Chip Supply Chain In-House—and That Could Create an OPEC-Style Cartel for the Digital Age." Fortune, March 28, 2024. https://fortune.com/asia/2024/03/28/chip-4-alliance-us-korea-japan-taiwan-semiconductors-china-opec-cartel-for-digital-age/.

Lee, Joyce. "South Korean Firms Get Indefinite Waiver on U.S. Chip Gear Supplies to China." Reuters, October 9, 2023. https://www.reuters.com/technology/samsung-sk-hynix-wont-need-approvals-supply-us-chip-gear-china-yonhap-2023-10-09/.

Lee, Yen Nee. "A Massive, 'Semi-Infinite' Trove of Rare-Earth Metals Has Been Found in Japan." CNBC, April 12, 2018. https://www.cnbc.com/2018/04/12/japan-rare-earths-huge-deposit-of-metals-found-in-pacific.html.

Lee, Yimou. "Taiwan Says China Lures Kiribati with Airplanes After Losing Another Ally." Reuters, September 20, 2019. https://www.reuters.com/article/idUSKBN1W50DH/.

Lee, Youkyung, and Debby Wu. "US, Asian Partners Discussed Supply Chains in 'Chip 4' Talks." Bloomberg, February 26, 2023. https://www.bloomberg.com/news/articles/2023-02-26/us-asian-partners-discussed-chip-supply-chain-reports-say?leadSource=uverify%20wall.

Leonard, Mark, ed. Connectivity Wars: Why Migration, Finance and Trade Are the Geo-Economic Battlegrounds of the Future. London: European Council of Foreign Relations, 2016.

Lewis, Mark. "Norway's Salmon Rots as China Takes Revenge for Dissident's Nobel Prize." Independent, October 6, 2011. https://www.independent.co.uk/news/world/europe/norway-s-salmon-rot-as-china-takes-revenge-for-dissident-s-nobel-prize-2366167.html.

Li, Chongjing, and Winnie Hsu. "Controversial Fukushima Nuclear Waste Plan Spurs Chinese Boycott of Japanese Cosmetics." Time, June 23, 2023. https://time.com/6289566/chinese-boycott-japanese-cosmetics-nuclear-plant-water/.

Li, Jane. "China Is Angry About Marvel's First Asian Superhero Movies." Quartz, July 23, 2019. https://qz.com/quartzy/1671394/china-is-angry-about-marvels-first-asian-superhero-movie.

Li, Shangfu. "Remarks at the Fifth Plenary Session, 20th Asia Security Summit: The Shangri-La Dialogue." International Institute for Strategic Studies, June 4, 2023. https://www.iiss.org/globalassets/media

-library---content--migration/files/shangri-la-dialogue/2023/final-transcripts/p-5/general-li
-shangfu-state-councilor-minister-of-national-defense-china---as-delivered.pdf.

Liang, Annabelle. "US-China Chip War: Japan Plans to Restrict Some Equipment Exports." BBC, March 31, 2023. https://www.bbc.com/news/business-65134017.

Lim, Darren J., and Victor Ferguson. "Chinese Economic Coercion During the THAAD Dispute." Asan Forum, December 28, 2019. https://theasanforum.org/chinese-economic-coercion-during-the-thaad-dispute/#40.

——. "Informal Economic Sanctions: The Political Economy of Chinese Coercion During the THAAD Dispute." *Review of International Political Economy* 29, no. 5 (2022): 1525–1548.

Lin, Bonny, and Joel Wuthnow. "The Weakness Behind China's Strong Façade." *Foreign Affairs*, published online November 10, 2022. https://www.foreignaffairs.com/china/weakness-behind-china-strong-facade.

Lithium for Future Technology. "Global Lithium Deposit Map." November 2021. https://lithiumfuture.org/map.html.

Lithuanian Radio and Television. "Calls to Support Taiwan 'Open Provocation,' Says China's Ambassador to Lithuania." April 30, 2020. https://www.lrt.lt/en/news-in-english/19/1169159/calls-to-support-taiwan-open-provocation-says-china-s-ambassador-to-lithuania.

——. "China Slams Lithuania's Move to Build Ties with 'Taiwan Separatists.'" March 5, 2021. https://www.lrt.lt/en/news-in-english/19/1358551/china-slams-lithuania-s-move-to-build-ties-with-taiwan-separatists.

——. "Lithuania Hands Note to China Over Incident During Hong Kong Support Rally in Vilnius." September 2, 2019. https://www.lrt.lt/naujienos/news-in-english/19/1093636/lithuania-hands-note-to-china-over-incident-during-hong-kong-support-rally-in-vilnius.

——. "Lithuanian President Doesn't Back Taiwan's WHO Membership—Aide." April 22, 2020. https://www.lrt.lt/en/news-in-english/19/1166291/lithuanian-president-doesn-t-back-taiwan-s-who-membership-aide.

Liu, Juliana. "China Proposes Fresh Export Curbs on EV Technology." CNN, January 3, 2025. https://www.cnn.com/2025/01/03/tech/china-ev-tech-export-controls-intl-hnk/index.html.

Liu, Siyi, and Dominique Patton. "China, World's Top Graphite Producer, Tightens Exports of Key Battery Material." Reuters, October 20, 2023. https://www.reuters.com/world/china/china-require-export-permits-some-graphite-products-dec-1-2023-10-20/.

Liu, Zongyuan Zoe. "How to Secure Critical Minerals for Clean Energy Without Alienating China." Council on Foreign Relations, May 25, 2023. https://www.cfr.org/blog/how-secure-critical-minerals-clean-energy-without-alienating-china.

Long, Jessica, and Jingtai Lun. "Vanadium Redox Flow Batteries: A New Direction for China's Energy Storage?" Fastmarkets, November 22, 2022. https://www.fastmarkets.com/insights/vanadium-redox-flow-batteries-a-new-direction-for-chinas-energy-storage/.

Lu, Shen, and Ginger Adams Otis. "Snickers Maker Apologizes to China for Referring to Taiwan as Its Own Country." *Wall Street Journal*, August 5, 2022. https://www.wsj.com/articles/snickers-maker-apologizes-to-china-for-referring-to-taiwan-as-its-own-country-11659727945.

Lukes, Steven. *Power: A Radical View.* 2nd ed. New York: Palgrave Macmillan, 2005.

Lv, Amy, Lewis Jackson, and Ashitha Shivaprasad. "China Expands Key Mineral Export Controls After US Imposes Tariffs." Reuters, February 4, 2025. https://www.reuters.com/world/china/china-expands-critical-mineral-export-controls-after-us-imposes-tariffs-2025-02-04/.

Lyons, Kate. "China Extends Influence in Pacific as Solomon Islands Break with Taiwan." *Guardian*, September 16, 2019. https://www.theguardian.com/world/2019/sep/16/china-extends-influence-in-pacific-as-solomon-islands-break-with-taiwan.

Magra, Iliana, and Christine Hauser. "Lululemon Fires Employee Over 'Bat Fried Rice' T-Shirt." *New York Times*, April 22, 2020. https://www.nytimes.com/2020/04/22/business/lululemon-bat-fried-rice-shirt-coronavirus.html.

Mai, Liqiang, Lin Xu, and Wei Chen. *Vanadate Nanomaterials for Electrochemical Energy Storage*. Cham, Switzerland: Springer, 2023.

Manley, Ross L., Elisa Alonso, and Nedal T. Nassar. "A Model to Assess Industry Vulnerability to Disruptions in Mineral Commodity Supplies." *Resources Policy* 78 (2022): 102889.

Mansfield, Edward D., Helen V. Milner, and B. Peter Rosendorff. "Why Democracies Cooperate More: Electoral Control and International Trade Agreements." *International Organization* 56, no. 3 (2002): 477–513.

Marsh, Vivien, Dani Madrid-Morales, and Chris Paterson. "Global Chinese Media and a Decade of Change." *International Communication Gazette* 85, no. 1 (2023): 3–14.

Marshall, Alys. "Federal Treasurer Orders Chinese-Linked Investors to Offload Shares in Australian Rare Earths Mine." ABC News, June 3, 2024. https://www.abc.net.au/news/2024-06-03/northern-minerals -jim-chalmers-yuxiao-fund-investors/103927762.

Marti, Pablo Abril, and Mariusz Maciejewski. "The European Commission." European Parliament, April 2024. https://www.europarl.europa.eu/factsheets/en/sheet/25/the-european-commission.

Martina, Michael, and Yew Lun Tian. "China Detains Staff, Raids Office of U.S. Due Diligence Firm Mintz Group." Reuters, March 24, 2023. https://www.reuters.com/world/us-due-diligence-firm-mintz -groups-beijing-office-raided-five-staff-detained-2023-03-24/.

Mazarr, Michael J. *Mastering the Gray Zone: Understanding a Changing Era of Conflict*. Washington, DC: US Army War College Press, 2015. https://press.armywarcollege.edu/monographs/428.

McCormick, John. "Trump Calls Tariffs the 'Most Beautiful Word.'" *Wall Street Journal*, October 17, 2024. https://www.wsj.com/livecoverage/harris-trump-election-10-16-2024/card/trump-calls-tariffs -the-most-beautiful-word--YMVPAupw4EjBRp6yobOy.

McDonald, Tim. "China and Taiwan Face Off in Pineapple War." BBC, March 19, 2021. https://www.bbc .com/news/business-56353963.

McElwee, Lily. "How Scholz's Unpopular Trip to Beijing Actually Served U.S. Interests." Center for Strategic and International Studies, November 7, 2022. https://www.csis.org/analysis/how-scholzs -unpopular-trip-beijing-actually-served-us-interests.

McGregor, Richard. "Chinese Coercion, Australian Resilience." Lowy Institute, October 20, 2022. https:// www.lowyinstitute.org/publications/chinese-coercion-australian-resilience#heading-6816.

McLaughlin, Seth. "Nikki Haley Calls for Ending Normal Trade Relations with China." *Washington Times*, June 27, 2023. https://www.washingtontimes.com/news/2023/jun/27/nikki-haley-calls-ending -normal-trade-relations-ch/.

McLean, Elena V., and Mitchell T. Radtke. "Political Relations, Leader Stability and Economic Coercion." *International Studies Quarterly* 62, no. 2 (2018): 357–370.

Meat & Livestock Australia. "State of the Industry Reports." October 18, 2023. https://www.mla.com.au /prices-markets/Trends-analysis/state-of-the-industry-reports/.

Mercer, Phil. "Australia Unveils $1.25 Billion Critical Minerals Plan." Voice of America, October 26, 2023. https://www.voanews.com/a/australia-unveils-1-25-billion-critical-minerals-plan/7327227.html.

Meunier, Sophie, and Kalypso Nicolaidis. "The Geopoliticization of European Trade and Investment Policy." *JCMS: Journal of Common Market Studies* 57 (2019): 103–113.

Miao, Hannah, and Rebecca Feng. "China Flexes Chokehold on Rare-Earth Magnets as Exports Plunged in May." *Wall Street Journal*, June 19, 2025. https://www.wsj.com/world/china/china-flexes-chokehold -on-rare-earth-magnets-as-exports-plunge-in-may-c1adac50.

Minister for Foreign Affairs [Australia]. "Resolution of Barley Dispute with China." August 5, 2023. https:// www.foreignminister.gov.au/minister/penny-wong/media-release/resolution-barley-dispute-china.

Minister for Resources [Australia]. "Milestone in India and Australia Critical Minerals Investment Partnership." March 10, 2023. https://www.minister.industry.gov.au/ministers/king/media-releases /milestone-india-and-australia-critical-minerals-investment-partnership.

Minister for Trade and Tourism [Australia]. "Australia Joins Global Minerals Security Partnership." July 12, 2022. https://www.trademinister.gov.au/minister/don-farrell/media-release/australia-joins-global-minerals-security-partnership.

Ministry of Commerce, People's Republic of China. "MOFCOM Regular Press Conference." July 6, 2023. https://english.mofcom.gov.cn/News/PressConference/art/2023/art_36fb2d80e4b4453891bb8fc83e2b3c4e.html.

——. "MOFCOM Regular Press Conference." October 26, 2023. https://english.mofcom.gov.cn/News/PressConference/art/2023/art_6fc7603ef80f4c819b79dba5baac76f6.html.

Ministry of Economy and Finance [South Korea]. "The Enactment of Framework Act on Supply Chain." December 27, 2023. https://english.moef.go.kr/pc/selectTbPressCenterDtl.do?boardCd=N0001&seq=5741.

——. "The 1st Supply Chain Stabilization Committee Meeting," June 27, 2024. https://english.moef.go.kr/pc/selectTbPressCenterDtl.do?boardCd=N0001&seq=5902.

——. *Gong-geubmang anjeonghwa chujinjeonlyag* 공급망 안정화 추진전략 [Supply chain stabilization strategy]. June 27, 2024. https://www.moef.go.kr/nw/nes/detailNesDtaView.do?menuNo=4010100&searchNttId1=MOSF_000000000069481&searchBbsId1=MOSFBBS_000000000028.

Ministry of Economy, Trade and Industry [Japan]. "As a Review of the Organization, METI Revises the Ordinance on the Organization of the Ministry of Economy, Trade and Industry." June 25, 2024. https://www.meti.go.jp/english/press/2024/0625_001.html.

——. "Japan's New International Resource Strategy to Secure Rare Metals." September 30, 2020. https://www.enecho.meti.go.jp/en/category/special/article/detail_158.html.

——. *Jūyō kōbutsu ni kakaru antei kyōkyū kakuho o hakaru tame no torikumi hōshin* 重要鉱物に係る安定供給確保を図るための取組方針 [Measures to secure a stable supply of critical minerals]. January 19, 2023. https://www.meti.go.jp/policy/economy/economic_security/metal/torikumihoshin.pdf.

——. "Press Conference by Minister Nishimura (Excerpt)." August 1, 2023. www.meti.go.jp/english/speeches/press_conferences/2023/0801001.html.

Ministry of Foreign Affairs, Japan. "G7 Hiroshima Leaders' Communiqué." May 20, 2023. https://www.mofa.go.jp/policy/economy/summit/hiroshima23/documents/pdf/Leaders_Communique_01_en.pdf?v20231006.

Ministry of Foreign Affairs, The People's Republic of China. "Full text of President Xi Jinping's 2025 New Year message." December 31, 2024. https://www.fmprc.gov.cn/mfa_eng/xw/zyxw/202412/t20241231_11524948.html.

Ministry of Foreign Affairs, Republic of China (Taiwan). "Diplomatic Allies." https://en.mofa.gov.tw/AlliesIndex.aspx?n=1294&sms=1007.

Ministry of Foreign Affairs, Republic of Korea. "Korea Assumes Chairmanship of Minerals Security Partnership (MSP)." June 27, 2024. https://overseas.mofa.go.kr/eng/brd/m_5676/view.do?seq=322611.

Ministry of Foreign Affairs (@MOFA_Taiwan). "We're Proud to Announce the Planned Establishment of the Taiwanese Representative Office in #Lithuania." X (formerly Twitter), July 19, 2021, 10:46 p.m. https://twitter.com/MOFA_Taiwan/status/1417314889236828165.

Ministry of Trade, Industry and Energy [South Korea]. *Cheomdansan-eob geullobeol gang-gug doyag-eul wihan haegsimgwangmul hwagbojeonlyag* 첨단산업 글로벌 강국 도약을 위한 핵심광물 확보전략 [Strategy for securing critical minerals to become a global leader in advanced industries]. February 2023. https://www.motie.go.kr/kor/article/ATCL3f49a5a8c/166862/view.

——. "Gong-geubmang anjeonghwa jiwon beobjeog giban malyeon" 공급망 안정화 지원 법적 기반 마련 [Establishment of legal basis to support supply chain stabilization]. May 25, 2023. https://www.motie.go.kr/kor/article/ATCL8764a1224/155118386/view.

——. "Special Act on National Resources Security." Law No. 20196, February 6, 2024. https://www.law.go.kr/lsInfoP.do?lsiSeq=259657&efYd=20250207#0000.

Moon, Chung-in. "Diplomacy of Defiance and Facilitation: The Six-Party Talks and the Roh Moo Hyun Government." *Asian Perspective* 32, no. 4 (2008): 71–105.

Murphy, Ben. "Chokepoints: China's Self-Identified Strategic Technology Import Dependencies." Center for Security and Emerging Technologies, May 2022. https://cset.georgetown.edu/publication/chokepoints/.

Musha Research. "Japanese Stocks Outstandingly High, U.S.-China Confrontation and Super Weak Yen Turned the Tide." June 5, 2023. https://www.musha.co.jp/short_comment/detail/333?lang=en.

Nadig, Smruthi. "Top Ten Nickel-Producing Countries in 2023." Mining Technology, March 25, 2024. https://www.mining-technology.com/features/top-ten-nickel-producing-countries-in-2023/?cf-view.

Nagahara, Masato. *Kakkoku oyobi chiiki rengō-tō no jūyō kōbutsu busshitsu risuto gairon* 各国および地域連合等の重要鉱物・物質リスト概論 [Introduction of the lists of critical minerals and materials around the world] Japan Organization for Metals and Energy Security, January 14, 2025. https://mric.jogmec.go.jp/reports/mr/20250114/185205/.

Nagata, Kazuaki. "Cabinet Approves Bill to Beef Up Japan's Economic Security." *Japan Times*, February 25, 2022. https://www.japantimes.co.jp/news/2022/02/25/business/economic-security-bill-cabinet/.

——. "Japan's New Economic Security Minister Sets Out Agenda Amid Global Supply Chain Woes." *Japan Times*, October 5, 2021. https://www.japantimes.co.jp/news/2021/10/05/business/economic-security-minister-agenda/.

Nakano, Jane. *The Geopolitics of Critical Minerals Supply Chains*. Center for Strategic and International Studies, March 11, 2021. https://www.csis.org/analysis/geopolitics-critical-minerals-supply-chains.

National Mining Association. "Energy Fuels: Strengthening Our Military Through Vanadium." December 2, 2019. https://nma.org/2019/12/02/energy-fuels-strengthening-our-military-through-vanadium/.

Ndolomingo, Matumuene Joe, Ndzondelelo Bingwa, and Reinout Meijboom. "Review of Supported Metal Nanoparticles: Synthesis Methodologies, Advantages, and Application as Catalysts." *Journal of Materials Science* 55 (2020): 6195–6241.

Needham, Kirsty, and Colin Packham. "China Halts Beef Imports from Four Australian Firms as COVID-19 Spat Sours Trade." Reuters, May 12, 2020. https://www.reuters.com/article/world/china-halts-beef-imports-from-four-australian-firms-as-covid-19-spat-sours-trade-idUSKBN22O0FA/.

New York Times. "Clinton's Words on China: Trade Is the Smart Thing." March 9, 2000. www.nytimes.com/2000/03/09/world/clinton-s-words-on-china-trade-is-the-smart-thing.html.

Ng, Sue, and He Huifeng. "Versace and Coach Spark Outrage in China for Selling Shirts That List Hong Kong Without a Country." Goldthread, August 12, 2019. https://www.goldthread2.com/culture/versace-coach-china-hong-kong/article/3022467.

Nick Friedell (@NickFriedell). "[Coach of the Golden State Warriors] Kerr Also Reiterated That the League Has Not Told Players or Coaches What They Can or Cannot Say in Regard to the Ongoing China Situation." X (formerly Twitter), October 12, 2019, 5:30 p.m. https://twitter.com/NickFriedell/status/1183132785684316160.

Nissen, Keith. "Global NBA Basketball Viewers, 2024." S&P Global, March 28, 2024. https://www.spglobal.com/market-intelligence/en/news-insights/research/global-nba-basketball-viewers-2024.

Nolan, Stella. "Nickel: Driving the Future of EV Battery Technology Globally." *EV Magazine*, October 25, 2024. https://evmagazine.com/technology/nickel-driving-the-future-of-ev-battery-technology-globally.

Nooruddin, Irfan. "Modeling Selection Bias in Studies on Sanctions Efficacy." *International Interactions* 28, no. 1 (2002): 59–75.

Norris, William J. *Chinese Economic Statecraft: Commercial Actors, Grand Strategy, and State Control.* Ithaca, NY: Cornell University Press, 2016.

North Atlantic Treaty Organization. "Washington Summit Declaration." July 10, 2024. https://www.nato.int/cps/cn/natohq/official_texts_227678.htm.

OECD. "OECD Inventory of Export Restrictions on Industrial Raw Materials 2024." September 16, 2024. https://www.oecd.org/en/publications/oecd-inventory-of-export-restrictions-on-industrial-raw -materials-2024_5e46bb20-en/full-report.html.

Office of Foreign Assets Control. "Hong Kong-Related Designations." U.S. Department of the Treasury, December 7, 2020. https://ofac.treasury.gov/recent-actions/20201207.

Office of the President, Republic of China (Taiwan). "President Tsai Meets U.S. Delegation Led by House of Representatives Speaker Nancy Pelosi." August 3, 2022. https://english.president.gov.tw/NEWS /6292.

Office of the United States Trade Representative. "United States and Japan Sign Critical Minerals Agreement." March 28, 2023. https://ustr.gov/about-us/policy-offices/press-office/press-releases/2023/march /united-states-and-japan-sign-critical-minerals-agreement.

Oh, Seok-min. "S. Korea Launches 'Early Warning System' on Supply Chains of 4,000 Key Industry Items." Yonhap News Agency, November 26, 2021. https://en.yna.co.kr/view/AEN20211126002700320.

——. "(LEAD) S. Korea Seeks to Cut Key Minerals Dependence on China to 50 Pct by 2030." Yonhap News Agency, February 27, 2023. https://en.yna.co.kr/view/AEN20230227003351320.

——. "S. Korea to Launch Pan-Gov't Commission on Enhanced Supply Chain Management." Yonhap News Agency, December 11, 2023. https://en.yna.co.kr/view/AEN20231211000951320.

——. "S. Korea, Vietnam Agree to Boost Cooperation on Critical Minerals." Yonhap News Agency, December 7, 2023. https://en.yna.co.kr/view/AEN20231207005400320.

Oi, Mariko. "Uniqlo Does Not Use Xinjiang Cotton, Boss Says." BBC, November 27, 2024. https://www .bbc.com/news/articles/c79zqdl7j2go.

Olsen, Kim B., and Claudia Schmucker. "The EU's New Anti-Coercion Instrument Will Be a Success If It Isn't Used." *Internationale Politik Quarterly*, January 10, 2024. https://ip-quarterly.com/en/eus-new -anti-coercion-instrument-will-be-success-if-it-isnt-used.

Olsthoorn, Kornel. "The EU's Anti-Coercion Instrument: A Return of Unlawful Unilateral Trade Countermeasures in Disguise?" *Legal Issues of Economic Integration* 51, no. 1 (2024): 47–86.

Onstad, Eric, and Yun Chee Foo. "EU to Set Up Central Buying Agency for Critical Minerals—Draft Law." Reuters, March 7, 2023. https://www.reuters.com/world/europe/eu-set-up-central-buying-agency -critical-minerals-draft-law-2023-03-07/.

Oram, Bill. "Oram: What It Was Like to Cover the Lakers in China When the Media Was Shut Out." *Athletic*, October 12, 2019. https://theathletic.com/1288670/2019/10/12/oramwhat-it-was-like-to-cover -the-lakers-in-china-when-the-media-was-shut-out/.

Oxford Analytica. "Digital Controls Give China an Edge in South-East Asia." Expert Briefings, 2023.

Oye, Kenneth A. *Cooperation Under Anarchy.* Princeton, NJ: Princeton University Press, 1986.

Pape, Robert A. "Why Economic Sanctions Do Not Work." *International Security* 22, no. 2 (1997): 90–136.

Parello-Plesner, Jonas. "An 'Economic Article Five' to Counter China." *Wall Street Journal*, February 11, 2021. www.wsj.com/articles/an-economic-article-5-to-counter-china-11613084046.

Parker, Tom. "Japan: Australia's Key Rare Earths Partner." Australian Resource and Investment, March 9, 2023. www.australianresourcesandinvestment.com.au/2023/03/09/japan-australias-key-rare-earths -partner/.

Patrick, Steward. "BRICS Expansion, the G20, and the Future of World Order." Carnegie Endowment for International Peace, October 9, 2024. https://carnegieendowment.org/research/2024/10/brics -summit-emerging-middle-powers-g7-g20?lang=en.

Paton, Elizabeth. "Versace, Givenchy and Coach Apologize to China After T-Shirt Row." *New York Times*, August 12, 2019. www.nytimes.com/2019/08/12/fashion/china-donatella-versace-t-shirt.html.

Patton, Dominique, and Andrius Sytas. "China Suspends Lithuanian Beef, Dairy, Beer Imports as Taiwan Row Grows." Reuters, February 10, 2022. www.reuters.com/world/china/china-suspends -lithuanian-beef-imports-taiwan-row-grows-2022-02-10/.

Peach, Brian, and Su-Lin Tan. "Explainer | How Iron Ore Is Powering China's Infrastructure Boom, and Why Securing New Sources Is So Vitally Important." *South China Morning Post*, February 14, 2021. www.scmp.com/economy/china-economy/article/3120761/how-iron-ore-powering-chinas -infrastructure-boom-and-why.

Pearson, Margaret M., Meg Rithmire, and Kellee S. Tsai. "China's Party-State Capitalism and International Backlash: From Interdependence to Insecurity." *International Security* 47, no. 2 (2022): 135–176.

Peksen, Dursun, and Timothy M. Peterson. "Sanctions and Alternate Markets: How Trade and Alliances Affect the Onset of Economic Coercion." *Political Research Quarterly* 69, no. 1 (2016): 4–16.

Perlez, Jane. "Dispute Between China and Philippines Over Island Becomes More Heated." *New York Times*, May 10, 2012. www.nytimes.com/2012/05/11/world/asia/china-philippines-dispute-over-island -gets-more-heated.html.

Philips, Mitch. "Clubs Unlikely to Bite the Chinese Hand That Feeds." Reuters, December 16, 2019. www .reuters.com/article/uk-soccer-arsenal-china/clubs-unlikely-to-bite-the-chinese-hand-that-feeds -idUKKBN1YK26H/.

Philstar. "Chinese Agencies Suspend Phl Tours." May 11, 2012. www.philstar.com/cebu-news/2012/05/11 /805553/chinese-agencies-suspend-phl-tours.

Prieger, James, Wei-Min Hu, Canhui Hong, and Dongming Zhu. "French Automobiles and the Chinese Boycotts of 2008: Politics Really Does Affect Commerce." Pepperdine University, School of Public Policy Working Papers No. 5 (2010). https://digitalcommons.pepperdine.edu/sppworkingpapers/5.

Prime Minister of Australia. "Australia–United States Climate, Critical Minerals and Clean Energy Transformation Compact." May 20, 2023. https://www.pm.gov.au/media/australia-united-states-climate -critical-minerals-and-clean-energy-transformation-compact.

Prime Minister of Canada. "G7 Leaders' Communiqué." June 28, 2022. www.pm.gc.ca/en/news/statements /2022/06/28/g7-leaders-communique.

Prime Minister's Office of Japan. "Partnership Between Japan's Ministry of Economy, Trade and Industry and Australia's Department of Industry, Science and Resources and Department of Foreign Affairs and Trade Concerning Critical Minerals." n.d. https://japan.kantei.go.jp/content/000116662.pdf.

——. "Press Conference by Chief Cabinet Secretary Matsuno (Aug. 1 - Morning)." August 1, 2023. https:// japan.kantei.go.jp/tyoukanpress/202308/1_a.html.

Putz, Catherine. "Which Countries Are For or Against China's Xinjiang Policies?" *Diplomat*, July 15, 2020. https://thediplomat.com/2020/10/2020-edition-which-countries-are-for-or-against-chinas-xinjiang -policies/.

Radford, Antoinette. "Winnie the Pooh Horror Film Will Not Be Shown in Hong Kong or Macau." BBC, March 21, 2023. https://www.bbc.com/news/world-asia-65030531.

Rajah, Roland. "The Big Bark but Small Bite of China's Trade Coercion." Interpreter, April 8, 2021. www .lowyinstitute.org/the-interpreter/big-bark-small-bite-china-s-trade-coercion.

Rasmussen, Anders Fogh, and Ivo Daalder. "Memo on an 'Economic Article 5' to Counter Authoritarian Coercion." Chicago Council on Global Affairs, June 2022. https://globalaffairs.org/research/policy -brief/memo-economic-article-5-counter-authoritarian-coercion.

Reilly, James. "China's Unilateral Sanctions." *Washington Quarterly* 35, no. 4 (2012): 121–133.

Reinsch, William. "The WTO's First Ruling on National Security: What Does It Mean for the United States?" Center for Strategic and International Studies, April 5, 2019. www.csis.org/analysis/wtos-first -ruling-national-security-what-does-it-mean-united-states.

Repnikova, Maria. *Chinese Soft Power*. Cambridge: Cambridge University Press, 2022.

Reuters. "Brazil Regulator Approves 5G Spectrum Auction Rules, No Huawei Ban." February 25, 2021. www.reuters.com/business/media-telecom/brazil-regulator-approves-5g-spectrum-auction-rules-no -huawei-ban-2021-02-26/.

——. "Brazil's Bolsonaro to Allow China's Huawei in 5G Auctions." January 16, 2021. www.reuters.com /article/us-brazil-huawei-tech/brazils-bolsonaro-to-allow-chinas-huawei-in-5g-auctions-newspaper -idUSKBN29L0JM/.

———. "China Denies Banning Rare Earths Exports to Japan." September 23, 2010. www.reuters.com/article /world/us/china-denies-banning-rare-earths-exports-to-japan-idUSTRE68M0PF/.

———. "China Expands Key Mineral Export Controls After US Imposes Tariffs." February 4, 2025. https:// www.reuters.com/world/china/china-expands-critical-mineral-export-controls-after-us-imposes -tariffs-2025-02-04/.

———. "China Issues Rare Earth Regulations to Further Protect Domestic Supply." June 29, 2024. www .reuters.com/markets/commodities/china-issues-rare-earth-regulations-further-protect-domestic -supply-2024-06-29/.

———. "China Suspends Tariff Concessions on 134 Items Under Taiwan Trade Deal." May 31, 2024. https:// www.reuters.com/world/asia-pacific/china-suspends-tariff-concessions-134-items-under-taiwan -trade-deal-2024-05-31/.

———. "China to Limit Antimony Exports in Latest Critical Mineral Curbs." August 15, 2024. https://www .reuters.com/world/china/china-limit-antimony-exports-latest-critical-mineral-curbs-2024-08-15/.

———. "Japan Passes Economic Security Bill to Guard Sensitive Technology." May 11, 2022. www.reuters.com /world/asia-pacific/japan-passes-economic-security-bill-guard-sensitive-technology-2022-05-11/.

———. "Ozil Removed from Computer Game in China Over Uighur Comments." December 18, 2019. www .reuters.com/article/idUSKBN1YM23C/.

———. "Pentagon Has Strategic Germanium Stockpile but No Gallium Reserves." July 6, 2023. www.reuters .com/markets/commodities/pentagon-has-strategic-germanium-stockpile-no-gallium-reserves-2023 -07-06/.

———. "South Korea's Posco to Invest $4 Bln in Lithium Project in Argentina." March 21, 2022. www.reuters .com/world/americas/south-koreas-posco-invest-4-bln-lithium-project-argentina-2022-03-21/.

———. "U.S. and Partners Enter Pact to Secure Critical Minerals Like Lithium." June 14, 2022. www.reuters .com/markets/commodities/us-partners-enter-pact-secure-critical-minerals-lithium-2022-06-14/.

Reynolds, Matthew, and Matthew P. Goodman. "China's Economic Coercion: Lessons from Lithuania." *Center for Strategic and International Studies*, May 6, 2022. www.csis.org/analysis/chinas-economic -coercion-lessons-lithuania.

Ross, Lester, and Kenneth Zhou. "MOFCOM Initiates Investigation Into PVH Group Under China's Unreliable Entity List Regime." WilmerHale, October 14, 2024. https://www.wilmerhale.com/en /insights/client-alerts/20241014-mofcom-initiates-investigation-into-pvh-group-under-chinas -unreliable-entity-list-regime.

Rozman, Gilbert. "The North Korean Nuclear Crisis and U.S. Strategy in Northeast Asia." *Asian Survey* 47, no. 4 (2007): 601–621.

Ruimy, Jordan. "Scorsese's 'Kundun' Banned by Disney, Much to China's Delight." World of Reel, November 10, 2023. www.worldofreel.com/blog/2023/11/10/rdep49sr2jiryudojiepyg34hqtha1.

Rutherford, Hamish, and John Anthony. "Air NZ Plane Forced to Turn Around After Airline Forgot to Remove Reference to Taiwan." Stuff, February 12, 2019. www.stuff.co.nz/business/110525974/air-nz -plane-forced-to-turn-around-after-airline-forgot-to-remove-reference-to-taiwan.

S&P Global Market Intelligence. "China Outbound Mining Investment." 2021. https://pages .marketintelligence.spglobal.com/rs/565-BDO-100/images/china-outbound-mining-investment -infographic-150421.pdf.

Saito, Yasufumi, Daniela Wei, Jinshan Hong, and Anton Wilen. "China Canceled H&M. Every Other Brand Needs to Understand Why." Bloomberg, March 14, 2022. www.bloomberg.com/graphics/2022 -china-canceled-hm/.

Sakaguchi, Yukihiro. "Quad to Discuss Joint Investments in Chips, Critical Minerals." *Nikkei Asia*, May 20, 2023. https://asia.nikkei.com/Spotlight/Supply-Chain/Quad-to-discuss-joint-investments-in-chips -critical-minerals.

Satter, Raphael, and Nick Carey. "China Threatened to Harm Czech Companies Over Taiwan Visit— Letter." Reuters, February 19, 2020. www.reuters.com/article/business/china-threatened-to-harm -czech-companies-over-taiwan-visit-letter-idUSKBN20D1BB/.

Sayers, Eric, and Brad Glosserman. "'Collective Resilience' Is the Way to Address the China Challenge." *Japan Times*, August 14, 2020. www.japantimes.co.jp/opinion/2020/08/14/commentary/world-commentary/collective-resilience-way-address-china-challenge/.

Schuman, Michael. "Why Biden's Block on Chips to China Is a Big Deal." *Atlantic*, October 25, 2022. www.theatlantic.com/international/archive/2022/10/biden-export-control-microchips-china/671848/.

Scissors, Derek. "Deterring Chinese Economic Coercion: Statement Before the House Committee on Rules." American Enterprise Institute, May 10, 2023. www.aei.org/wp-content/uploads/2023/05/Derek-Scissors_Written-Testimony.pdf?x85095.

Seaman, John. "China's Weaponization of Gallium and Germanium." French Institute of International Relations, July 27, 2023. https://www.ifri.org/en/memos/chinas-weaponization-gallium-and-germanium-pitfalls-leveraging-chokepoints.

Segal, Adam. "China-Philippines Hacking War: A Missed Opportunity for Beijing?" Council on Foreign Relations, May 10, 2012. www.cfr.org/blog/china-philippines-hacking-war-missed-opportunity-beijing.

Sevastopulo, Demetri, and Kathrin Hille. "Washington Risks Beijing Ire Over Proposal to Rename Taiwan's US Office." *Financial Times*, September 10, 2021. www.ft.com/content/07810ece-b35b-47e7-a6d2-c876b7b40444.

Shepherd, Christian, and Pei-Lin Wu. "Their Fruit Forbidden in China, Taiwan's Pomelo Growers Feel Squeeze." *Washington Post*, August 29, 2022. www.washingtonpost.com/world/2022/08/29/china-import-ban-taiwan-fruit-pomelo/.

Shin, Hyonhee. "South Korea, Africa Leaders Pledge Deeper Ties, Critical Mineral Development." Reuters, June 4, 2024. www.reuters.com/world/asia-pacific/south-koreas-yoon-calls-greater-cooperation-with-africa-minerals-trade-2024-06-04/.

Shin, Kyung-Jin. "Retaliation by Beijing Extends to Bidet Imports." *Joongang Ilbo*, January 19, 2017. https://koreajoongangdaily.joins.com/2017/01/19/economy/Retaliation-by-Beijing-extends-to-bidet-imports/3028897.html.

Šimalčík, Matej, and Adam Kalivoda. "Sister-City Relations and Identity Politics." *Diplomat*, February 25, 2020. https://thediplomat.com/2020/02/sister-city-relations-and-identity-politics-the-case-of-prague-beijing-taipei-and-shanghai/.

Slaughter, Anne-Marie. "America's Edge: Power in the Networked Century." *Foreign Affairs* 88, no. 1 (2009): 94–113.

Smith, Michael. "China's Sanctions Against Australia Have Been a Spectacular Failure." *Australian Financial Review*, December 21, 2022. www.afr.com/world/asia/china-s-sanctions-against-australian-have-been-a-spectacular-failure-20221220-p5c7vl.

Smith, Peter, Jonathan Soble, and Leslie Hook. "Japan Secures Rare Earths Deal with Australia." *Financial Times*, November 23, 2010. www.ft.com/content/63a18538-f773-11df-8b42-00144feab49a.

Smith, Sheila A. "Japan Turns Its Attention to Economic Security." Council on Foreign Relations, May 16, 2022. www.cfr.org/blog/japan-turns-its-attention-economic-security.

Snyder, Glenn H. *Deterrence and Defense: Toward a Theory of National Security.* Princeton, NJ: Princeton University Press, 1961.

Snyder, Scott. "Six-Party Talks: 'Action for Action' and the Formalization of Regional Security Cooperation in Northeast Asia." *International Journal of Korean Unification Studies* 16, no. 1 (2007): 1–24.

Solís, Mireya, and Mathieu Duchâtel. "The Renaissance of the Japanese Semiconductor Industry." Brookings Institution, June 3, 2024. https://www.brookings.edu/articles/the-renaissance-of-the-japanese-semiconductor-industry/.

Son, Ji-hyoung. "Yoon Names New Security Office Deputy, Vice Foreign Minister." *Korea Herald*, January 10, 2024. www.koreaherald.com/view.php?ud=20240110000742.

Sopcisak, Joseph. "China Imposes Export Controls on Medium and Heavy Rare Earth Materials." Holland & Knight, April 4, 2024. https://www.hklaw.com/en/insights/publications/2025/04/china-imposes-export-controls-on-medium-and-heavy-rare-earth-materials.

Stanford Advanced Materials. "Precious Metal Catalysts for the Petroleum Sector." December 27, 2023. www.samaterials.com/precious-metal-catalysts-for-the-petroleum-sector.html.

State Security Department of the Republic of Lithuania. "National Threat Assessment 2019." February 2019. www.vsd.lt/wp-content/uploads/2019/02/2019-Gresmes-internetui-EN.pdf.

Stein, Marc. "China Conflict Mutes N.B.A.'s New-Season Buzz." *New York Times*, October 12, 2019. www.nytimes.com/2019/10/12/sports/basketball/nba-china-hong-kong.html.

Stevenson, Alexandra. "China Raises Tariffs on U.S. Imports to 125%, Calling Trump's Policies a 'Joke.'" *New York Times*, April 11, 2025. https://www.nytimes.com/2025/04/11/business/china-tariffs-125.html.

Stumpf, Dan, and Shruti Srivastava. "What Trump's Reciprocal Tariffs Mean for India." Bloomberg, April 3, 2025. https://www.bloomberg.com/news/articles/2025-04-03/trump-tariffs-on-india-how-is-country-economy-impacted-what-is-modi-doing.

Su, Qiang. "Rare Earth Will Not Be Used as Bargaining Chip: Wen." *China Daily*, October 8, 2010. www.chinadaily.com.cn/china/2010-10/08/content_11382162.htm.

Sverdrup-Thygeson, Bjørnar. "The Flexible Cost of Insulting China: Trade Politics and the 'Dalai Lama Effect.'" *Asian Perspective* 39, no. 1 (2015): 101–123.

Swanson, Ana. "Netherlands and Japan Said to Join U.S. in Curbing Chip Technology Sent to China." *New York Times*, January 30, 2023. www.nytimes.com/2023/01/28/business/economy/netherlands-japan-china-chips.html.

Sytas, Andrius. "Lithuania to Get U.S. Trade Support as It Faces China Fury Over Taiwan." Reuters, November 19, 2021. www.reuters.com/business/lithuania-get-us-trade-support-it-faces-china-fury-over-taiwan-2021-11-19/.

Sytas, Andrius, and John O'Donnell. "German Big Business Piles Pressure on Lithuania in China Row." Reuters, January 21, 2022. www.reuters.com/world/europe/german-big-business-piles-pressure-lithuania-china-row-2022-01-21/.

Szadziewski, Henryk. "A Search for Coherence: The Belt and Road Initiative in the Pacific Islands." In *The China Alternative: Changing Regional Order in the Pacific Islands*, ed. Graeme Smith and Terence Wesley-Smith, 283–318. Sydney: Australian National University Press, 2021.

Tabeta, Shunsuke. "China Bans Exports of Rare-Earth Magnet Technologies." *Nikkei Asia*, December 21, 2023. https://asia.nikkei.com/Economy/Trade/China-bans-exports-of-rare-earth-magnet-technologies.

Taipei Times. "'Fab 4' Discuss Supply Chain Early Warning System." February 27, 2023. www.taipeitimes.com/News/front/archives/2023/02/27/2003795105.

Taiwan Today. "MOFA Announces Plans to Establish the Taiwanese Representative Office in Lithuania." New Southbound Policy Portal, July 21, 2021. https://nspp.mofa.gov.tw/nsppe/content_tt.php?unit=2&post=204651.

Tan, Su-Lin. "Explainer | What Happened Over the First Year of the China-Australia Trade Dispute?" *South China Morning Post*, October 28, 2020. www.scmp.com/economy/china-economy/article/3107228/china-australia-relations-what-has-happened-over-last-six.

Tang, Didi. "China Has Threatened Trade with Some Countries After Feuds. They're Calling 'the Firm' for Help." Associated Press, May 27, 2024. https://apnews.com/article/china-trade-economic-firm-state-department-42655e067386a20b22f1317ce298f334.

Tarasov, Katie. "ASML Is the Only Company Making the $200 Million Machines Needed to Print Every Advanced Microchip. Here's an Inside Look." CNBC, March 23, 2022. www.cnbc.com/2022/03/23/inside-asml-the-company-advanced-chipmakers-use-for-euv-lithography.html.

Terazawa, Tatsuya. "Chairman's Message: The Rare Earths Embargo of 2010 and Its Lessons." Institute of Energy Economics, Japan, October 2023. https://eneken.ieej.or.jp/en/chairmans-message/chairmans-message_202310.html.

——. "How Japan Solved Its Rare Earth Minerals Dependency Issue." World Economic Forum, October 13, 2023. www.weforum.org/agenda/2023/10/japan-rare-earth-minerals/.

Thibaut, Kenton. "Chinese Discourse Power: Aspirations, Reality, and Ambitions in the Digital Domain." Atlantic Council, August 24, 2022. https://www.atlanticcouncil.org/in-depth-research-reports/report /chinese-discourse-power-ambitions-and-reality-in-the-digital-domain/.

Tian, Yew Lun. "China Sanctions Lithuanian Deputy Minister for Taiwan Visit." Reuters, August 13, 2022. www.reuters.com/world/china-sanctions-lithuanian-deputy-minister-visiting-taiwan-2022-08-12/.

Tillett, Andrew. "Australia Hits Back at China's 'Economic Coercion.'" *Australian Financial Review*, April 27, 2020. www.afr.com/politics/federal/payne-blasts-beijing-s-economic-coercion-over-virus -probe-push-20200427-p54nig.

Tillett, Andrew, and Phillip Coorey. "PM Wants Weapons Inspector–Like Powers for WHO." *Australian Financial Review*, April 22, 2020. www.afr.com/politics/federal/pm-wants-weapons-inspector-like -powers-for-world-health-organisation-20200422-p54m5x.

Tilman Fertitta @TilmanJFertitta. "Listen. . . . @dmorey does NOT speak for the @HoustonRockets. Our presence in Tokyo is all about the promotion of the @NBA internationally and we are NOT a political organization. @espn." X (formerly Twitter), October 4, 2019, 11:54 p.m. https://twitter.com /TilmanJFertitta/status/1180330287957495809.

Tobin, Meaghan, John Liu, Ana Swanson, and Tripp Mickle. "China Opens Investigation Into Nvidia Over Potential Antitrust Violations." *New York Times*, December 9, 2024. https://www.nytimes.com/2024 /12/09/technology/china-nvidia-investigation-antitrust-ai.html.

Toh, Michelle, and Anna Cooban. "Germany's Leader and Top CEOs Have Arrived in Beijing. They Need China More Than Ever." CNN, November 4, 2022. https://www.cnn.com/2022/11/03/business /germany-china-olaf-scholz-visit-trade/index.html.

Toh, Michelle, and Laura He. "All of the NBA's Official Chinese Partners Have Suspended Ties with the League." CNN Business, October 9, 2019. www.cnn.com/2019/10/09/business/nba-china-partners /index.html.

Tsang, Denise. "Uproar Against Firms Such as Pocari Sweat, Tempo, Yoshinoya, and Pizza Hut Shows Brands Tread Dangerous Ground by Taking Sides on Hong Extradition Protests, Say Marketing Experts." *South China Morning Post*, July 14, 2019. www.scmp.com/news/hong-kong/politics/article /3018539/uproar-against-firms-such-pocari-sweat-tempo-yoshinoya-and.

Tsuge, Mamoru, and Shoya Okinaga. "Japan Takes First Stake in Heavy Rare Earths to Reduce China Reliance." *Nikkei Asia*, March 9, 2023. https://asia.nikkei.com/Spotlight/Supply-Chain/Japan-takes -first-stake-in-heavy-rare-earths-to-reduce-China-reliance.

Tucker, Sean. "Average New Car Prices Sets Record." *Kelley Blue Book*, December 12, 2022. www.kbb.com /car-news/average-new-car-price-sets-record/.

United Nations. *Responsibility of States for Internationally Wrongful Acts, G.A. Res. 56/83, U.N. GAOR, 53rd Sess.* (December 12, 2001).

UN Comtrade Database. 2024. https://comtradeplus.un.org/.

U.S. Department of Commerce. "U.S. and IPEF Partners Establish Supply Chain Bodies and Convene First Virtual Meetings Under Landmark Supply Chain Agreement." July 30, 2024. www.commerce.gov /news/press-releases/2024/07/us-and-ipef-partners-establish-supply-chain-bodies-and-convene-first.

——. "U.S. Department of Commerce Publishes Text of Landmark Indo-Pacific Economic Framework for Prosperity (IPEF) Supply Chain Agreement." September 7, 2023. https://www.commerce.gov/news /press-releases/2023/09/us-department-commerce-publishes-text-landmark-indo-pacific-economic.

——. "U.S. Identifies Critical Sectors and Key Goods for Potential Cooperation Under the IPEF Supply Chain Agreement." August 23, 2024. www.commerce.gov/news/press-releases/2024/08/us-identifies -critical-sectors-and-key-goods-potential-cooperation.

U.S. Department of Defense. "Defense Production Act Title III Presidential Determination for Critical Materials in Large-Capacity Batteries." April 5, 2022. www.defense.gov/News/Releases/Release /Article/2989973/defense-production-act-title-iii-presidential-determination-for-critical-materi/.

U.S. Department of State. "How the People's Republic of China Seeks to Reshape the Global Information Environment." September 28, 2023. https://2021-2025.state.gov/gec-special-report-how-the-peoples-republic-of-china-seeks-to-reshape-the-global-information-environment/.

——. "Inaugural C5+1 Critical Minerals Dialogue Among the United States and Kazakhstan, the Kyrgyz Republic, Tajikistan, Turkmenistan, and Uzbekistan." February 9, 2024. https://2021-2025.state.gov/inaugural-c51-critical-minerals-dialogue-among-the-united-states-and-kazakhstan-the-kyrgyz-republic-tajikistan-turkmenistan-and-uzbekistan/.

——. "Inaugural U.S.-Mongolia-ROK Critical Minerals Dialogue Held in Ulaanbaatar." June 27, 2023. www.state.gov/inaugural-u-s-mongolia-rok-critical-minerals-dialogue-held-in-ulaanbaatar/.

——. "Joint Statement of the Fourth Round of the Six-Party Talks Beijing, September 19, 2005." September 19, 2005. https://2001-2009.state.gov/r/pa/prs/ps/2005/53490.htm.

——. "Joint Statement of the Minerals Security Partnership." March 4, 2024. www.state.gov/joint-statement-of-the-minerals-security-partnership/.

——. "Minerals Security Partnership." June 14, 2022. www.state.gov/minerals-security-partnership/.

——. "The Minerals Security Partnership Announces Collaboration in Minerals Exploration, Production, and Processing Between GECAMINES in the Democratic Republic of Congo and JOGMEC in Japan." February 5, 2024. www.state.gov/the-minerals-security-partnership-announces-collaboration-in-minerals-exploration-production-and-processing-between-gecamines-in-the-democratic-republic-of-the-congo-and-jogmec-in-japan/.

——. "Reaffirming and Reimagining America's Alliances." March 24, 2021. www.state.gov/reaffirming-and-reimagining-americas-alliances/.

——. "State Sponsors of Terrorism." www.state.gov/state-sponsors-of-terrorism/.

U.S. Department of the Treasury. "Fact Sheet: President Biden Issues Executive Order Addressing United States Investments in Certain National Security Technologies and Products in Countries of Concern; Treasury Department Issues Advance Notice of Proposed Rulemaking to Enhance Transparency and Clarity and Solicit Comments on Scope of New Program." August 9, 2023. https://home.treasury.gov/system/files/206/Outbound-Fact-Sheet.pdf.

——. "Treasury Designates Banco Delta Asia as Primary Money Laundering Concern Under USA PATRIOT Act." September 15, 2005. https://home.treasury.gov/news/press-releases/js2720.

——. "Treasury Releases Proposed Guidance on New Clean Vehicle Credit to Lower Costs for Consumers, Build U.S. Industrial Base, Strengthen Supply Chains." March 31, 2023. https://home.treasury.gov/news/press-releases/jy1379.

U.S. Geological Survey. *Mineral Commodity Summaries 2025.* 2025. https://pubs.usgs.gov/periodicals/mcs2025/mcs2025.pdf.

——. "U.S. Geological Survey Releases 2022 List of Critical Minerals." February 22, 2022. www.usgs.gov/news/national-news-release/us-geological-survey-releases-2022-list-critical-minerals.

"Rare Earths Statistics and Information," https://www.usgs.gov/centers/national-minerals-information-center/rare-earths-statistics-and-information

U.S. Mission Korea. "Readout of the United States–India–Republic of Korea Trilateral Technology Dialogue." U.S. Embassy & Consulate in the Republic of Korea, March 13, 2024. https://kr.usembassy.gov/031324-readout-of-the-united-states-india-republic-of-korea-trilateral-technology-dialogue/.

Upadhyay, Shreya. "Covid-19 and Quad's 'Soft' Reorientation." *Research in Globalization* 3 (2021): 100069.

Van Ness, Peter. "Why the Six Party Talks Should Succeed." *Asian Perspective* 29, no. 2 (2005): 231–246.

Venzon, Cliff. "China Uses Banana Diplomacy in Philippines to Edge Out Japan." *Nikkei Asia*, July 26, 2019. https://asia.nikkei.com/Politics/International-relations/China-uses-banana-diplomacy-in-Philippines-to-edge-out-Japan.

Vivek, N. D. "The Quad: Can This Democratic Coalition Bolster Global Health Security?" *Diplomat*, March 2, 2024. https://thediplomat.com/2024/03/the-quad-can-this-democratic-coalition-bolster-global-health-security/.

Vlasov, Artem. "Five Interesting Facts to Know About Zirconium." International Atomic Energy Agency, February 1, 2023. https://www.iaea.org/newscenter/news/five-interesting-facts-to-know -about-zirconium.

VOA News. "China Scolds Germany over Meeting with Hong Kong Activist." September 11, 2019. www .voanews.com/a/east-asia-pacific_china-scolds-germany-over-meeting-hong-kong-activist/6175623 .html.

Wallbank, Derek, and Alfred Cang. "How a Quickly-Deleted Tweet About China Got Pretty Much Every-one Mad at the NBA." *Time*, October 7, 2019. https://time.com/5694150/nba-china-hong-kong/.

Wang, Christoph Nedopil. "China Belt and Road Initiative (BRI) Investment Report 2023 H1." Green Finance and Development Center, August 1, 2023. https://greenfdc.org/china-belt-and-road-initiative -bri-investment-report-2023-h1/.

Wang, Vivian. "Chinese Military Drills Aim to Awe, Both Abroad and at Home." *New York Times*, August 6, 2022. www.nytimes.com/2022/08/06/world/asia/china-exercises-taiwan.html.

Waxman, Sharon. "China Bans Work with Film Studios." *Washington Post*, November 1, 1997. www .washingtonpost.com/archive/lifestyle/1997/11/01/china-bans-work-with-film-studios/9f3a23e3 -4d83-4749-898c-bd1fef276f03/.

Wayland, Michael. "Chip Shortage Expected to Cost Auto Industry $210 Billion in Revenue in 2021." CNBC, September 23, 2021. www.cnbc.com/2021/09/23/chip-shortage-expected-to-cost-auto -industry-210-billion-in-2021.html.

——. "How Covid Led to a $60 Billion Global Chip Shortage for the Auto Industry." CNBC, February 11, 2021. www.cnbc.com/2021/02/11/how-covid-led-to-a-60-billion-global-chip-shortage-for-automakers .html.

Wee, Sui-Lee. "Giving In to China, U.S. Airlines Drop Taiwan (in Name at Least)." *New York Times*, July 25, 2018. www.nytimes.com/2018/07/25/business/taiwan-american-airlines-china.html.

Weeks, Jessica L. "Autocratic Audience Costs: Regime Type and Signaling Resolve." *International Orga-nization* 62, no. 1 (2008): 35–64.

Weiß, Wolfgang. "The EU's Strategic Autonomy in Times of Politicisation of International Trade: The Future of Commission Accountability." *Global Policy* 14, no. S3 (2023): 1–11.

Westcott, Ben. "Australia Knocks Back China-Linked Investment in Rare Earths." Bloomberg, March 1, 2023. https://www.bloomberg.com/news/articles/2023-03-01/australia-knocks-back-china-linked -investment-in-rare-earths.

——. "Iron Ore Is Saving Australia's Trade with China. How Long Can It Last?" CNN, May 6, 2021. www .cnn.com/2021/05/05/economy/australia-china-iron-ore-trade-intl-hnk/index.html.

Whalen, Jeanne. "In Detroit, the Chip Shortage Has Left the City Eerily Short of Cars." *Washington Post*, July 23, 2022. www.washingtonpost.com/technology/2022/07/23/chip-shortage-detroit-manu facturing/.

Whalen, Jeanne, and Cate Cadell. "Pelosi Dined with Taiwan Computer Chip Executives During Her Brief Visit." *Washington Post*, August 3, 2022. www.washingtonpost.com/technology/2022/08/03/pelosi -tsmc-meeting-lunch-semiconductors/.

White House. "America First Investment Policy." February 21, 2025. https://www.whitehouse.gov /presidential-actions/2025/02/america-first-investment-policy/.

——. "Australia-United States Climate, Critical Minerals and Clean Energy Transformation Compact." May 20, 2023. https://bidenwhitehouse.archives.gov/briefing-room/statements-releases/2023/05/20 /australia-united-states-climate-critical-minerals-and-clean-energy-transformation-compact/.

——. "Fact Sheet: Biden-Harris Administration Announces Supply Chain Disruptions Task Force to Address Short-Term Supply Chain Discontinuities." June 8, 2021. https://bidenwhitehouse.archives.gov /briefing-room/statements-releases/2021/06/08/fact-sheet-biden-harris-administration-announces -supply-chain-disruptions-task-force-to-address-short-term-supply-chain-discontinuities/.

——. "Fact Sheet: In Asia, President Biden and a Dozen Indo-Pacific Partners Launch the Indo-Pacific Economic Framework for Prosperity." May 23, 2022. https://bidenwhitehouse.archives.gov/briefing -room/statements-releases/2022/05/23/fact-sheet-in-asia-president-biden-and-a-dozen-indo-pacific -partners-launch-the-indo-pacific-economic-framework-for-prosperity/.

——. "Fact Sheet: President Biden Takes Action to Protect American Workers and Businesses from China's Unfair Trade Practices." May 14, 2024. https://bidenwhitehouse.archives.gov/briefing-room /statements-releases/2024/05/14/fact-sheet-president-biden-takes-action-to-protect-american -workers-and-businesses-from-chinas-unfair-trade-practices/.

——. "Fact Sheet: President Donald J. Trump Imposes Tariffs on Imports from Canada, Mexico and China." February 1, 2025. https://www.whitehouse.gov/fact-sheets/2025/02/fact-sheet-president -donald-j-trump-imposes-tariffs-on-imports-from-canada-mexico-and-china/.

——. "Fact Sheet: President Donald J. Trump Secures a Historic Trade Win for the United States." May 12, 2025. https://www.whitehouse.gov/fact-sheets/2025/05/fact-sheet-president-donald-j-trump-secures-a -historic-trade-win-for-the-united-states/.

——. "Fact Sheet: Quad Leaders' Summit." September 24, 2021. https://bidenwhitehouse.archives.gov /briefing-room/statements-releases/2021/09/24/fact-sheet-quad-leaders-summit/.

——. "Fact Sheet: Securing a Made in America Supply Chain for Critical Minerals." February 22, 2022. https://bidenwhitehouse.archives.gov/briefing-room/statements-releases/2022/02/22/fact-sheet -securing-a-made-in-america-supply-chain-for-critical-minerals/.

——. "Fact Sheet: The Trilateral Leaders' Summit at Camp David." August 18, 2023. https:// bidenwhitehouse.archives.gov/briefing-room/statements-releases/2023/08/18/fact-sheet-the -trilateral-leaders-summit-at-camp-david/.

——. "G7 Hiroshima Leaders' Communiqué." May 20, 2023. https://bidenwhitehouse.archives.gov /briefing-room/statements-releases/2023/05/20/g7-hiroshima-leaders-communique/.

——. "G7 Leaders' Statement." December 6, 2023. https://bidenwhitehouse.archives.gov/briefing-room /statements-releases/2023/12/06/g7-leaders-statement-6/.

——. "G7 Leaders' Statement on Economic Resilience and Economic Security." May 20, 2023. https:// bidenwhitehouse.archives.gov/briefing-room/statements-releases/2023/05/20/g7-leaders-statement -on-economic-resilience-and-economic-security/.

——. "Japan-U.S. Joint Leaders' Statement: Strengthening the Free and Open International Order." May 23, 2022. https://bidenwhitehouse.archives.gov/briefing-room/statements-releases/2022/05/23 /japan-u-s-joint-leaders-statement-strengthening-the-free-and-open-international-order/.

——. "Leaders' Joint Statement in Commemoration of the 70th Anniversary of the Alliance Between the United States of America and the Republic of Korea." April 26, 2023. https://www.whitehouse.gov /briefing-room/statements-releases/2023/04/26/leaders-joint-statement-in-commemoration-of-the -70th-anniversary-of-the-alliance-between-the-united-states-of-america-and-the-republic-of-korea/.

——. "Memorandum on the Establishment of the Countering Economic Coercion Task Force." December 12, 2024. https://bidenwhitehouse.archives.gov/briefing-room/presidential-actions/2024/12/12 /memorandum-on-the-establishment-of-the-countering-economic-coercion-task-force/.

——. "President Biden Signs Executive Order on Addressing United States Investments in Certain National Security Technologies and Products in Countries of Concern." August 9, 2023. https:// bidenwhitehouse.archives.gov/briefing-room/statements-releases/2023/08/09/president-biden-signs -executive-order-on-addressing-united-states-investments-in-certain-national-security-technologies -and-products-in-countries-of-concern/.

——. "Quad Joint Leaders' Statement." May 24, 2022. https://bidenwhitehouse.archives.gov/briefing -room/statements-releases/2022/05/24/quad-joint-leaders-statement/.

——. "Readout of the Trilateral United States–Japan–Republic of Korea Economic Security Dialogue." February 28, 2023. https://bidenwhitehouse.archives.gov/briefing-room/statements-releases

/2023/02/28/readout-of-the-trilateral-united-states-japan-republic-of-korea-economic-security
-dialogue/.

——. "Remarks by President Trump at APEC CEO Summit | Da Nang, Vietnam." November 10, 2017.
https://trumpwhitehouse.archives.gov/briefings-statements/remarks-president-trump-apec-ceo
-summit-da-nang-vietnam/.

——. "Remarks by President Trump in Joint Address to Congress." March 4, 2025. https://www.whitehouse
.gov/remarks/2025/03/remarks-by-president-trump-in-joint-address-to-congress/.

——. "Remarks by Vice President Al Gore." January 11, 1994. https://clintonwhitehouse6.archives.gov/1994
/01/1994-01-11-remarks-by-vice-president-al-gore.html.

——. "United States–Japan Joint Leaders' Statement." April 10, 2024. https://bidenwhitehouse
.archives.gov/briefing-room/statements-releases/2024/04/10/united-states-japan-joint-leaders
-statement/.

Wilkinson, Bard. "Taiwan Slams China After Burkina Faso Cuts Ties." CNN, May 24, 2018. www.cnn
.com/2018/05/24/asia/taiwan-china-burkina-faso-intl/index.html.

Williams, Lou @TeamLou23. "That's Your Opinion. I Like Peak. I'm My Own Boss Over There. And
I've Made More in One Season with Them than 8 with Nike. Ha." X (formerly Twitter), January 21,
2017. https://twitter.com/TeamLou23/status/822925786713915392.

Wintgens, Sophie. "China's Footprint in Latin America." European Union Institute for Security Studies,
September 2022. www.iss.europa.eu/sites/default/files/EUISSFiles/Brief_9_China%20in%20
Latin%20America_web.pdf.

Wischer, Gregory. "The U.S. Military and NATO Face Serious Risks of Mineral Shortages." Carnegie
Endowment for International Peace, February 12, 2024. https://carnegieendowment.org/2024/02/12
/u.s.-military-and-nato-face-serious-risks-of-mineral-shortages-pub-91602.

Won, Ho-jung. "Duty Free Struggles as THAAD Crisis Persists." Korea Herald, September 1, 2017. https://
www.koreaherald.com/view.php?ud=20170901000682.

Wong, Audrye. "How Not to Win Allies and Influence Geopolitics." Foreign Affairs 100, no. 3 (2021). www
.foreignaffairs.com/articles/china/2021-04-20/how-not-win-allies-and-influence-geopolitics.

Wong, Foster, and Yian Lee. "China Ends Tariff Exemptions on Some Taiwan Agricultural Imports."
Bloomberg, September 18, 2024. https://www.bloomberg.com/news/articles/2024-09-18/china-scraps
-tariff-exemptions-on-some-taiwan-imports.

Woo, Ryan, Albee Zhang, and Casey Hall. "China Lifts Tariffs on Australian Wine, Ends Three-Year
Freeze in Trade." Reuters, April 2, 2024. www.reuters.com/markets/commodities/china-lifts-tariffs
-australian-wine-ends-three-year-freeze-trade-2024-04-02/.

World Bank. "Lifting 800 Million People Out of Poverty—New Report Looks at Lessons from China's
Experience." April 1, 2022. www.worldbank.org/en/news/press-release/2022/04/01/lifting-800
-million-people-out-of-poverty-new-report-looks-at-lessons-from-china-s-experience.

World Integrated Trade Solution. "Bananas, Including Plantains, Fresh or Dried Imports from Philippines
in 2011." World Bank, 2011. https://wits.worldbank.org/trade/comtrade/en/country/ALL/year/2011
/tradeflow/Imports/partner/PHL/product/080300.

World Trade Organization. "Article XXI Security Exceptions." www.wto.org/english/res_e/booksp_e
/gatt_ai_e/art21_e.pdf.

——. "The Process—Stages in a Typical WTO Dispute Settlement Case." www.wto.org/english/tratop
_e/dispu_e/disp_settlement_cbt_e/c6s1op1_e.htm.

Wright, Stephen. "China Warns New Zealand Against Squandering Trade Ties." Wall Street Journal,
June 2, 2022. www.wsj.com/articles/china-warns-new-zealand-against-squandering-trade-relationship
-11654147681.

Wright, Thomas. "Sifting Through Interdependence." Washington Quarterly 36, no. 4 (2013): 7–23.

Wu, Sarah. "First US-Led 'Chip 4' Meeting Held, Featuring Taiwan." *Taipei Times*, October 1, 2022. www
.taipeitimes.com/News/front/archives/2022/10/01/2003786225.

Xinhua. "China Maintains Quarantine on Philippines Fruit." May 26, 2012. www.chinadaily.com.cn
/business/2012-05/26/content_15392626.htm.

Yang, Zeyi. "China Just Fought Back in the Semiconductor Exports War. Here's What You Need to Know."
MIT Technology Review, July 10, 2023. www.technologyreview.com/2023/07/10/1076025/china-export
-control-semiconductor-material/.

Yeung, Jessie. "Prague's Tryst with Taipei Sees Shanghai Spurned in Sister City Love Triangle." CNN, January 15, 2020. www.cnn.com/2020/01/15/asia/prague-taiwan-china-intl-hnk-scli/index.html.

Yin, Yeping. "Piano Firms Expect Hit After Czech Senate Speaker's Taiwan Visit." *Global Times*, September 7, 2020. www.globaltimes.cn/content/1200167.shtml.

Yonhap News Agency. "S. Korea Joins Minerals Security Partnership." June 15, 2022. https://en.yna.co.kr
/view/PYH20220615081100325.

——. "S. Korean Gov't Bolsters Supply Crunch Early Warning System Abroad." January 16, 2022. https://en
.yna.co.kr/view/AEN20220116000800325.

——. "THAAD Row with China Costs S. Korea Dear: Report." September 15, 2017. https://en.yna.co.kr
/view/AEN20170915008300320.

Yong, Nicholas. "China: Fans Rejoice as Marvel Films Return After Apparent Ban." BBC, January 17, 2023.
https://www.bbc.com/news/world-asia-china-64300182.

Yoon, Ja-young. "China Bans Import of 19 Korean Cosmetics." *Korea Times*, January 10, 2017. www
.koreatimes.co.kr/www/biz/2023/06/602_221794.html.

Young, Jabari. "Sports Agents Warn NBA Players to Avoid China Talk as Athletes, Executives Walk 'Fine
Line.'" CNBC, October 10, 2019. https://www.cnbc.com/2019/10/10/sports-agents-warn-players-to
-avoid-china-talk-as-nba-walks-fine-line.html.

Youngmisuk, Ohm. "LeBron James: Daryl Morey Was 'Misinformed' Before Sending Tweet About China
and Hong Kong." ESPN, October 14, 2019. www.espn.com/nba/story/_/id/27847951/daryl-morey-was
-misinformed-sending-tweet-china-hong-kong.

Zahn, Max. "What to Know as Tariffs Go Into Effect on Mexico, Canada, China," ABC News, March 4,
2025, https://abcnews.go.com/Business/tariffs-effect/story?id=119380711.

Zarate, Juan. *Treasury's War: The Unleashing of a New Era of Financial Warfare*. New York: Public Affairs,
2013.

Zhang, Ketian. "Cautious Bully: Reputation, Resolve, and Beijing's Use of Coercion in the South China
Sea." *International Security* 44, no. 1 (2019): 117–159.

——. *China's Gambits—Explaining Chinese Coercion*. Cambridge: Cambridge University Press, 2024.

Zhang, Phoebe. "Chinese Netizens Boycott South Korean TV Show, 'Running Man.'" *South China Morning Post*, December 8, 2020. www.scmp.com/lifestyle/entertainment/article/3113196/chinese
-netizens-boycott-south-korean-television-show.

Zhang, Yunbi. "Protest Lodged at Harassment by Manila Ship." *China Daily*, April 12, 2012. https://usa
.chinadaily.com.cn/china/2012-04/12/content_15026889.htm.

Zhao, Tong. "Sanction Experience and Sanction Behavior: An Analysis of Chinese Perception and Behavior on Economic Sanctions." *Contemporary Politics* 16, no. 3 (2010): 263–278.

Zheng, William. "Chinese Internet Users Call for Boycott of BNP Paribas Over Worker's Support for
Hong Kong Protest." *South China Morning Post*, September 18, 2019. www.scmp.com/news/china
/politics/article/3027962/chinese-internet-users-call-boycott-bnp-paribas-over-workers.

Zhong, Raymond, and Sopan Deb. "Celtics Games Are Pulled in China After Enes Kanter's Pro-Tibet
Posts." *New York Times*, October 21, 2021. www.nytimes.com/2021/10/21/sports/basketball/celtics
-kanter-china-tibet.html.

Zhou, Cissy, and Thompson Chau. "China Bans Thousands of Taiwan Food Imports and Pelosi Trip Riles." *Nikkei Asia*, August 2, 2022. https://asia.nikkei.com/Politics/International-relations/US-China-tensions/China-bans-thousands-of-Taiwan-food-imports-as-Pelosi-trip-riles.

Zoellick, Robert B. "Whither China: From Membership to Responsibility?" U.S. Department of State, September 21, 2005. https://2001-2009.state.gov/s/d/former/zoellick/rem/53682.htm.

INDEX

Entries for tables and figures are in *italics*.

GPSR Authorized Representative: Easy Access System Europe, Mustamäe tee 50, 10621 Tallinn, Estonia, gpsr.requests@easproject.com

www.ingramcontent.com/pod-product-compliance
Lightning Source LLC
Chambersburg PA
CBHW022131020426
42334CB00015B/850